1 MONTH OF
FREE
READING

at

www.ForgottenBooks.com

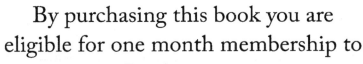

By purchasing this book you are eligible for one month membership to ForgottenBooks.com, giving you unlimited access to our entire collection of over 1,000,000 titles via our web site and mobile apps.

To claim your free month visit:
www.forgottenbooks.com/free444896

ISBN 978-0-331-23159-5
PIBN 10444896

This book is a reproduction of an important historical work. Forgotten Books uses
state-of-the-art technology to digitally reconstruct the work, preserving the original format
whilst repairing imperfections present in the aged copy. In rare cases, an imperfection in
the original, such as a blemish or missing page, may be replicated in our edition. We do,
however, repair the vast majority of imperfections successfully; any imperfections that
remain are intentionally left to preserve the state of such historical works.

Published by Licence of the Board of Trade under the " Trading with the Enemy Amendment Act, 1916."

DEMENTIA PRÆCOX

AND

PARAPHRENIA

BY

Professor EMIL KRAEPELIN of Munich

TRANSLATED BY

R. MARY BARCLAY, M.A., M.B.

From the Eighth German Edition of the " Text-Book of Psychiatry,"
vol. iii., part ii., section on the Endogenous Dementias

EDITED BY

GEORGE M. ROBERTSON, M.D., F.R.C.P. (Edin.)

Lecturer on Mental Diseases in the University of Edinburgh
and Physician to the Royal Asylum, Morningside

EDINBURGH

E. & S. LIVINGSTONE

17 TEVIOT PLACE

1919

EDITOR'S PREFACE.

DEMENTIA PRÆCOX has excited more interest and speculation than any other form of insanity in our time, with the possible exception of general paralysis of the insane. I therefore value highly the usefulness of the work that Dr Mary Barclay has done in thus bringing before English-speaking physicians a faithful translation of the views of Professor Kraepelin, who is the recognised authority on this subject. In no country has there been less inclination to accept his doctrines without qualification than in this, but so important are they, that every physician of the mind, who would keep himself abreast of modern clinical research, must be familiar with them. The present work therefore supplies a want in giving in an accessible form the complete and latest account of this subject by Professor Kraepelin. In addition, there is no other publication in the English language which deals solely with dementia præcox in all its various aspects.

Professor Kraepelin informs us that he got the starting point which led to dementia præcox being regarded by him as a distinct disease, in the year 1896. He admits "that Clouston also, who spoke of an 'adolescent insanity,' had evidently before everything dementia præcox in view, though he did not yet separate it from manic-depressive cases, which likewise often begin about this time." The identity of Clouston's "secondary dementia of adolescence" with the chief forms of dementia præcox is quite apparent to anyone reading the remarkable address on dementia which he delivered in 1888 when President of the Medico-Psychological Association. While, however, Sir Thomas Clouston regarded some of his cases of adolescent insanity as being of an unfavourable type which often ended in secondary dementia, Professor Kraepelin would regard these very cases, from their initial symptoms onward, as being examples of a distinct form of disease, namely dementia præcox. This situation therefore recalls in an interesting manner the circumstances connected with the discovery of general paralysis of the insane. Esquirol and his pupils had for seventeen years been observing cases of "insanity complicated with paralysis," when Bayle, in 1822, boldly asserted that the symptoms of this clinical condition were those of a separate and definite disease. This hypothesis has proved true ; is it too soon yet to say the same of the former ?

i

Professor Kraepelin's task in depicting the characteristic features of dementia præcox has not been an easy one, and even now he has not reached finality in his opinions. He is not satisfied with his delimitation of its boundaries, nor with all the sub-divisions which he has created, though he believes that his main thesis has been substantiated. Neither terminal dementia nor precocity is, however, an essential element of the clinical picture, though his reluctance to discard the former is very evident, and this masterly summary has been as a matter of fact prepared solely from observation of cases which actually became demented.

Now that general paralysis of the insane, after a century of observation and research, has yielded up most of its secrets, by far the most important practical problem facing the psychiatrist and the community, in the domain of mental hygiene, is that of dementia præcox. The patients suffering from this disease form the major part of the inmates of our mental hospitals. The heavy financial burden imposed upon the public for the treatment of the insane, resolves itself therefore very largely into the outlays needed for the lifelong care of the almost hopeless victims of this disorder. Moreover, as the disease does not directly cause death. and as such patients lead protected lives and live long, they tend to accumulate. They thus form the chief reason for the periodical necessity of enlarging our mental hospitals, and of erecting new ones. Could a study of the causes and treatment of this disorder result in its prevention or diminution, its cure or alleviation, a practical benefit to society of the most direct and valuable kind would be conferred. Such an enquiry should have the support of the Ministry of Health as this disease costs the State more than any other. How to avert this dementia continues to be the cardinal problem of psychiatry.

It is hoped that the publication of this translation will stimulate the interest of English-speaking physicians in these peculiar states of mental enfeeblement, promote further clinical observation and research, and lead to greater accuracy of diagnosis and prognosis, with a better understanding of the nature of the disease.

GEORGE M. ROBERTSON.

UNIVERSITY OF EDINBURGH,
    July 1919.

TRANSLATOR'S PREFACE.

As the aim of this translation is to bring the views of Professor Kraepelin, of Munich, on dementia præcox before the English-speaking members of the medical profession who may not be intimately acquainted with German, I have made it as literal as seemed consistent with readable English. Professor Kraepelin's *Psychiatry* is the leading German text-book on disorders of the mind, and I therefore willingly acceded to the wish of Dr George Robertson to make a complete translation of the section on dementia præcox. This special disease still requires much elucidation, and in its study medical practitioners, educationalists, and criminologists may well work together. It is especially on the educational side that Professor Kraepelin's observations or investigations appear to be deficient. It should not be difficult in this country to collect the required facts relating to individual cases, and to a certain extent this is being done already. When these facts are classified, much benefit should accrue to education, medical advancement, and the public welfare.

To Dr George Robertson I have to express my thanks for many useful suggestions, and to Dr Walker for the unwearying care with which he has revised the proofs.

R. MARY BARCLAY.

EDINBURGH, *July* 1919.

CONTENTS.

LIST OF ILLUSTRATIONS.

ILLUSTRATIONS

SPECIMENS OF WRITING.

INTRODUCTION.

THE ENDOGENOUS DEMENTIAS.

A series of morbid pictures are here brought together under the term "endogenous dementias" merely for the purpose of preliminary inquiry. Their clinical relations are not yet clear, but they all display two peculiarities, that they are in the first place, so far as can be seen, not occasioned — from without but arise from internal causes, and that secondly, at least in the great majority of cases, they lead to a more or less well-marked mental enfeeblement. It appears that this form of mental weakness, in spite of great differences in detail, exhibits many features in common with other forms of dementia, such as are known to us as the result of paralysis, senility or epilepsy. For this reason I have hitherto described under the one name, dementia præcox, the morbid pictures under consideration. Bleuler also has taken them together in his "group of the schizophrenias," without trying to make a further division of this group. I consider it an open question whether the same morbid process is not after all the cause of the divergent forms, though differing in the point of attack and taking a varying course. It appears to me expedient at the present stage to separate out a number of these clinical pictures from the domain of dementia præcox, which in any case is very extensive. Nevertheless it is dementia præcox which we must take as the first division of the endogenous dementias to be reviewed.

These clinical pictures referred to differ considerably in one direction or another from the current conceptions of dementia præcox. It would perhaps have been possible to carry this separation still further, and, for instance, allow a separate place also to the forms which have a periodic course, or which lead to confusion of speech. Meanwhile this has not been done, and therefore, to begin with, only those forms have been singled out and placed together subsequently[1] which are distinguished in their whole course by very definite manifestations of peculiar disturbances of intellect while lacking enfeeblement of volition and especially of feeling, or at least such symptoms are only feebly indicated. It seems to me that the term "paraphrenia," which is now no longer in common use, is in the meantime suitable as the name of the morbid forms thus delimited which are here by way of experiment brought together.

[1] Chapter xiii., p. 283.

CHAPTER I.

DEMENTIA PRÆCOX.

Dementia præcox[1] consists of a series of states, the common characteristic of which is a peculiar destruction of the internal connections of the psychic personality. The effects of this injury predominate in the emotional and volitional spheres of mental life. To begin with, the assertion that this is a distinct disease has met with repeated and decided opposition, which has found its strongest expression in the writings of Marandon de Montyel and of Serbsky.[2] But even though in many details there are profound differences of opinion, still the conviction seems to be more and more gaining ground that dementia præcox on the whole represents a well characterised form of disease, and that we are justified in regarding the majority at least of the clinical pictures which are brought together here as the expression of a single morbid process, though outwardly they often diverge very far from one another.

The objections have been directed even more against the name than against the clinical conception. I got the starting point of the line of thought which in 1896 led to dementia præcox being regarded as a distinct disease, on the one hand from the overpowering impression of the states of dementia quite similar to each other which developed from the most varied initial clinical symptoms, on the other hand from the

[1] Finzi e Vedrani, Rivista sperim. de freniatria, xxv. 1899; Christian, Ann. médico-psychol. 1899, 1, 43; Trömner, Das Jugendirresein (Dementia præcox), 1909; Sérieux, Gaz. hebdomad. Mars 1901; Revue de psychiatrie, Juin 1902; Jahrmärker, Zur Frage der Dementia præcox. 1902; Meeus, de la démence précoce chez lez jeunes gens. 1902; Masselon, Psychologie des Démences précoces; de la démence précoce. 1904; Stransky, Centralblatt für Nervenheilkunde xxvii. 1; Uber die dementia præcox. 1909; Bernstein, Allg. Zeitschr. f. Psychiatrie, lx. 554: Deny et Roy, la démence précoce. 1903; Pighini, Rivista Sperimentale di freniatria, xxxiv. 3; Hoche, Deutsche Klinik von Leyden-Klemperer, vi. 2, 197; Hecht, American Journal of nervous and mental diseases, 1905, 689; Evensen, Dementia præcox. 1904; Rizoi, Archiv f. Psychiatrie. xliii. 760; Wieg-Wickenthal, Zur Klinik der Dementia præcox. 1908; Bleuler-Jahrmärker, Allgem. Zeitschr f. Psychiatrie, lxv. 429; Bleuler, Dementia præcox oder Gruppe der Schizophrenien, Aschaffenburgs Handbuch der Psychiatrie, 1911 (Literatur) Deny et Lhermitte, Traité international de psychologie pathologique, ii. 439, 1911.

[2] Serbsky, Annales médico-psychologiques 1903, 2. 379; Marandon de Montyel, ebenda 1905, 2, 246; Soutzo, ebenda 1907, i. 243.

experience connected with the observations of Hecker that these peculiar dementias seemed to stand in near relation to the period of youth. As there was no clinical recognition of it, the first thing to be done for the preliminary marking off of the newly circumscribed territory, was to choose a name which would express both these points of view. The name "dementia præcox," which had already been used by Morel[1] and later by Pick (1891), seemed to me to answer this purpose sufficiently, till a profounder understanding would provide an appropriate name.

It has since been found that the assumptions upon which the name chosen rested are at least doubtful. As will have to be explained more in detail later, the possibility cannot in the present state of our knowledge be disputed, that a certain number of cases of dementia præcox attain to complete and permanent recovery, and also the relations to the period of youth do not appear to be without exception. I certainly consider that the facts are not by any means sufficiently cleared up yet in either direction. If therefore the name which is in dispute, even though it has been already fairly generally adopted, is to be replaced by another, it is to be hoped that it will not soon share the fate of so many names of the kind, and of dementia præcox itself in giving a view of the nature of the disease which will turn out to be doubtful or wrong.

From this point of view, as Wolff showed, a name that as far as possible said nothing would be preferable, as dysphrenia. The name proposed by Evensen "amblynoia," "amblythymia," further the "demenza primitiva" of the Italians, or the one preferred by Rieger, which meanwhile has certainly been already used in a narrower sense, "dementia simplex," might also be taken into consideration. Bernstein speaks of a "paratonia progressiva," a name that would suit only a part of the observed cases. Other investigators accentuate the peculiar disturbance of the inner psychic association in our patients and call the disease "dementia dissociativa," "dissecans," "sejunctiva" or with Bleuler "schizophrenia." It remains to be seen how far one or other of these names will be adopted.

[1] Morel, Traité des maladies mentales, 566, 1860.

CHAPTER II.

PSYCHIC SYMPTOMS

The complexity of the conditions which we observe in the domain of dementia præcox is very great, so that their inner connection is at first recognizable only by their occurring one after the other in the course of the same disease. In any case certain fundamental disturbances, even though they cannot for the most part be regarded as characteristic, yet return frequently in the same form, but in the most diverse combinations. We shall therefore try to give a survey of the general behaviour of the psychic and physical activities before we describe the individual clinical manifestations of the disease.[1]

Perception of external impressions in dementia præcox is not usually lessened to any great extent as far as a superficial examination goes. The patients perceive in general what goes on around them often much better than one would expect from their behaviour. One is sometimes surprised that patients to all appearance wholly dull, have perceived correctly all possible details in their surroundings, know the names of their fellow patients, and notice changes in the dress of the physician. By more accurate observations, however, such as were carried out by Busch and by Gregor, it becomes evident that the extent and especially the trustworthiness of perception are decidedly decreased. This is chiefly so in the acute phases of the malady, and then again in the last periods of its course. It was specially striking in the experiments of Busch to find that the patients usually made, along with a few correct statements, a great many wholly false ones. For instance, in the perception of letters they uttered repeatedly the same arbitrary series or sometimes parts of the alphabet. It was evident that they could not make the effort to retain and to reproduce what they really saw ; instead of this they named at random whatever happened to occur to them.

Attention.—This behaviour is without doubt nearly related to the disorder of attention which we very frequently find

---

[1] Albrecht, Allgem. Zeitschr. f. Psychiatrie lxvii. 659.

conspicuously developed in our patients. It is quite common for them to lose both inclination and ability on their own initiative to keep their attention fixed for any length of time. It is often difficult enough to make them attend at all. The patients do not look up when spoken to, and betray neither by look nor by demeanour in any way that they are sensitive to external impressions. Although this is so, they have perhaps perceived all the details, but have not experienced any real internal appreciation of their significance. Sometimes in cases of profound stupor or in many other insane states it is no longer possible, even by the strongest stimulus, to force the patients to show any interest.

But the patients do not take any notice of what they may perceive quite well, nor do they try to understand it ; they do not follow what happens in their surroundings even though it may happen to be of great importance for them. They do not pay attention to what is said to them, they do not trouble themselves about the meaning of what they read. On this depends what was observed by Ossipow in some of the patients, "photographic" reading, the thoughtless repetition of what is printed with all the signs of punctuation. Further there is seen the tendency of groups of patients, when they transcribe to copy carefully all mistakes, corrections, interpolations, and marginal notes. In psychological experiments the patients cannot stick to the appointed exercise ; they feel no need to collect their thoughts in the appointed manner, or to reach a satisfactory solution. Perhaps the experience related by Dodge and Diefendorff, that patients do not usually follow a moving pendulum continuously, as normal persons do, but intermittently and hesitatingly, may be explained by a similar disorder of attention.

With this loss of capacity to follow a lead is connected *a certain unsteadiness of attention* ; the patients digress, do not stick to the point, let their thoughts wander without voluntary control in the most varied directions. On the other hand *the attention is often rigidly fixed* for a long time, so that the patients stare at the same point, or the same object, continue the same line of thought, or do not let themselves be interrupted in some definite piece of work. Further it happens that *they deliberately turn away their attention* from those things to which it is desired to attract it, turn their backs when spoken to, and turn away their eyes if anything is shown to them. But in the end there is occasionally noticed a kind *of irresistible attraction of the attention* to casual external impressions. The patients involuntarily introduce into their speech words that they have heard, react to each movement of their neighbours, or imitate them. Leupoldt describes patients who instinctively had to touch or count objects as they came within their field of vision. On the disappearance of stuporous conditions a distinct inquisitiveness sometimes appears in the patients: they surreptitiously watch what happens in the room, follow the physician at a distance, look in at all open doors, but turn away if any one calls them. We shall later see that all these disorders of that inner activity of volition, which we call attention, represent only partial manifestations of general morbid changes in the processes of volition.

Hallucinations.—Sensation is very often profundly disordered in our patients as is evident by the occurrence of hallucinations. They are almost never wanting in the acute and subacute forms of the disease. Often enough they accompany the whole course of the disease; but more frequently they gradually disappear, to reappear more distinctly from time to time in the last stages. By far the most frequent are *hallucinations of hearing*. At the beginning these are usually simple noises, rustling, buzzing, ringing in the ears, tolling of bells ("death-knell"), knocking, moving of tables, cracking of whips, trumpets, yodel, singing, weeping of children, whistling, blowing, chirping, "shooting and death-rattle"; the bed echoes with shots; the "Wild Hunt' makes an uproar; Satan roars under the bed.

And then there develops gradually or suddenly the symptom peculiarly characteristic of dementia praecox, namely, the *hearing of voices*. Sometimes it is only whispering, "as if it concerned me," as a patient says, a secret language, "taunting the captive"; sometimes the voices are loud or suppressed, as from a ventriloquist, or the call of a telephone, "children's voices"; a patient heard "gnats speak." Sometimes they shout as in a chorus or all confusedly; a patient spoke of "drumming in the ear"; another heard, "729,000 girls." Sometimes the voices appear to have a metallic sound, they are "resonant voices," "organ voices," or as of a tuning-fork. At other times they do not appear to the patients as sense perceptions at all; they are "voices of conscience," "voices which do not speak with words," voices of dead people, "false voices," "abortive voices." A patient said: "It appeared to me in spirit, as though they would find fault, without having heard it." There is an "inner feeling in the soul," an "inward voice in the thoughts"; "it is thought inwardly in me"; it "sounded as

if thought "; " it was between hearing and foreboding "—
in such ways the patients express themselves about these
sensory disturbances.

The illusions not infrequently are connected with real
noises. The clock speaks as if it were enchanted; the
rushing of water is changed into words; each step under
the patient speaks; a patient "heard the thoughts of others
out of the soles of his boots." Here and there the voices
have a rhythmical cadence, probably in connection with the
carotid pulse.

The voices are often referred to the ear or the head; they
are "voices in the ear"; there are evil spirits in the ear, a
telephone, a receiver, a phonograph in the head; "the brain
talks." One ear may be exclusively concerned in it, or at
least more so; sometimes the voices of the two ears have a
different character. A patient asserted that the voices went
in at one ear and out at the other. Many patients hear the
voices in the whole body; the spirits scream in the belly, in
the feet, and possibly also wander about; a patient heard
them speaking in his purse. Another wrote down:—

Voice in the right ear: "Never," for example as answer to a wish.
Voice in the left ear: "Stupid—Jesus—God." Voice in the stomach:
"Blackguard. Point. Good." Voice in the nose: "Munich; Oho-
boy." Voice at the heart: "Boy." Voice in the right side of the
abdomen: "Yokel."

But for the most part the origin of the voices is sought
for in the external world. The patient feels himself influenced
by the telephone, is a "living telephone"; "it all came by
telephone to the bed"; said a patient. The question is
about the "address," about "the communicated voices of
human beings," about "murmurings and natural spirit-
voices," about underground voices from the air, from the
ground, voices from Further India and Siberia, whispering
voices from the whole of mankind, "voices of spirits which
are quite near," of God, the saints and the blessed, of the
guardian angel, but especially of all conceivable persons in
the neighbourhood. A patient heard a bird whistle from a
picture; another saw threads from which voices spoke. Often
the voices torment the patient the whole day long, and at
night also he hears "telephone gossip," or perhaps he only
hears them now and then, not infrequently in the form of
single detached remarks.

It is, however, usually difficult to get trustworthy accounts
of these occurrences from the suspicious and reserved patients:
they usually deny that they still hear voices, and only allow
on pressure that yesterday or the day before perhaps some-

thing happened. Sometimes the patients are only able to give general information about the voices : " They were voices as if the battle was lost," " as if I had set about something "; " the conversation was about the king and royalty," " of life and the soul and divine love," of " marriage and death "; " the clergyman whispered something into my ear, that could not be understood." But much more frequently they catch the exact wording as in real perceptions ; some patients make notes of what they hear.

What the voices say is, as a rule, *unpleasant* and *disturbing.* " The voices rushed in on me at all times as burning lions," said a patient. The patient is everywhere made a fool of and teased, mocked, grossly abused, and threatened. People speak about him ; everyone is occupied with him ; the whole workshop screams ; there is " a petty espionage," " like legal proceedings"; he hears voices, " as one reads of them in stories of murder and Indians." Some one calls out : " Rascal, vagrant, miserable scoundrel," "incendiary, parricide," " good-for-nothing," " blackguard," " anarchist, rogue, thieving murderer," " filthy fellow, filthy blockhead, filthy beast," " vagabond," " scamp," " swine," " filthy swine," " sloven fury," " town whore," " convict," " criminal, criminal," " offended, offended." The patient is said to have assaulted a child, seduced a girl with 80,000 marks, had sexual intercourse with his children, eaten human flesh. He is threatened with having his ears cut off, his feet chopped off, with being sawn asunder, with being beheaded ; there is a command from the Government to stab him. " He must come along ; he must be arrested : he has seduced the girl," it is said : ' That's he," " I've got him," " Wait, Kaiser Franz, we've got you ! " " The fellow must go to the cemetery," " I'll shoot the convict through the wall," " Just come along, and you'll be killed," " Now we've given him a shot," " We'll do for him, he must come here," " We'll squirt water on him, we'll stab him," " He'll be milked," " There'll be an end put to the blackleg's children," " The beast's going to die, she's going to be fetched down, this creature." Most frequently they are indecent and filthy things that are called out in which impurity and self-abuse play a large part. In many of the utterances a certain feeling of disease comes to light. His comrades whisper secretly about the patient, saying that he is mentally affected, " an absolute fool," " He is studying, he has something in his head," " He has neurasthenia," " That is megalomania," " He must go the madhouse."

On the other hand there are also frequently " *good voices*," "good wishes," "praise," "That's the real Simon Pure." God makes known to the patient that he will proclaim him, send him into the world as his son. "Here he is," cries a voice from heaven. He hears that he is a king's son, an officer's son, that he is very musical; he has a splendid life; "To-day we won't do anything to him." The voice calls out: "King, King!" "Saint Joseph!" "I am God"; a dove says at night: "You have already the divine bride."

Many of the voices make remarks about the thoughts and the doings of the patient: "He has good hearing," "Damn it, what ears the fellow has!" "He has done for himself; the filthy fellow must get away from this," "Do you hear the reflector upstairs? Now they have the sound-hole open again": "Mary, you're talking nonsense, the policeman has seen you already," "But what have we done to him? He never listens to us now." "The voices knew what I did," said a patient. Another when she exposed herself to the sun heard, "She is melting"; to one patient the voices named the people he met, "analysed his inside." They narrated events in his life, asked him about family affairs. "The director and the nuns disturb my rest at night, they tell me all that has happened in my life," complained a patient. "When I leave the house all the telephones know where I am going and what I am thinking of: the whole town is in excitement when I go out," said another. A patient who later became quite insane furnished the following notes:

"In the Prince Charles I should have got a shilling tip—I should have been a conceited boy—The man would have been on his travels—Now the boy too is still laughing—Now I'd just like to know why the boy is here—He's not yet at an end—Now I don't like it any more—O God! I'm sorry for the boy—He does write well—That goes on swimmingly—How well that all agrees—He writes each line in a different writing (The writing was really quite changed.)—The Jew can't help himself any more for discontentment—".

Often, however, in the beginning of the disease or in the more advanced stages what the voices say is indifferent or quite nonsensical and incomprehensible. The patient hears a call from England that he is to pay a visit, "always another way about, always new names"; he hears "Banker, rich farmer, crash, salt roll"; "Stallion," "They help me or they don't help me," The military come to-morrow early," "Education," "Lavender and crossroads are the strongest explosive," and similar expressions.

From the very varied notes of a patient, who was quite sensible and reasonable, I give the following example taken at random—notes of his hallucinations which consisted of detached sentences without connection, of the meaning of which in detail he was not able to give any account :—

"She is said to have run after him—Oh you blockheads I always hear something and see nothing—I would just make a start—Get out with your trash—We have done our duty ; now he can do what he likes—It won't be finished immediately ; if it goes far wrong, the law is still there—Get yourself licked at A. ; here you must have two ears, in at the one, out at the other, here the heirs can still wrangle, here twenty shillings, there twenty shillings, yes, why not?—How is he ever to think of it ; for he doesn't know what has happened—d'ye see him—shall we send him a servant—A tree isn't hewn down so quickly ; it did not grow all at once, at night all cows are black—Cheating innkeepers—O, du mein lieber Augustin, 's Geld ist hin—Trees and the roots with them—Oh I must undress," and so on.

Another patient, also quite reasonable, wrote down the following words as being what the voices said :—

"He—veni—I came—Cham—Saul—Absalom—lyric—dropping—roast—lust—Turks—rukidiku—trilling—singing—tins—tinker—skr—ram—fail—dog—fruit—Ko—vault—complaint—flax—holy water—pasture—inspired—drone—dull—pressing—funnel—Druid—tremens—squeezing—dropping—quail—clever—formerly—sausage—lynx—vult—question—crime—splendour."

In some places " veni—kam—Cham," " Saul—Absalom," "trilling—singing"—"tins—tinker," there is a certain connection, if only external, of the ideas which follow each other. But, except for these, the words are connected without any obvious link of ideas or sound ; at most the slight similarity of sound in "roast—lust" and in the series "drone" to "dropping" [in German, Drohne—trübe—drängen—Trichter—Druide—tremens—drücken—tröpfeln] could be regarded as the connecting link. This series reminds one of similar inventions of alcoholics in delirium when they read from a blank sheet of paper ; and in reading during dreams such expressions, wholly without connection, occur.

Many patients hear perpetually, in endless repetition or with slight changes, the same meaningless sentences, so that there is a kind of hallucinatory *verbigeration*. The following notes give an example of it. They were written down by an otherwise thoroughly clear and intelligent patient :—

"For we ourselves can always hope that we should let ourselves pray other thoughts. For we ourselves wish to wish to know who would let the swine's head be tormented to death with us foolishly. No, we ourselves are no longer so stupid, and do not always trouble ourselves, if we shall let ourselves be spared drinking like beasts. Because we just behave as fools and would let ourselves be cheated like silly swine."

In a series of cases the voices *give commands* which in certain circumstances are very precisely obeyed. They forbid the patient to eat and to speak, to work, to go to church; he must run barefoot. "Go on, strike him, beat him," it is said, "go on, go on!" "Hands up!" "Slope arms!" "Put the chair here, stand up!" "Jump in!" A patient said that he heard: "You must do that," then "You must not do that"; "it is a chaos, one can't get out."

But it is quite specially peculiar to dementia præcox that the patients' own *thoughts appear to them to be spoken aloud.* In the most varied expressions we hear the complaint of the patients constantly repeated that their thoughts can be perceived. They are said loud out, sometimes beforehand, sometimes afterwards; it is "double speech," the "voice trial," "track-oratory," the "apparatus for reading thoughts," the "memorandum." A patient heard her thoughts sounding out of noises. In consequence of this everything is made public. What the patients think is known in their own homes and is proclaimed to everyone, so that their thoughts are common property. "I have the feeling, as if some one beside me said out loud what I think," said a patient. "As soon as the thought is in my head, they know it too," explained another. "When I think anything I hear it immediately," said a third. People look into the brain of the patient, his "head is revealed." When he reads the newspapers, others hear it, so that he cannot think alone any longer. "We can read more quickly than you," the voices called out to a patient. "Everyone can read my thoughts, I can't do that," complained a patient. Another said, "A person can have his thoughts traced by another, so that people can learn everything." A patient himself had "to whistle" his secrets "through his nose."

Influence on Thought.—Still more characteristic of the disease which is here discussed seems to be the feeling of one's thoughts being influenced, which often occurs. People speak to the patient in his thoughts, guide them, contradict him, "offer" him thoughts, suggest them to him, transfer to him words, thoughts, pictures, smells and feelings. A patient said, "My senses don't belong to me any more, they are being unlawfully taken from me." Strangers send him thoughts silently and speak in his head, it is "a remembrance, a memory, a memorial," a "receiving of thoughts." In this way his own thoughts are disturbed, "drilled," "drawn off"; he cannot think when the voice speaks. A patient explained, "They take my thoughts from me and nothing comes back but a ragamuffin." What he thinks himself is distorted; his thoughts are "plundered, organised and published." "The voices and my brain are one, I must think what the voice says," said a patient, and a woman complained ; "The voices work on my thoughts from morning to evening, suggest dreams to me and torment me unceasingly." Many of the patients must utter aloud their own thoughts or those that are given to them, "low by movements of the lips," "say silly stuff to oneself." "It flows into the brain as a thought and expresses itself as words in the mouth," said a patient. Another heard "dead" and had to answer "bread."

On the other hand the patient sometimes *knows the thoughts of other people*, is "connected by telephone with M'Kinley," can "speak with the Kaiser," "tones constantly with God," "is in constant communication with the Holy Ghost." He can also think for others, he passes on the thoughts, carries on conversations, dialogues, with his companions, with people in other houses ; it is an "electrical glee." "There is talking going on in my head and body," said a patient. "I close my throat and sing the most beautiful songs, and you do not hear it."

These most extraordinary disorders, quite foreign to healthy experience, are at first usually kept secret by the patient, so that one only hears something about them when they have already existed for a long time. The patients frequently connect them with malevolent people by whom they are "watched through the telephone," or connected up by wireless telegraphy or by Tesla currents. Their thoughts are conveyed by a machine, there is a "mechanical arrangement," "a sort of little conveyance," telepathy. A patient said, "I don't know the man who suggests that to me." Another supposed that it might perhaps be done for scientific purposes by a professor. A third explained, "I am perfectly sane and feel myself treated as a lunatic, while hallucinations are brought to me by magnetism and electricity." Or the patients think of supernatural powers, of "demi-spirits which perceive the thoughts," "little souls and little figures," their guardian angel, God and Christ ; they are inspirations, revelations. A patient heard the unborn Virgin Mary speak in his belly ; another carried God's voice in his heart.

Many patients feel themselves very much troubled by telephony, they stop their ears, "do not like such treatment by voices." One patient begged that "the blessed nonsense should be taken away." Others regard themselves as specially privileged. "I hear from a distance ; not everyone can do that," said a patient. Some patients try, by ingenious devices, to protect themselves against their thoughts being influenced ; a patient translated foreign words in order to ward off the receiving of thoughts. Others exert themselves to conceal their real line of thought to a certain degree, by a second carried on alongside of it, which shall then receive the outside influences.

Hallucinations of **sight** begin with variegated rings in front of their eyes, plays of colour, fiery rays and balls, seeing sparks, everything looks awry and wrong. The patients are troubled by reflections, by blinding light, their eyes are irradiated and blinded by reflectors. On the wall appear white figures, reflections, the mother who is dead, paintings, imaginative pictures, death's heads, a heart with a dagger, ghosts, shadow figures half beast, half human, southern landscapes, saints from all eternity; it is photography at a distance and double sight. In front of the window a clown is tumbling about, good and evil spirits appear, angels and the Virgin Mary in a blue mantle offer the cup, Satan with horns and a fiery tail dances about the room, death appears as a figure with a mask; at night men approach the bed. Black birds of prey hover overhead; people appear who are not there; the Emperor of China comes and speaks; gentlemen in white suits, lions, people who are dead, pretty girls, red men with black heads appear; a black figure grins. The patient sees "a shining crown and a threatening star," "theatrical stuff," naked women, improper pictures, an automobile in the air, two men in a balloon, the "Wild Hunt"; a green shadow flies beside him. There are snakes in his food, in the water for his bath. Supernatural appearances are seen in the air, fire in the sky, a halo, Luther in the clouds, spirits in the fields. Acquaintances look strange, everything is as though accentuated, pieces of furniture are changed into the form of wife and children; the figures in paintings and sculpture make obeisance. A patient saw the "voices" in the form of small, grey, four-footed beings hopping round about and whirling in the air; they were accompanied by small flames, which could be separated from them. Another offered in a very definite way "extrakampine" hallucinations; he "saw" a gun-barrel on his back, red and white mice in his heart, two tortoises in his shoulder.

Smell and **taste** frequently share in the morbid condition. Evil-smelling substances are scattered about; there is a smell of sulphur; of corpses and chloride of lime, of blood, of fire, of the fumes of hell, of "stinking poison," of dynamite. A patient smelled human souls; another felt the devil standing behind her, "it stank." Cold vapours are blown in at the one nostril, warm vapours at the other. Many patients smell the fragrance of roses, or notice that they are being chloroformed or stupefied by perfumed handkerchiefs. Th soup has a curious taste of creosote; in the food there is petroleum or arsenic, in the beer morphia or iodoform, the drinking water is brackish, or contains chloroform.

(Morbid tactile sensations and common sensations meanwhile gain considerable importance in the clinical picture. They are usually very varied.) The patient feels himself laid hold of, touched over his whole body, he feels tickling in his thigh and right up to his neck, pricking in his back and in his calves, a curious feeling in his neck, heat in his face; hot sand is strown over his face, filth is put in his hair; something is squirted on his feet; a hundred mice run over his neck. At night he is pricked with needles, he gets blows in the ribs, invisible powder is sprinkled over him; warm air plays on his body. He has a feeling as if his feet were rising from the ground; his bed is pushed at night, moves about, swings. Vermin and itch powder are in his bed; a patient felt lion cubs. There is a tearing feeling in his head and in his back, a burning in his stomach, pain in his teeth, a rolling in his brain, a tugging at his heart, lumbago shoots through his body and loins. A patient felt it in his right ear, if other people turned up their noses.

Not infrequently these imaginations, connected apparently with organic sensations, receive a very strange *interpretation*. The patient is terribly tormented in his body, notices that something is taken away from him, blood is taken, that "every part of his body is misused"; he feels "internal stirrings." emptiness inwardly, currents and strains in his body. Water flows away out of his body, food goes immediately out at his head. His body is twisted; his mouth is torn asunder; his gums are broken open; his eyes are clawed out; his hair is tugged out; his shoulders are pulled apart, his testicles are burst; her ovaries and stomach are torn out; his cheeks are pared off. His brain is crushed, his throat is blown out; his whole intestine is drawn up; fire bursts out at his mouth. The patient has injections made behind; God pierces his foot with a wire; he is disfigured. A man is laid across him, his back is broken, his breath is sucked up. Ears and head are blown up, his strength is drawn out, his toes are burned off, his ears are cut off. A patient kept saying that he was being "deprived," another that he was being "undone." A third complained of "intersections"; a fourth said, "It is always as if something were being shoved into me," a fifth felt "a thousand dolls sliding down inside him."

Very commonly these sensations are associated with *electricity* and similar action at a distance. The patient feels

himself fastened to the receiving and also to the discharging
station, electrified from a distance, raised from the ground by
electric shocks, blown up by electricity, he feels the current in
his pleuræ, a prick in his heart from the apparatus, he becomes
warm by the rays ; electric currents flow through his bed ; an
electric current comes from the sun. A patient thought that
she was illuminated with Röntgen rays under her petticoats
and was thus exposed to the general gaze.

As the result of these hallucinations the conviction is
often developed in the patients that they have become the
sport of all sorts of *influences*.[1] A patient described this in
writing in the following words :—

"I felt myself touched in such a way as if I were hypnotised,
electrified, or generally controlled by some sort of medium or some other
will. My several organs of sense were influenced in such a way, that I
always heard the will of the medium from great distances, to which I had
then unconditionally to surrender myself. I feel and hear the will in
all parts of my body, in my whole organism. I must do what I hear
according to the will of the so-called medium which can assume the voices
of all people known to me, of whom others daily appear before my soul.
In this way as regards my person there are no secrets for the medium as
a whole. All that has passed through my brain, or that still influences it,
is reproduced by the medium, and indeed as often as it likes, and my
brain has always to take part in this proceeding, which extends not only
to thoughts but also to speech. The characteristic feature is that I
also have these hallucinations of hearing when my hearing is deafened
by a real noise, so that I am sure that these proceedings take place in
the brain itself. I have also already had hallucinations of sight, visions,
and all this happens according to the will of the medium and as a
consequence of my power of imagination. The visions only appear
when I have my eyes closed."

Notice here the curious mixture of insight into disease
and ideas of influence, but especially the feeling of *internal
compulsion*, which we shall meet with again and again in our
descriptions.

Sexual sensations play a considerable rôle in our
patients' experiences. The patient has a feeling of contraction
in the testicles and penis, experiences "a sultry feeling" on
meeting people, notices signs in his fingers which the girls
make. Love-charms are employed, the penis is erected by
the electric current, a gold needle is stuck into it. At night
lustful deeds are committed, his nature is electrically withdrawn from him ; lustful men approach him. A patient felt

[1] Haslam, Erklärungen der Tollheit, übersetzt von Wollny, 1889 ; Wollny ;
Über Telepathie, 1888 ; Sammlung von Aktenstücken. 1888 ; Teffer, Über die
Tatsache des psycho sexualen Kontaktes oder die actio in Distans. 1891 ;
Schreber, Denkwürdigkeiten eines Nervenkranken. 1903.

that she was kissed at night by a Capuchin. Another patient described her experiences at night in the following way :—

"It seemed to me in the night as though I were divinely and spiritually married, or rather that my innocence was taken from me. The pains were considerable, but I did not scream though for some minutes I had to breathe violently. It then seemed to me as though I were several times married, when I had to lie down on the bed with better clothes on. But there never was a human being with me."

Orientation is not usually disordered. The patients know as a rule where they are, recognize people, are clear about the reckoning of time. It is only in stupor and in states of intense anguish that the correct perception of the environment may occasionally be more profoundly disordered. It is indeed often just the characteristic of the patients that they remain surprisingly clear in spite of the most violent excitement. On the other hand, however, orientation is not infrequently encroached upon by hallucinations. The patients name their place of residence and persons incorrectly, give a wrong date, are in a wrong hospital, in an imitation madhouse, in a prince's house ; the physician is God, the attendant Satan ; his relatives have been exchanged, his fellow patients are females or disguised policemen. But here it is clearly not a case of falsification of perception but of insane interpretation of impressions in themselves correctly perceived.

The **consciousness** of the patients, if we leave out of account the terminal condition of dementia, is in many cases clear throughout. Only in conditions of excitement and stupor is it occasionally dulled, though the dulness is not usually so great as it appears at the first glance. The patients complain frequently of passing dulness of consciousness which should probably be regarded as a condition of very slight stupor. They say that they were " stunned," " disembodied, magnetically repressed"; they became suddenly incapable of thinking or of working. These are " mental conditions artificially induced through hypnosis," " spiritual visitations," " magnetic conditions of sleep," caused by the physician. A patient thought he suffered from " somnambulism " ; another narrated about the " nightly narcosis with Röntgen in which she was cross-questioned ; it would all appear in the newspaper in which people would hear about it."

Memory[1] is comparatively little disordered. The patients are able, when they like, to give a correct detailed account of their past life, and often know accurately to a day how

[1] Gregor und Hänsel, Monatsschr. f. Psychiatrie, xxiii. 1.

B.

long they have been in the institution. The knowledge which they acquired at school remains sometimes with surprising tenacity until they are sunk in the most profound dementia. I remember a peasant lad, mentally quite dull, who could point to any town on the map without hesitation. Another startled you by his knowledge of history. Others again solve difficult problems in arithmetic with ease. Weygandt ascertained that a prebendary of the Julius Hospital, who suffered from mental disease and was quite confused, still retained forty-seven years after the beginning of his illness a fair knowledge of Latin, mastery of the multiplication table, and also recollected all sorts of historical facts, although these ideas had certainly not been roused for decades.

Retention is also often quite well preserved. Gregor however, found in his experiments very dissimilar values for successive repetitions in consequence of great wavering of attention. Mistakes and senseless combinations were not corrected, but rather showed an inclination to become established; continuance of the repetition was of comparatively little use. Vieregge also reports great wavering of attention. In spite of that it is usually easy to impress numbers or names even on quite indifferent patients, which they correctly reproduce after days and weeks. Certainly inappropriate answers are often given first, but after more searching interrogation it is clear that the patients have quite understood ·the exercise. After deep stupor it sometimes happens that the patients have no recollection, or only a very dim recollection, of what has occurred during a long space of time, it may be that because of the dulness of consciousness, they were unable to perceive, or that the impressions were not permanent.

Pseudo-memories.—Here and there we meet also with *confabulations* which point to *pseudo-memories*. It must, it is true, seem very doubtful if one ought to speak of such when the patients relate that they have been in hell, in heaven, in America, have travelled over the moon and all parts of the world, that at six years of age the marrow was burned out of their legs, and their feet were chopped off. A patient declared that he had already been beheaded, but his head had not fallen off. In other cases, however, it is easier to assume pseudo-memories. The patient remembers having been in a beautiful castle as a little child and having sat on the knee of a grand gentleman, and to have been kidnapped on a cloudy night. Kaiser Wilhelm on a journey through the town gave him a medal which in an unaccountable way has been mislaid. Others assert that they already knew beforehand where they were to be brought, and what would happen, that in the madhouse they would meet this and that person, that there would be a fire, and they would get a bride. A patient asserted that the Spirit had prophesied to him the death of an acquaintance ; another explained that God inspired him so that he could foretell what should happen. Or the patients think that they have already been in the hall, that they have seen the pictures before; they consulted the physician once two years ago. A patient declared he had himself planted the trees in the hospital garden. Usually the tendency to such insane pseudo-memories passes off quickly.

Train of Thought.—This sooner or later suffers considerably. There is invariably at first a *loss of mental activity* and therewith a certain poverty of thought. The patient "has little life in him"; his nerves are under such tension that he can no longer think or speak. Thinking is difficult to him ; "he trifles about the whole day," occupies himself "with tearing off the last leaf of the calendar and tidying up." His thoughts have been taken out of his head ; he has lost the joy of life ; it is as if a fur cap were on his brain, he is "as stupid as a pig"; his head is empty and hollow. A patient complained that "he had no more earnestness."

Association experiments.—Bouman frequently observed repetition of the word used as stimulus, irrational associations, omissions ; disinclination to make the attempt seemed to play a considerable rôle. Bleuler brings forward, among others, as further peculiarities of "schizophrenic" associations, great irregularity of association-time, connecting up with former stimuli or answers, frequent repetition of the same associations, tendency to indirect associations, change of answer on repetition of the experiment. Marcus found in his patients specially lively visual ideas. Further, Pfersdorff has proved that in the combination of ideas *linguistic constituents* gain a certain preponderance ; the patients show a tendency to rhyme, to introduce assonances, to play with words, to twist them, behaviour to which we shall later have to return.

But above all, as Bleuler especially has shewn in detail, the patients lose in a most striking way the faculty of *logical ordering* of their trains of thought. On the one hand, the most self-evident and familiar associations with the given ideas are absent. It seems as if these were only partially illumined, and therefore were not in a position to call into consciousness thoughts that lie quite near. On the other hand again, the most unnatural combinations of heterogeneous ideas are formed, because their incongruity is not perceived on account of some purely external relation, as similarity in sound, or coincidence in time. The most evident truths are not recognised, the greatest contradictions are thoughtlessly accepted. " Doctor, is your name Julia ? " asked a patient, and another called the physician " Mrs Colonel." By these disorders, which in many respects remind one of thinking in a dream, the patients' mental associations often have that peculiarly bewildering incomprehensibility, which distinguishes them from other forms of confusion. It con- stitutes the essential foundation of *incoherence of thought*.

In less severe cases this is shown only in increased facility of distraction and increased desultoriness, in passing without any connection from one subject to another, in the interweav- ing of superfluous phrases and incidental thoughts. Similarly, Pfersdorff found in continuous reading a tendency to make meaningless mistakes, to perseveration of certain words, to changes and omissions, even when single 'words or short sentences were correctly rendered ; he concludes rightly that there is a failure of attention. A patient who was quite sensible, when asked to copy the fable of the " greedy dog," performed the exercise correctly as far as the sentence : " But when he snapped at it, his own piece of meat fell from his mouth, and sank in the water," then, however, continued :—

"And as now her present condition depends wholly on what Dr J. M. plans for the future, who wishes to make himself acquainted with what is in connection with it, and of whose condition she wished to be again acquainted with, which he wished on his own desire. Now he had nothing at all but what was yours, which seems to lose what was his, but he himself tried to lose it, the fortune which for him was trying to be acquired," and so on.

The line of thought here leaves the appointed exercise and moves in indistinct spheres of ideas, which otherwise occupied the patient, and then, without any connection, again brings in parts of the fable (" Now he had nothing at all," " Who wants to take the goods of others loses his own "). Still more striking is the departure from the given idea in the answer of a patient who was asked what year it was :—

" O I know nothing, what shall I say ? Fire, fire ! O you old beast, devil, wretch, dog, slaughtered, slaughtered ! It's cold in the wood ; hurrah ! Damn it a million times, beast of a cat, slaughtered ! "

In certain circumstances the incoherence may go on to complete loss of connection and to confusion. An example of this is given in the following answer of a patient to the question : Are you ill ?—

" You see as soon as the skull is smashed and one still has flowers (laughs) with difficulty, so it will not leak out constantly. I have a sort of silver bullet which held me by my leg, that one cannot jump in, where one wants, and that ends beautifully like the stars. Former service, then she puts it on her head and will soon be respectable, I say, O God, but one must have eyes. Seats himself and eats it. Quite excited, I was quite beside myself and say that therefore there should be meanness and there is a merry growth over. It was the stars. I, and that is also so curious, the nun consequently did not know me any more, I should come from M. because something always happens, a broken leg or something, they've had a quarrel with each another, the clergyman and she ; a leg has just been broken. I believe it is caused by this that such a misfortune happens, such a reparation for damages. I have also said I shall then come in the end last, with the sun and the moon, and too much excitement, and all that makes still a great deal of trouble. Kings do not collect the money, in this way the letters have been taken away from me, as I at last specially think from the that, and all are burned. You can imagine that comes always from one to the other."

In a few places here, a certain connection between the ideas can perhaps be recognised :—" ill—skull smashed," " held by my leg—not jump in," "something happens—broken leg," "misfortune—reparation for damages," "excitement—trouble," "letters taken away—burned," "excited—quite beside myself." Also " silver bullet " and " stars," and further on " sun and moon " and " nun " and " clergyman," who " have had a a quarrel with each other," point to associations of thought. On the whole, however, we have before us a completely unintelligible and aimless series of words and fragments of thoughts. It must certainly be taken into consideration that the actual train of thought is possibly much less disordered than the expression of it in speech, because the patients, as indeed happened in this case, can in certain circumstances not only perceive correctly, but also further elaborate what they perceive and behave fairly rationally.

Stereotypy.—We almost always meet in the train of thought of the patients indications of stereotypy, of the persistence of single ideas. If the patient continues talking, the same ideas and expressions usually turn up again from time to time. Occasionally the persistence gets the mastery of the train of thought to such an extent that the patients for weeks and months always move in the same monotonous sphere of ideas, and cannot be brought out of it by any means.

Evasion. — Further peculiar disorders of the train of thought which here and there are observed, are evasion and a feature which Bleuler more accurately characterised as " *intellectual negativism.*" Evasion or *paralogia* consists in this, that the idea which is next in the chain of thought is suppressed and replaced by another which is related to it. It appears most distinctly in the patients' answers to questions ; but it might be possible that the complaints of

the patients that their thoughts are "drawn off" from them,
"distorted," refer to similar occurrences. An example is
given in the following answers of a patient to the physician's
questions :—

What is the name of this gentleman? (Dr A.), "Little man." What
is his name? "Florschütz" (The name of a fellow patient). How many
fingers am I holding up? (3) "Four." How many now? (4) "Five."
And now? (2) "One." How much money is that? (three pennies)
"Sixpence." No, you know quite well, "Twopence." No, how much?
"Fourpence." Now name the number that was left out, how much
then? "Twenty-five thousand." What do you mean by twenty-five
thousand? "That I'm all right."

It is here easily seen that the patient deliberately
avoids the right answer which he certainly has at his
command, a proceeding which at first makes the impression
of intentional dissimulation. A patient replied to the
question how old she was; "One day.' Clearly this
phenomenon is nearly related to the negativistic disorders
of thought. They appear in the difficulty to carry on a
series of ideas as one wishes, the patient's thoughts are
"taken" from him. So it sometimes comes to pass that he
is obliged to think the opposite of what he really wishes.
There are "quarrels in his head." One patient said, "My
ideas have quarrelled," while another, perhaps with reference
to such occurrences, said, "Swindling is constantly going on
in my inside." This state appears more clearly in the
utterances of other patients, that they "are forced to think
otherwise," that they "have to think the opposite of what
other people with normal understanding do."

Constraint of Thought. — From these and similar
experiences the feeling which has already been discussed
often develops in the patients, that their thinking is constrained, has been withdrawn from the dominion of their
will by irresistible influences. On the one hand thoughts
arise in them which they feel as strange, as not belonging
to themselves ; there is a "thronging of thoughts," a "pushing
of thoughts," sometimes in tempestuous form. A patient
had to "drive through his brain in four hours nineteen years";
another thought he would have to write a book if he were
to note down everything that came into his head. But on
the other hand the patients cannot think as they wish; their
thoughts are withdrawn from them, slip away from them,
although they exert themselves to hold them fast and to
think them out. Owing to this there can be a sudden
"blocking" of their thought, producing a painful interruption in a series of ideas.

They never tire of describing this constraint of theirs

in ever varying ways. The patient's *thoughts are influenced*, inspired, pressed on him; he must receive them like a telephone; they are forced on him by hypnotism and suggestion, act on him "by suggestion." Everything that he thinks or says is thought or said under compulsion. A patient had always to fight against the idea that he was Christ. Reading is interrupted by thoughts and explanations; thoughts are arrested, blurred, the patient has to exert himself to squeeze them out; he must think what people say. He feels as if his brain stood still, as if he had two brains. He is no longer himself, he has a kind of double consciousness; the voices pull a thread, so that he has to think such stupid things. The thoughts can be taken out of people's brains; the patient is confused in his head, he cannot grasp any clear ideas, he cannot bring order into the jumble of his thoughts, there is an "entanglement in his mind." A patient wanted to strangle herself because she had not her thoughts any longer. Thoughts are made by others in the distance, in Berlin, read off, taken away, carried over. "It was blown into me that way" said a patient. His thoughts escape from the patient, he cannot catch them up, he is no longer independent. A patient "had to speak about politics," another had always to think of "business arrangements," a third "had to despise people." Frequently, as before described in detail, the powers which carry out such thought-influences, take on the form of voices which take away, turn aside, or suggest thoughts.

Mental efficiency is always diminished to a considerable extent. The patients are distracted, inattentive, tired, dull, do not take pleasure in work, their mind wanders, they lose the connection, they "cannot keep the thought in mind," they have no perseverance. It is true·they are often able to carry out quickly and correctly tasks depending solely on memory or practice, sums, repetition of what they have previously learned, but fail completely as soon as it is a question of independent mental activity and the overcoming of difficulties. A striking example of this is the photographic reading and transcription, which was previously mentioned. In work the patients soon become negligent, they get bad certificates, pass no examinations, are turned off everywhere as useless, and easily fall into the condition of beggars and vagabonds. They sit about idle and the most they do is to turn over the pages of an old calendar or to stare at the advertisements in a newspaper. Others develop great diligence, "study all night long," but accomplish nothing at all, take up trifling or aimless occupations, begin to compose bombastic, incomprehensible rhymes, to copy a foreign dictionary, or they lock themselves up in order to learn poems off by heart.

Experiments in calculation yield further insight into the changes in mental efficiency. These experiments were employed in a number of patients according to the procedure formerly employed for alcoholics. Fig. 1 gives a graph of the results. Here the work done in the first five minutes and in the second five minutes, on the days when no pause was made, is represented by a continuous line; the value of the second five minutes, on the days when a pause was

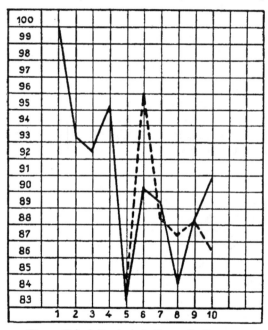

Fig. 1. Calculation tests in Dementia Præcox.

made, by a broken line, while the average work done in the first minute is put down at a hundred. We recognize in the first place that the values in the first part of the experiment sink very much more quickly than in the directly comparable normal attempts, a behaviour, that may be caused either by specially great liability to fatigue or through very rapid yielding of the original will-tension. The striking oscillations of the values of the average minutes particularly in the second part of the curve as also the high values attained even here in single minutes (sixth and tenth) is in some measure contrary to the assumption of unusually great effect of fatigue. It is still more decidedly disproved by the insignificance of the general effect of the pause which we know may be regarded within certain limits as the measure of fatigue. The work performed rises considerably, it is true, in the sixth minute on the days when there was a pause, but sinks again immediately and keeps after that within the limits of the values reached on the days when there was no pause. Comparison with the curves of normal persons and still more with those of the very easily fatigued alcoholics shows quite distinctly the difference in the effect of the pause. The even and rapid fall of the values in the first beginning of the task, as well as immediately after the pause, points here also to a very rapid yielding of will-tension, as in alcoholics, but it is not connected with heightened liability to fatigue, but with the direct and very considerable oscillations of the work done, which clearly correspond accurately to the oscillations of attention observed by Busch and Gregor which also usually appear in the clinical picture.

Judgment.—Further the faculty of judgment in the patient suffers without exception severe injury. What always surprises the observer anew is the quiet complacency with which the most nonsensical ideas can be uttered by them and the most incomprehensible actions carried out. It is true that they often move with tolerable certainty in accustomed paths, but in the psychic elaboration of new experiences, in the judgment of circumstances not hitherto experienced, and in particular of their own state, in the drawing of obvious conclusions, in the bringing forward and trial of objections, they not infrequently commit the grossest blunders. One has the impression that the patients are not in a position to accomplish that mental grouping of ideas which is requisite for their survey and comparison, their subordination among one another and for the discovery of contradictions. In this respect they resemble dreamers in whom likewise the ability to sift the ideas which come into the mind, to arrange them and to correct them according to the standards gained by former experiences and general ideas is abolished. These disorders, on whose great fundamental significance Bleuler also lays most emphatic stress, suggest an encroachment on the inner action of will.

The patients often have a distinct feeling of the profound change which has taken place in them. They complain that they are "dark in the head," not free, often in confusion, no longer clear, and that they have "cloud thoughts."

They cannot grasp a thought, cannot understand anything; their mind is scattered; their thoughts have flowed away; their brain is no longer competent, is enfeebled. " My thoughts went away and will never come back," said a patient. " My mind has been taken away by spiritual influence of speech and will." " My whole mental power has disappeared, I have sunk intellectually below the level of a beast," " I am quite out of my mind," " I am being punished a little by my imagination," " I have become very stupid lately," " I've got something in my head," " My mind sometimes goes away," " The stupid fellow is confused," are similar expressions. Others call themselves " Half-fools" " easily weak-minded," " idiotic"; they are afraid they are going out of their mind, becoming insane, falling ill of softening of the brain. " Things go round about inside me, thoughts which belong to a sanatorium," said a patient. Another said that he had lost the faculty of perception and energy, that he was wholly changed. A patient declared she was quite well, but stupid, and would like to be cured, while another begged that she might be freed from spirits, she did not wish to be mad, to be the plaything of other people, but wished to be like other human beings, she couldn't stand it any longer, she was quite incurable. Many patients begin to read medical books, connect their complaint with onanism, begin all sorts of cures. A patient was absorbed in the books ; " How Can I Become Energetic?" and " Guide to an Imposing Appearance," and he diligently carried on medical gymnastics, deliberately gazing at the sun as long as possible every day in order by so doing to improve his health. In contrast to these indications which sometimes characterize the situation with surprising clearness, under-standing of the disease disappears fairly rapidly as the malady progresses in an overwhelming majority of cases even where in the beginning it was more or less clearly present.

Delusions, either transitory or permanent, are developed with extraordinary frequency on the foundation of the morbid change which is created by dementia præcox. In the first period of the disease they are usually by preference of a sad character, hypochondriacal, or ideas of sin or of persecution. The feeling of disease takes on insane forms; the brain is burned, shrunken, as if completely gone to jelly, full of water, the mind is " drawn like rags from the brain"; the patient " has only a little knuckle of brain left"; the nerves are teased out. The tongue is made of iron, the lungs are dried up, blood is in the spinal marrow, wax in the body, the heart is dried up, the flesh is loosened from the bones, the blood vessels tremble, threaten to fall down, the spinal marrow runs out by the genitals. The patient is not a human being any longer, he has not got his life any more, carries a death skull in his head, gets a rogue's skull, clown's wrinkles. Not infrequently these bodily changes are traced to interference from outside. The patient is "cut to pieces inside," "vivisected," his soul is torn out of him, his brain is blown out, his heart is torn out by poison, the physicians have stolen his brain at an operation, and looked into his inside, they change his figure, his legs, his genitals, and eyes, tear out his intestines. "Something else is made of my hands every day," said a patient.

Ideas of Sin.—These delusions are frequently accompanied by ideas of sin. The patient has by a sinful life destroyed his health of body and mind, he is a wicked fellow, the greatest sinner, has confessed unworthily, has committed lese-majesty, has denied God, scorned the Holy Ghost, neglected his gifts. The devil dwells in him, will fetch him, God has forsaken him, he is eternally lost, he has been driven out of the church, is going to hell. A patient felt "as if the devil wished to take hold of him." He is brought into relation with a murder, he is considered a spy, he is under police control, is watched by detectives, he must appear in court, must be the scapegoat for others, is to be driven to death. Many patients abuse and revile themselves in connection with such ideas. A patient expressed himself as follows :—

"O you filthy beast, you are lying down again on an honoured bed—you are again to blame for it—there is a new waitress there again, nothing but princesses, whom you are bringing into confusion. If you only had the courage to get drunk! Insolent beast! Thunder and lightning shall strike in! If I had defended myself better yesterday. The thunderstorm shall strike in and damn you, beast—everyone's falling ill! I should long ago have been drunk!"

Ideas of Persecution.—In connection with these ideas of sin ideas of persecution are invariably developed, in the shaping of which hallucinations of hearing generally play an important part. The patient notices that he is looked at in a peculiar way, laughed at, scoffed at, that people are jeering at him, are spitting in front of him, the clergyman makes allusions to him in the sermon. He is grossly abused and threatened, his thoughts are influenced, he is surrounded by a "spiteful revolution." People spy on him ; Jews, anarchists, spiritualists, persecute him, poison the atmosphere with poisonous powder, the beer with prussic acid, generate magic vapours and foul air, do not let him take a single good breath, try to wash him away with musk water. He must die, will be shot, beheaded, poisoned by the State, petroleum is poured over him and set on fire, he comes into the iron maiden, into a vault with toads and broken glass. His house is blown into the air, his wife is imprisoned, his brother has his "flesh torn off," his family is shot; the patient must drink the blood of his relatives. The peculiar sensations of influence lead to the idea that witchcraft and charms are

Fig. 2.   Representation of bodily influences.

being practised. The patient feels himself hypnotized by a magnet, bewitched, " possessed by the god Pluto," surrounded by spirits. " A nest of spirits lives in my brain." He has been taken for a telephone post, the telephone goes through him.

Ideas of Influence.—From the examples which have already been given it can be seen that very often the delusion of influence through external agents is developed ; " In a natural body such things do not happen." A patient sketched the picture reproduced in Fig. 2, from which at least so much can be gathered that in his opinion his persecutors took the most varied parts of his body as the points of attack for their malevolent importunity. Many patients are entangled in an inextricable net of the most painful ideas by the feeling of forced and powerless dependence on strange influences. The following fragment of a letter gives some insight into that kind of train of ideas :—

" I am in terrible anxiety. There is the greatest danger that my life is coming to an end with fear, because the whole institution is arranged like clock-work, which is managed, not by reason, but by crazy heads in the cells, which are regulated like toothed wheels, and not only are the cells so arranged that one must move to and fro in haranguations as on a telegraphic cobweb of nerves, also in the passages each square yard is a division that demands a hanging-man to appear from anywhere whether it is for a view or a brutal person. At the same time vapours, waves of heat are developed in the divisions which produce a dreadful degree of embarrassment on the one hand, brutal fascinating power and rapidity on the other ; with that there is a continuous sound of medium sounds, mediation voices which in a cruel manner perterrorize the mind with contradictions. It is quite indescribable with what wicked refinement these dialogues are carried on, which by the aid of influences are transferred in destructive manner treacherously from body to body and give witness that so-called crazy stationary in combination with all sorts of drivers and haranguers are the most cruel criminals in life which there are, who are yet surpassed only by another class which in certain circumstances take hold of one and crush him with poisoned fingers in an unscrupulous way like a stuffed lifeless mass in another condition. . . "

Exalted Ideas.—In a large number of cases ideas of exaltation are added to the ideas of persecution, sometimes from the beginning, more frequently first in the further course when they often come quite into the foreground of the clinical picture. Here and there perhaps only ideas of exaltation are observed. The patient is " something better," born to a higher place, the " glory of Israel," an inventor, a great singer, can do what he will. He is noble, of royal blood, an officer of dragoons, heir to the throne of Bulgaria ; Wilhelm Rex, the Kaiser's son, the greatest man in Germany, more than King or Kaiser. Or he is the chosen one, the prophet, influenced by the Holy Ghost, guardian angel, second Messiah, Saviour of the world, the little God, who distributes grace and love, more than the Holy Ghost, the Almighty. He has carried on the battle of life, conquered death, turned the axis of the earth, can make weather, can walk on the waves. He lives in Berlin, gets a uniform, must go to the Kaiser, can become minister and pope, will be a good match, will get a great inheritance, gets milliards from

God ; at the war-office there is gold deposited for him.
Female patients are countesses, princesses, queens ; they
possess the whole world, have the dignity of the Mother of
God, get gold-embroidered clothes, children from the Grand
Duke and from the Kaiser, will marry the surgeon-major or a
prince, their uncle has left millions.

Sexual Ideas.—A conspicuously large place in the
clinical picture of dementia præcox, seems to me to be
occupied by sexual delusions which are often connected with
the sexual sensations described above. The ideas of sin are not
infrequently connected with this domain. The patient has
committed sin with his stepdaughter, with his sister, has had
intercourse with cows so that hybrids have been produced ;
he has committed a crime against decency, has ruined himself
by sexual excess, is homo-sexual, is a sadist. He has
become impotent through onanism, the ' neurosis ' proceeds
from onanism, onanism can be recognised in his face. A
patient kept a record of his seminal emissions. Another
was always obliged to think of filthiness (sexual intercourse
with his mother) ; a third "could not get rid of the thought
that his wife committed lewdness with animals in order to
punish him for onanism." Improper thoughts always came
to a patient against her will. Female patients notice that
men wish to seduce them, policemen and soldiers wish to
have them all. A dog with a muzzle on seemed to a patient
to indicate his sexual restraint ; when his landlady brought
him an egg for breakfast he regarded that as an invitation to
sexual intercourse and prepared to accept it. Another patient
felt impelled to have intercourse with his sister.

But above all things patients feel themselves sexually
influenced in the most varied ways. A neighbour's wife
occupied herself at night with the genitals of the patient, nuns
constantly withdraw seminal emissions from him and behave
immodestly before him. ' Love-stories ' are given him in his
coffee, grated flesh-flies are mixed in his food so that his penis
becomes blue. Sexual dreams are suggested to him, proposals
are made to him from a distance, women with butterfly wings
come to live with him, the landlady "will force nature on
him." He is weakened in the genitals, loses sexual power,
something is stuck in from without, he is enticed to onanism,
he is castrated because of self-abuse, the students want to
"dock" him. Women feel that they have lost their
virtue, that their honour has been tarnished ; their father,
their clergyman has abused them ; their master, the Kaiser
comes at night to them. Gentlemen are sent to them for
sexual intercourse, someone lies on them every night. They

are raped in anæsthesia, " spiritually abused," are pregnant by a cup of coffee, by a shadow, by the devil, by Lohengrin, have children in their body, must always bring forth ; things are said as if they were expecting to be confined and were committing abortion ; their womb rises into their head. The institution is a brothel, a house of ill-fame, in which filthiness is carried on.

In connection with these insane ideas an irritable aversion to the other sex is not infrequently developed. A patient spat at the girls he met. Women fall into lively excitement as soon as the physician comes near, speak abusively in obscene language about debauchery and whoredom, will not have anything to do with men. A patient cut off her hair in order to displease her followers.

Ideas of Reference.—The events of the outside world are brought into manifold connection with the delusions by means of "conjecturing thoughts." Indifferent remarks and chance looks, the whispering of other people, appear suspicious to the patient. " I feel myself referred to there," said a patient. A passer-by shows off his big nose, his red face on purpose to mock at the patient. News in the papers contain allusions, he finds in them thoughts which he has had. " My instinct tells me that," asserted a patient. His fellow-patients are appointed to watch him ; a patient who heard others speaking about him said, " I think to myself that the doctor gives people the commission to make me mad, the thunderstorm must help too." On the street he meets girls with whom he formerly had intercourse ; the tramway gives signs with the bell ; the sentries present arms. A patient recognised by the finger nails of his superior that he was his brother. People are astonishingly friendly; it is all a farce ; there is a change in his military pass. A patient thought it better to go from home when a gas pipe was going to be repaired in his house. Another read from the clothes of the physicians their thoughts about him ; a star in the sky pointed out his grave to a third ; the fern in his buttonhole indicated war to a fourth ; all labels and buttons that he found were important papers and pieces of money to a fifth. A patient held the opinion that misfortunes were brought into connection with her menses and she would be called to account for it. Frequently the delusions are connected with dreams which are regarded simply as actual experiences or as significant portents.

The delusions of our patients often show, as the given examples do, an extraordinary, sometimes wholly *nonsensical* stamp. As a rule also they are either not at all, or only in a very superficial way, worked up mentally and are scarcely brought into inner connection with one another. The patients do not try to give any account of the reliability of their observations and conclusions, do not search for explanations of their remarkable experiences, their persecutions, their good fortune ; they make no difficulties and pay no regard if any are pointed out to them, but rather hold the more to their insane ideas without further proof. " I have innumerable proofs and not one," said a patient."

But always here and there we meet with a certain systematisation of the morbid ideas mostly indeed only temporary ; they are connected with one another by all sorts of unwarranted assumptions or subtle arguments. For example a patient wholly out of his mind demanded as compensation for his supposed unjust detainment in the institution simply the civil list of the King, as he explained that the denial of justice, if only towards a single subject, signified the virtual abdication of the King as the stronghold of justice ; he, the injured party, must accordingly demand what the King by the permission of injustice voluntarily resigned.

In accordance with their generally very *loose inner connection* the delusions are for the most part by no means constant, but they change their content more or less quickly by the disappearance of former and the addition of new constituents. At times the patients produce nearly every day new delusional details in spite of certain persistently returning characteristic features, and perhaps let themselves be stimulated to further delusions by suggestion. In the overwhelming majority of cases, however, the delusions which are at first often very luxuriant, gradually cease. At most a few insane ideas are for some time adhered to without being further developed, or they appear once again from time to time, or finally they fall into oblivion permanently and completely. Only in that group of observations with which we shall later become acquainted as paranoid dementia are the delusional ideas generally more connected for a longer time, perhaps for some years, and appear unchanged in the main point, but here also they become gradually more confused and more contradictory.

Emotion.—Very striking and profound damage occurs as a rule in the emotional life of our patients. The most important of these changes is their *emotional dulness.* The disorders of attention which have already been mentioned might be essentially connected with the loss of interest, the loss of inner sympathy, with the giving way of those emotional main-springs which move us to exert our mental powers, to accomplish our tasks, to follow trains of thought. The singular indifference of the patients towards their former emotional relations, the extinction of affection for relatives and friends, of satisfaction in their work and vocation, in recreation and pleasures, is not seldom the first and most striking symptom of the onset of disease. The patients have no real joy in life, "no human feelings"; to them "nothing matters, everything is the same"; they feel "no grief and no joy," "their heart is not in what they say." A patient said he was childish and without interest, as he had never been before. Another said that nothing gave him pleasure, he was sad and yet not sad. Again another stated that he had "inward peace in his soul"; a fourth said "I am as cold as it is possible to be." "Everything is frightfully indifferent to me, even if I should become quite insane," said a female patient.

Hopes and wishes, cares and anxieties are silent; the patient accepts without emotion dismissal from his post, being brought to the institution, sinking to the life of a vagrant, the management of his own affairs being taken from him; he remains without more ado where he is put "till he is dismissed," begs that he may be taken care of in an institution, feels no humiliation, no satisfaction; he lives one day at a time in a state of apathy. The background of his disposition is either a meaningless hilarity or a morose and shy irritability. One of the most characteristic features of the disease is a frequent, causeless, sudden outburst of *laughter*, that often is strikingly in evidence already at the very commencement. "His thoughts always made him laugh," said the relatives of a patient.

Moral sentiments also and their regulating influence on action suffer severe loss. Not only in the former history of the patient do we find manifold contraventions of the penal code and public order, but also during the disease itself deeds are frequently committed which are dangerous to the common weal. Pighini found that among 114 mental patients who were sentenced, 49·1 per cent. were cases of dementia præcox.

Loss of sympathy is shown in indifference and want of understanding for the misfortunes of others, in the roughness with which the patients occasionally ill-use their companions in misfortune on the most trifling occasion; a woman tried to strangle the patient in the next bed in order to free her from her troubles. Even the fate of his nearest relatives affect the patient little or not at all. He receives their visits without a greeting or other sign of emotion, does not enquire how they are, takes no share in their joys or sorrows. A patient remained quite indifferent to the death of his mother, and then excused himself, as he could not help it ; " Life is nothing to me and death is nothing," he said.   A patient who had cut the throats of her three children because they were bewitched and would not be rightly brought up, did not show afterwards the slightest emotion ; her children were now angels and well taken care of, she explained.

Another phenomenon of emotional dementia is the *disappearance of delicacy of feeling*.   The patients have no longer any regard for their surroundings ; they do not suit their behaviour to the situation in which they are, they conduct themselves in a free and easy way, laugh on serious occasions, are rude and impertinent towards their superiors, challenge them to duels, lose their deportment and personal dignity ; they go about in untidy and dirty clothes, unwashed, unkempt, go with a lighted cigar into church, speak familiarly to strangers, decorate themselves with gay ribbons.   The feeling of disgust and of shame is also lost.   The patients do not preserve control of the sphincters.   They pass their excreta under them, they ease themselves under the bed, in the spitoon, in their hat, in the dishes, they make little balls of fæces, collect their evacuations in handkerchiefs or cigar-boxes, smear themselves with urine, wash their hand-kerchief in the full chamber ; they take their food with their fingers, they spit in their bed or in their hand, or on their bread, they devour beetles and worms, sip dirty bath-water, or empty at one draught the full spittoon.   The want of a feeling of shame expresses itself in regardless uncovering of their persons, in making sexual experiences public, in obscene talk, in improper advances, and in shameless masturbation.

It appears also that the patients often become *less sensitive to bodily discomfort* ; they endure uncomfortable positions, pricks of a needle, injuries, without thinking much about it ; burn themselves with their cigar, hurt themselves, tear out the hair from their genitals, let the glaring noonday sun shine in their face for hours, do not chase away the flies which settle on their eyelids.   Often, however, food retains for a long time a special power of attraction.   When their relatives visit them the patients are seen hurriedly rummaging through their bags and baskets for things to eat, which they immediately devour to the last crumb, chewing with their mouths full.   In the terminal conditions of the illness, perfect indifference towards all that goes on in the neighbourhood is often enough one of the principal features of the clinical picture.

On the foundation of the more or less strongly marked

emotional dulness, however, *sudden oscillations of emotional equilibrium* of extraordinary violence may be developed. In particular, sudden outbursts of rage with or without external occasion are not infrequent and can lead to most serious deeds of violence. The patients destroy objects, smash windows, force open doors, deal out boxes on the ear. A patient stabbed a girl's arm, another killed his master, a third killed a companion by whom he felt himself influenced. On the other hand the patients may suddenly fall into the most unrestrained merriment with uncontrollable laughter, seldomer into states of intense anguish. All these emotions are distinguished by the suddenness of their onset and disappearance and the often quite sudden change of mood. At the same time they have often no recognisable connection with the experiences or the ideas of the patients. Bleuler, however, brings forward the view that in such states it is usually a case of contact with the "complexes," the sensitive traumata of life. I have not been able to convince myself of that, but believe much rather that we have essentially to do with the loss of that permanent colouring of the background of mood which in normal people influences all chance oscillations of the emotions, equalising and checking them and which only then lets them appear in greater strength when an important occasion finds a powerful echo in our being.

Stransky has, therefore, not without justification, said that it is a case in our patients less of an emotional devastation, than of an "*ataxia of the feelings*," a loss of connection with other mental occurrences. I am inclined to assume that this confusion in the emotional life is caused essentially by the weakening of the higher permanent feelings, whose task it is on the one hand to check sudden oscillations of feeling, on the other hand to give to our inward states permanently equable tension and temperature, and so to become security for the agreement of our emotional relations with the outer world. Exactly in the terminal conditions with pronounced dementia one frequently observes emotional irritability with sudden, violent outbursts, and also excitement which appears without cause with more or less regular periodicity.

The comparatively great independence on outer influences of the temper has as a consequence that it often remains for a very long time extremely *uniform*. Many patients constantly exhibit a silly cheerfulness, others always a lachrymose dull depression or an ill-humoured strained behaviour. They are not brought out of their careless contentment either by unpleasant occurrences or by the blows of fate, nor can they be comforted, nor can their affection be won. But the course of the illness itself can bring about unexpectedly some day a sudden change in their mood.

Here and there it may be observed that the disposition of the patients is exactly *contrary to the actual state of affairs.* The patients laugh while they narrate an attempt at suicide, or the death of a near relative, and weep bitterly on any occasion for mirth. Sometimes it is only a case of want of relationship between mood and expression—of paramimia. The most frequent occurrence of the kind is senseless laughing without mirthfulness. The patient cannot help laughing ; he does it even when he does not wish to ; he has "laughing fever," said a patient. Also the mingling of crying and laughing, crying in tune, dancing about with fixed and furrowed features belong to the paramimic phenomena.

But further there sometimes takes place in the patients a *complete reversal of their emotional relationships,* which may be the first sign of the approaching illness. Former feelings of affection are changed into downright aversion. In especial the nearest relatives suffer frequently. Towards his parents of whom he has hitherto been fond, the patient behaves rudely, haughtily, threateningly ; he abuses them in obscene language ; his mother is an old spitfire, his father is a rogue, a perjured dog. His mother stupefies him, is a witch ; his father causes him headache ; his sister is the devil, " the whore who has ruined his life." His brother has signed the deed for his execution ; his brother-in-law shoots him. The former lover becomes an enemy and persecutor, who stirs up the people and is everywhere in evidence. And senseless jealousy is not rare. His wife has secretly married another man ; the nurses wish to alienate the loved one ; the husband has been changed. A patient suddenly tried to poison her new-born child, as it seemed to her it was not the right one ; she asked the public prosecutor by telegraph to arrest her husband as he wanted to murder her.

Like the thoughts, the feelings of the patient can also occasionally be " transferred " in his opinion ; " there are transferences of grief " ; " feelings of anguish come from outside by the ears, inward thoughts of persecution," said a patient. Another asserted that his sister had an apparatus for speaking at a distance, 150 to 300 miles ; by the current one could be made to fall in love, to grieve, to have bad thoughts. The patient " has no peace at work because some one always sits beside him." " The laughing is made by voices," explained a patient ; " that is not laughing, my mouth is drawn askew," said another ; " the nerve of laughing is irritated," said a third, it is an electrical laughing. " The laughing comes to me from beneath upwards ; it makes me laugh, and yet it is not laughable," said a fourth ; and a patient complained, " Now again another quite stupid fit of laughing is caused in me !"

Volition.—Hand in hand with the profound disorders of the emotional life go the extensive and varied morbid manifestations in the domain of *work and conduct*, which specially give the clinical picture its peculiar stamp. They are composed of a series of diverse fundamental disorders. In the first place we have commonly to do with a general *weakening of volitional impulses*. The patients have lost every independent inclination for work and action ; they sit about idle, trouble themselves about nothing, do not go to their work, neglect their most pressing obligations, although they are perhaps still capable of employing themselves in a reasonable way if stimulated from outside. They experience no tediousness, have no need to pass the time, " no more joy in work," but can lie in bed unoccupied for days and weeks, stand about in corners, " stare into a hole," watch the toes of their boots or wander aimlessly about. For work they have " no inclination"; " their nerves can't stand it." A patient did no work for two years, " in order not to deprive people of gain "; another had in view, after having used his last sovereign, to go into the Lake of Constance ; a third asked " for an easy job, perhaps as a clergyman."

Automatic Obedience.—This loss of instinct for occupation, even though its clinical manifestations may be inconspicuous, represents without doubt an *unusually severe disorder*, as the activity of the will forms the most important foundation of psychic personality. To it there stands in close relationship that *susceptibility of the will to influence*, which finds its most distinct expression in the phenomena of automatic obedience. As the inner activity of volition fails, the resistance which outside influences meet within us is also easily lost. The patients therefore are usually docile, let themselves be driven as a herd, so that they form the necessary nucleus of those crowds which conform willingly to the monotonous daily round in large institutions. A not inconsiderable number join without resistance the crowd of vagabonds which chance leads to-day hither, to-morrow thither.

But also fully developed automatic obedience is extremely frequent. It is found in all stages of the disease, at the beginning as well as at the end, not infrequently also as the one noticeable remaining feature of the disease in otherwise apparently complete recovery. It is seen in *waxy flexibility*, in the preservation of whatever positions the patient may be put in, even although they may be very uncomfortable. This very striking disorder is plainly seen in the group in Fig. 3, which brings together a series of patients suffering from dementia præcox. They were put without difficulty in the peculiar positions and kept them, some with a sly laugh, others with rigid seriousness. The patient sitting on the right was already fairly demented, while the three patients on the left were still in the initial stages of the disease.

Fig. 3. Group of schizophrenic patients.

Further the Figures 4, 5, 6 show the same patient in different positions in which he was put, of which specially the last one could obviously be preserved only by a considerable expenditure of force. " I have to do it," said a patient, when he was asked about the cause of his cataleptic behaviour; another said, " It happens to order."

Again automatic obedience, as its name expresses, appears in *involuntary obedience* when called upon to do things, even those which are visibly disagreeable to the patient. He continues to put out his tongue when commanded to do so although one threatens to stab it, and causes him pain with a needle, as can be seen by the grimaces he makes.   It might also be considered as automatic obedience that the patient submits to unpleasant touching of his face, tickling of the mucous membrane of his nose, piercing a fold of his eyelid without defending himself, in as far as these proceedings

Fig. 4. Waxy flexibility (a).*

contain the unspoken command not to prevent them.   Again *echolalia* and *echopraxis* belong to this group of phenomena, the involuntary repetition of words said to them, the imitation of movements made in front of them, or the continuance of movements passively initiated.   "I do it because you wish it so."   "I place myself according to what is commanded."

" I was unconscious, I had to do everything," say the patients. But in the end a curious *constraint of the movements* is invariably connected with automatic obedience, which apparently stands in relation to the inner want of freedom of the patient, with the uncertainty of the patient's own will and its susceptibility to influence from all possible accidental occurrences. Often indeed is it so distinctly marked that it

Fig. 5. Waxy flexibility (*b*).

makes the conclusion very probable that there will be other disorders of automatic obedience.

Impulsive actions.—The weakening of the dominion of will in the psychic life provides further, as it appears, the conditions favourable for the appearance cf the impulsive actions which attain such great significance in dementia præcox. The relaxing of those restraints, which keep the activity of normal people in well defined paths, provides chance impulses with the freedom to turn themselves un-hesitatingly into action without regard to the end in view or to suitability. So it happens that the patients commit a great many of the most nonsensical and incomprehensible acts of which they themselves are usually unable to explain

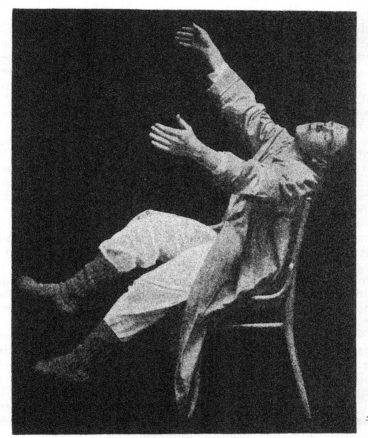

Fig. 6. Waxy flexibility (*c*).

the cause. "I have a sort of feeling as if I must do that," explained a patient who was screaming and biting everything. "I had no free course left me, I had often to do things without knowing why," said another. A third said, "I must shuffle and do gymnastics," a fourth, "I must scream in order not to burst"; a fifth sang, "because it was desired";

a sixth asserted that "God made him spit." The patients suddenly break a mirror in pieces, knock over tables and chairs, take down pictures, throw objects out at the window, climb on to a cupboard, set fire to their hair, run naked into the street, ring bells, put their heads in the basin of the water-closet, set the chamber on their head, creep under the table, smash a lamp. Usually such senseless actions are carried out with great violence, suddenly, and with lightning rapidity, so that it is impossible to prevent them; the patients also oppose themselves in the most insolent way to every attempt to keep them from doing these things. "I had a feeling as though I were not doing my duty; there was an impulse in me," were the terms in which a patient described his inner perceptions. Another smashed the fire-alarm, "because he had the impulse in his arm"; a third, who with all his might was struggling and drumming called out, "I cannot do it any more vigorously! Am I to do it still more vigorously?"

In certain circumstances the impulsive actions of the patients may become extraordinarily dangerous. The patients suddenly give a box on the ear to any one they meet, make a furious attack on a neighbour, set fire to beds, tear off a gas-bracket. A patient tried to throttle his uncle's grandchild; another smashed the bell at a level-crossing and wanted to tear up the rails as well; he alleged as his motive that he had been shut up in Roumania and made insane. Others bite their arm, strike their face, squeeze their testicles together, drink up any bottle of medicine, put beetles or stones in their ears, make continuous attempts at suicide, suddenly hang themselves, jump out at the window, throw themselves in front of the tramway; a patient broke a tea-spoon in order to stick it into his neck.

Often sexual impulses are also very lively. The patients masturbate without regard for their surroundings, or in the examination by the physician, snatch at the genitals of their fellow-patients, take hold of their sister under her skirts. A patient raped his brother's cook and tried to do the same to his sister-in-law. A female patient for years made regardless sexual attacks on the physicians, in order through intercourse "to be freed from the oppression on her breast."

Catatonic Excitement. — The peculiar condition of catatonic excitement consists of a collection of senseless actions and movements with which we shall have later to occupy ourselves more in detail. Besides impulsive actions we meet at the same time in large number and variety with discharges of will-power, in which every relation to the realisation of fixed aims is wanting, but which appear in the form of completely aimless movements. They have no connection either among each other or with ideas or emotions, but have the tendency to repeat themselves very often either in the same form or with all manner of changes. Here and there they still bear the character of mutilated movements of purpose or expression, from which partly at least they may arise. The patients hop, jump, turn somersaults; scream, grunt, see-saw, drum, screech, go through the movements of ringing, of playing the violin, usually with the expenditure of all their energy, but without any recognisable aim.

Stereotypy.—With the disorders of volition which have already been considered, there is very frequently connected in dementia præcox, as has already been indicated, another, the tendency to the instinctive persistence of the same volitional movements, stereotypy. It shows itself in continuance in the *same positions* as well as in the repetition of the *same movements* or *actions*. The will is here to a certain extent influenced for a considerable time by previous activities, in the same way as in automatic obedience. Stransky therefore speaks, probably with right, of an "auto-echolalia" and "auto-echopraxis." The patients stand or kneel for hours, days, or still longer, on the same spot, lie in the most uncomfortable positions in bed, fold their hands spasmodically, even till pressure-sores appear, take up the position of fencing. Usually it is possible only with the most extreme force to bring them out of such a position, which they usually take up again as soon as the hindrance has ceased.

Much more varied are the stereotypies of movement which we often meet in the most marked form, especially in states of catatonic excitement. In the milder degrees it is more a matter of a certain uniformity of volitional expression, the persistence of definite activities. The patients always make the same gestures, go the same ways, pull their hair out like the patient represented in Fig. 7; they make bread pellets, continually scratch their faces, slide down on their knees, make peculiar noises, make grimaces, play all day long the same tune on the piano; a patient "threw his roll on to the table a hundred times." In the same category there belong also twitching movements in different groups of muscles, raising a shoulder, "contortionist movements," waving with the hands, touching definite parts of their bodies with their fingers, conspicuous clearing of their throats, smacking of their lips, snorting. A patient who always twitched with his alæ nasi, explained, "That is just my way."

Sometimes the whole ·volitional expression of the patient is dominated by stereotypies for a long time, so that his doings resolve themselves into an almost uninterrupted series of senseless movements which are either monotonous, or repeat themselves with slight changes. A certain *rhythm* invariably results. The patients rock themselves from one leg on to the other, keep time, "pull letters away from their fingertips," spread out their fingers with a quavering movement, clap their hands, shake their heads, bellow keeping time, give themselves boxes on their ears, run up and down

Fig 7. Hair-pulling patient.

in double quick time. About the motives for these proceedings, no satisfactory account is got from them. A patient who always rocked himself rhythmically from side to side, simply explained, "It happens so in me," "I must shake my head or else I am in terror," "I must constantly say things," "I must scream without wanting to, there is that impulse in me," "I must throw myself about at night in bed as if a strange power threw me," "I must turn round, as when a magnet draws a needle," "I could not have rested till I had done that," are similar expressions.

We may well suppose that also the development of such stereotypies, which later give such a peculiar appearance to the terminal states of the disease and likewise to many forms of idiocy, is specially favoured by the failure of healthy volitional impulses, perhaps first made possible. Many experiences at least indicate that the mechanism of our will possesses arrangements acquired long ago, which favour a rhythmical repetition of the same discharges ; their influence will be able to make itself felt as soon as the impulses disappear which serve for a realisation of intentions.

Mannerisms. The uncertainty and weakness of the volitional movements which are accompanied with consciousness of purpose, and further the ease with which all possible impulses can influence volitional expression perhaps explain how it is that the actions of our patients often end in *morbidly changed forms*. Even simple movements can show such changes. Sometimes they are carried out with too great an expenditure of force, or unnecessary groups of muscles take part in them, or too much of the limb is employed, so that they become ungraceful and clumsy ; or they are not rounded off, they begin and end jerkily and appear therefore stiff, wooden, and angular. Other patients again arrive at the aim of the movement not by the nearest way, but by round-about ways with all sorts of changes and interpolations ; they add flourishes by which the movements become unnatural, affected and manneristic. Through such peculiarities, which are called mannerisms, the processes of breathing, speaking and writing, standing and walking, dressing and undressing, shaking hands and eating, smoking, gestures, and the mode of setting to work, can be influenced and transformed in the most manifold way. Grasping is done with fingers spread out ; speaking is accompanied with loud hawking and grunting or with smacking movements of the lips, the face is distorted by spasmodic grinning ; among masons every stone is first turned round several times before it is laid in position. Many patients lift their legs in walking "like the stork in the lettuce" ; a male patient promenaded about with his shirt solemnly lifted ; a female patient played the piano with gloves on.

The process of taking food especially may be changed by the most manifold side impulses. Frequently the patients simply thrust their hands into their plate, fall upon the common dish, hurriedly stuff their mouths as full as possible and swallow their food down almost without chewing, or the spoon is grasped quite lightly with their finger-tips, often at the extreme end and the handle is used for eating ; their food is invariably stirred about with their forks two or three times before each mouthful, the vegetables are divided into a row of equal little heaps, their hands are first wrapped up in their coats, their nose is stuck into the soup, or there must be a mouthful drunk between each two mouthfuls of food till twelve are counted and so on. Others lap the soup like a dog or pour it with profuse spilling into their mouth without more ado, press the vegetable dish flat on to their face and steadily lick it clean. One of my patients took hold of the spoon quite correctly with the right hand, but brought it round her head by the left side to her mouth; another crept under the bed cover at meals.

Not infrequently the aim of the action is wholly or at least partially frustrated by the changes and made unrecognisable, so that the impression arises of oddness and senselessness. To this group belong such peculiarities as giving the edge of the hand or the fingertips in shaking hands, lying crosswise in bed, speaking with closed teeth. A patient covered himself with paper; another sucked passionately at the corner of the bed, a third dipped the corners of his pillow into his coffee. All these mannerisms have a pronounced tendency to persist, and they may form part of the behaviour of a patient without change for decades. Through them especially arise the half-repulsive, half-ludicrous impressions which strike the laity on visiting an institution for the insane, and it is those therefore above all from which the popular picture of "lunatic" is usually composed.

It is made still more complete by the oddities in the outer adornment of the patients, the extraordinary modes of dressing the hair, the earrings made of pieces of wire, the gay ribbons in the hair and in the button-hole, the peculiar ornaments of the clothes. A patient drew his socks over his trousers; another wore them folded together on his head; a third adorned himself with bracelets of paper. Frequently also the patients adopt very peculiar attitudes and deportment, balance themselves on one leg, put their head between their legs, lie on the edge of the bed, spread out their arms in cruciform attitude, twist themselves together in the most remarkable manner. A patient answered as follows to the question why he did such things:—

"The feeling is called forth by influence from the outer world. It is then as if with certain degrees of unity of the small parts with no reasonable handling by oneself small parts of the body (at the finger and other limbs) were pulled away from the entire whole with unspeakable pains. If I feel anywhere in my body much discomfort, which it with its whole mental ability must endeavour to put right, in order not to will to produce these extraordinary pains, I must change my position in all the small parts."

Parabulia.—Gradual transitions from the simple changes of every-day purposeful actions lead to those disorders of volition which we may gather together under the name of parabulia. The side impulses which at first bring about only flourishes in action may gradually become cross impulses which lead to complete derailment of volition. Some examples belonging to this class we have already brought forward in which to a certain extent a distorted picture of natural actions arises by the employment of unsuitable means. But further, an action at first perhaps correctly begun is turned away in quite another direction by cross impulses or perhaps simply stopped before completion (Ergodialeipsis according to Moravsik). The hand that will stretch out and take hold of the spoon, goes to the nose to scratch there; the patient who will put on his coat, puts his legs into the sleeves. In shaking hands the movement comes to a standstill half way; the patient breaks off in the middle of a sentence; he stirs his food about keeping time as he does so, without bringing the fork with food on it to his mouth.

Whether we have here to do with the turning away of actions in a different direction or with the stopping before completion of actions already begun, the cross or contrary impulse can further suppress the volitional movement itself even as it is already coming into being, so that the action which is about to be done is not even begun, but from the outset is replaced by another or simply suppressed. The patient who is to show his tongue, opens his eyes wide instead, he flings the cup away instead of putting it to his mouth. We shall consider these "parergasias" more in detail in the discussion of the movements of expression.

Negativism.—By far the most important form of parabulia is the suppression of volitional movements by contrary impulses, negativism. It is natural that of the innumerable side impulses which in themselves are possible, those should take up a special position which are exactly *contrary* to the attainment of the end in view; on the appearance of a volitional intention they are at the same time most strongly stimulated in consciousness by the action of contrast. Negativistic obstruction of volition plays therefore an extraordinarily large rôle in the clinical picture of dementia præcox. To begin with it leads to the instinctive suppression of all reaction to external influences, further to stubborn opposition to interference of all sorts, and in the end to the performance of actions which are exactly opposed to those which are suggested by the circumstances or required by the environment.

It is, however, certain that the disorders commonly collected under the term negativism have not all the same origin, as Bleuler [1] in particular has shown in detail. At first insane ideas or ill-temper, especially anxiety or irritability, cause the patients to shut themselves up from their environment. They do not touch their food because they think it is poisoned, do not lie down in bed because they imagine that they are threatened with the danger of syphilitic infection there, do not shake hands because they distrust the physician, or fear his influencing them, and they will not have anything to do with him. In a similar way probably one should regard the resistant attitude of the bewildered and confused patients to whom everything appears changed, incomprehensible, and mysterious ; here also anxious distrust may be assumed as the mainspring of their opposition. In none of these cases is it a question of negativism in the sense of a disorder specially peculiar to dementia præcox. It appears to me also that the behaviour of such patients towards the stimuli which they encounter does not differ from that of other anxious or irritable persons ; in especial on stronger provocation they fall into excitement, make lively movements of defence, or even pass over to attack.

Various experiences meantime indicate that there is another form of resistance to outside influences, which comes into existence wholly by impulse that is without foundation on ideas or emotions. Imperative negativism, the carrying out of action exactly contrary to that wished, scarcely allows of any other interpretation. Only exceptionally could there be any palpable motive in the question, as when a patient forces his way out on being told to stay where he is. But when a patient begins to sing as soon as he is asked to be quiet, when he goes backward on being ordered to march, it is difficult to find an explanation in deliberation or emotional influences. To this it may be added that the patients in many cases of marked negativism actually exhibit neither delusions nor emotions, which could in any way justify their peculiar behaviour. But finally for this question the utterances of the patients themselves are very important which are almost always to the effect that they felt themselves forced without being able to explain the reasons to themselves. "I must often do the opposite of what I am asked," said a patient, "I do not will as the people will," explained another. Certainly here and there delusions or hallucinations are mentioned as causes of the negativistic behaviour. The patients feel themselves under a " ban," eat

[1] Bleuler, Psychiatrisch-Neurol. Wochenschr. xii., 18.

nothing for a day "because God does not wish them to," "must not speak," "remain lying," "on a higher command," "because the mediums wish it," "the voices command it." It may, however, rightly be assumed that such reasons are nothing else than formulas for the characterisation of hindrances to volition which are inexplicable to the patient; the voices also might in this respect only give expression to what the patient feels in himself.

Still more distinct does the peculiarity of this disorder become by the fact specially emphasised by Bleuler of "inner negativism." As already mentioned above, obstacles place themselves in the way not only of external commands, but also of the internal volitional impulses, obstacles which lead sometimes only to the omission of the intended action, but also to the performance of a contrary one or even of an action of a totally different kind. "I never arrive at what I want to do," said a patient, "I cannot do what I wish," "I had no free will," "I had to do something without myself wishing to, sometimes to go backwards," "I had to do what was repugnant to my character," "Reason fights against the external influence," others explain. Also "intellectual negativism," which has already been discussed, the appearance of negativistic hindrances in the train of thought, can scarcely be otherwise explained than by immediate disorders of that inner activity of volition which regulates the rising into consciousness and the connection of ideas.

Autism.—The clinical phenomena, in which negativism shows itself, are extremely varied. It is a common experience that the patients with dementia præcox are more or less inaccessible, that they shut themselves off from the outer world. Bleuler has described this important symptom as *autism*. The refusal of all psychic contact is often shown in the whole behaviour of the patients as soon as one begins to occupy oneself with them. They do not look up when spoken to, perhaps turn away their head, or turn their back directly to the questioner. The hand offered in greeting is refused, "It is not proper," "In bed the hand is not given," "Only women greet each other that way," say the patients; they have given the hand too often formerly. Many patients close their eyes, cover their faces with their hands, cover themselves up, draw the bedcover over their head, and convulsively hold it fast; "This position is pleasant for the eyes and more restful for the inner life," explained a patient. Often the patients refuse all information; "That is their own affair," "That is no one's business," "People are cross-questioned in that way," "They should not be there, did not require to give explanations." A patient first asked the physician to show him his diplomas that he might know with whom he had to do. Others give perverted or quite insufficient answers.

Stupor.—But even when they do express themselves, one notices very distinctly by their niggardly, resisting, forced statements which tell nothing, the resistance which they oppose to any searching into their inner life. Frequently the patients have already shut themselves off from their family and their surroundings long before the appearance of the more striking symptoms, say only the most necessary things, do not appear any more at the common meals, avoid all friendly intercourse, bolt themselves in, take lonely walks. They bluntly refuse visits from the physician and friendly relations with their fellow-patients. As the disorder becomes further elaborated there is developed the picture of negativistic stupor, the rigid, impenetrable shutting up of themselves from all outer influences, which is connected with a suppression driven to the limit of the possible of all natural emotions. We shall later have to describe the clinical picture in detail.

Causation of Negativism.—As has already been indicated in the general part, the understanding of negativism in the sense here depicted requires to be connected with the fact that our thinking and acting constantly have to make decisions between different, often contrary, ideas and volitional resolves. In especial our whole relationship to the environment is governed throughout by volitional movements of inclination and disinclination, and the suitable choice of these possesses fundamental importance for our existence. Bleuler speaks of an "ambivalence" and an "ambitendency" of psychical processes, in the sense that they are accompanied at the same time, by contrary emotional stresses and can lead to contrary emotional movements. He assumes on the basis of his experiences that this discord in feelings and impulses comes under observation specially frequently and strongly in dementia præcox, and forms an important foundation for the development of negativism.

But of course even if that discord be granted, still further explanations are needed, not indeed why the choice between resistance and yielding oscillates in an unaccountable way which certainly often enough happens, but why so frequently during a long period the negativistic movements govern the sum total of the actions in so decided a way. So far as morbid moods or delusions play a part, I believe, as has been mentioned above, that it is not a case of genuine negativism. At most it might be admitted that with their

help the tendency to the appearance of negativistic
•phenomena which is present in any case, may be strengthened,
as conversely negativism perhaps also exercises some
influence on the content of hallucinations and delusions, as
on the tone of the mood.

In the last place, however, there must be other causes
which determine the governing position of the contrary
impulses, because of their instinctive origin and their
independence of the remaining contents of consciousness.
Besides erotic emotions which are usually even in healthy
life already accompanied by discordant processes of
emotion and volition, Bleuler regards as such, principally
the "autistic" tendency of the patients to withdraw themselves into themselves, the existence of specially sensitive
"life traumata," and the "forcing of thoughts," the deficient
command over the train of thought. He reckons, however,
for the explanation of "inner negativism" also with influences
unknown as yet.

The significance of erotic emotions is in my opinion to
be judged of in a similar way to those other feelings and
therefore to be left out of account in the fundamental
explanation of genuine negativism. That in the behaviour
of the patients "life traumata" play a part to any great
extent, so that they shut themselves up from their surroundings
as a protection from contact has, as I believe, till now neither
been proved nor even made probable; also the fact that
negativism frequently appears and disappears so suddenly
seems to me to argue very much against such an interpretation.
In contrast the "autism" of the patients stands certainly
without doubt in near relation to their negativism, only I
should think that it represents not so much a cause but much
rather a manifestation of negativism. The tendency to shut
themselves off from their surroundings is frequently found
in our patients already many years before the real onset of
the disease and it is a very common phenomenon in the
terminal states. But I very much doubt if it, as Bleuler
thinks, is caused by the withdrawal of the patient to his
own phantasies, and if he on this account feels every diverting
of attention as an intolerable disturbance. Stubborn inaccessibility is often enough shown by patients on the one
hand, in whom there can be no thought of special imaginings
in which they could lose themselves, and it is lacking on the
other hand in innumerable other delusional forms of disease,
as specially in paralysis in which the patients certaintly do
dream themselves into a world of imaginings which are
greatly disturbed by the influences of the surroundings.

It seems far more probable to me that negativism and "autism" which is only its forerunner, are not at all connected with ideas or "complexes," but with the general constraint of volition which is so specially peculiar to dementia præcox. Already on the most varied occasions we have had to point to the fact that the patients *lose the mastery over volition* and often feel this profound disorder more or less distinctly. They are heard describing their inner constraint always in new and emphatic expressions. Their will has been taken from them; it is weak, they have no will of their own any more, are not masters over it; there is no independence in them. "I am not melancholy, and not senseless," said a patient, "I only lack a will of my own, an impulse of my own." The patients feel themselves not free, influenced, dominated by external will, by invisible might, by magic powers possessed by superhuman beings "like an automaton"; they suffer from "auto-suggestion and high grade suggestibility," stand "as under compulsion," are in "slavery to suggestion"; "I am a man under compulsion," explained a patient." An external force has power over them under whose ban they must wholly exist and act; they must do what others wish, other people have power over them; "Another person works in me; who that is, I do not know," said a patient. Another complained, "For a year I have no longer had any will of my own, I am dependent on other people; my will becomes weaker from day to day; it is a dreadful bungling of work; I have no power to begin another life." A servant girl said she got orders as if she were in a situation, she was already accustomed to it.

Sometimes the influence on volition is referred to certain sources. God leads the patient; the patient is wholly under the influence of a companion; he "must do what his brother-in-law suggests to him by thought-transference by electrical means." A female patient felt herself ruled "by a gentleman and a lady," another by her fiancé who used enchantments and mystic measures in order to fetter her; still another noticed that a gentleman who passed had power over her. A patient thought that people were sent to him, who were to study suggestions, and they gradually went over to hypnosis; experiments were being tried on him; another saw an "eye like a half-moon, and had to follow it, he had sworn to." One of my patients, who thought he was put on trial by the authorities, asked them in thought often and urgently now at last to make an end of it; he crossed the French frontier in order to see if there also the suggestions took place. When he had convinced himself that the currents went over the frontier, probably by railways and telegraphs, he had only the one wish left, to cross the sea in order to take his life in case the action at a distance could be carried over also by cable.

We have already mentioned that even the isolated peculiar acts are caused as a rule without further motive by irresistible impulses. The patient "must" lie down, "assume a strange appearance," "spit on the physician," "assume attitudes," walk till he can "walk no longer," "by order" run from one place to another, imitate everything, laugh, "even when he is sad"; he "can do nothing against it," he must scratch his face; "that is caused." A female patient complained there was something wanting in her head; her understanding was weak; she therefore "talked stupidly, was really insane, had to do such things from want of sense." Here and there the impulses take on the form of auditory hallucinations without the nature of the process being thereby essentially altered; voices summon the patient to do this or that, and he "must do all that they ask."

Personality.—From these and similar utterances of the patients it clearly follows that their thinking, feeling, and acting have lost the unity and especially that permanent inner dependence on the essence of the psychic personality, which provides the healthy human being with the feeling of inner freedom; "I can't get hold of my will," said a patient. We may assume that this profound change in the psychic life, which indicates a complete destruction of the personality, must in itself influence the attitude towards the outer world in the most decisive way. The most natural protective measure of the weak consists in shutting himself up and hiding. The more or less distinct feeling of inner constraint and powerlessness which accompanies our patients along with childish susceptibility to influence, could therefore on the other hand play an essential part in the development of their obstinate seclusion. If the disorder of volition can influence the conduct of the patients in both directions and if it at the same time makes it more difficult for them to hold fast to a uniform attitude towards their surroundings, we should also have come nearer to the understanding of the frequent oscillations between heightened sensitiveness to influence and stubborn negativism. It is self-evident here that we must not, as has already been pointed out, think of conscious deliberation. Much rather is it the general change of the personality and its behaviour towards the ordinary events of life that come into consideration as it is conditioned by the perception of its own inner want of independence. If one wishes, one may with more right in my judgment regard the feeling of the *destruction of the will*, which may precede the real onset of the disease under certain circumstances certainly by many years, as a "life trauma" which cannot endure any contact and therefore causes the patient to shut himself up, rather than the influence of other chance events of life.   That

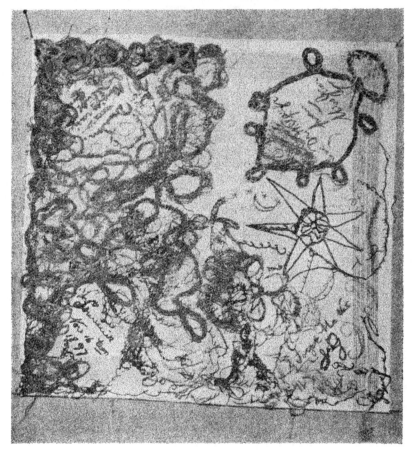

Fig. 8.   A handkerchief embroidered with silk.

disorder would also to a certain extent explain the tendency of many of the patients to spin themselves round with imaginings ; he who is not able to control his own will and with it his life, gladly takes refuge in the realm of dreams.

Practical Efficiency.—As the mental, so also the practical efficiency of the patients is invariably greatly encroached on by the disorders of volition. They come to a standstill at every difficulty, must always be driven on again, work extremely unequally, do a great deal of their work wrongly, are completely unreliable, spoil material and tools. At the same time, however, a certain technical skill can be preserved. In their handiwork the loss of taste often makes itself felt in their choice of extraordinary combinations of colour and peculiar forms. The accompanying figure gives an example of the singular works of art of the patients ; it represents a handkerchief embroidered with thick silk. I also reproduce in Fig. 9 a stocking which was knitted by a patient who had had catatonic stupor for years. The measure placed beside it is 20 cm. The patient knitted for a number of days simply a long pipe, and then when she was told brought the stocking at last to an end. She next added the two remarkable loops and further the point. At the same time the work was without fault in detail. Many patients produce very queer handiwork, a glove made of human hair, linen coverings for horses' hoofs, dolls made of cotton wool. The musical performances of the patients also show distinctly the decline of fine artistic feeling as they play sometimes without expression, sometimes in an arbitrarily incorrect way. After the more stormy manifestations have run their course, it is often possible to educate the patients again to simple work which they then accomplish without circumspection or self-reliance, and often with all sorts of caprices, but still with the regularity of a machine. A few patients continue work without showing any sign of fatigue or annoyance, till they are told to stop.

Fig. 9.
Singular stocking (Catatonia).

Self-expression.—The general disorders of volition often take many peculiar forms in the movements of expression of the patients.[1] The *cessation of the need to express oneself* corresponds to the disappearance of volitional activity. The

[1] Mignot, Annales médico-psychol, 1907, II. i. Morawsik, Allgem. Zeitschr. Psychiatrie, 1907, 733.

patients become monosyllabic, sparing of their words, speak hesitatingly, suddenly become mute, never relate anything on their own initiative, let all answers be laboriously pressed out of them. They enter into no relations with other people, never begin a conversation with anyone, ask no questions, make no complaints, give their relatives no news. They write no letters or only those with almost nothing in them, stop after writing a few lines. Their facial expression also is vacant and dull ; their gestures are limp, few, and monotonous. On this foundation echolalia easily appears, which makes itself known in the involuntary repetition of questions asked or other things said to them, as well as in the introduction of fragments of speech caught up into their own utterances.

In the states of excitement in place of taciturnity a pro-digious *flow of talk* may appear which does not correspond to a need for expression, but usually unburdens itself without any reference to the surroundings. Often it consists of out-bursts of filthy abuse, piercing shrieks or singing ; a patient whistled tunes all day on a water-bottle ; many patients carry on monologues or answer voices loud out, often cursing and abusing, especially in the night. The following is a record of a fairly lively dialogue of this kind, which a patient carried on with his voices :—

"What does it matter to me then what you think ! That has nothing to do with me, is in the highest degree indifferent to me.—What? I must think that? That I must not at all. I can think what I like, and you think what you like !—That would be still better? No, that would not be better at all ! I can certainly do with my head what I will ! I must wholly misunderstand you ! That is entirely your affair if you share your thoughts with me ! It is not I who am ill. —You are the patient ! I am a real, sensible person, and the superintendent is carrying on the most infamous game, is carrying on criminal fabrication !—What ? Am I to shoot myself ? I don't think so ! Shoot yourself if you like ! I am not going to do you this pleasure !—What? I am stupid ? No you are stupid ; I am cleverer than you all ! I am too clever for you ; that's why you want to keep me in here—It doesn't help me at all? We'll see that, if it doesn't help ! There is still a Bavarian State with guaranteed rights, and you will be put in jail ! As far as I'm concerned lick me—— ! "

Incoherence of the train of thought, as we have already depicted it, is usually distinctly noticeable in the conversation of the patients. The most different ideas follow one another with most bewildering want of connection, even when the patients are quite quiet. A patient said "Life is a dessert-spoon," another, "We are already standing in the spiral under a hammer," a third, "Death will be awakened by the golden dagger," a fourth, "The consecrated discourse cannot be over split in any movement," a patient, " I don't

know what I am to do here, it must be the aim, that means
to steal with the gentlemen."

The page, which is reproduced as a specimen of writing

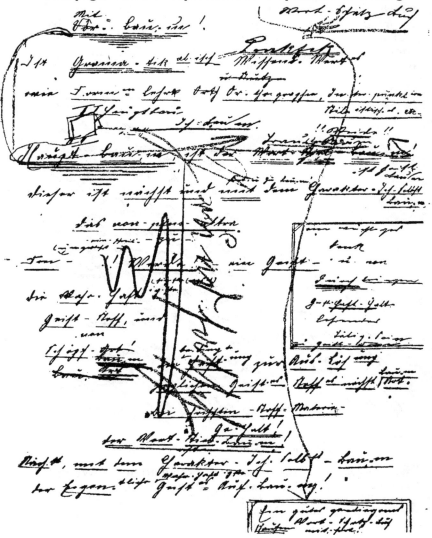

Specimen of writing 1. Incoherence.

No. 1 with notes of a patient, as he used to produce them
in large number, gives a good impression of this incoherence.
The arrangement of the notes, the handwriting changing in

size and form, the irregular grouping, the underlining of different kinds and colours make it appear peculiar and incomprehensible. In detail we have a varied mixture of broken words and fragments of sentences before us, among which there is no connection whatsoever. We only notice the recurrence of single parts (" Bau," " baum," " Hauptbau," " Charakter," " Wortschatzbuch," " Wort-stiel-baum," " Geist-Stoff," " Haft," " wahrhaftigste," " fort."). The affected use of hyphens is further noticeable (" Bau-m," " Grama-tik,"

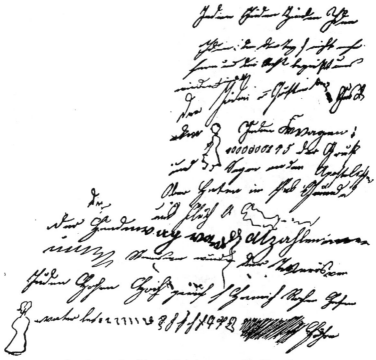

Specimen of writing 2. Incoherence with Stereotypy.

" Or-tho-graphie ") and of marks of exclamation (" !! Weide !!," "!! Werde !!"), and the writing above the line of the last letters in numerous words, and lastly among the other notes the curiously encouraging remark " (sig-ste-was??)," and " grundfalsch " written with a flourish across it.

Still more incoherent is the above piece of writing. (Specimen of writing 2.) Here there are certainly still some connected words decipherable (" the day's no longer far off and the night greets us again,' " salutation and blessing from the apostolic over "), but intermixed there are irregularly strewn incomprehensible aggregations of letters, childish drawings, single signs like letters and numbers, a group of similar strokes, which let the tendency to *persistence* of the movements of writing appear clearly, as do also the words that return in various forms, "Juden," "Gus-Gruss-Grund," "Hohen-Hoch-Höhre." The extraordinary irregularity of the hand-writing should also be noticed here.

In the drawings of the patients also there invariably appears on the one hand incoherence, on the other hand *persistence* of impulse to movement. Fig. 10 reproduces one of the senseless, childish drawings which a patient

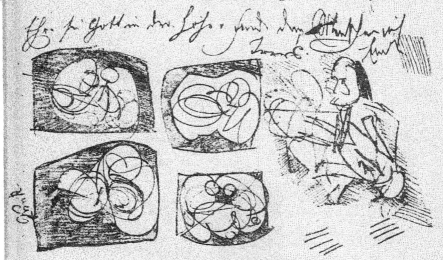

Fig. 10. Drawings in Dementia Præcox (Metamorphoses).

produced in large numbers daily; there are wonderful combinations of strokes and flourishes with hints of stereotypy. They correspond completely with what Pfersdorff has named metamorphoses; there were endless variations of the same recurring fundamental form.

The second example, Fig. 11, gives the impression at the first glance of a pen and ink drawing. It is composed, however, of senseless combinations of strokes. Besides these there are notes with written verbigeration, enumerations and plays on words ("Irre-Irrengarten - Irrenspaziergänge, Irrenreichman" and so on, "Irrenwurz, Eierwurz," "Abtritt-Pissoir, Latrine-Scheisskerle," "Lukretia, Metardus, Onophrius, Primus-Benignus"). Such expressions of quite divergent stamp are interpolated in the most elegant and regular handwriting. The third example also (Fig. 12) shows besides the startling senselessness and tastelessness of the design, the monotonous recurrence of the same details, and lastly the incoherent inscriptions in which " Semiramus," " Jeremias," " Apollo " are joined with ' Ludowicum Napoleon," " Markus," " Chamisso " and " Woltaires."

Fig. 11.   Senseless Drawing.

Similarity in Sound can be recognised here and there as a certain link in the disconnected utterances of the patients. They rhyme, " Ott Gott," " simbra-umbra "; they play senselessly with words and sounds.   A patient spoke of " Ehebrecher and Beinbrecher," another of " verhört und verstört," a third of " Sauspiel and Schauspiel."   A fourth explained his spitting

Fig. 12. Queer Drawing.

with "Zufluss, Einfluss, and Ausfluss"; a fifth said "jetzt müssen Sie mich herunterfragen, damit es wieder heruntergeht," a sixth, "Ich bin der Besitzer und Ihr seid die Schwitzer"; a seventh wished "Vorrichten statt Nachrichten"; an eighth called himself "Gottes Sohn und Gottes Schwur"; a patient spoke of Albicocca, Kokken, Kokain.

How the train of thought may be interrupted by meaningless plays on words is shown by the following passage which was written by a young patient who amused himself a great deal with writing:—

"da droben auf dem Gebirge war einmal ein Jäger aufgefunden worden. Auf der Felsenwand in der Nähe der Sennhütte, Senner und Sennerin hat ein eines schönen Tages ein von Felsenwand achasant drihahol-drietal am droben auf der Wand. Vesuv, Vilz, Ventus, Verlend, Vaterland, Vrist, Vogel. Veinstningerstadt, Venus, Vondertan Vogt, Vugler, Vangfisch, Vidtrich, Versendung, Viendling, Vach, Vieh, Viehzucht, Versicherung, Velzler, Vanter, Ente, Entrich, Elsass, Erlangen, Eidling, Eidschwur, Eid, Endlang, Esel, Ellenbogen, Eiter, Edling, Entdeckung, Erfindung, Erdboden, Erdenhügel, Erdenwall, Engel. (There follow still forty-seven words beginning with E, partly quite senseless, then thirty-two words with U, thirty-five with K; then comes Die Wacht am Rhein, "Morgenrot," "Zu Strassburg auf der Schanz," "Ich hab' mich ergeben," "Der gute Kamerad," lastly 127 words beginning with K, twenty-two with P, two with A, two with B, three with Sp, fifteen with W.)

Besides the purely outward connection of ideas by similarity of sound there appears here clearly the persistence in the direction of the thought which has once come into view [mountain, huntsman, cliff, herdsman, Vesuvius and so on].

Stereotypy is shown in the frequent recurrence of the same turns of expression which occasionally are "done to death." A patient added on to everything; "We Germans don't have that," another always answered, "Certainly, certainly," a female patient invariably interpolated "bitt schön." The following passage is another characteristic example:—

"Ein venerisches Feldherrentalent, ein venerisches Arzttalent; Sie haben über zu sein, wenn ich will. Die Anstalt ist ein renerisches Feldherrentalent; ist sie nicht über, ist sie nicht über; sie ist nicht renerisch, über zu sein; dann bin ich aber der L., wo ich über zu sein bin. Ich bin über zu sein, was ich bin. Jeder Anstreicher ist hier am Geiste zu sprechen. Sie kommen hinausel; das ist ja über Esel, hinausel! Und da ist dieser renerische Maler; so tappig ist er am Geist zu sprechen, 17-18 Jahre alt, über zu sein, was ich bin. Kein vernünftiges Wort ist über zu hören im Geist. Einer muss über werden. Kommt da ein Baron, so ein Baron, der über sein will; der is gar nicht über. Der ist ja gar nicht über zu sein, was ich bin; der B. ist nicht über; der ist eigentlich über was ganz gefährlich über zu sein."

In this senseless rigmarole single words and phrases are

always brought forward again, sometimes exactly the same, sometimes with all sorts of changes, specially " über sein," " venerisch-renerisch," " Arzttalent-Feldherrntalent," " was ich bin," " im Geist-am Geist," " hinausel."

If stereotypy is still more strongly pronounced, the morbid symptom of *verbigeration* is developed, the endless repetition of the same sentences, usually in measured cadence. A female patient repeated the following sentence from seven o'clock to half-past nine :—

" I beg you to put me in another bed, in the bed where it was got ready yesterday ; else I shall not get out of hell any more. Jesus, dear Master mine, let me rely faithfully on thee ; lead me in the right path, O do lead me heavenward. You are my mother's lady's maid, and my mother is also there."

If the endless repetition seems here to be partially explained by the form of prayer, the following examples of verbigeration from the same patient show distinctly that it is a case of monotonous instinctive flow of speech : " Mutterle, führ mich ums Kirchlein herum bin um uns um zu verfüttern," " Zar mein Milchen ums Eckbrett in alle Zimmer." Sometimes verbigeration takes the form of a senseless ringing of the changes on a syllable. A patient connected the following with the word " Bett " which was called out to him :—

" Bett, Bett, Bett, dett, dett, dett, ditt, dutt, dutt, daut, daut, daut, dint, dint, dint, dutt, dett, datt. Wenn ich angefangen habe, fahre ich fort bis zu Ende." [When I begin, I continue to the end.] " Behindelt, bedandelt, bedundelt, bedindelt und bedandelt, umgewandelt, umgedandelt, umgewandelt, umgedandelt. Krone, krone, krone, gekrönt, gekrönt, gekrönt, gekrant, gekrant, gekrant, beschwant, beschwant, beschwant, sie sind beschwant und sind belohnt, sie sind betont, betonen, betonen, betonen, sie betonen, sie belohnen." " Es muss halt so sein, wenn es herauskommen soll." [It must just be so, if it is to come out].

In writing also we again find stereotypy, it may be in frequent reappearance of the same expressions and phrases, or in innumerable slavish repetitions of the same strokes and words, sometimes with certain changes. Such an example is given in the specimen of writing 3. Besides the senseless persistence there is to be noticed here the peculiar spelling (" God " instead of " Gott," " Godhatz," " Godwilz," " Godiche kannz nicht Anders," " Willenz," " Sollenz," aber " Müssens "). The specimen of writing 2, as well as Figs. 10, 11, 12, show a less obtrusive stereotypy. From the writing of a patient, which will be discussed later, consisting partly of senseless accumulation of syllables, I take the following extract which exhibits the monotony of such productions :—

" Von allen Rocky-Mountygrenzen ; in der ganzen Welt ; 9 Klm. (nach allen Massen). Von allen Catalonien-grenzen : in der ganzen

Welt : 9 Klm. (nach allen Massen). Von allen Hispanien-Neuspanien-San Juan—in der ganzen Welt : Seiten : Mittelpunkt : Ecken : u. s. w. 9 Klm. (nach allen Massen). Von allen San-Salvator ; in der ganzen Welt : (Mittelpunkt : Ecken : Seiten : 9 Klm. nach allen Massen) " usf. It continues in the same way : " Von allen Mooderfontein," "Transvaal," " Zinninseln," " Johannesburg," " Gewürzinseln," " Zimmtbaum-inseln," " Unter allen mit Gras bewachsenen Rainboschung," "unter allen europäisch-asiatischen Kap,". " Von allen Cappadocien : grenzen," " Baotokuten-grenzen," " Kanea-Kretagrenzen," " Karfunkel (Amethist) gruben," "Kaplandplätzen," "Garibaldis Ziegeninsel," "Unter allen Cottillontanzplätzen," " Panamarepublikgrenzen," "unter allen Panamaskandalplätzen," " allen Lumpenfabriken," "allen Minen," "Adelaideplätzen," and so on and so on, invariably with the addition : " überall in der ganzen Welt : 9 Klm. (nach allen Massen)."

This senseless narration which endlessly repeats the same

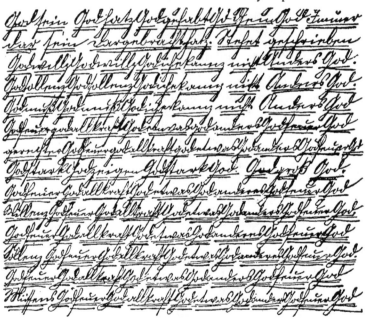

(Specimen of writing 3. Stereotopy).

details deals with the country which it is " self-evident " the patient lays claim to for himself and his children.

Negativism shows itself in the domain of speech activity, on the one hand in *mutism*, on the other hand in *resistive* or *evasive answers*. Many patients answer every question with another question or with " How ? " and then perhaps without further ado give the required information ; others simply repeat the question. Answers are often given that say nothing, are indefinite, or quite without relation to the subject. Negativism appears more distinctly when the patients answer to all remarks, " I don't know " or " I don't need to tell you that." " You know that yourself already," a patient constantly answered, " I know everything, oui, oui.", It frequently comes to " speaking past the subject.' To the question always repeated; " How are you ? " a patient replied in succession, "On the bridge," then " Mustardseed," next " Prayer-book," lastly, " Not at all ; I am sitting."

Sometimes the patients obstinately maintain silence, as long as one is occupied with them, and begin to talk when one turns away from them, or they try to speak, utter a few words, but suddenly break off and cannot be moved to any further utterance; a few patients speak with certain people, but are wholly inaccessible to others. Many patients speak low, scarcely move their lips, murmur unintelligibly to themselves. In the end it comes to complete mutism, which lasts for months or years, but which may be suddenly interrupted by outbursts of the most violent abuse or screaming. In certain circumstances the patients in this state still give utterance in writing to their thoughts, sometimes expressing them comprehensively and for the most part very confusedly ; a patient declared that he wrote because he could not find words readily. As a rule, however, expression in writing is also suppressed by negativism. The patients cannot be persuaded to write at all, or they break off after a few letters, go playing over the paper, only scrawl a few unintelligible flourishes, or tap with the pencil on the desk keeping time. In measurements of pressure in writing one sees sometimes a continuous fall of pressure which is to be accounted for either by a simple failure of will-tension or by negativistic disorder. A patient wrote Roman mirror writing in order that no one might be able to read it.

Linguistic movements of expression also seem to the patients to be often under the power of external forces. We have already stated above, that many patients are forced not only to think but also to say aloud what is suggested to them. Others " must " scream, " rage and abuse," call out suddenly " Halleluia," " Pfui " or " Kaiser and King "; a patient " was obliged " involuntarily to " speak Bambergerisch." In the same way the patients sometimes cannot answer because the voices have forbidden them.

Derailments in linguistic expression form a specially important domain in the speech disorders of dementia præcox. Vocal speech itself can be changed in the most varied way by side and cross impulses. The patients in speaking, bellow, screech, murmur or whisper, scarcely move

E

their lips, keep their teeth closed, or often pass suddenly from low whispering to loud screaming. The flow of speech is frequently hurried and rapid even in low speaking, sometimes varying quite irregularly, or speech is jerkily broken up, or produced keeping time with sharp rhythmical modulation. The cadence often lacks the risings and fallings, the melodies of speech; the timbre of the voice may also be changed. The patients speak in falsetto, through their noses, in an artificial bass voice, pass suddenly from one key to another. Mignot rightly calls attention to the fact that the changes in strength of tone, height of tone, rapidity and rhythm in our patients are throughout lacking in that close relation to thought and mood, which in healthy people makes the voice such a pliant means of expression of inward states; the individual peculiarities of vocal speech are changed without relation to each other or to the psychic occurrences by which they are usually ruled.

Later there are introduced into speech not infrequently clicking and smacking sounds, sniffing, and snorting, bleating words without sense, stock phrases with tiring repetition. Many patients *speak affectedly* with excessively distinct pronunciation, with distortion of single letters and with senseless intonation; others of set purpose in a childishly awkward manner, deliberately careless, indistinct, limp, or in the rudest dialect; others again join on diminutives or other capricious additions, and still others speak in an unctuous preacher's tone. A patient mutilated and distorted the words, said "glank" for "krank," "nuten Hag" for "guten Tag," "Feinbeg" for "Heidelberg," spoke of the "Soktor" (Doktor) "Notessor" (Professor). Many patients answer singing; a female patient sang her own conversation and answers.

In their *writings* there is found an arbitrary, peculiar disorder with whimsical misuse of punctuation marks and orthography invented by themselves. The letters show for the most part a very changing character, are sometimes large, and pretentious, sometimes small and scrawling, sometimes irregular, slapdash or punctiliously uniform, as the specimens of writing given above show. Many patients write mirror-writing. Gregor found in his enquiries slowing of writing. The writing pressure also shows many oscillations. Gross was able to establish at one time very high, at another time very low pressure values, also lengthening of the pauses, and lastly extraordinarily great fluctuation of all values, even in quite short periods of time, a sign of great fluctuation in the attention and volition of our patients.

Internal Speech.—But much more significant are the disorders of internal speech, of the transformation of ideas into linguistic movements of expression. The consideration of the disorders of speech in dreams has shown that the variety of such errors is very great. Unfortunately in dementia præcox there have not been as yet any satisfactory enquiries into the corresponding phenomena; nevertheless it seems to me that we find here the most important of the anomalies observed there with surprising similarity. Certainly the difficulty of the interpretation is greater here, as we, unlike the experience of dreams, can seldom ascertain what the patient has exactly wished to say.

Paraphasia.—We shall have to keep apart two chief forms of paraphasic disorders; firstly, *derailments in finding words*, secondly, *disorders in connected speech*. In the first group there may be, to begin with, a simple mutilation, a change or partial fusion of words in common use. A patient said: "Ich schäm" instead of "Ich shäme mich"; another complained that he was "schmerzend, schädigt and genötigt"; another spoke of "Reglierung." "Das Herz ist schwankig," "hilfbar" instead of hilfsbereit," "Zaubrigkeiten" instead of "Zauberei," "direktiv" ("I can't pronounce anything") instead of "direkt" are examples of word-transformations. A patient spoke of the "Wundneiarzt," when he was evidently bringing together "Wundarzt" and "Arznei"; another felt himself "kopfbewusstlos," "unbewusstlos."

Another occurrence which is frequent in dreams, the substitution of one word for another usually *similar* in *sound* or *meaning*, an occurrence which plays a large part in ordinary paraphasia also, is difficult to trace in our patients since the meaning of such utterances is mostly unrecognisable. But we may well suppose that many of the unintelligible expressions of the patients arise by paraphasic word-substitution. They speak of the "Totenwahn," of the "Mondteufel," of the "Dolchmesser mit Hochzeitszettel," of the "sozialdemokratischen Jagdstock," of the "souveränen Neuner," "Papstneuner." A patient worked "mit dem Vernunftgott"; one felt himself "gaumenschwach"; to another something appeared "schwarzwälderisch"; a fourth declared, "Ihr seid Unterwalder"; a fifth called the physicians "Falschzugeschworene"; a sixth said that a "Wecker vom Kriegsgericht" had been there; a female patient complained that someone was pulling the "Frevelschnur." A male patient complained that his senses were "checked"; "The doctor has collected my four senses."

Neologisms.—There are intimations here already of a

further form of paraphasic derailment, which may become of very great extent in dementia præcox, neologisms. In several of the examples quoted it was already a case of new unintelligible words, but they were, however, composed of sensible component parts. ("Papstneuner," "gaumenschwach," "Frevelschnur".) But there may be produced also quite senseless collections of syllables, here and there still having a sound reminiscent of real words. A patient spoke of the "Gestübe und Angstbetrieb"; another of the "Totendumpf"; a third of the "Lebepuppe"; a fourth of the "Oxypathie," from which he was suffering; a fifth was "krikeliert"; a sixth did not want to belong "zur Tätowie"; a seventh drivelled in an unintelligible way of "Reichsleben und Gerichtsleben." A female patient obstinately demanded "ihre Scheidung, ihr Amtsgericht, ihr Jahr 1888, ihre Sallesichten und Sarasichten"; another complained about the "Physizieren und Mechanisieren," by which she without doubt wished to indicate sexual molestation. Many neologisms may, as happens in dreams, be expressions of more complicated or morbid ideas, for which no words exist. Formations such as "Äquinoktialhimmelskönigskind," "Wasserpädagogium," "Bombardongehör," "Verkörperungsunternehmen" make such a supposition probable. A patient explained that he would travel to Constantinople "auf dem Luftkompressionswege"; another had "bengalische Gehirnerweichung durch Simulantenbehandlung"; a female patient spoke of the "Gliederauswachsung," and the "Blutvergiftungswasser."

The tendency to silly plays on words and neologisms can get the upper hand in our patients to such an extent, that they fall into a wholly *incomprehensible gibberish*; they usually then give it out as a foreign language which by slight changes in the syllables may be changed into any other you like. A patient gave as his first name, "Detscheneinaninadrenn." Another called himself, "Jesasus Christasusäsus Heilandasus" and wrote down as his address "Aewa owa Ouwou Aewouwio sanco to totosaak saakiou sahaia siri tou toutou, Hoch Waiowauoxyowiüowäüoxyoohoeho hächi hihi"; it was the name of his castle. Another example is given in the following fragment from a petition to the district court which began at first quite sensibly :—

"Urrass Asia peru arull pelluss Pisa anuell pelli.

"Madrass ihsa Peru parell mull illuss thesu thariass mehluss pinta aperu allesa, medut prusa exel ill Farrawall.

"Cap Nansen ell Pisa uruhl nell palle ixo piso panthe alluss pesass esu tull maxima perrett ill panse arruse ill perrell Thatciduss usa ibru maltell pe uxa thyrra, pia apentia rubsa iss tbeto, cralluss Asia peni vendi arrull, mesa. Uss Adda pia mellu Exter a probro; Mess Killian esu panem Dante, illo pisa thesu arrendt, mess pasi Ural pill palli mesa essu Acus Cantone, ell Albydill, Anschill, Kulla Apia Nestor," and so on.

In this senseless collection of syllables there are scattered a number of correct or somewhat altered proper names (" Asia," " Pisa," " Madrass," Peru, Nansen, Adda, Exter, Killian, Dante, Ural, Apia, Nestor, Farrawell, Thatciduss, Albydill) ; some (Pisa, Asia) appear again, as also a series of other newly formed words (arull, perell, ill, thesu, mesa, esu, pia). There are also innumerable similarities of sound (pellus-pelli-pill-palli, mehluss-alluss-cralluss, arull-uruhl-arruse-ruhsa, peru-perell-perett, pinta-panthe-apentia-peni-penem-pasi), though not in unbroken sequence, but like the repetitions scattered irregularly thoughout the whole series. If the whole comprehensive piece of writing had been reproduced, that would have been still much more distinct. An inner connection is only recognisable in so far as the names introduced all apply to towns, countries or persons ; in Farewell (" Farrewell ") and Cap Nansen there could also perhaps be found a still nearer relation. The patient interrupted his gibberish with the remark, " Now again to the subject " and then writes of his " discoveries," among which a great number of countries are mentioned ; he concludes with more gibberish as above. In the middle sentence there is the following silly play on words ; " Puntas : Punte : Punto : Punti : Punta : Puntes : Puntal : Puntales : Puntu : Punto : Puntel : Puntelus."

Sometimes it comes to senseless *rhyming* as in the following transcript :—

"Sei ruhig, ich werde ein lichter Träger mit seiner dummes Zeug Kläger—er fetter schon die Arm im Schnauzen mit seiner gimmen guten Bauzen. Er hat nicht schlucken voll Erbarmen aus voller Schmerz in seiner Karmen—Von Lichter schlägt er mir die Lichter in Donnerwetter Höllenrichter, ein Donnerwetterrichter, ein schwarzer Seljon ein Secht in meine Hinterlader spricht einst ein junger halb in Kräter. Ein Vater Himmel Donnerwetter Licht—ich lade alle Teufel aus und trug die Höllenmarke naus."

This wholly incomprehensible talk made up of neologisms, similarities of sound, rhymes and repetitions brings to mind the speech of dreams as also the reading of a delirious alcoholic from a blank page. We find the same thing again in the next piece of writing :—

"Weiss blau bin ich gnau soh der Pfau. Weiss und gelb soh die Quell. Schwarz und weiss soh das Eis. Rot und schwarz soh der Bass und soh das Fass. Weiss wieh Schnee rot im Kleeh soh die Höh oh welches Glück. Mäuschen grau rot und grau rot und blau. Wenn und wann soh die Tann. Holz zum Kranz soh der Tann. Mäuschen gleih soh das Blau."

Almost still more peculiar do the lyric poems appear to

us, which a female patient composed in a language invented by herself, though usually she could express herself without difficulty. I give one verse here:—

> Stanzuru vimmt den Bark zum Obendrob
> Heuschend lagert ein Blgart im Striehen Obss
> Leulend, lagernd, bimmt die Bimbii im Hyurisch
> Bordent blickt Aug im Drugsag des Auggehoks
> Rastand blickt die Staniza im Herz eingelallt
> Schwächend irrt Corpus im trausen Lauf gedalt
> Zu einem armen kranken Cornt von Erdgedob.

A few words (" Bark," " lagert," " blickt," " Aug," " rastend," " Herz," and so on) are still intelligible, but for the most part it is a case of wholly senseless neologisms, At the same time a certain tendency to assonance and a childish playing with sounds cannot be lost sight of (" vimmt—bimmt—Bimbii," " Obendrob—Erdgedob," " Stan-zuru — Staniza," " Aug — Auggehoks," " Corpus — Cornt," eingelallt,—gedallt," "heuschend—leulend—lagernd—bordent, —rastend—schwächend ").

Akataphasia.—Not less worthy of note than the disorders in word-finding are those which influence in a morbid way the form of speech. At first we have to do with those derailments in the *expression of thought* in speech which we call akataphasia. In this case the patients either do not find the expression appropriate to their thoughts, but only produce something with a similar sound ("displacement paralogia"), or they let their speech fall into quite another channel ("derailment paralogia"). A patient said he was "wholly without head on the date" for "he did not know the date"; another complained he "lived under protected police" instead of "under the protection of police" a third declared to his father he "was the greatest judicial murder" instead of "on him the greatest judicial murder was practised." Similarly a patient remarked he was "the disguise in all ways" instead of "he had disguised himself in all ways." Another patient said he had "his fiancée always in speech" instead of "his fiancée still continued to speak to him" (through voices); a female patient asserted she knew "in a miracle" that her father was a priest instead of " she had learned it in a miraculous way." To this series also the expression of a patient mentioned before belongs, he "toned with God," instead of "he heard tones from God," and the utterance of another that he "was instructed in the experimentally approved specialty."

The following utterances give us ground for concluding that the expression of thought in speech glides off into *side-ideas* which intrude themselves; " I have a suspended appetite," "I have voluntary disease of the eyes," "They are threaded at the head," "I am national-liberal chased away." A patient said that he had danced, "lay in mortification." To this group should perhaps be reckoned some of the bewilderingly nonsensical utterances, which were quoted above as examples of the incoherence of speech of our patients, and which apparently represent a senseless jingling of words. A patient used the word "Log" a great deal and explained that it was shortened from "logic," and then leaving the track he continued "Lot-overlog-underlog; philologists have outlived themselves; these are individual expressions." Here the relation to childish playing with sounds is distinct.

Construction of Sentences.—A further form of impairment of speech springs from *disorder in the construction of sentences.* In the examples of incoherence of the train of thought which were given before, the *syntax* is also confused in different places ("Former service and then she does it," "I, and that is also so curious, therefore the nun." "I should come from M. because always something happens, leg broken or something, they have quarrelled," "as I that at last of those that particularly believe"). A patient wrote in an anonymous letter, "Mortimer in reference to two kings"; another said he was sad "on account of the national economic interests, concerning foreign commerce." In more pronounced disorder speech may develop into the style of a *telegram*, doing without all superfluous phrases, and in the end there may be complete disappearance of sentence-formation. An example of this is given in the following petition to the chief of the police which is called "Cabinet affair honesty":—

"By the grace of God are the Emperor of the present analogy of the spirit 'in spiritu' of radical sworn upon oath subjects of proved alarm-satisfaction of my stamped masculine disposition 'centre Çalvin' of academic birth-stamp of analogy of party liable to military service of declarative property customary of honest palatinate despotism of the highest of all honesty 'contrary disposition' of freely intelligently right of acquisition of foreign rank of financial-joint legal contract of psychiatric truth of forgotten wound-fever of frugally imperial bureaucracy of secured-capital profitable persecution of the Christians most obediently S., imperial parliamentary IV. service-laced prize-seal. Affair of an oath! Radical 'brevi manu'!"

In this singular piece of writing besides the verb "sind" only dependent genitives are found as the one indication of syntax. For the rest it swarms with newly-formed compound words, the parts of which in themselves are rational (Geistesanalogie," "radikaleidlich," "Alarmgenugtuung," "meingestempelt," and so on). "Geistesanalogie" is soon followed by " Parteianalogie," " meingestempelt " by " Geburtsstempel," " Mannesgesinnung " by " Gegengesinnung." " radikaleidlich " by " Eidessache " as indication of the persistence which is invariably noticeable in such documents. " Dienstgeschnürte Prisensiegel " might be regarded as displacement paralogia (" Dienstsiegel "). The whole is a sample of confusion of speech in which moreover, in spite of complete want of connection, there is still a certain general colouring of the ideas recognisable.

Train of Thought.—The last group of examples brings us to derailments in the train of thought itself, which certainly often accompany the forms hitherto discussed. As already mentioned, we hear from our patients a great many quite imcomprehensible and disconnected utterances, in which it can scarcely be only a question of disorders of linguistic expression, even though it is impossible in the individual case to discover the inner mechanism by which the utterances arose. Thus a patient spoke of the " brain-navel of the merchants' association "; another said, " One cannot take the direction from the reflection." But sometimes a derivation of the train of thought from the series of ideas which is immediately present, to another, as frequently happens in dreams, is clearly seen. A patient when asked what year it was, replied, " It may be Australia," wandering from the series of years to the series of continents; another to the question what month it was, answered Strassburg. A third complained that the attendant had " forced the tax-duty " on him, and so passed from the idea of some sort of unpleasant influence to that of paying taxes. Perhaps the utterance of defence made by a patient " Get away from the reins " is to be regarded in a similar way, in as far as the approach of anyone awakened the idea of the putting on of reins. When a patient said, " Suffering hunger is stronger than in all deaf-mutes," the supposition may be made that here the idea of deaf-mutes has taken the place of a more general thought comprehending want or misfortune. Also the saying, " I have gone through much for the German language," may be considered as a derivation of the train of thought, as also the expression relating to some or other indifferent occurrence; " That can be written with blue ink."

One will scarcly go wrong if one assumes a derivation in those forms of talking past a subject, in which a negativistic evasion of the right answer is not clear. A patient replied to the question in which town the hospital was by saying, " The house stands in the gospel of Luke of the eighth, and if one has swine, one can slaughter them." [German . . . des achten . . . schlachten.] Here after the first derivation of the train of thought to another domain of ideas another follows which is conditioned by the rhyme. The same patient on being asked to enumerate the names of the months, did so in the following manner: "Jas je ji jo jan jan dran drin draus dann Mainz, dann Worms." He first fell into the vowel series, then into similarities of sound and into practised combinations of letters ("drin-draus"), and lastly, into the enumeration of names of towns.

From these disorders the transition is easy to those pnenomena with which we became acquainted before as *speaking past a subject.* Here it is no longer the transference to expression in speech that is morbidly influenced, but the ideas aroused by the circumstances are themselves already in their origin pushed aside or suppressed by ideas related but lying remote or opposed to the original ones.

CHAPTER III.

GENERAL PSYCHIC CLINICAL PICTURE

NOW if we make a general survey of the psychic clinical picture of dementia præcox, as it has presented itself to us in the consideration of about a thousand cases which belong to the subject, there are apparently two principal groups of disorders which characterise the malady. On the one hand we observe a *weakening of those emotional activities which permanently form the mainsprings of volition.* In connection with this, mental activity and instinct for occupation become mute. The result of this part of the morbid process is emotional dulness, failure of mental activities, loss of mastery over volition, of endeavour, and of ability for independent action. The essence of personality is thereby destroyed, the best and most precious part of its being, as Griesinger once expressed it, torn from her. With the annihilation of personal will, the possibility of further development is lost, which is dependent wholly on the activity of volition. What remains is principally what has been previously learned in the domain of knowledge and practical work. But this also sooner or later goes to ruin unless the failing inner mainspring is replaced by outer stimulus which rouses to continual practice and so obviates the slow disappearance of ability. Whether and how far the malady directly injures the mental faculties apart from their gradual disappearance through disuse of mental function needs further inquiry. The rapidity with which deep-seated and permanent dementia sometimes develops in the domain of intellectual work makes the suggestion easy, that it also may itself be drawn by the disease into a sympathetic morbid state, even though it is invariably encroached on to a much less degree than emotion and volition. It is worthy of note in any case, that memory and acquired mental proficiency may occasionally be preserved in a surprising way when there is complete and final destruction of the personality itself.

The second group of disorders, which gives dementia præcox its peculiar stamp, has been examined in detail especially by Stransky.[1] It consists in the *loss of the inner*

[1] Stranksy, Jahrb. f. Psychiatrie, xxiv., 1903, 1 ; Wiener med. Presse 1905, 28.

unity of the activities of intellect, emotion, and volition in themselves and among one another. Stransky speaks of an annihilation of the "intrapsychic co-ordination," which is said to loosen or destroy the articulations of the "noopsyche" and the "thymopsyche" themselves as well as their mutual relations. This annihilation presents itself to us in the disorders of association described by Bleuler, in incoherence of the train of thought, in the sharp change of moods as well as in desultoriness and derailments in practical work. But further the near connection between thinking and feeling, between deliberation and emotional activity on the one hand, and practical work on the other is more or less lost. Emotions do not correspond to ideas. The patients laugh and weep without recognisable cause, without any relation to their circumstances and their experiences, smile while they narrate the tale of their attempts at suicide: they are very much pleased that they "chatter so foolishly," and must remain permanently in the institution; on the most in-significant occasions they fall into violent terror or outbursts of rage, and then immediately break out into a neighing laugh. It is just this disagreement between idea and emotion that gives their behaviour the stamp of "silliness." Stransky traces the soiling of the bed also to a morbid connection of this procedure with feelings of pleasure.

The work of the patients is not as in healthy people the expression of their view of life and temperament, it is not guided by the elaboration of perceptions, by deliberation and moods, but it is the incalculable result of chance external influences, and of impulses, cross impulses, and contrary impulses, arising similarly by chance internally. A patient sang as he jumped into the Neckar; others burn or scatter their money, try to cut the throat of a beloved child, or with pitiful screaming maltreat themselves in the most regardless way. The phenomena of paramimia belong to this group also, the side activities, as well as the oddities which result from them, but especially do the disorders of inner speech find their place here, which may likewise be understood from the point of view of a relaxation of the relations between idea and actual speech. By this destruction of inner concatenation and causation the whole of active life receives the stamp of the incalculable, the incomprehensible, and the distorted.

As it seems to me, there exists an inner connection between the two groups of disorders, which are here distinguished. What fashions our experiences into a firmly mortised building, in which each part must fit the other and sub-ordinate itself to the general plan, are general conceptions and ideas. The even calm of our temper, the swift victory over sudden shocks, are guaranteed by the higher general emotions ; on the one hand they work by acting as a check, and on the other hand they give to the background of our mood a definite colouring even when no emotional stimuli are caused by special internal or external experiences. Lastly, the inner unity of our will is conditioned by the general trend of volition which is always alive in us, and which is the product of our racial and personal development. We may therefore expect that a weakening or annihilation of the influence which general conceptions, higher emotions, and the permanent general trend of volition exercise on our thinking, feeling, and acting, must draw after it that inner *disintegration*, those "schizophrenic" disorders, which we meet with in dementia præcox. It seems to me that the disorders observed in the patients and the complaints to which they give utterance, point exactly to injury to the general scheme of our psychic development, as it fixes the substance of our personality. The general trend of volition and also the higher emotions might form the first point of attack. But further the instrument of general conceptions with its regulating influence on the train of thought would then also become worthless, if the will were no longer capable of using it. Weygandt speaks, obviously following a similar line of thought, of an "apperceptive dementia" in as far as the injured "active apperception" signifies the dominion of volition over the formation and the course of psychic processes.

CHAPTER IV.

BODILY SYMPTOMS.

BESIDES the psychic disorders there are also in the physical domain[1] a series of morbid phenomena to record, whose more exact relations to the fundamental malady are not yet, it must be admitted, proved in all points.

Headaches are frequent, to which Tomaschny has specially directed attention; they are referred to forehead and temples, but also to the vertex or the occiput, mostly in the form of oppression, a pressing together. To these may be added unpleasant sensations of all kinds in the most different parts of the body, of which we have to a certain extent made mention already, also those irritative phenomena which are so frequently present in the higher mechanisms of sense. Sensitiveness to pain seems not infrequently diminished, even though no certain opinion can be arrived at owing to the psychic dulness of the patients; Mayor often found tenderness in the hypogastrium and the breasts.

Behaviour of the Pupils.—This is of great significance. They are frequently in the earlier stages of the disease and in conditions of excitement conspicuously wide, according to Meyer in 10 per cent. of the cases, as Weiler explains, because of an increase, caused by the morbid process, of that cortical excitement which reduces the tone of the sphincters. Here and there one observes a distinct difference in the pupils. The light-reaction of the pupils[2] often appears sluggish or slight. Westphal sometimes found distortion of the shape of the pupils, obliquely oval position, and also passing failure of the reaction to light and accommodation especially in states of profound stupor, sometimes unilateral, sometimes bilateral. He suggests morbid tension of the musculature of the iris in connection with the general muscle tension. According to Sioli's observations similar disorders can be produced even

[1] Trepsat, Etude des troubles physiques dans la démence précoce. Thèse. 1905 ; Tomaschny und Meyer, Allgem. Zeitschr. f. Psychiatrie, 1909, 845 ; Pförtner, Monatsschr. f. Psychiatrie u. Neurol. xxviii. 208 ; Sérieux, Annales médico-psychol. 1902, Nov.-Dez.

[2] Westphal, Deutsche medizin. Wochenschr. 1909, 23 ; Bumke, Münchener medizin. Wochenschr. 1910, 51 ; Weiler, Zeitschr. f. die ges. Neurologie und Psychiatrie ii., 101.

after the disappearance of the stupor by strong voluntary straining of the muscles. All the disorders which have been mentioned appear to be subject to much change.

The pupillary reaction to *pain* and *psychic stimuli* as well as the pupillary movement which continuously accompanies the *psychic life* has disappeared, as Bumke found, in a considerable number of cases. It must be allowed that the statements about the frequency of this disorder are extraordinarily discrepant which, considering the difficulty in ascertaining the facts, does not appear surprising. Bumke did not once find the psychic reactions normal in 33 cases, in 69 per cent. he found it lost; he states that first the pupillary movement, the permanent slight variation of the width of the pupils, which is only recognisable with the loupe, disappears, then the dilatation of the pupils caused by psychic impressions, lastly the pain reaction. Hübner failed to get the psychic reflexes in 75 per cent. of 51 cases. Still higher numbers were got by Sioli who found in 48 cases belonging to the domain of dementia præcox the psychic reaction and the pupillary movement absent. On the other hand, Wassermeyer in 39 cases observed absence of the psychic reflexes only in 15 per cent. Weiler saw it in 36 per cent. of 126 cases; in another 20 per cent. they were diminished. In detail it was shown that absence of pain reaction could be ascertained only in 36 per cent., a diminution in a further 20 per cent.; against that an increased reaction on psychic and sensory stimulation in 40 per cent., a diminution in 34 per cent. of the cases. The disorders of all these reactions appeared 24 times among 35 hebephrenics, 41 times among 79 catatonics, 6 times among 12 paranoids; they were therefore most frequent among the first. Weiler is inclined to account for the numerical difference of his results from those of other observers, disregarding slight differences in the carrying out of the observations, essentially by the circumstance that he had mostly more recent cases. The disappearance of the reaction was observed in general more in advanced stages of the disease, but was occasionally to be seen in the early periods. One can scarcely be mistaken, if one brings this failure of the psychic reaction into connection with the disappearance of the emotional activities in our patients, by which they are probably caused. It must, however, be noted that Wassermeyer in 174 healthy soldiers, could establish in 6 cases a considerable diminution and once absence of the psychic pupillary reaction, while Sioli found it present in 25 attendants, though to a very varying degree.

The **tendon reflexes** are often more or less considerably increased, according to Meyer in 45 per cent. ; according to Trepsat in 59 per cent. ; diminished in 14, relatively 12 per cent. Weiler often got, especially in stuporous patients, absence of the brake-action, and in consequence repeated after-oscillation. Meyer found in 398 cases patellar-clonus 6 times, ankle-clonus twice. Skin and mucous membrane reflexes are often weak ; Trepsat found the plantar reflex in 64 per cent. of the cases diminished, in 26 per cent. increased.

Psycho-motor Domain.—Various and profound disorders are found here. Dufour has described disorders of equilibrium, staggering, adiadochokinesia, and tremor, which he regards as the expression of a " cerebellar " form of dementia præcox. Ermes[1] has recorded curves of attitude in cataleptic patients. He found that a fall of the leg held horizontally only began after 205 seconds, while in healthy persons it made its appearance on an average after 38 seconds, at latest after 80 seconds. There followed then either a repeated jerky falling off with tremor or a gradual sinking. Before complete relaxation 20 minutes elapse with the patients; in healthy persons rather more than 7 minutes. The principal cause of this power of endurance is certainly to be sought for in peculiar disorders of volitional impulse. Meanwhile Ajello[2] has after very comprehensive investigations arrived at the result, that the muscles of those patients, whom we shall later come to know as catatonics, show a peculiar reaction to electrical stimuli. It consists according to his experiments in the simultaneous appearance of tonic contractions along with genuine muscle-twitchings. He connects this phenomenon with a heightened irritability of the sarcoplasm, as it is only found otherwise in embryonic, fatigued, anæmic, or degenerated muscles, and he brings it into relation with the idiopathic muscular swellings, which indeed can be demonstrated not infrequently in our patients at the same time as heightened sensibility of the muscles to percussion.

Gregor and Hänsel found in *experiments with the ergograph* that the patients made only a few curves of approximately the same height, and then suddenly gave out. Isserlin and Lotmar have investigated the course of simple flexion and extension movements of the right index finger in

[1] Ermes, Uber die Natur der bei Katatonie zu beobachtenden Muskelzustände. Diss. 1903.
[2] Ajello, Ricerche sulle proprietà fisiológiche generali dei muscoli nella catatonia, 1907.

our patients. Fig. 13 [1] shows the course of a finger movement consisting of flexion and rapid extension in a healthy person; Figs. 14 to 17 the same in catatonic patients; the rapidity of the revolving drum which in Fig. 15 is reproduced in fifths of a second was in all approximately the same. Fig. 14 shows

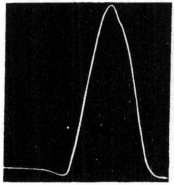

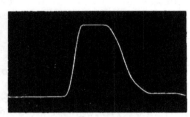

FIG. 14.
Simple Finger Movement in Catatonia (*a*).

FIG. 13. Normal Finger Movement.

apart from the smaller excursion of the movement, an abnormality which frequently appears in catatonics, though not invariably, the interpolation of a perceptible pause between flexion and extension which always follow each other immediately in healthy persons, at the same time

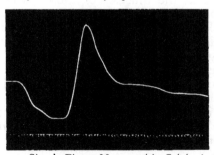

FIG. 15. Simple Finger Movement in Catatonia (*b*).

extension is slower than normal. We are here reminded of the stiffness and rigidity which strike us so frequently in catatonic movements. The abnormalities seen in Fig. 15 are much greater, though certainly they do not appear so frequently. Here there is first a preliminary extension before flexion, that is an opposing impulse which is seen in healthy persons, as in Fig. 13, at most as a slight " depression."

[1] The whole series is reduced two-thirds.

The recoil of the finger immediately succeeds flexion, but it is suddenly checked in the middle of its descent and then the finger returns with oscillations to the original position. The straightforward course with which the required move-

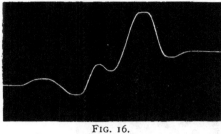

FIG. 16.
Simple Finger Movement in Catatonia (c).

ment is performed in healthy persons is accordingly influenced in patients occasionally by all sorts of counter impulses and checks. The other curves got from the same patient, as they are reproduced in Figs. 16 and 17, show still other results. In Fig. 16 a repeated oscillation of opposing impulses meets us ; at the end the finger persists in the flexed position. Fig. 17 shows a similar proceeding after a movement of flexion carried out correctly at the beginning. Among these curves there were frequently some that followed a normal course.

Rhythmical movements also, which in healthy persons run their course in the form of flexion and recoil just like a machine, show at the transition to extension the same hesitation as the simple "reaction movements." Fig. 18 represents such a series of continuous pendulum movements, which keep

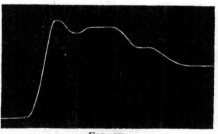

FIG. 17.
Simple Finger Movement in Catatonia (d).

time, of a finger of a healthy person ; Fig. 19 shows the same in the case of a catatonic; the time record which is reproduced gives the hundredth parts of a second.

The **seizures** which have already been very well described by Kahlbaum and Jensen deserve special notice. They are mostly attacks of vertigo, fainting fits, or epileptiform convulsions, which occur in our patients, sometimes as an isolated occurrence, sometimes more frequently. More rarely there are spasms in single muscle groups (face, arm), tetany or even apoplectiform seizures with paralysis which lasts for a considerable time, but I was told of some such cases in the previous histories. Once I saw profound collapse with spasms on the left side and in the right facial nerve. A seizure is not very infrequently the first sign of

F

the approaching disease.   I observed among others the case
of an older student who had been specially gifted from youth.
He was suddenly attacked by profound coma from which he
only gradually awoke.   Except for a slight difference in the
pupils, facial phenomenon, and great increase of the reflexes,
there was no trace of cerebral symptoms, but when I

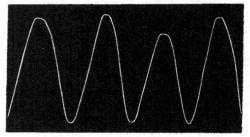

FIG. 18. Normal Rhythmical Finger Movements.

examined the patient a few weeks later, he exhibited the
well-marked picture of premature weak-mindedness, which
continued for years.   Hüfler describes also equivalents of
catatonic seizures, in which he includes transitory disorders
of the innervation of the arm, of the musculature of the face,
of the tongue, paræsthesiæ, pains, vascular and pupillary

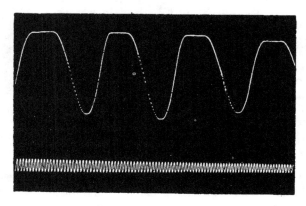

FIG. 19. Rhythmetical Finger Movements in Catatonia.

disorders, vomiting, attacks of sweating with or without
clouding of consciousness.   All these seizures are more
common in the female sex than in the male.   I found them
in my series in about 16 per cent., and in the Heidelberger
patients, who were observed for a longer time, in 19 per
cent. of all cases.   But besides that in a whole series of

patients (6 per cent. of the men, 3 per cent. of the women) spasms or fainting fits had occurred previously in youth, about which it must for the present remain doubtful whether any connection with the psychic disorder may be ascribed to them. Some patients had suffered from chorea. Urstein records seizures in 8 per cent. of the men and in 19 per cent. of the women. In one case I saw the development of a profound catatonia after the existence for many years of undoubted epileptic seizures to which then hysteroid seizures were added. And otherwise hysteroid spasms and paralyses are often observed besides aphonia, singultus, sudden erection, local contractures, and similar phenomena.

The **spasmodic phenomena** in the musculature of the face and of speech, which often appear, are extremely peculiar disorders. Some of them resemble movements of expression, wrinkling of the forehead, distortion of the corners of the mouth, irregular movements of the tongue and lips, twisting of the eyes, opening them wide, and shutting them tight, in short, those movements which we bring together under the name of making faces or *grimacing*; they remind one of the corresponding disorders of choreic patients. Nystagmus may also belong to this group. Connected with these are further, smacking and clicking with the tongue, sudden sighing, sniffing, laughing, and clearing the throat. But besides, we observe specially in the lip muscles, fine lightning-like or rhythmical twitchings, which in no way bear the stamp of voluntary movements. The same is the case in the tremor of the muscles of the mouth, which appears sometimes in speaking and which may completely resemble that of paralytics. In a great number of patients I observed distinct twitchings of the musculature of the mouth on tapping the lower branches of the facial nerves. Occasionally one sees uneven muscle-tension on the two sides of the face temporarily or for a longer time, on which Hüfler has laid stress. The out-spread fingers often show fine tremor. Several patients continually carried out peculiar sprawling, irregular, choreiform, outspreading movements, which I think I can best characterise by the expression "athetoid ataxia."

Aphasia.—In two cases it was possible during a state of dull stupor to demonstrate distinct aphasic disorders. The patients were unable to recognise and to name the objects laid in front of them although they could speak and were evidently exerting themselves to give the required information. Repeatedly after long consideration the wrong names came out. The disorder disappeared again after a few hours.

Vasomotor disorders are very wide spread in our patients. Above all one notices cyanosis of the hands, less of the feet, the nose and the ears; from the deep blue colour of the skin, dilated arterial areas are sometimes distinguished as bright red, sharply circumscribed spots, which can be artificially produced by pressure. Further there are found circumscribed areas of œdema, congestion of the head, vivid blushing, dermatography in all degrees, especially in the beginning of states of stupor. Trepsat was able in one case after 48 hours to make the dermatographic writing again visible by light rubbing with the finger-tip; he reports also eruptions and even ulcers of "trophic" origin. The activity of the heart is subjected to great fluctuations; sometimes it is retarded, more frequently it is somewhat accelerated, often also it is weak and irregular; many patients complain of palpitation.

Blood-pressure is as a rule lowered; it fluctuates, however, considerably. Weber found for systolic and diastolic pressure, pulse pressure and pulse frequency low or at most average values especially in stuporous patients. Lugiato and Ohannessian, as well as Lukacs, were able to ascertain frequently a disproportion between blood-pressure and pulse frequency. Bumke and Kehrer observed in plethysmographic experiments in catatonic stupor absence of decrease in volume, as well as of changes in pulse and respiration, on the application of the stimuli of cold and pain, and they point out the relationship of this disorder to the absence of the psychic pupillary reaction.

Respiration is according to d'Ormea's statements somewhat accelerated and very deep, and it shows many irregularities especially in expiration. Sometimes severe outbursts of perspiration are observed.

The **secretion of saliva** is frequently increased, usually only temporarily, much seldomer permanently; I was able from one patient to collect in 6 hours 375 ccm. of saliva. The analysis carried out by Rohde in one case gave a specific gravity of 1·0026 and a nitrogen content of 0·191 per cent., values which are at the lower limit of the normal, and do not point to the origin of the flow of saliva by stimulation of the sympathetic. In some patients rumination is observed, especially in the terminal states.

Temperature is usually low, sometimes sub-normal with occasional reversal and small range of the daily fluctuations. Fig 20 shows the course of the temperature in the last weeks of life of a patient who was considerably excited and who did not exhibit any apparent bodily ailment. The

readings, which had already for more than 3 weeks previously
almost always been under 37° C. and on one occasion had
sunk to 34·2° C., are repeatedly lower in the evening than
in the morning ; they sink in the two last weeks of life first
to 33·4° C. and then with a single jump rise again to 38·5° C.
and even to 39·1" C. towards the end of life.

The **menses** are usually absent or irregular, according
to Pförtner's statements in two-thirds of the recent cases.

Blood Changes.—The obscurity that hangs over the
causes of dementia præcox has been a frequent motive for
the examination of the blood-picture and of metabolism,
but the findings up to now are not very satisfactory.   Lund-

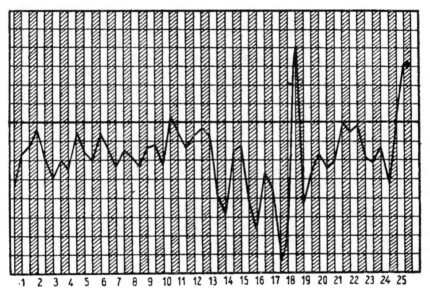

Fig 20.—Course of the body temperature at the close of life of a catatonic
patient.

wall found in general no change in the blood, but "blood
crises" with decrease in the red and increase in the white
corpuscles which appeared periodically.   Bruce and Peebles
describe in the acute periods of the disease a moderate
increase ·specially of the polynuclears and the large mono-
nuclears, which in stupor, but still more in the terminal
stages, gives place to a decrease, specially in the polynuclear
leucocytes.   Bruce has even made the attempt to establish
blood-pictures peculiar to each form of insanity and from
them to draw prognostic conclusions, an undertaking, which

in face of the many diverse statements must be regarded as premature. Heilemann also reports a small increase of the white blood cells with comparative decrease of the polynuclear forms. Sandri emphasised similar findings especially in catatonic states. Dide and Chenais[1] observed an increase of the eosinophil cells, Pighini and Paoli an increase in the size of the red blood corpuscles with a ring-shaped arrangement of the hæmoglobin. Itten was not able to establish any characteristic findings in the blood. However, in some chronic, resistive, demented patients fairly high leucocyte counts were found, and in some dull depressed patients comparatively low counts.

Berger has made the attempt to prove the presence of toxic material in the blood of catatonics by injecting serum of the patients into the occipital lobe of dogs; he found that muscle twitchings, apathy and a tendency to forced attitudes appeared.

Investigations in metabolism[2] have also frequently been carried out. In acute cases Pighini observed increased excretion of nitrogen, phosphorus, and sulphur, of urea, uric acid, and xanthin bases, which he connects with increased breaking down of nucleoproteins containing phosphorus and sulphur. Allers has called attention to the fact that here possibly insufficient nourishment might play an essential part in the states of excitement. During the chronic course, on the contrary, there is said to be retention of phosphorus and nitrogen, and a loss of lime and sulphur. Rosenfeld invariably observed retention of nitrogen, 1-2 grm. daily. A considerable lowering of the need for oxygen which cannot be removed by thyroidin was shown by the researches of Bornstein. The restriction of the oxidation processes which is in healthy persons already noticeable between the 15th and 25th years undergoes here according to his investigations a morbid increase. Grafe[3] also found in catatonic stupor a distinct slowing of metabolism, a lowering of heat production to 39 per cent. of the normal, the increase of oxidation after the intake of nourishment showed a slower development. In the urine of the patients, sugar is occasionally found; it probably is always a case of alimentary glycosuria, which could be fairly frequently demonstrated. Lugiato found retarded excretion of injected lævulose. The elimination of methylene blue and iodide of potassium began

---

[1] Dide et Chenais, Annales médico-psychologiques 1902, 2, 406.
[2] Pighini, Rivista sperimentale di frenia'ria xxxiii, 566 ; d'Ormea e Maggiotto, Riforma medica, 26, 1905.
[3] Grafe, Deutsches Archiv f. klin. Medizin, 102, 15.

according to the researches of d'Ormea and Maggiotto considerably later than in healthy persons and lasted longer. In the cerebro-spinal fluid Pighini found in 43 per cent. of his patients cholesterin which he never could demonstrate . in healthy persons.

In a series of cases I observed diffuse enlargements of the thyroid gland, occasionally the disappearance of such enlargements immediately before the first appearance of morbid phenomena, also repeated rapid change in the size of the gland during the development of the malady. Occasionally exophthalmos and tremor were present. Lastly we noticed, as the relatives of the patients also did, not infrequently a turgid appearance and a thickening of the skin reminiscent of myxœdema, especially in the face. Unfortunately these

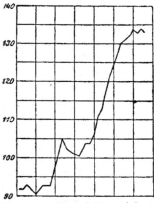

Fig. 21.—Body-weight in catatonic stupor with dementia.

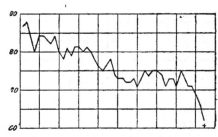

Fig. 22.—Body-weight in catatonic excitement.

findings cannot be made use of further in the meantime because of the frequency of thyroid disease amongst us. Very frequently anæmic and chlorotic conditions appear to be present.

Sleep and Food.—During the whole development of the disease the *sleep* of the patients is frequently disturbed even when they are lying quiet. The *taking of food* fluctuates from complete refusal to the greatest voracity. The *body-weight* usually falls at first often to a considerable degree, even to extreme emaciation, in spite of the most abundant nourishment. Later, on the contrary, we see the weight not infrequently rise quickly in the most extraordinary way, so that the patients in a short time acquire an uncommonly well-nourished turgid appearance. Sometimes, in quite short periods, very considerable differences in the body-weight are noticed, probably in connection with fluctuations of the amount of water contained in the tissues. Of the curves which are here reproduced, Fig. 21, shows the body-weight in the usual course of a case of catatonic stupor terminating in dementia of middle grade. Although after the awakening from stupor slight excitement set in, the weight increased very much. Fig. 22 was obtained from the patient whose temperature curve is given above, and who in spite of the most careful nursing and abundant nourishment sank in marasmus of the highest degree without any organic disease. Very great fluctuations of the body-weight, from the initial weight to the double of it, is shown in Fig. 23, which was

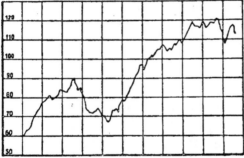

Fig. 23.—Body-weight in alternation of stupor and excitement with dementia.

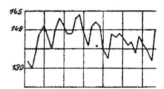

Fig. 24.—Fluctuations in bod weight in the beginning o case of dementia præcox.

obtained from a young catatonic. The patient after an initial alternation of stupor and excitement came to us, recovered at first, but then sank with diminution of the body weight again into deep stupor, from which he awoke after some months to increase rapidly in weight to an extraordinary extent; but at the same time the transition to depressive dementia with some features of silly affectation had taken place. Lastly, Fig. 24 shows in a commencing dementia præcox a series of fairly regular fluctuations which kept pace with an alternation of stupor and greater clearness. Later this regularity ceased, and it came to permament dementia.

CHAPTER V.

CLINICAL FORMS.

THE presentation of clinical details in the large domain of dementia præcox meets with considerable difficulties, because a delimitation of the different clinical pictures can only be accomplished artificially. There is certainly a whole series of phases which frequently return, but between them there are such numerous transitions that in spite of all efforts it appears impossible at present to delimit them sharply and to assign each case without objection to a definite form. We shall be obliged therefore, as in paralysis, to content ourselves at first for the sake of a more lucid presentation with describing the course of certain more frequent forms[1] of the malady without attributing special clinical value to this grouping.

As such forms I have hitherto separated from each other a *hebephrenic*, a *catatonic*, and a *paranoid* group of cases. This classification has been frequently accepted with many modifications, specially concerned with the clinical position of the paranoid diseases, as also by Bleuler in his monograph on schizophrenia; he adds, however, to it the insidious "dementia simplex" as a special form. Räcke has made other attempts at classification; he separates out "depressive," "confused excited," "stuporous," "subacute paranoid" forms and a "catatonia in attacks." Wieg-Wickenthal differentiates "dementia simplex," "hebephrenia" with pseudomanic behaviour, "depressive paranoid forms" and catatonia.

The undoubted inadequacy of my former classification has led me once more to undertake the attempt to make a more natural grouping, as I have in hand a larger number of possibly more reliable cases. For this purpose there were at my disposal about 500 cases in Heidelberg which had been investigated by myself, in which according to their clinical features, as well as according to the length of the time that had passed, the ultimate issue of the morbid process could be accepted with considerable probability. "Recovered" cases were not taken into account because of the uncertainty of their significance which still exists, but only such cases as

---

[1] Sante de Sanctis, Rivista sperimentale de freniatria, xxxii, 141.

had led to profound dementia or to distinctly marked and permanent phenomena of decreased function. On grounds which will be discussed later, it is, as I believe, not to be assumed that by this choice definite clinical types have quite fallen out of the scope of our consideration ; at most a certain displacement in the frequency of the individual forms would be conceivable.

The result of this attempt at a classification agrees in many points with the statements of the above-mentioned investigators. First I also think that I should delimit simple insidious dementia as a special clinical form. Next in the series comes hebephrenia in the narrower sense of silly dementia which was first described by Hecker. A third group is composed of the simple depressive or stuporous forms, a fourth of states of depression with delusions. In a fifth form I have brought together the majority of the clinical cases which go along with conditions of greater excitement ; one could speak of an agitated dementia præcox. To it is nearly related the sixth form, which includes essentially the catatonia of Kahlbaum, in which peculiar states of excitement are connected with stupor. A more divergent picture is seen in the seventh and eighth groups, in which the cases are placed which run a paranoid course, according to whether they end in the usual terminal states of dementia præcox or in paranoid, relatively hallucinatory, weakmindedness. We shall then subject to special consideration the small number of observations, which present the remarkable phenomenon of confusion of speech along with perfect sense and fairly reasonable activity.

DEMENTIA SIMPLEX.

Simple insidious dementia as it was described by Diem [1] under the name dementia simplex, consists in an *impoverishment and devastation of the whole psychic life which is accomplished quite imperceptibly.* The disease begins usually in the years of sexual development, but often the first slight beginnings can be traced back into childhood. On the other hand Pick has also described a " primary progressive dementia of adults," but it is certainly very doubtful whether it may be grouped with dementia præcox. In our patients a deterioration of mental activity becomes very gradually noticeable. The former good, perhaps distinguished, scholar fails always more conspicuously in tasks which till then he could carry out quite easily, and he is more and

[1] Diem, Archiv f. Psychiatrie xxxvii. 111.

more outstripped by his companions. He appears absent-minded, thoughtless, makes incomprehensible mistakes, cannot any longer follow the teaching rightly, does not reach the standard of the class. While pure exercises of memory are perhaps still satisfactory, a certain poverty of thought, weakness of judgment and incoherence in the train of ideas appears always more distinctly. Many patients try by redoubled efforts to compensate for the results of their mental falling off, which is at first attributed by parents and teachers to laziness and want of good will. They sit the whole day over their work, learn by heart with all their might, sit up late at night, without being able to make their work any better. Others become idle and indifferent, stare for hours at their books without reading, give themselves no trouble with their tasks, and are not incited either by kindness or severity.

Hand in hand with this decline of mental activity there is a change of temperament, which often forms the first conspicuous sign of the developing malady. The patients become depressed, timid, lachrymose, or impertinent, irritable, malicious ; sometimes a certain obstinate stubbornness is developed. The circle of their interests becomes narrower ; their relations to their companions become cold ; they show neither attachment nor sympathy. Not infrequently a growing estrangement towards parents and brothers and sisters becomes noticeable. The patients remain indifferent to whatever happens in the family circle, shut themselves up, limit the contact with their relatives to the least possible. Bleuler brings forward here as a frequent explanation the " Œdipus complex," the concealed sexual inclination to one of the parents and the jealous emotions which arise from it. I consider that the generalization of that kind of case, which is certainly very rare, as belonging to the system of Freud, is wholly without foundation. It seems much more natural to me to explain the antagonism to relatives by the gloomy feeling of inferiority and the defiant resistance to it, but above all by the common experience that for a long time it has been the habit of the relatives to trace the morbid phenomena back to a moral offence, and to meet them with painful reprimands and measures. Similar antagonism is also seen quite commonly to develop in the relations with degenerate, wayward children.

Ambition and pleasure in the usual games and occasional occupations become extinct ; wishes and plans for the future are silent ; inclination and ability for useful occupation disappear. The patient has neither endurance nor understanding, works confusedly, begins everything the wrong way about, tries as far as possible to withdraw himself from claims on him.   He remains lying in bed for days, sits about anywhere, trifles away his time in occupations of no value, devours perhaps without choice and without understanding chance and unsuitable literature, lives one day at a time without a plan.   A few patients have indeed at times a certain feeling of the change, which takes place in them, often in hypochondriacal colouring ; but the majority sink into dulness without being in any way sensible of it.   Sometimes a certain restlessness is shown which causes the patient to take extended walks, to run away without any plan, to undertake aimless journeys.   Alcohol is for him a special danger, he gives way to its temptations without resistance, and then very rapidly comes down in the world, and comes into conflict with public order and criminal law.   That happens the more easily as many patients are very sensitive to intoxicating drinks.

In these circumstances the inability of the patients to undergo the preparatory training or to attain to the calling which was planned for him becomes always more clear.   He passes no more examinations, is sent away as useless from every apprenticeship, does not fit in anywhere, nor does he feel at home in anything.   After all possible unsuccessful attempts to get them settled, many patients in the end remain idle at home, where they either lead a quiet existence without activity and without desire, without any disorder of note, or they live their own lives, and as capricious oddities try the patience of their relatives severely.   Other patients succeed in getting a foothold in some subordinate calling, especially in gardening and agriculture, where in narrow surroundings they are in a position to fulfil a limited number of duties.   Others again, as no other expedient is known, are provided with some money and sent to America, where they immediately go to the bad ; some manage to enter the Foreign Legion and are there again turned away after severe discipline and punishment.   A considerable number in the end fall into the crowd of beggars and vagabonds, and oscillate hither and thither in a half-witted state from year's end to year's end between public highway and workhouse, where ever anew the hopeless attempt is made " to turn them into useful people again."

The development of this clinical picture invariably takes a series of years.   It may stand still for a shorter or longer time, but on the other hand it may occasionally experience a more sudden exacerbation.   The terminal result to which the malady leads is of varied character, as it may make a final halt on each step of its development. Thus then we see in a series of cases a very slight loss in the psychic life remain, which only becomes noticeable by comparison with former behaviour, while in others a marked psychic decline comes into existence.

The frequency of the malady is probably fairly large, even if only a small number of the cases are considered as morbid at all or even fall into the hands of the alienist. Who cannot call to mind companions of his youth who at first gave just ground for certain, perhaps brilliant, hopes, but then from some point of their development onwards failed in an incomprehensible way? It is here a question of these young people who, without palpable cause and without any special morbid phenomena, simply trifle away the time, or are only able to gain a position in life far under their original prospects. Neither they nor their relatives have perhaps any idea that a morbid process has taken place; only the knowledge of cases which run a severer course, suggests the thought that such slight losses in psychic ability might also be due to dementia præcox. Here and there, perhaps, also individual caprices, peculiarities or temperamental inadequacy in people who are otherwise well developed psychically are to be regarded as residua of slight morbid disorders of the same kind as the disease here discussed, if it can be proved that they were first developed in a definite period of life.

When the disease comes to a standstill, it may mean a final, though incomplete, recovery; but sooner or later the morbid process may again progress. We are not able at present to say whether the latter is always possible, or if in many cases it is excluded. A really profound dementia, without fairly acute exacerbations, with a continuous development of the malady, only slowly progressive, does not seem to occur. On the contrary, a dementia simplex which lasts for many years, even for decades, forms often enough the introduction to one of the forms of dementia præcox which goes on to profound dementia, and which will be discussed later on. If one will, one may also regard dementia simplex in a certain way as the first period of dementia præcox. The cases which belong to it halt on one of the steps which form this period, while in the remaining forms there occurs progress of the malady beyond that point. But a first period in the sense of the term dementia simplex can certainly not always be proved, except in a certain number of observed cases.

SILLY DEMENTIA.

That form of dementia præcox which we have called above "silly dementia," is in many respects nearly related to simple insidious dementia. In its clinical picture there appears besides the progressive devastation of the psychic life *incoherence* in thinking, feeling, and action. It corresponds, as already mentioned, in its principal features to the clinical picture of *hebephrenia* which was described by Hecker[1] in 1871 as a type in connection with the researches of Kahlbaum. Hecker at that time brought together under this term a group of cases in which, after an introductory stage of melancholy, a stage of mania develops and then rapidly makes room for a quite peculiar weak-minded condition. Daraszkiewicz[2] then enlarged the idea of hebephrenia by including also the "depressed forms" which lead to profound insanity.

The development of the disease is accomplished in almost four-fifths of the cases quite gradually; often an insidious change of the psychic personality precedes the appearance of more distinct morbid phenomena by many years. In the remaining patients the disorder begins in subacute form; in a few cases it breaks out suddenly. In the preliminary stage there are sometimes nervous troubles, complaints of lassitude, headaches, feeling of giddiness, fainting-fits, irritability, disorders of sleep. The patients become absent-minded, forgetful, negligent; they tire easily, they cannot collect their thoughts any more; they appear lacking in ideas and understanding, they are silly and lazy; they fail in daily tasks, change their occupation, because it is too difficult for them, set aside their work, or give it up entirely.

Here and there hallucinations appear. The patients see apparitions, witches, dead people, will-o'-the-wisps, the devil with a white beard, little black mannikins, which sit down on their breasts. A patient saw "the three most beautiful crowns in the world"; "black points were flung at" another. They hear good or evil spirits, the Edison phonograph speaking, voices "talking always of love"; things are spoken into their head; their thoughts become loud, their suspenders turn into snakes; their food appears green from arsenic; it smells of the water-closet.

Delusions.—Not infrequently passing states of depression are developed. The patients are dispirited and dejected,

---

[1] Hecker, Virchows Archiv lii. 394.

[2] Daraszkiewicz, Über Hebephrenie, insbesondere deren schwere Form. Diss. Dorpat, 1892.

they think they are syphilitic, have got the itch or dyspepsia ; they have a feeling of oppression in their brain ; they search out all possible physicians and quacks ; the disease is in all their limbs. Their morbid sensations sometimes assume the most nonsensical forms. They have no brain any longer ; their back is broken in two ; their blood has been taken from them ; their body has died ; their legs are exchanged. A female patient thought that she had the Kaiser in her stomach, every human being in her body, a telephone, small dolls, a bicycle in her head, that she had a wooden head ; five people had been made out of her. Other patients become anxious, are to blame for everything, are damned, have committed sins, are said to have killed someone ; they wish to make confession, read the Bible zealously, search out clergymen. People are looking at them, speaking about them, making fun of them, hatching out abominable crimes, are persecuting them, are selling them for immoral purposes, are hypnotising them, are making fools of them. Little girls make sexual assaults on them ; everywhere there are enemies, "enchanters," conspirators ; it is a year of revolution, a hereditary feud ; the arch-enemy has a hand in it. Stuff is blown into the spinal marrow of the patient ; his nature is electrically withdrawn from him ; his forehead is bent in ; people blow up his testicles, cut his boots to pieces, give him poison in his food, assault him at night, mutilate him ; he gets a headache if he enters a church. He must be slaughtered, he is taken prisoner, stamped to pieces, "sawn asunder and broken on the wheel." His wife is unfaithful, has secret intercourse with two other men, wishes to poison him. Thoughts of suicide often rise to the surface; a patient thought he would have liked to kill his child in order that it might not be so unhappy as himself.

Exalted Ideas.—On the other hand we meet also, but in smaller range with *exalted ideas*. The patient feels that he has a special call, is something more than everyone else, has a proud spirit, an enormous will-power, is "the ornament of his feelings," is sent from God, will be Christ, receives revelations ; the feast of the atonement is there. He is Maurice Monfort of Scotland, is surrounded with princes and emperors, is descended from his grandfather Billbull, has 10-20,000 marks capital, will be a rich man ; the hospital belongs to him. He will attain to great things, will make a fortune by national bankruptcy ; he will have permission given him to carry on a temperance restaurant, and then he will dispense wine, beer, and brandy. A patient hoped to become "a general with 250 marks yearly income "; a female patient thought that she was divorced and had children by a captain in the army; another declared that she was the Empress Augusta. Many patients do not acknowledge their father any longer, they speak of their "so-called parents."

At the time the patients are giving utterance to these nonsensical delusions they are for the most part fairly quiet and quite sensible, clear about time and place, about their surroundings and their affairs, but incoherent and desultory in their train of ideas; they are not in a position to occupy themselves seriously and with perseverance in mental work; they are childishly incapable of making a decision and susceptible to influence. Their delusions even appear mostly only as sudden thoughts, which are not further worked up or retained. Memory, especially what was learned at school, and the recollection of recent events may be quite undisturbed.

Emotions.—These are for the most part in harmony with the ideas to which the patients give utterance, but are not very deep and they show quite sudden fluctuations. The patients laugh and weep without recognisable cause, sometimes convulsively, fall abruptly into violent excitement, but quieten down again just as suddenly. Sometimes there predominates an imperturbably exalted, self-satisfied mood; in other patients, a childish hilarity which passes easily into a lachrymose state or a pitiable faint-heartedness; or the patients are mistrustful, peevish, impertinent, rough and rude, break out into obscene abuse on the most insignificant occasions, threaten and become violent. A patient without more ado shot a railway employee with whom he had fallen into an altercation. A few patients incline to exaggerated religiosity; a patient wished to change his religion; others plan to go into a cloister. Many are sexually excited, plan to be married; show a "pathetic desire for love," masturbate, expose themselves, make sexual assaults on little girls; a patient wished to go to bed with his mother and sister. Women put matrimonial advertisements into the newspapers, "scream for a husband," give themselves without regard to anyone, let whole troops of young men on the highway misuse them, and fall into prostitution.

Conduct.—The disease makes itself noticeable in by far the most striking way in the activities of the patients. Already in the beginning of the malady a change in their behaviour invariably sets in. They become dreamy, shy of their fellow-beings, withdraw themselves, shut themselves up, do not greet their friends any more, stand about in corners, stare intently in front of them, give no answer, talk with themselves. Others become stubborn, self-willed, difficult, insubordinate, or unrestrained, restless, loquacious. Their capacity for work suffers severely. They do not trouble themselves any more about their obligations, do everything the wrong way about ; a patient cleaned his boots with mud. They leave everything where it is, suddenly throw the shovel away, go to bed, look out at the window all day long, busy themselves with trifling affairs, make wreaths of flowers; they exert themselves to learn poems off by heart, or to begin Latin ; a patient said "he took as great pains as possible to investigate thoroughly what the real meaning of positive and negative electricity was." Many patients stop working, because they have enough to live on ; others because of their performances being of less value, work "for board" without wages ; they frequently change their situations because they are of no use anywhere. One of my patients suddenly appeared unasked at the house of strangers with a stolen manure-fork in order to spread manure ; another time when he again escaped he joined some workmen and unloaded stones with them, then went to a strange stable and began there to saw wood. A few patients have in view to change their occupation. A patient who till then had wished to study theology, decided to study medicine because theology was "too stupid" for him, another planned to go on the stage, a third who had never shown any musical inclinations wished to study the theory of music ; a fourth patient wished for himself "a little post in the hospital."

The whole conduct of life of the patients becomes senseless and incoherent. They cannot any longer manage money ; they make aimless purchases, give away and squander their property ; a female patient threw good fruit to the pigs. A poor patient fooled away an inheritance of 5000 marks within two years ; another stopped taking money for the wares which he sold. Many patients fall into drinking habits and in this way come down in the world with remarkable rapidity. In their outer appearance they become disorderly, negligent, dirty, peculiar. They do not wash themselves any more ; they wear conspicuous clothing, tie cigar ribbons in their button-hole, stick paper in their ears ; a patient put on a truss without any reason ; a lawyer bound flowers on to his stick and umbrella, hung a garland round his neck, stuck brooches and pictures on himself, blackened his face, painted a large paragraph sign on his coat.

With these are associated a multitude of incomprehensible and childishly aimless actions. The patients throw stones, lie down in cruciform attitude on the floor, cut off their hair, undress, bathe publicly in the middle of the town, begin to play the harmonica at night, run about on the rails of the shunting-station, burn their own hair and beard and those of other people with their cigar, cut up their linen and clothing; they destroy the furniture and throw it about; they lie sprawling on the floor, turn somersaults in bed, climb on to the stove, slide about the room with chairs. A patient smashed a crucifix and a gravestone; a second tolled the big bell during divine service; a third lit the candles on the high altar and imitated the clergyman, a fourth lay down in a. fountain. A teacher played tag with his scholars, lay down in a crib in the cow-house "from love of mischief," put his head into the well, because on account of his great sins he could do very well with another baptism, lay down on the floor in order to measure how long his coffin would have to be; a lady fed her dolls with coffee. A female patient abused herself grossly with the strongest expressions, others try to throttle themselves, to cut their throat, to cut off their fingers, usually without special energy, often in full publicity. A patient asked for gunpowder; another scratched himself with his knife in order to lessen the influences; a female patient wished that her body should be cut up.

Very frequently we observe in the patients a certain restlessness. They run away suddenly from their work, roam about, wade barefoot in the snow, insist on going out even at night, become deserters, hide themselves away, make senseless journeys, often without money and without a ticket, want to get into the Castle, to go to America; a patient wandered for days in the forest without food. In consequence of this they easily become vagrants, beg, commit small thefts, and land in this way in prison and the work-house, where then a deterioration of their condition often sets in; nearly a quarter of my male patients met this fate.

The *conduct* of the patients invariably shows many peculiarities. They are very changeable in their behaviour, sometimes accessible, childlike, docile, at other times repellent, inapproachable, resistive, irritable, flaring up easily, at one moment loquacious and verbose, at another taciturn and mute. Their mode of speech is frequently manneristic, unctuous, didactic, sometimes noisy or purposely obscene. The substance of their conversation is often confused and unintelligible, or there is nothing in it. Frequently they ride to death certain phrases; they indulge in stale jokes and insipid doggerel; they introduce unusual or foreign expressions or dialect. Many patients startle us by extraordinary turns of expression and abrupt nonsensical questions; a patient said, " He blows his nose, and I blow mine; who then is right, I or he?" Others have a tendency to foolish plays on words and to peculiar symbolism.

Writing.—These peculiarities often appear more distinctly in the *writing* of the patients which are usually in "Karlchen-Miesnik-style," according to Hecker's description. Besides negligent want of connection in the train of thought, repeated change of construction in long spun-out periods, mixed metaphors, abrupt interspersing of sudden ideas, rhymed effusions, we find a slovenly external form, irregular handwriting, flourishes on single letters, underlining, deficiency or superfluity in marks of punctuation, and monotonous contents often with verbal repetitions. An example is given in the following extract from a letter written by a student who was up for his leaving examinations. The extract forms the introduction to the specimen of writing 4 which is reproduced here :—

"When you on the 19th May of this year, namely on a beautiful Sunday afternoon, constructed the plan for yourself to do me the honour to visit me by the railway in the Hospital for the Insane at H., care of Professor K., Littera Voss-strasse Nr 4, you thought then perhaps to give your dear and good son a special pleasure, visiting him in the institution !—Or was it not so ? !—When I further recapitulate again the many unjust things and abusive epithets which I threw at the head of my dear mama, I think that I really cannot avoid being obliged to confess that I should have rather expected a visit first from the maternal side. Supposing namely the case that the above mentioned should not only have been ill, but had actually been so, so would my humble self have first strongly advised in her case a visit to her first-born ! Now as *happily* my 22nd birthday coincided with Ascension day, as God and fate would have it, but in the Asylum, the visit of my mother in person certainly caused me a great momentary joy, especially as she from motherly love showed me the honour and kindness to promise to bring me another cake and a silver chain, but in any case her visit would not and could not be a visible comfort for me for the old reason, namely my father's dissatisfaction with my diligence at home, regarding conscientiousness ! Further I thank you also most heartily for the beautiful artistic card with the special signature Family G. But wait ! Who should the Family G. be then in this case, if its principal member is crouching in a madhouse ? " and so on.

The shallowness of the contents, the incomprehensibility, the laboured style, the incoherence of the train of thought, as well as the slovenly external form, which is scarcely decipherable on account of the many crossings-out and alterations, all these features of the specimen of writing appended here show the profound mental incapacity, which is in sharp contradiction to the cultural standing of the patient who was originally highly gifted. For comparison, I place beside it a letter very similar as regards handwriting, written by a day-labourer likewise· hebephrenic. The letter is better

Specimen of writing 4. Letter of a Hebephrenic.

arranged in external form, but the contents are still more incoherent. The abrupt breaking-off of the ideas, the vacuity of thought, the meaningless expressions of speech are accompanied here by a certain feeling of disease :—

"Dear parents and brothers and sisters, Do not be anxious about me, my thoughts are directed in the right way, I hope you will not experience that again. I am convinced that you meant well with me and still mean well. Social relations make it necessary to pay taxes. To live and let live is the main principle of the purely human thought especially of a day-labourer as I am. The arrival has done me good ; but I am somewhat weak in my nerves. I shall take pains to direct my thoughts wholly according to the nat. liberal circumstances, not socialist. I am also no longer so melancholy, have lost m knowledge terribly.

In the following extract from a letter of a young business man the feeling of disease also appears distinctly along with the peculiarity of expression :—

"There is no prospect that an after-effect event, of my symptoms come to a decision, but it is certain that the contained sensations unfold their arrangement. . . . As regards my condition, end-symptoms of epileptic combination show themselves and I am always prepared, if that should come, which I did not expect. The depressive phenomena corresponding to subj. psych. neurasthenic combination are of a permanent kind and now you will perhaps yourself know what is impending. . . . With my psychological and psychiatric studies also will it now soon be done, for my condition is itself composed of psychiatry . . ."

Another patient, who afterwards became drivellingly demented, wrote to a married woman in a lengthy document from the "madhouse H." a declaration of love in German, English, French, and Greek with the assurance, that he had to get air for his oppressed heart, and must explain what he could not keep any longer for himself alone without being obliged to fear that he would get palpitation or that his senses would take a different direction from that which nature had traced out for them. A young student of divinity composed the following poem, in which the vacuity of the jingle of words as well as the loss of artistic feeling comes very clearly to expression :—

Ferner Länder Städte hab' ich viel gesehen,
Wunderbar gebaut und riesengross,
Und es herrschte drin ein eigenartig Wehen,
Barg manch' süss Geheimnis in dem Schoss.
Und die Rätsel blieben ungelöst,
Hätte nicht die Liebste heimlich mir verraten,
Was uns anzieht, was uns von sich stösst,
Und dies alles bei dem besten Wein und Braten.

The *bearing* of the patients is often constrained, forced, affected, or slack and negligent, "not military," as was ascertained in the case of a soldier; they frequently also commit breaches of military discipline, laugh in the ranks, do not stand erect.   They make faces, assume peculiar attitudes, lie on their faces, make strange gestures, scratch themselves till the blood comes, spit, are occasionally filthy, produce nonsensical drawings and needlework.   Not infrequently automatic obedience, especially catalepsy, can be demonstrated.   ·

The *sleep* of the patients is frequently disturbed, sometimes by excitement at night.   The *appetite* is irregular ; the patients are sometimes voracious; at other times they eat nothing or only certain articles of food, cram them hastily into their mouth, eat in an extremely unmannerly way, seize the food with their hands.   A patient declined food, giving as his motive that he lived on the supernatural ; another asked for better food and at the same time called out : "Waiter, a glass of water !"

The **Further Course** of the disease in the very great majority of cases which I have brought together led to profound dementia in which for the most part the peculiarities of the previous morbid condition, silly conduct and incoherence of the train of thought, were still distinctly recognisable.   In a quarter of the cases the patients became wholly dull and devoid of thought, in a further number of cases manneristic or negativistic.   Only in about 12 per cent. of the observed cases the disorders disappeared so far that a simple weak-mindedness remained without other striking morbid phenomena.   Improvement lasting somewhat longer, 8 or 10 years, with later relapse, was ascertained in about 7 per cent. of the cases.   Not infrequently the condition exhibited fluctuations, sometimes within a fairly regular return, it may be in connection with the menses.   As the *issue* in states of slight weakness was noted in about 19 per cent. of the total number of our cases of dementia præcox, and considerable and more lasting improvement occurred in nearly 26 per cent. of the cases, we must regard silly dementia as an *unfavourable* form of the disease.   It includes about 13 per cent. of our observed cases.   Seizures, in nearly 21 per cent., appear to be a little more frequent than in the average. The age of the patient corresponds fairly accurately with that of dementia præcox as a whole ; 59 per cent. of the patients had not yet reached their 25th year ; the male sex was represented by 63 per cent., which is considerably more than the average (56 per cent.)

SIMPLE DEPRESSIVE DEMENTIA.

As the third group of dementia præcox I should like to take together under the name of simple depressive or stuporous dementia, those cases in which after an introductory state of depression with or without phenomena of stupor a definite psychic decline gradually develops. The beginning of the disease is in something more than half of the cases slowly progressive; still in nearly 20 per cent. it is acute, especially in the forms in which there is stupor. Sometimes for a number of years before the actual onset of the disease there is a history of a quiet, shy, depressed behaviour. The introductory phenomena are those already described—headaches, vertigo, disorders of sleep, failing appetite, great need for rest, now and then fainting fits, hysteriform or epileptiform seizures. The patients stop working, neglect the household, go to bed, withdraw themselves, stare into a hole, are continually brooding, run away, hide themselves, carry on confused conversations.

Hallucinations.—Not infrequently hallucinations appear, although they do not usually take up much room in the clinical picture. The patients see the Virgin Mary on the ceiling, heavenly apparitions, God and the devil, mice; they hear people gossiping, spirits making a noise, the voice of their father or of their neighbour, of the "men from the churchyard," of the "tormentors from above downwards," of the maidens; their companions are jeering. Reproaches are made to them and commands bestowed on them, thoughts are given to them which must be repeated. "The voices work the system of thought and breath," said a female patient; she heard that she was damned, that she was no longer pure, that she was to be hacked to pieces. To other patients eating is forbidden; "that has crept in so for the last five or six years," said a patient. The feeling of sexual or hypnotic influence also occurs.

Depression.—As a rule all sorts of depressive ideas appear on the surface, especially those of *hypochondriacal* content. The patient suffers from all possible diseases, from softening of the brain, is weak in his head, ill in his nerves, has foul blood, has contracted atrophy of the nerves by onanism, has lost his reason; one half of his body is already gone; he never has his life. His sense is torn asunder, his body is melted up, his heart is worn out; "reason, understanding, and sense have gone out of my brain," said a female patient; another asserted that he had "the half exhalation of a woman." The following extracts from a comprehensive description of himself written by a patient who was permanently quite sensible and reasonable, may give an idea of these hypochondriacal trains of thought which gradually develop alongside of the most various hallucinations and dysæsthesiæ :—

"Already in June very great excitement became noticeable in me. . . . Remarks about me could excite me in the highest degree. In studying I began sometimes at one place, sometimes at another . . . ; in writing I then very often made mistakes. . . . All at once it happened to me that studying was no longer at all possible ; the sentence that had been read shortly before did not stick. In a rather long excerpt, which I had already begun, I noticed a considerable change in my handwriting, and that the handwriting changed in the course of the copying of a few pages. I carried on my studies in a most extraordinary hurried way, and did not allow myself any more the necessary rest and recreation ; I was unwilling to take any more the necessary time even for eating. . . . My memory left much to be desired already for a considerable time. . . . My sleep was bad ; I could not fall asleep for a long time, and in the morning I was not properly strengthened and refreshed. . . . Physically I became gradually weaker ; the skin of my face became pale and was pasty to the touch. I constantly had the inclination to look in the mirror. I saw that my eyes had a peculiarly dull lustre. If I turned my head quickly, immediately a peculiar cracking was heard. I was struck by the rapid diminution of my visual power, in spite of the fact that I spared my eyes. . . . I had accustomed myself for a long time when I went a walk to wend my steps where I had the prospect of meeting only a few people. . . . I did not trust myself any longer to look at people. . . . Later I then began to have a certain fear of everything ; I did not trust myself any longer to look at anything, and thought that enjoyment of nature was also forbidden to me ; ideas, as if I dared not any more touch myself or look at myself, came to me occasionally. When I then, under medical treatment, took bromides, I got curious pricking sensations in my brain. In walking I thought that the right leg was thrown out in front of me, sometimes also the left leg. . . . Till sleep came over me I had a sensation in my legs as if they were squeezed firmly and as if the skin were contracted on the shin bones and feet. On the left side of the body I thought a paint brush was being stroked downwards, especially in the region of the heart. Often till I fell asleep I could not get enough breath ; I had the feeling as if it always drove the belly higher up, and as if there were an impediment against the breastbone in my breast, so that my breast could not sink any more. In my head I thought balls rolled up and then fell down. Besides that I had also the following sensations ; my skull-cup was like glass to the touch and my hair like fur ; my skull could be pressed together at will ; my head was sometimes light and sometimes heavy ; my teeth were sometimes knocked out, sometimes knocked in. My tongue was sometimes too long for speaking so that it came close against my teeth, sometimes it was too short and contracted. In my gums I was aware of all kinds of oppressive and dragging feelings ; my nose was sometimes knocked inwards, sometimes outwards. There was sometimes a bad smell of the mouth ; sometimes there was a fragrant odour. Often also such a smell was blown on me. Cold air was blown over my face. Someone sat down beside me on the bed. My buttocks were rough like a grater. There were noises in my heart, there was a rubbing as of two millstones on each other. Sometimes I felt my body light, sometimes heavy. I thought someone was sleeping close beside me and sometimes also over me. I heard loud hammering on the wall and whizzing in the air. The bedstead sank downwards at my feet and rose upwards at my head, or it turned over sidewards. I flew away, the bed with me. The voices were often preferable to these sensations; I could more easily fall asleep with the former. I heard pilgrims pass by in two choruses; the one said: 'He must die,' or 'He is dying'; the other: 'He is becoming again.' First I heard the great bell ring, then small bells, then great and small confusedly. When reading I was disturbed by a voice on my left which read quickly along with me in an unpleasant way. . . . The back of my head appeared to me, when I laid it on the pillow, all wobbling and soft. At and in my head I had the following sensations:—pricking above, squirting from my hair, the falling down of big drops out of my head on to the pillow. Besides that, I often thought that drops were falling on the bedcover or on the sleeve of my night-shirt, on the back of my hand, on my finger-nails. . . . I saw people with two shadows in place of eyes, then blind: then again I thought they had scintillating fire in their eyes; once only for a short time I saw people black in the face. . . . I had a feeling as if a worm would creep around in my brain; then would creep through my gums and tongue into my spinal marrow; in my neck I felt crackling crashing noises. . . . I heard the following voices: 'Nothing rare,' 'Nothing special,' 'Carrion,' 'Rascal,' 'Onanist,' and especially in the last part of the time nothing but my name."

The patient who while suffering from the phenomena described was slowly becoming weak-minded, not only observed himself most accurately but also recognised quite clearly the morbidity of the disorders reported by himself; the remarkable point in his case was only the equanimity with which he reproduced all his tormenting perceptions.

Ideas of Sin and of Persecution.—Not infrequently ideas of sin also appear, and in connection with them ideas of persecution. The patient has sworn falsely, committed a mortal sin, is a "sinful serpent," is accused of sodomy, wants to die. He must atone, be sacrificed, has fallen into the hands of the evil one who is now going to wring his neck. He is shut out from society, is afraid of an assault by night; people are not kind to him. He is watched, is going to be fetched, is to be dragged away in the knacker's cart, is to be beheaded, is to be killed by a painful death. His food is filthy, contains poison. Often these ideas are very indistinct and obscure and only find utterance on questioning. Here and there an exalted idea is also perhaps on an occasion brought forward; the patient is a substituted child, must strive after something higher, must meet with Kaiser and Kings, is in Paradise. The patient, from whom the above description of himself came, thought some years later that he would quite likely yet become a professor.

Perception usually exhibits at first no very serious disorders, yet the patients are for the most part inattentive, indifferent, often also repellent, melancholy. People and surroundings are as a rule correctly recognised, while the patients are often not clear about time-relations. The train of thought of the patients changes abruptly, is at times confused, is easily diverted. Memory, acquired knowledge and expertness remain sometimes fairly well preserved, sometimes they undergo considerable loss. Sooner or later, however, a certain mental decay makes itself felt; the patients become poor in ideas and weak in judgment; "I often don't know at all what is the matter with me," said a patient. The relatives of a female patient declared, "She couldn't think rightly and did not know what she was talking about."

Mood is in the beginning usually anxious, dejected, lachrymose and despondent; the patients have no more joy in life, are about to despair, do not trust themselves; they weep and lament, would like to die because things do not please them any more. They frequently make attempts at suicide, often in very nonsensical ways. They try to throw themselves out at the window, dash their head against a wall, go into a stream to turn back again immediately, run into the forest to let themselves freeze to death there. A female patient drank petroleum; a patient hung his head out of the bed in order that it could be hewn off. Sometimes periods of exalted and even *unrestrained* mood temporarily intervene. Other patients are irritable, morose, violent. Sexual excitement vents itself in impulsive masturbation and in sexual intercourse regardless of consequences; a patient made a proposal of marriage to a lady who was wholly unknown to him. In the further course, however, often very soon, the emotional life becomes *duller*; the participation of the patients in the events around them becomes always feebler. They do not trouble themselves about their fellow-patients, remain indifferent to exciting events, do not move a muscle if one occupies himself with them or even causes them pain. At the same time they become dirty, spit into the dishes used for food, smear themselves with urine, play with lumps of fæces, make messes.

Volition.—In the whole conduct of the patients the *devastation of their will* makes itself conspicuous above everything. They are tired, weak, lazy, without initiative, irresolute, let themselves become destitute, live carelessly a day at a time, fling away money and possessions senselessly, let themselves drift according to chance influences and therefore come quickly down in the world especially when they begin to drink. Many become vagrants, as an elementary school-teacher did in my observation who gradually had become unfit for his calling. Occasionally the stupidity and irritability of the patients lead to very risky actions. A female patient did not turn off the gas; a patient threatened his wife with his knife; another bought a revolver to defend himself. Many patients must be washed and dressed like children. Very frequently *automatic obedience* can be demonstrated in them.

Besides this weakness of will there is often a certain *restlessness*; the patients change their calling and situation, run away, make aimless journeys; a patient sailed three times to America and back. To that may be added all kinds of impulsive actions. The patients speak away to themselves, collect everything possible in their pockets, play the piano all day, scream suddenly for hours, force their way out howling, pray, sing, laugh uncontrollably, become violent without cause, slide about on the floor, climb up on to the windows. Stereotyped movements also occur, rhythmical movements of the body, odd movements of arm and finger, wringing of the hands, picking and pulling the fingers, running up and down. A patient always squeezed his urethra together; another squeezed his forearm continually with his fingers spread out. He gave the following account of the motives of his behaviour :—

"I must do that; if I do not lift it I have on the side no complete course, no inner life; it is just bad since I had the congestion, the disturbance in the inner vascular passage. Sometimes I am outwardly so animated, so emotional, sometimes again inwardly. My blood is always so unfaithful, my animation is, however, different, sometimes inward life, sometimes outward life; I feel that so. I am just weak in my nerves, weak and weakened in my whole body; I must do that; otherwise I can't hold out. The drainage through the limbs must be there; otherwise the constituent parts could not circulate through the pores, the blood, even the moisture. I will yet live; I am yet a young being; I must always look after the drainage. . . ."

The remaining volitional disorders of dementia præcox usually appear also in more or less pronounced fashion. *Mannerisms* show themselves in making faces, in whimsical ways of shaking hands, in stirring food about, in parade step in marching, in solemn and affected gestures, in rattling in the throat and smacking movements which are interpolated in conversation. Many patients lie on their belly, anywhere on the floor, on the edge of the bed, take up uncomfortable positions, keep the corner of the bedcover in their mouth. The conversation of the patients is incoherent, sprinkled with meaningless words, odd phrases, bewildering expressions.

A patient abruptly approached the physician and said:
"Would ask you for the divine highness." Many patients
lisp, whisper, speak in affected High German, speak French,
scream with a disguised voice. *Negativism* meets us in the
unapproachable, repellent behaviour of the patients. They
do not return a greeting, do not look up when they are
addressed, give evasive, nonsensical answers or even none
at all, stop in the middle of a sentence, begin to speak when
one turns away. They draw back when one approaches
them, go backwards round the room, creep under the bed,
resist obstinately every regulation. Their deportment is
stiff, rigid, constrained; their limbs become stiff at every
interference; many patients lie in bed with their heads
lifted up, or sit with bowed heads and closed eyes. They
do not remain in bed, endure no shirt, stand about naked,
do not eat anything or only eat if they think they are
unobserved; many take greedily other people's food or only
eat standing in a corner.

These negativistic phenomena, united with and alternating
with those of automatic obedience, characterise the *states of
stupor* which develop in rather more than one-third of our cases.
These states follow closely the introductory sad or anxious ill
humour after a shorter or longer period, and may be of very
various duration. Not infrequently they are interrupted by
quickly passing states of excitement; the patients suddenly
sing a song, jump out of bed, have a fit of laughter.

The number of cases brought together in this group
amounts almost to 10 per cent. of the cases worked up here.
As 69 per cent. of the patients had not yet passed their 25th
year, we have here to do with a form which by preference
attacks young subjects. The male sex was represented by
53 per cent. therefore differing little from the average, but it
seemed to have a greater share in the cases in which stupor
occurred.

The **further course** of the disease was interrupted in
something over 10 per cent. of the cases by improvement
which sometimes continued for several years; it appeared
to me to be more frequent in the stuporous cases. In one
female patient such improvement occurred four times; relapses always of longer duration followed each time after
childbirth till at last a state of dementia developed which
lasted without change till death 5 years later. As *issue* there
was in 27 per cent. of the cases a moderate weak-mindedness
to be recorded; the form which is considered here has therefore a substantially more favourable prognosis than silly
dementia; seizures appeared in 17 per cent. somewhat

seldomer than in the latter. Among the states of profound dementia forms with complete apathy or with negativistic features were the most frequent, the latter specially as termination of stupor.

DELUSIONAL DEPRESSIVE DEMENTIA.

Those cases, in which delusions gain a considerable expansion and an extraordinary form, we take together as a fourth form of dementia præcox, depressive dementia with delusions. The beginning of the disease is quite similar to that of the last group, but apparently somewhat more frequently *subacute*. Often after changes in the behaviour of the patients have already gone on for years, they become quiet, depressed, anxious, restless, complain of headaches, giddiness, sleeplessness, noises in the ear, and they leave off working; a patient suffered for a considerable time from agoraphobia.

Hallucinations. — Gradually or suddenly numerous hallucinations now make their appearance. The patients see "horrible pictures," naked females, three little men of the woods, long processions of decorated people, fiery beams, the Mother of God, " God, two lions and the Kaiser," figures in heaven ; angels and the Virgin Mary offer him the chalice. A female patient saw " her thoughts."

Hallucinations of *hearing* are usually the most strongly marked. There is a noise in the house ; burglars are forcing their way in ; the children are wailing ; there is a noise of crashing and banging in the air. The patients hear scream- ing, " whizzing," " chatting in the ear," " frightful talking," " wholly peculiar matters," improper things ; " coarse and refined things " are said to them ; it is a " secret language"; there are voices from heaven, beneath, voices with electric wires ; sometimes the whole body speaks. The voices torment them all day long, reproach them that they have lived an immoral life, that they have committed a moral offence on themselves, that they are wanted by the police. " That is the wickedest man of all " they say, " a bastard "; he should have a sound thrashing, his ears should be cut off ; he should be executed, slaughtered, he can make poison ; she has a child. On the other hand it is said to the patient that he is to get a uniform, is to become a policeman, is to marry. The voices question him, give him thoughts. His thoughts become loud, so that others know them, and he can com- municate with the whole world by telephone ; it is said to him that he cannot think. A female patient stated that she often felt as if she got something placed quite softly in her mind when she was thinking of nothing. Strange people, physicians, speak in the patient and he must speak after them, " confirmations to be spoken out in a low tone " ; his mother forbids him to eat ; a voice calls upon him to slaughter his wife ; a female patient was directed to take off her clothes.

Food has a peculiar taste, of petroleum, it contains " shoenail juice and potash " ; it smells " of poison," of sulphur ; the patient is ·conscious of oil in his mouth, of the smell of powder, he is being chloroformed. Something comes against his face, he feels that he is being pricked all over, that his neck is being cut off, that sand is being spirted into his ears, that he is being electrified ; a female patient got prickings in her heart when anyone died. A few patients feel sensations in their body ; others have the feeling " that gentlemen do wicked things to them," " so tickling things, which are not pretty." Often such sensations are interpreted in an extraordinary way ; a female patient noticed that the physician went backwards and forwards in her body ; a male patient felt that a man was fastened to him.

An excellent idea of the early development of the malady is afforded by the following extracts from the description written by the patient herself, a musician, who fell ill very acutely and quickly became weakminded. She wrote it five weeks after the beginning of the illness on her own initiative :—

"In the following night I was electrified. I conclude that from the fact that the following morning I felt quite peculiar pains and twitchings, and it was called out to me a few days before by an electrical machine, which had inspired me with all possible moods and thoughts, and by means of which each thought is understood ; 'We have electrified you' . . . As a great criminal was conjectured in my person or even an anarchist (1), I was several times examined electrically on my conscience with the greatest pains. Since that day I have had terrible stories of murder and theft in my head, which, as I know that the machine is still always working on me, can absolutely not be controlled. . . . Had I foreseen that I would be tormented so long, I should have noted down this quite remarkable torture already from the first day onwards ; now unfortunately I can still remember only a little. I make notes of all this for myself because I am now fearfully unhappy. I feel that by the machine I am mentally always more irritated, and have already often asked that the current should be stopped and my natural thinking be given back to me, as otherwise within measurable time a catastrophe could easily occur. Moreover, it appeared to me ·as if papa and mama were also electrified in the first days, as I very distinctly recognised by the movements and by the expression of the face of my parents at my often dreadful thoughts. . . . I must here mention another point which let me understand quite well that the machine was still working. This is that horrible smells from time to time, I don't know how, are transmitted to me. When the physician examined me such plague smells also streamed out, that the doctor went backwards terrified. . . . One evening it was called out to me by the machine : ' We conjecture in you the murderer of the Empress of Austria (! ! !)' . . . It was suggested to me by electrical means, that I wished to murder L.; as I was for some time speechless about it, it was called out to me by the machine : "You have brought great shame on yourself' . . . As on this I had to endure frightful pains—the electric current went as already before through my whole body—it was called out to me: 'You will now be lynched (l !)' . . . In particular the last word (anarchist) was for several minutes formally wound round my head. . . . How my thoughts are all so exactly understood and whole sentences are thrown back to me by the machine—this is fact, that I know definitely that these for the greatest part are not my own thoughts—is a great riddle to me. This must be a very complicated machine, which has put me myself in any emotional mood whatever, as earnest, cheerful, laughing, crying, furious, humorous—at different times it was also adjusted to grim humour, that I understood very well—amiable, morose, energetic, absent-minded (very frequently employed), attentive, dwelling of thoughts on one point to unconsciousness, yes, even to madness—I remember one evening when I actually did not know what I was thinking—melancholy, confused and so on. The very remarkable machine is also able to give me sleep suddenly, to keep away sleep, to develop dreams in me, to wake me up at any time, to lead me to any thoughts whatever as also to a definite point by greater tension of the electric current (or however this is managed) further to lead off the thoughts, indeed even to suggest any movement whatever to me. My mind is excited to such an extent and the most incredible thoughts come to me chiefly on awaking early in the morning. . . . I try to control them with the utmost energy ; but with the best will it does not suceeed, so long as the machine is active and I must always remember it as, besides, my thoughts are directly drawn out. Also in reading, it may be anything whatever, I cannot give sufficient attention at all to the contents of the book and a side-thought comes to me almost at each word. . . . I should like to take hold of another point ; that is an exaggerated laughing which has often already moved me quite peculiarly, though not tormented me, and which I could hardly control at all. This laughing, which is by no means painful, was transmitted to me just when I had thought something especially stupid. When one reads all this it seems to be the greatest nonsense, that ever was written down ; I can, however, make known nothing further than that I have actually experienced all this but unfortunately have not understood it. Probably only he will understand this who by means of such a machine has been already tormented just as I have been ; probably only an expert will be able to give further information about it."

Perception, orientation and the **working up of external impressions** are frequently disordered. The patients often mistake persons and surroundings, they are perplexed and bewildered, and do not understand their position and what is happening around them. They complain that they are no longer as they were, that their mind is failing, their thoughts are all confused, that they cannot collect their thoughts any more ; their memory also is failing. In fact, they sometimes make the impression of stupidity and silliness, are confused and easily distracted ; 'my mind and sense go lost during conversation,' said a female patient. Sometimes to the simplest questions nonsensical answers quite away from the subject are given, while at other times the patients do arithmetical calculations quickly and correctly or display a fair amount of school knowledge.

Delusions.—A great number of delusions now invariably develop, some of which are most amazing. The anxious confusion of the patients is expressed in the idea that everything is falsified, that false statements are made, that there is war in the whole world, that the world is being ruined, that they are "in an enchanted house." "It is a mystery," said a patient; the greatest events happen, the greatest secret, the greatest wonder of the world, that devils come into heaven. The house is on fire, is full of dead bodies; the provincial court was taken by storm, the clergyman was stabbed; the French are coming; the physician is the examining magistrate, the Kaiser; every event has a weird significance.

Ideas of Sin.—Very frequently there are also ideas of sin especially in the beginning. The patient has misgivings about his past life, reproaches himself. He is a wicked fellow, has made mistakes, has told lies and committed theft, has deceived his wife, has killed his children, has said something about the Kaiser, has destroyed religion, has thought "Godswine," is to blame for the war, for the death of a nobleman, is bringing misfortune on his family; everyone has died on his account. He is the last Judas, is rejected, is damned for time and eternity, is the anti-Christ, cannot be saved, is to vow allegiance to Satan; his children are in hell. He is looked on as a great criminal, accused of theft, of indecent assault; he must die for the sins of the world.

Ideas of Persecution.—Not less various are the ideas of persecution that are developed. Allusions are made to the patients; they are watched, stared at, spied on, laughed at. They are influenced by sympathy, bewitched, stunned, chloroformed, hunted like a wild animal in flight. Suspicious personages meet them in the street; there are people in the cellar; the slater will kill them; the policemen are coming to drag them to court. A raven appears at the window, which will devour their flesh; there are serpents in their bed; the black cat is coming; hellish spirits are threatening. The physicians give them poisonous pills, sprinkle poison in their ears; the air is also poisoned; the breakfast is made dirty with urine; there is human flesh in the food. The patient is murdered, executed, burned, cut to pieces, sawn asunder, dissected alive, trampled by a horse. His children are ill;

his wife is in prison ; his daughter has been killed ; his brother is dead ; his little boy has fallen out at the window ; all Jews are being beheaded ; a mother who thought her children were in danger, prepared to drown them. At night they are ill-treated ; their flesh is tampered with, their breath is twisted off, their neck is broken by pressure, their strength is drawn out of them, their blood is driven off, the nape of their neck is broken, their skull is being proved ; one can "tear him with words from below upwards" ; with words his "legs can be shaken off." His brain is injured ; in his head everything is taken part in, thoughts are "made incarnate" ; there is another spirit in his body. His nature is excited, his semen is driven off, an assault is made ; the nurse makes sexual advances. As has been mentioned formerly, the persecutions are frequently connected with the nearest relatives. His family will bring the patient to the gallows ; his father will kill him ; his mother is a witch ; a female patient asserted that she had been sexually ill-used by her father. The wife is contaminated by others and will poison the patient.

The idea of the change which has taken place in the patient, often takes very singular forms. The patient feels himself weak, gloomy, not right in his head, "not as it ought to be." His head is "a rubber tube filled with blood" ; everything is rebellious in him. His brain will burst, is heavy, has broken through ; his understanding is destroyed by onanism ; the patient cannot think alone, so cannot live outside. He had eaten the disease with a sausage, said a patient ; another said that he was ill because of a disappointment in England and in Kaiserslautern. His face is a death-mask, his heart is dried up, hardened, swollen ; his bones rattle ; loops of his intestine come out at his ear ; his blood-vessels are burst ; the connection between intestine and stomach is broken off ; everything is torn off and drawn together. The patient has no longer a stomach or an intestine or a motion ; he has little children in his neck, serpents and snails in brain and body, a glazier's diamond, a church tower in his breast, a frog in his stomach. He will not get better, he will not be alive to-morrow, is not a human being any more, is a guinea-pig, the northern lights, is dead, no longer in the world, is in another world ; "I am as if dead-born," said a female patient. A patient said that he must make the Talmud, his wife the Acropolis of Athens and then marry a grand gentleman, while he was being murdered. Perhaps such senseless utterances are connected with hallucinations ; Bleuler suggests obscure associations caused by remote similarities of ideas or sounds perhaps also indirect associations.

H

Exalted Ideas.—In a number of cases exalted ideas are present also, mostly for the first time in the more advanced periods. The patient will be rich, will have good things to eat, get a situation on the railway of the Grand Duke, has an excellent memory, possesses means to make people omniscient, has the "imperial attack," must go to the Kaiser. An inheritance of a million is being kept back from him ; his mother is not his own mother, his father is a Count, Prince of Leiningen, the Grand Duke, the Emperor Frederick ; he himself is a millionaire, Prince of Hesse, possesses a third part of the world ; " Everything belongs to me, but there are also shareholders," declared a patient. The patient is divinely gifted, is the vicar of Christ, the son of almighty God, feels the spirit of the Saviour, is inspired, fights for the faith, has the Bible and the world in his head, lives eternally ; the spirit goes forth from him ; a patient declared he was the bride of the Holy Ghost. Women are "the bride of a gentleman in a white suit," hope "to get a husband, gentlemanly and aristocratic"; they are countesses, angels, "mother of the world," the bride of Christ, their sons are princes ; a female patient said she was the Mother of God, but had also earned it.

Mood is at first anxious and depressed. The patients mourn, they howl, they break out into convulsions of weeping, even though they often seem singularly indifferent in comparison with the delusions to which they give expression. Very frequently ideas of suicide come to the surface ; the patients beg that something should be put into their coffee, that they should be killed because they cannot live any longer; that they should be beheaded as they will not get really well again. Many patients also make attempts at suicide, sometimes impulsively with great energy, sometimes more as in play. Several patients jumped out at the window ; a patient threw himself before a train ; a female patient stabbed her breast with a knife   A man lay down in front of a beer-wagon in order to let himself be run over : another beat his head against the wall ; a female patient "tried how drowning feels." Not at all infrequently exalted moods are interpolated in the periods of anguish, giggling, grinning, and laughing, especially in the further course of the malady ; also states of irritated excitement, outbursts of obscene abuse, and sudden dangerous assaults on the surroundings often occur. A few patients display in the beginning of the disease an exaggerated piety ; they kneel, they pray, they read pious books continuously, they wish to go into a cloister ; a female patient procured the robe of a penitent ; another reproached the clergyman in church that he did not preach rightly. Sexual excitement is expressed by undressing, taking down their hair, improper talk, violent masturbation, which sometimes is ascribed to constraint; a female patient lay down in a missionary's bed; a male patient urinated on his sister-in-law.

The **Activities** and **Behaviour** of the patients have in part a certain connection with their hallucinations and delusions. They listen at the window, speak secretly against the wall, exert themselves to ward off invisible people; a patient begged to be allowed to sleep in the cellar, that he might not hear the voices; another was afraid of the alarum-clock. Many preach, wish to confess their sins, ask the public prosecutor for protection. A female patient hid herself for several days and nights in the forest for fright. The aversion to relatives leads not infrequently to hostile assaults. A patient threatened his mother with a knife; another was going to kill his father with his scythe.

Very frequently, however, a motive for the conduct of the patients cannot be found at all; we have rather to do with impulsive actions, such as are so frequent in dementia præcox; for ought we know vague delusions may often play a part. The patients throw things on the floor, tear the clothes off their body, seize hold of the physician by his face, steal things from their neighbours, bite their handkerchiefs; a patient who was given an injection immediately bit the part of the skin away. Another set the mill going by night, and then set fire to a hay stack, in doing which he was severely hurt. Many patients devour bees-wax, dirt, drink the bath water. The assaults on the surroundings also may be wholly impulsive; a patient felt himself urged without any comprehensible motive to kill his sister, and stabbed her without more ado in the arm.

But further we meet in the patients here also all the *peculiar volitional disorders* which were discussed before. They often show waxy flexibility, often also echo-phenomena; they let themselves be pricked without offering any resistance; they assume singular attitudes "on command," make faces, blink, utter inarticulate cries, shake their heads, make senseless gestures, pull out the hair on their genitals, lie about in corners, salivate into their handkerchiefs, behave in a silly way, "like a flapper." They speak in a whisper, affectedly, mincingly, in a singing tone, using many foreign words, a foreign language; they address the physician by his first name, carry on confused, drivelling conversations, verbigerate, give utterance to silly plays on words and senseless doggerel, suddenly break out into bleating laughter. Negativism is also frequent. The patients become unapproachable, give either no answer or an evasive one, "because they do not need to say it," do not shake hands, "because they have no time," hold their hand before their mouth, do not eat because they think they must not, or "because they live on the word of God," but they take food secretly or appropriate their neighbours' food. They force their way out, they resist, they do not let themselves be undressed, or they keep no clothes on, they lie the wrong way in bed, disown their name, do not trouble any more about their surroundings, do not occupy themselves, remain lying in bed in a state of indifference. Occasionally there is developed a pronounced stuporous behaviour ; ten years after the appearance of severe morbid phenomena a patient sank for the first time into stupor of long duration.

The **Course** of the disease, which generally is progressive, was in 14 per cent. of the cases collected here interrupted by improvement more or less complete, which lasted as a rule one to five years, but occasionally six or seven or even nine years, till another exacerbation ushered in a terminal state. This *issue* was in 20 per cent. of the cases a simple weak-mindedness, in which certainly the possibility of dementia progressing still further must be reckoned with. Nearly quite as frequent was the sinking into states of dementia, sometimes of dull, drivelling, negativistic stamp, seldomer manneristic. *Seizures* were observed in 27 per cent. of the cases. The form here discussed corresponds, therefore, with respect to the final issue to about the average, but inclines little to remissions and is accompanied with striking frequency by seizures. It includes not quite 13 per cent. of all the cases. Of the patients 55 per cent were men, this corresponding just about to the average ; 48 per cent. had not yet passed their twenty-fifth year. This form seems accordingly to prefer somewhat the more advanced periods of life, a circumstance to which we shall later have to return.

THE AGITATED DEMENTIAS.

The next of the larger groups of the cases includes those in which *states of excitement* more severe and lasting longer are developed. According to the kind of clinical symptoms which appear, but specially according to the clinical course, we shall here be able to separate out some subordinate groups. Further, I think that on historical grounds I should keep apart and later discuss separately that form of dementia præcox in which peculiar states of excitement are associated with stupor, as it essentially corresponds to the picture of catatonia delineated by Kahlbaum.

CIRCULAR DEMENTIA.

The first subordinate group, which on account of the nature of its course we may perhaps name the circular form, at first shows a relationship with the clinical form just dis. cussed, in as far as it also begins with a period of depression and generally is accompanied by vivid delusions. The development of the disease takes places gradually in about 56 per cent. of the cases often after trifling symptoms have appeared a long time in advance ; about 18 per cent. of the cases begin acutely. The patients become melancholy, anxious, resistive, morbidly contemplative, monosyllabic, stare steadfastly in front of them, and express thoughts of death. They complain of sleeplessness, nightmares, oppression in their head, sleepiness ; they are indifferent, forgetful, have an aversion from work, are sometimes restless, irritable and violent, suffer from poverty of thought, weak-mindedness, have great ideas, but no energy, as the relatives of a patient stated. Not infrequently a distinct morbid feeling exists at the same time. The patients are afraid that they are becoming insane and ask for help. A patient desired admission to the hospital because he had become insane ; such improper thoughts were always occurring to him. Another stated that he had suffered from his head for a year and his thoughts were weakened. A third said that he had been slightly weak-minded for three years through onanism.

Hallucinations are very commonly present, specially those of *hearing*. The patients see shadow-pictures, ghosts, dead people, their dead parents, one of their children without a head, two devils ; light is reflected on to them and they are dazzled. They hear the children screaming, a band of robbers with chains rattling in the wall; the bed speaks, the devil chats in their ear ; a man who has been hung speaks. Their name is called out ; they are hoaxed, mocked, grossly abused, tormented with the telephone. Unhappy souls are calling ; whole poems are sounded in front of them ; there are "secret gossipings," voices as from a distance, inward voices of thought, suggestions, inspirations, the thought-telephone. Thoughts are drawn off from the patient, manufactured, suggested ; people try to tempt him to suicide ; he must kill his child ; God forbids him to work ; he carries on dialogues in the distance. "It is the hopper of Nürnberg ; one has it simply inside one's head ; the machine is always going on," explained a patient. His feet are besprinkled, a stream is carried through his head ; a patient had the feeling as if his eyes were being pressed out ; a female patient complained of a vulvar smell.

Delusions are predominantly of a *depressive* character. The patient feels himself constrained, "inwardly repressed," he is "utterly confused"; "my mind sometimes goes away," said a patient; another said that he was dead; a female patient said that she had lain in chloroform. Their heads are hollow, their brains are rent, burnt, their blood and their stomachs are in bad condition, their bowels are detached, their voice is frozen, their throat is going to close. Something is being done to their ears; the patient feels himself influenced especially in the night; there is a transference, "something false in things"; "electricity is the whole business." Signs are given; people march with the patient keeping step with him, look at him suspiciously, wish to thrash him; agents, policemen, parsons persecute him. He is bewitched, laughed at, teased, sold, and sold for immoral purposes, dragged about the whole house by night, is an object of scorn and derision; he is stunned, beaten on his head with a hammer. Filthy and unchaste deeds are committed; a female patient thought that she was always having children.

The husband is dead; the children are executed; the physician administers poisonous powders; the patient is to be killed, burned, he will have a leg cut off; he knows "what happens underground." He is to blame for everything, he is the devil himself, has stolen money, blasphemed God, dishonoured his children and mother, is possessed of the devil, is going into the convict prison; he is being tried by God, will suffer, will eat snails for three months and die of hunger; will be forged to chains: his feet are to be cut off; the devil is sitting in the wall. His wife wishes to poison him, takes sides with parsons; his father will strike him dead; his sister-in-law is a poisoner; father and brother take the part of the persecutors; he must therefore provide himself with weapons. Everything is changed; the brother is exchanged; the husband is quite different; a female patient asserted that two different men came by turns to her. The physician is the Kaiser, the Crown Prince of Sweden; the companions in the bedroom are not patients; the hospital is the house of the kingdom of God, is the girl's school. Everything is on fire; the home is burned down; famine fever will break out; there is war; the end of the world is approaching. At the same time there are a few *exalted* ideas. The patient has a higher divine calling, is William I., General, Admiral, is successor to the Prince of Lippe-Detmold, Prince, son of Count Cotta; he has written three books, is getting an order from the Prince Regent of Sweden, has castles; everything is of gold. He is Christ, is being redeemed, has restored dead people to life.

Women are empresses, redeemers of the world, are going to marry the physician; the Kaiser was there disguised; a female patient thought she was a foundling born of a man.

As already appears from the utterances of the patients which have been quoted, their *consciousness* is frequently somewhat clouded; they often have an obscure idea, perverted by delusions, of the persons and events in their surroundings and of their own position. Many of the patients, however, perceived quite well and even were always perfectly clear in the most severe states of excitement. The *train of thought* is confused and incoherent; in conversation there appears heightened distractibility, interweaving of words just heard, prolixity along with persistence in single, ever-recurring ideas. A few of the patients wrote sensible letters, while others furnished, also in writing, wholly disconnected productions; a patient sent us for a long time innumerable confused postcards.

Mood is subjected to very severe and sudden change. The patients are sometimes "inwardly oppressed," "dejected," sometimes immoderately happy; they implore pardon one moment, lament their profligacy, beg that they may be saved, and in the next moment they break out in horse-laughter. Just as suddenly they fall into the most senseless despair, shriek, cling to someone, pray passionately "in anguish and distress," cry and scream like little children; then again they are irritated, grumble, make impertinent remarks, threaten, have frightful outbursts of rage, scold without measure till they are exhausted. "It always comes suddenly in ebullition," said a patient.

Activities.—The disorders of activity are invariably extremely manifold and striking. The actions of the patients are only in small part connected with recognizable, though morbid motives. They listen for the voices, try to drive away invisible forms, pray "for the whole of mankind," prophesy, preach, make confession, drink holy water on account of their sins, are rude towards their relatives, by whom they believe themselves persecuted. A shoemaker asked an aristocratic lady in marriage assuming that she was interested in him; a patient with jealous ideas summoned his wife before the sheriff-court.

The volitional expressions of the patients are really governed by an innumerable number of the *most varied impulses* which arise in irregular sequence from the peculiar excitement which is developed here. Many of these impulses lead to methodical, although senseless, actions. The patients run off aimlessly, even in their shirt, wander about in a circle, adorn themselves with gay ribbons, paint the walls, scribble over every scrap of paper or stuff, appear bare-footed in the public-house, climb on the door, throw themselves over the head of the bed "in order to get exercise," suddenly lift the physician up in their arms, cut their hair off, undress, make aimless journeys, put their hands in the soup, force their way with the greatest effort out of the door, wind threads round their fingers and ears, play with a torn-off button, wear stockings of different colours, go to the water-closet innumerable times.   Not at all infrequently they become really dangerous to their surroundings.   They try to light a fire under the bedstead, they throw stones, they spit in people's faces, throw patients out of their beds without consideration. A patient smashed the sewing-machine to pieces, another seized his wife by the throat and threw his children on the floor ; a third wanted to cut his children's throats ; a female patient tried to kill her youngest child.   Many patients ill-use themselves, and for days and weeks almost continuously they make attempts at suicide before the eyes of the people round them, try to throttle themselves, climb up the window in order to throw themselves down.   Feelings of shame and disgust go into the background.   The patients strip themselves, hold their hands on their genitals, carry on improper conversations, spray dirty bath water through their mouth and nose, wash themselves with urine, pass urine into their slippers, collect their fæces in their pocket-handkerchiefs, smear themselves with their excreta and eat them.

But by far the most characteristic features of the excitement of our patients are the aimless, impulsive *single movements* which sometimes overrun the whole of volition and which either give place the one to the other in variegated change or are repeated with slight alterations innumerable times.   The patients rub their hands or clap them, shake their heads, turn somersaults, throw the bed-clothes about, tumble about on the floor, frisk about, hop, carry out turning, scrambling, spreading movements with the arms, twist themselves, tremble, shake themselves, touch or tap objects, bore their fingers into their noses, put out their tongues, make faces, squint, make singular gestures, squirt, splash and whirl in water.   Excitement makes itself conspicuous also in the movements of expression.   They bellow, screech, scream, give commands, preach, recite, shout, cry, sometimes with a trumpet voice, sometimes in sweet affected tones ; they sing, whistle, pant, snort, clear their throats.   As a rule they are talkative, mix up different languages, speak with nonsensical intonation, verbigerate, let themselves go in silly plays on words and scraps of doggerel.

With these are associated singular *positions,* theatrical attitudes. The patients press their body together with their hands, lie on their belly or in cruciform attitude on the floor, twist their legs round each other. Indications of automatic obedience and negativism are also frequently encountered. The patients are cataleptic, imitate what is done in front of them, scream in concert when others scream ; a patient wrote words that were called out to him, in the bath water. Others close their eyes, press their lips together, throw away their food, crumble the bread that is offered to them, and then eat secretly or snatch food from others ; they sleep standing, go naked to bed or lie the wrong way, do not shake hands, lie down in other people's beds, hide themselves away, retain their urine. The patients are often to some extent aware of the volitional disorders which come to light in their actions. " I can't work as I should like," said a patient. "The will is there, but I can't get it out," said another ; a third declared " Others work outside with my mind." The patients' explanation of the nonsensical actions is that they were under compulsion, that there was constraint in them.

The severity of the states of excitement here described is subject to great fluctuations. It can rise from the slightest restlessness even to unheard-of violence endangering life. There are patients who for weeks and sometimes even for months are almost continuously in a state of the most senseless excitement. Meantime as suddenly as the excitement appeared, just as abruptly it may again disappear ; it is exactly the alternation between complete quiet and stormy excitement, which often occurs in the most surprising way and is frequently repeated, which is specially peculiar to the disease. The duration of these states is also very variable. Sometimes there are only short interpolations lasting a few days or weeks ; in other cases a constant restlessness continues for months and even for years, which frequently rises to more severe states of excitement even in fairly quiet interludes.

The **course** of the disease, which in general progresses from depression through excitement to a terminal state, was interrupted in 53 per cent. of the cases by periods of considerable improvement, in nearly 14 per cent. even several times. These remissions lasted in the half of the patients concerned up to three years, in the other half up to ten years. In 70 per cent. of the cases the improvement was interpolated after the preliminary depression ; several times periods of depression preceded, separated by more lucid intervals.   After the improvement the disease then generally continued with a state of excitement leading to dementia ; less frequently a state of depression was again interpolated and the first excitement followed.   In those cases which only improved after a preliminary depression with excitement following, the relapse usually began again with a state of excitement leading now to dementia ; less frequently a state of depression was once more interpolated, or psychic weakness was developed gradually after the expiration of the more lucid interval without more striking morbid phenomena.   The duration of the attacks till the terminal state was reached, was sometimes only a few weeks or months, more rarely one to two years. · The *issue* was in almost a quarter. of the cases simple weak-mindedness ; the same number of patients sank into complete dulness, while in the remaining cases sometimes more a talkative incoherence, sometimes more an odd manneristic behaviour, here and there also negativism, accompanied the psychic decline.   A patient died in the course of a very severe and lasting state of excitement without organic disease.   Seizures occurred in one-fifth of the patients.   According to the course and issue the form here described may therefore be termed a comparatively favourable form of dementia præcox.   It includes something over 9 per cent. of the cases made use of in this enquiry.   The share of the male sex with 53 per cent. corresponded nearly to the average ; as 61 per cent. of our patients had not yet passed their twenty-fifth year, it seems in comparison to the general average number of 57 per cent. that in these forms which run a more favourable course, the younger patients are somewhat more largely represented.

AGITATED DEMENTIA.

As second subordinate group, an agitated form, we bring together those cases in which the disease begins with a state of excitement and then directly or after more or less numerous remissions and relapses, passes into the terminal state.   The development of the disease is accomplished in 45 per cent. of the cases suddenly, while in about a third of the cases for a considerable time prodromal morbid phenomena have been noticeable.   As a rule the patients become excited, irritable, insubordinate, violent ; they run away, carry on nonsensical, disconnected conversations ;   sometimes a condition of great confusion appears quite abruptly.

Hallucinations, especially of hearing, play a considerable part here also.   The patients see fiery balls, must " watch the

light day and night," must watch the "dazzling lights."
Pictures are put before them; they see four people swinging
who have been hung; they see mice, ants, the hound of hell,
a white star, devils, angels, black men, people with knives,
scythes and axes. They hear cocks crowing, shooting, birds
chirping, spirits knocking, bees humming, murmurings,
screaming, scolding, voices from the cellar, or from above
downwards; the walls speak, ghosts talk, there is chatting
going on in their body. The voices say "filthy things," "all
conceivable confused stuff, just fancy pictures"; they speak
about what the patient does, "as if he had arranged something," they reproach him for eating too much, they comfort
him. They say: "That man must be beheaded, hanged,"
"Swine, wicked wretch, you will be done for"; his wife calls
out, "Beast of a fellow!" the death of the patient is discussed.
Visual and auditory hallucinations are often connected. A
patient saw an angel who announced to him, "Make atonement, I will crown thee"; it was said to a female patient by
a child whom she saw lying beside her: "Wait, till I get
you!" The voices proceed sometimes from God, sometimes
from the devil, from spirits and ghosts, from the mayor's
daughter; there are people under the bath. Machines repeat
what the patient thinks, his thoughts are open to others; they
are drawn off, and strange unfavourable thoughts, such as
come from the devil, are suggested. The angel Gabriel commands; "voice-interference" takes place. The patient is
stupefied by smelling-stuff; the air, the food is stinking, they
contain dirty things; the water is salt. People spit in his
face, treat him with electric currents; he feels the shocks, is
strangled, is rocked; at night a lieutenant pulls him by the
genitals; he is cupped every evening; he can get no air; in
his bed there are fleas and vermin; "they make a man tired."
A patient had a feeling as if everything were breaking down,
and called out: "I am falling."

Perception and **Understanding of the Surroundings**
are frequently disordered. Many patients are as if lost in a
dream, are perplexed, say that everything is muddled, everything turned upside down; the world is being ruined; there
is a religious war; the axis of the world is tilted over. They
mistake people, call the physician their father, the local
member of the School Board the Duke of Orleans, the
Saviour; they call a fellow-patient their sister; they are in
a manufactory, in France, in a nunnery, in church, in the
"Schnallenhallenhaus." At the same time they are as a rule
poor in ideas, distractible, monotonous in their utterances,
they weave in words which they have heard without under-

standing. Through this the condition acquires the features of acute confusion, especially when vivid hallucinations are present, and is frequently so interpreted. Other patients, however, always remain surprisingly clear, make suitable remarks, solve problems in arithmetic quickly and correctly.

Delusions are connected at first with the feeling of the change experienced. The patients feel themselves "confused and constrained," "not right in the head," "scattered in their mind," quite bewildered, "so confined"; they have "such childish things in them," they do not know what they should say. Everything is destroyed in their head, "evaporated," "completely done for." "I was a stupid fellow from the beginning," declared a patient; another said, "I am no longer as I was, had no more thoughts, did not know where I was going;" a third said, "I am quite stupid, I know nothing more"; a fourth, "I am becoming half mad, I can no longer understand anything." Other hypochondriacal ideas are also expressed. The patient has fever, phthisis, pains in his body; he cannot breathe, has just almost died; his blood is not moving; his arms are cut off, are sometimes fatter, sometimes thinner; his limbs are changed, his body burned, his legs are broken; a little monster is sitting on his chin, a bludgeon on his back; there is wax in his body, cold in his brain; a patient thought that the one half of him was male, the other female.

Ideas of Sin, of Persecution, and of Influence.—Ideas of sin play a small part. The patient has done everything bad, is a Jacobin, anarchist, and nihilist, is going into the convict prison; the evil one is fetching him. Neither are ideas of persecution much in evidence. The patient leads the life of a martyr, gets hard, mouldy bread and the smallest pieces of meat, does not get the right wages, is being poisoned with prussic acid, is being persecuted by the magistrates, by a servant girl, is regarded as a spy, is chosen by his family as the sacrificial lamb; at night his bed and clothes are soiled; people are going to take his money from him. He is to be murdered, thrown into a grave, does not want to go to the scaffold. A misfortune is going to happen; a flash of lightning is coming; his parents are burned; his sister has died; his wife has hanged herself. Not infrequently we meet ideas of influence. The patient feels himself magnetized, under a ban, as if electrified, influenced by God, by the look of the attendant; he has a machine in his body; everything that he does is destiny; he must stay in bed "on command." His cough is made by the physicians; people attack him at night, torment him, will make him mad: "the beastly swine were at me," said a patient. Female patients are raped, chloroformed, and dishonoured ; a female patient believed that she had become pregnant by a shadow and that abortion had been committed.

Exalted ideas are the most frequent. The patient feels himself destined to great things, works beside royalty, can put anyone into prison, speaks many languages, is to be a professor, will teach at a university, is getting an inheritance from the Australian Kaiser, possesses fifty estates, millions. He is Li-Hung-Chang, Prince, son of the King of Würtemberg, Majesty, Napoleon, Kaiser ; a patient asked on admission if the European Concert had been informed. The patient receives revelations from God, is going to write a book about a new Christianity, is going to redeem the world, has wrestled with the devil, was in heaven ; he is the "father of his own mother," mediator between God and men, "Lord Holy·Ghost," is waiting for redemption, for the last judgment. He can heal the sick ; he will do away with menstruation in women ; no one is going to die any more. Female patients become rich women, have money in the savings-bank for their children, are getting a Lord Mayor for a husband, are to marry a priest. A female patient declared she was the Queen of Heaven, and wished to have a private water-closet. ·The following extract from a letter may give an idea of the senselessness and incoherence of the delusions :

"Let it be your business, dear T., that you in the new year have the empty room put full of continents and increase your fortune and your fame to the infinite. In this case you will take the second place in the world and will have a happy future. Millions of continents are given to your care and providence and happy in your theism. That you till now are still lethargic, that can finally be redressed and we shall hope the best for you. Lethargy is devil's work and needs presumably time for removal. But how to remove your argie? It's that that causes me trouble. Drink plenty of wine and beer and move about a great deal in society, then it will pass. You will not finally get rid of your creation-stain at all—A merry life and fortunate future.
With hearty partial honour-sympathy your friend and brother
H.H. (Name of the superintendent of the institution).
"Holy Ghost and third person in the Godhead.
"Nota bene : obediently to serve that I must later generate a son from myself; he will receive the title 'Son of God,' and will be generated as from the holy third spirit and received as second person in the Godhead. Otherwise we have with us no splendour and no consideration. Upon you, dear T., I bestow as New Year's present the title 'glorious, sole councillor and dear almanac.'"

Mood is in general exalted, more rarely anxious, but always subject to extraordinarily sudden and severe fluctuation. Whimpering, bewilderment, wild laughing, frightful outbursts of abuse, unrestrained merriment may make place for each other without intermission. The behaviour of the patients towards their relatives shows complete indifference. Sexual excitement is expressed in masturbation, indecent assaults, jealous ideas, and exposure of themselves; a female patient hung her bloody chemise in front of the window. A patient was very much irritated by his father who, he said, always forced him to masturbate; another felt himself constrained to cohabit with his sister. Now and then homosexual tendencies come to the front.

States of excitement have the same features as in the group last described. Only within narrow bounds does the behaviour of the patients appear to some extent comprehensible. Thus there might be a connection with religious delusions when a patient rings the bells by night, lights the altar candles, begins to preach in church, takes objects from the altar, wishes to open graves, burns the stigmata on himself with his cigar. Ideas of persecution lead to the patients wishing to appeal to the police, to provide themselves with a revolver, to make a visit "only with a strong escort," to cut their wife's throat. Patients with exalted ideas make purchases, make senseless presents, forge plans for getting engaged, write letters to Grand Duke and Kaiser, wish to go to Rome to liberate the Pope. Those with ideas of sin kneel, pray, beg for forgiveness; a female patient put on her Sunday clothes and was going to jump out at the window in order to reach God, because she had not confessed everything. Hallucinations have as a consequence that the patients stop up their ears with paper and bread, and try to chase away spirits ("away with the devil!"); a female patient threw the goldfish into the water-closet because they carried on blasphemous conversation.

But on the whole the excitement consists of *impulsive actions* and *senseless movements*. The patients run aimlessly about, play tricks, mix up their bedclothes altogether, tear up and destroy things, throw chairs and spittoons about, smash panes of glass, fling their food about the room, throw their watch down the water-closet; they march out naked, they throw things at the burning lamp. Others scratch their faces, dash headlong out of bed, stick the handle of a spoon into their anus, pull out their teeth, try to strangle themselves, beat their faces, pull at their genitals, at their ears, all being done impulsively, suddenly, with great violence and without recognizable motive. The very frequent and dangerous attacks on their surroundings also bear the same stamp. The patients without any consideration throw their relatives on the floor, knock down a neighbour, rush at an unknown person with a fork, bite the arm of the attendant ; a patient took hold of an attendant's finger so firmly with his teeth that he could only be made to let go under an anæsthetic. The senselessness of these actions is made clear by the fact that the patients one moment impetuously embrace a person and next moment perhaps belabour him with their fists.

But besides these actions, which after all have a certain relation to the surroundings, a disorderly series of completely *aimless* movements are further carried out, usually with a tendency to innumerable, uniform repetitions and to rhythmical arrangement. The patients run round at a gallop. always the same way, run round the house till they are exhausted, they jump up and down with great leaps, march in the garden "as if they had the strictest order from the colonel," cut capers, dance about singing, carry out military movements, "physical drill," flourish their arms, beat time, knock and drum on the bedstead, turn round about, write figures in the air. They let themselves fall on the floor, waltz round about bellowing, prance, fall over and roll about, grind their teeth, pull hideous faces, spray and spit about them. In its most simple forms this restless movement becomes stretching, shaking, trembling, choreic jerking of the hands, tripping and stamping, balancing and rocking, distorting of the arms and legs, as we find it again in the terminal states as a residuum of the severe and acute volitional excitement. In the domain of the movements of expression the excitement makes itself conspicuous in singing and playing the harmonica for hours, in shrill screaming and screeching, in the inarticulate utterance of senseless sounds, in ceaseless flow of words, reciting, rhyming, scolding, panting, groaning, hissing, whistling, sighing ; some patients say everything singing ; others speak in gibberish invented by themselves.

Besides the impulsive discharges the signs of the other *volitional disorders* which are peculiar to dementia præcox are also invariably found here. The movements, actions and attitudes of the patients are frequently manneristic, sometimes clumsy and awkward, sometimes affected and florid. The patients assume odd attitudes, twist themselves together, balance themselves, hold the lobe of one of their ears tight for months, behave in a theatrical manner, only give the finger-tips in shaking hands, bolt their food without chewing it, dress their hair in an extraordinary way. A female patient sewed white figures on to her jacket ; a patient knelt down each time he came in or went out. Others speak in a stilted manner, with high-sounding phrases ; a patient wrote letters in dog-Latin. Frequently automatic obedience is present, the patients imitate and follow closely. Negativistic phenomena also meet us almost everywhere. The very inaccessibility of the patients and their want of susceptibility to influence might be interpreted in this sense. They do not listen to what is said to them, obey no injunctions, do not let themselves be disturbed in any way in their senseless ongoings, not even by force, do not show the slightest consideration for their surroundings. They give no answers to questions or else nonsensical or unrelated ones; they arbitrarily apply names to people whom they recognize correctly. They crouch under the bed-cover, stick their head under the pillow, endure no clothes, do not remain in bed, do not change their shirt, do not let themselves be undressed, retain their urine and then soil the bed, eat only when unobserved or eat the food of other people, keep their bread for hours in their mouth. A patient let himself be only half shaved, then ran away ; a female patient tied on her apron the wrong way.

Here also the severity of the excitement may be of very varying degree, from slight silly restlessness to raving mania of the most severe type. The impulse to movement may become so uncontrollable and so regardless that it seems scarcely possible to procure any rest even for a short time for the patients and their surroundings. Bruises and abrasions and even more serious injuries can in certain circumstances not be prevented at all. At the same time the sense of many of the patients is very surprising ; they may be quite clear about their situation and surroundings, but just as surprising is then the abrupt commencement and the equally sudden cessation of the excitement which often appears in the form of limited attacks of shorter or longer duration.

Course.—The states here described may pass after many fluctuations directly into incurable states of weakness. In 36 per cent. of the cases, however, after the first attack there is a remission of all morbid phenomena, which in 10 per cent. of the cases may even be repeated once or indeed several times before the terminal state is reached. The duration of these periods of improvement fluctuates from a few months to twelve or fourteen years ; it is most frequently about three years. The recurrence of the disease occurs usually with fresh states of excitement, somewhat seldomer in the form of progressive dementia, now and then also perhaps with a state of depression to which excitement may again follow, terminating in dementia. When there are repeated remissions of the disease the states of excitement may return more frequently. In one case I observed first four states of excitement separated by periods of improvement lasting for some years, of which two terminated in depression; then there followed after a clear interval of fifteen years a state of confusion which led to a final state of dementia, which I followed for eight years.

A simple weak-mindedness of varying degree was the *issue* in 27 per cent. of the cases of the form here described. Nearly in the same ratio a state of dementia with marked mannerisms was the result, somewhat seldomer a psychic decline with predominating incoherence or with dull indifference; one patient died by suicide. Seizures were observed in approximately a fifth of the cases. Evidently we may regard this form also of dementia præcox as relatively favourable. It includes about 14 per cent. of the total number of our cases. The male sex was represented by 60 per cent., and the ages under the twenty-fifth year were the same; in both directions, therefore, the numbers are somewhat over the average. It is perhaps not without interest to remark that the form described seemed to me to be by far the most frequent among the numerous cases of dementia præcox observed among the natives of Java.

Periodic Dementia.

In close connection with the cases brought together in the last section we have still to mention a small group which runs a pronounced periodic course either in the introductory stages of the disease or during its whole duration; its number amounts to not quite 2 per cent. of all cases. The outbreak of the disease occurred in two-thirds of my cases before the twentieth year, sometimes at fourteen years of age. With shorter or longer intervals, often very few weeks, sometimes only once a year, confused states of excitement appear which run a rapid course. In the female sex they are frequently connected with the menstrual periods in this way, that the attack begins with the commencement of the menses or even a short time before, and then lasts about one or two weeks till it makes way for a clear interval lasting usually somewhat longer ("menstrual insanity"). The commencement of the excitement is as a rule quite sudden. After at most slight indications of the commencing attack, causeless laughter, blinking of the eyes, wandering about, have preceded, there is developed from one day to another, often in the middle of the night, the picture of maniacal excitement. Sometimes it is limited to heightened irritability, change of mood, restlessness, incessant chatter ; but gradually the excitement becomes worse, going on even to raving mania of the most severe type, often with delusions and hallucinations. The *body weight* invariably decreases rapidly, sometimes as much as five to eight pounds in twenty-four hours (Fürstner). Fig. 25 shows the fluctuations during a prolonged series of attacks up to death. The excitement often lasts only a few days or weeks, more rarely it continues for months and then is interrupted by only a few quiet days. Usually the intervals are somewhat longer, a few weeks or months. In course of time the duration of the attacks may be extended.

The commencement of the quiet period takes place usually just as quickly as that of excitement, even though one can generally notice already towards the end of the attack a slight decrease of confusion and restlessness. The patient

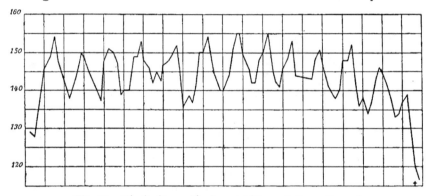

Fig. 25.   Fluctuations of body weight in periodic excitement.

is now all of a sudden reasonable, but remarkably quiet, indifferent, dull, and has not as a rule complete insight into the morbid nature of his state even though he still remembers well many details. He rather tries to represent the excitement, which he has gone through, as something quite harmless or as caused by the surroundings, the restraint in the institution and that sort of thing. He considers himself already on the first day of the commencing state of quiet as completely recovered, and urgently desires to be discharged. A certain physical improvement usually takes place rapidly, but during the interval which now follows the body weight frequently remains lower than it was before the onset of disease.

After a considerable number of attacks there frequently occurs a considerable, or even lasting, cessation. Or the attacks are prolonged and are only interrupted by short, comparatively clear intervals. In a small number of cases there may finally be developed a quite regular alternation lasting for decades between short periods of the most severe excitement and of quietness. In a patient whom I observed there had developed a daily alternation, setting in with the greatest punctuality between behaviour in every way suitable for society and the most violent raving mania, which lasted at least for ten years. But it invariably comes to the development of marked psychic decline, which sometimes has more the features of a simple weak-mindedness with poverty of thought, lack of judgment, emotional dulness and weakness of volition, sometimes is accompanied by incoherence and affectation. In contrast to the excess of men in the other forms, two-thirds of these patients were women, in whom obviously the *periodicity* of *sexual life* favours the development of the form which runs this course.

Formerly I regarded these forms as belonging to manic-depressive insanity. Without doubt in this disease also there are attacks of similarly short duration. Meanwhile the states of excitement here described which are repeated in short periods of time often form only an episode in the course of a disease which otherwise undoubtedly is dementia præcox; further, the states of weakness which are developed, bear the features throughout of the decline generated by that malady. These experiences have made me change my opinion. There is also the fact that the states of excitement themselves, with their monotony, impulsive character, and poverty of thought, resemble much more those of dementia præcox than those of mania. Again the circumstance might be pointed out, that periodic states of excitement are also otherwise very frequent in dementia præcox. Lastly, one might bring forward the fact that occasionally inherited relationships can be proved between this and other forms of dementia præcox. Accordingly one may represent it to oneself somewhat in this way, that a peculiarity of the malady, which usually only develops later, dominates the clinical picture in the cases here discussed specially early and in specially high degree.

CATATONIA.

The states of excitement of dementia præcox form also an important constituent part of that clinical form to the consideration of which we have now to turn, catatonia.[1]   Under this name Kahlbaum has described a clinical history which presents in series the symptoms of *melancholy*, of *mania*, of *stupor*, also in an unfavourable course those of *confusion* and *dementia*, and besides is characterized by the appearance of certain motor *spasmodic* and *inhibitory phenomena*, just the "catatonic" disorders.   The description given by him, in many respects masterly, should demonstrate that all conditions till now named melancholia attonita, stupor, acute dementia, and so on, are in reality only manifestations of a single psychosis, which, like dementia paralytica, in spite of external differences in the course, still exhibits a number of wholly peculiar bodily and psychic morbid symptoms.

As far as we can take a general view of it to-day, the statement of Kahlbaum must be regarded in a certain direction as too narrow but in another as too wide.   Later experience has taught that the catatonic morbid conditions can nowhere be sharply separated from the remaining forms of dementia præcox.   Much rather not only are certain fundamental features of the clinical picture common to both, but single catatonic morbid symptoms frequently meet us also in forms of the disease otherwise wholly divergent.   As further in all remaining respects, in the conditions of development, in the course and specially in the issues, and lastly, so far as a judgment on the subject is possible to-day, also in the post-mortem findings, no decided differences are recognizable, we may regard the catatonia of Kahlbaum as in the main a form, though peculiar, of dementia præcox.   On the other hand "catatonic" morbid phenomena are undoubtedly also observed in many quite different morbid processes to a greater or less extent, so that its appearance alone does not justify the conclusion that catatonia in the sense just indicated is present.   In this direction accordingly we must limit the conception mentioned, that only such cases of disease belong to it, in which the morbid process of dementia præcox is the foundation.   How far and by what symptoms we are able already to recognize that to-day, must be discussed later.

The course of catatonia in the single periods above

---

[1] Kahlbaum, Die Katatonie oder das Spannungsirresein. 1874; Brosius, Allgem. Zeitschr. f. Psychiatrie, xxxiii. 770 ; Neisser, Uber die Katatonie. 1887 ; Behr, Die Frage der Katatonie oder des Irreseins mit Spannung. Diss. Dorpat. 1891 ; Schüle, Allgem. Zeitschr. f. Psychiatrie, liv. 515, lviii. 221 ; Aschaffenburg, ebenda, 1004 ; Meyer, Archiv. f. Psychiatrie xxxii. 780 ; Tschisch, Monatsschrift f. Psychiatrie vi. 38. 1899 ; Arndt, Centralblatt f. Psych. xxv. 81. 1902 ; Claus, Catatonie et stupeur. 1903 ; Pfister, Allgem. Zeitschr. f. Psychiatrie. 1906, 275.

mentioned is, as Kahlbaum himself has already said, not inviolable, but it represents only in a certain degree the general framework, in which the divergent cases approximately find a place. The really characteristic pictures of the state are rather the "mania" of Kahlbaum, which to-day we more correctly name catatonic excitement and stupor. I think, therefore, that I may group together as catatonic forms of dementia præcox those cases in which the *conjunction of peculiar excitement with catatonic stupor* dominates the clinical picture. It is true that states of stupor are occasionally interpolated for quite a short time or by slight indications also in the states of excitement hitherto described. In this way gradual transitions arise to the catatonic forms now about to be discussed, in which both conditions, apparently so opposed to each other, come under observation along with or after each other.

The development of the disease takes place in 41 per cent. of the cases acutely, in 31 per cent. insidiously, otherwise subacutely. In 47 per cent. of the cases a *state of depression* forms the introduction ; an acute commencement is in these cases somewhat seldomer. The patients become reserved, shy, introverted, absent-minded, distracted, indifferent, irritable, taciturn ; they stand about, carry on unintelligible conversations, pray, go often to church, get up at night, eat and sleep badly. At the same time they give utterance to a great many *delusions* frequently quite extraordinary ; there come "temptations," "presentiments." They have evil thoughts, feel themselves lost and abandoned, proscribed. They feel uneasy, as if someone were persecuting them ; their life is no longer of any value ; everything has turned out badly ; no one can help them. They are mocked by bad women, maligned, spat on, grossly abused ; they are to be taken to the convict-prison, condemned to death, slaughtered, buckled on to the railway ; their house is to be blown up ; their family is trying to take their life, wants to be rid of them. The chopping-knives are already being sharpened ; people are coming to fetch them ; their daughter is being murdered ; their children are going to the scaffold. Everything is being taken away ; the stove-pipe is stopped up ; murder and robbery are being committed on their mother. Their food is poisoned, lard is in the coffee ; in the soup there are worms and human flesh ; poison is being blown on them ; the flies must bite the patient ; his hair is being torn out.

Ideas of sin are frequently associated with these delusions. The patient is more wicked than Judas is the "old eternal swine," a traitor, not worthy to look in the mirror ; he has led a dissolute life, has not prayed enough, has nailed the Saviour to the Cross, murdered his children, is bringing everyone to misfortune.   He has three evil spirits in his head ; he must always remain in life because the devil is hiding in him ; he wishes to do penance.   People reproach him that he has stolen, that he has assaulted a child ; he is to renounce his faith, is in alliance with the evil one ; he is to get a prayer-book and holy water, is to have his head chopped off.   Many patients defend themselves against the supposed reproaches ; they have done nothing, do not want to be killed.   The ideas of sin are expressed very clearly in the following document written by a patient :

"I am a whole world of mean actions and of secret and open vice, I believe, therefore, that I only do damage with my filth of mean actions and evil deeds, in short in all domains just where I am.   I am too cowardly to die a hard death or a lingering death and think therefore it is now about time to die entirely by means of a revolver.   A noxious person in every way, I am really not worth powder and shot, and have never been an iota of use to you, on the contrary only done you a thousandfold damage, just for this reason away with me, completely exterminated."

Often a state is developed of perplexity and confusion. Everything is enchanted, changed, full of entanglements and complications, bewitched ; the patient believes that he is in an enchanted castle, in China, in heaven ; he fights battles with death and devil.   There is war ; the heavens are falling ; there is a fire ; the house is falling in ; the end of the world is imminent, the Palatinate is being consumed by fire.   The patient is being made ill by treacherous people, does not know himself any more, feels himself "quite darkened," appears strange to himself ; the furniture does not belong to him ; the visitors are not the right people.   He takes his fellow-patients for his relatives, for princes, the physician for the black devil, for Jesus, for the King.   All human beings have been destroyed ; there is no one any longer at home ; everything is being taken away, the safe is being broken into.

Hypochondriacal ideas.—These occur very frequently. The patient has pain in his limbs, pressure in his throat, poison in his body, phthisis, dropsy, he must die.   His semen has gone inwards ; his bones are growing out of his body. His feet are black, his hands have rotted ; a patient thought that he was dirty and washed himself continuously.   His stomach runs up and down ; blood forces its way out at mouth and nose ; fire issues from his mouth ; his fæces are alive. His throat and anus have closed up; his limbs become smaller; his eyes have been gouged out; the patient has a club-foot, chloride of lime in his bones, is full of grass and moss, is shut up with a pane of glass. He suffers from headache, his head is empty, he has diphtheria in his brain, beetles in his head, cannot speak; his memory has suffered much.

The **Feeling of Influence** also often plays a part in the delusions. The patients feel themselves "influenced by magic power," "governed by invisible power." At night "electro-magnetic practices are carried on"; their nature is caused to pass from them; they are made crazy; they must think filthy thoughts, do what the mediums wish; they are hypnotized by the physician.

Exaltation.—Here and there ideas of exaltation appear beside those of depression. The patient is Gustavus Adolphus, King of Hungary, a great athlete, will go to Vienna and there become Kaiser, inherits money from his *fiancée*, gets 60,000 marks from God, wishes to marry, to go to America by the lightning-express, to redeem mankind, to make other laws; he is the emperor-angel, has revelations in the spirit, wants milk from angels. Female patients are "Queen on the Rhine," "Heaven's child," become engaged to the Kaiser, wish to marry Jesus, an officer, have a secret love affair, are pregnant, possess castles, ten millions. A servant girl asserted that the son of her employers had offered 70,000 marks for her; another related that she was getting three crowns before her execution. Usually these delusions are fairly fleeting and indefinite, and are given expression to without special emphasis. A patient said he did not know whether his mother was Queen of England, or Kaiserin, or a cook.

Hallucinations are invariably present, especially those of sight and hearing. The patients see apparitions of light, figures, three faces at the altar, devils, dogs, snakes, soldiers, policemen. They hear music, voices of birds, cries for help, voices from the stove and water pipes, from their own body, "from the hind." There is singing in the wall; the apparatus is crazy under the bed; the clocks are speaking; outside they are blustering; the Christ-child speaks; their mother is weeping; husband and daughter are calling out; dogs are barking. Gentlemen are telling wicked stories; the devil calls out the name of the patient; God announces to him that he must die, carries on conversations with him; the Kaiser challenges him to a duel with pistols; people mock him, call him abusive names ; " Goose," " Good-for-nothing," " wicked fellow," threaten to tear out his throat ; a voice in his head reproaches him. A female patient perceived that she had a secret love affair, and said, " I have that so in hearing." Many patients have their thoughts said to them ; others receive commands, " Hands up " ; a female patient heard " all the letters of the alphabet," and had to count. Here and there the voices have a rhythmical cadence. Some patients feel themselves breathed on, blown on, tormented with rays, electrified, feel needles in their hands, smell the smell of corpses ; one patient stated that he had " experienced much in his genitals."

States of Excitement.—After the introductory depression there usually next follows a state of stupor, especially in men, and then excitement ; more rarely is it the other way. On the other hand the cases setting in without depression begin according to my experience somewhat more frequently in the form of a state of excitement, the picture of which essentially corresponds to that of the agitated form previously described. The patients become restless, sleepless, run about, carry on absurd conversations ; their actions are impulsive and aimless, and they fall more or less rapidly into severe excitement ; sometimes raving mania may break out quite suddenly, even in the middle of the night, perhaps after insignificant prodromal symptoms which have not been noticed at all. Mood is usually exalted. The patients laugh, try to be witty, make jokes, tease other patients, boast, carry on unrestrained conversations ; here and there religious ecstasy is observed. But very frequently the patients are also irritated, angry, threatening ; they break out into wild abuse, fly into a passion on the slightest occasion, make dangerous attacks without consideration. More rarely they are anxious, whine, cry, groan, wring their hands, beg for their life, scream " murder ! " " Satan, begone ! " ; they do not wish to go to the war ; they prepare for death. But invariably the colouring of the mood is subjected to swift and astonishing change. Angry irritation is abruptly interrupted by a jocular remark ; the patient who has just been lamentably afraid of Satan, suddenly calls out laughing, " The wicked one has gone ! " Many patients laugh and weep confusedly, and sing merry couplets amid tears. Very frequently there is extreme sexual excitement, which is made known by jealous ideas, shameless utterances, movements of coitus, regardless exposure and masturbation. A female patient tore her chemises down the front ; others grasp at the genitals of the physicians ; a male patient tried to urinate on a nurse. During the menses the states of excitement usually grow worse.

While the excitement in many cases only affects the patients with a certain restlessness, we meet in others the most severe raving mania. But even in the same case the most violent excitement may very rapidly develop from nearly complete quiet, and then just as suddenly again disappear.

The **Behaviour** of the patients has only a slight connection with their ideas and moods. Anxious patients pray, kneel, run off by night, hide away in the forest, try to throttle themselves, jump out of the window; the irritable mood leads to sudden deeds of violence, megalomania to the squandering and giving away of their goods and chattels, the exalted mood to wonderful decorations. A patient, who wished to become a poet, copied out Goethe and Schiller with this aim in view; another practised indoor gymnastics "against globus hystericus and psychic pains."

As a rule, however, no satisfactory motive can be found for the activities of the patients, which are often extremely peculiar; they seem much rather to follow blindly whatever impulses may happen to arise in them. They make aimless journeys, want to go to America, run about naked, clear out the beds, destroy the stove, burn important papers, smash panes of glass, bite to pieces plates and glasses, suddenly fall round someone's neck and kiss him, and then spit in his face or give him a resounding box on the ear. They drag other patients out of bed, strike out senselessly in every direction, throw their shoes about, dance about with the door of the room which they have lifted off its hinges, gallop away buck-jumping in position for fencing, bite a neighbour, shove the furniture about the room, take possession of any object with blind fury, climb hastily on to a table or on to the window-sill in order to defæcate there. A female patient laid small pieces of bread in rows on the edge of her bed, kissed the grating of the hot-air apparatus for hours, and dragged her mattress continually round her in a circle, each time at a definite place knocking on the wall; another stood with arms extended on the night-stool; a third wished to dig up her dead father again; a male patient, when the party was gathered together for counting, climbed up a tree, took off his clothes, whistled and yodeled.

Activities.—In more severe excitement the activities of the patients are resolved into a disordered series of unconnected and unrelated impulses. They dart through the room with arms stretched out in front of them, slide on the polished floor, run violently up and down or round about in small circles so that their track is gradually marked out like that of a beast of prey in a cage.   Others lie down on their belly and carry out swimming movements, glide, roll about on the floor, frisk about, hop, stamp with their feet, turn round about on their toes, drum with their fingers, throw out their arms, grasp everything round them, creep round, go a few steps forward then back again, lift up the beds, bite tight into the pillows.   At the same time it very commonly comes to frequent, rhythmical repetition of the same actions or movements.   The patients bounce up and down, swing hither and thither, clap their hands, make arm movements of exorcising, drawing water, fanning, turning, circling; they revolve their fists round each other; they grind their teeth, lift their legs high, turn about, shrug their shoulders, throw their hair sometimes over their face, sometimes back-wards, blink their eyelids, squint, breathe with forced breaths, pant, blow, nod, seize, pull, pick, rub their hands, tap on the table.

Remains of such stereotypies are usually preserved in the terminal states.   To them are related all kinds of monotonous repeated actions which may become habits very difficult to root up.   Many patients pull their clothes to pieces, bite their nails, scrape the lime from the walls, collect rubbish in their pockets, tie threads round their fingers or genitals, devour buttons and stones, stick objects in their ears, burn themselves with their cigar, tear and scratch definite parts.   A patient perpetually destroyed his shirt buttons in order to bore the little metal ring through the lobes of his ears.   Here also belongs probably the continual spitting which sometimes threatens the whole surroundings ; a patient said that he did " saliva gymnastics."

Besides stereotypy we invariably meet in the activities of the patients indications of the *volitional disorders* formerly discussed.   Automatic obedience is shown in the distractibility of the patients ; they weave words they hear into their conversation, join in other people's singing, sometimes take part in everything that goes on round them.   They are frequently cataleptic, occasionally also echolalic or echopractic. In other patients or at other times negativistic features are more in evidence.   The patients do not trouble themselves in the least about their surroundings, give no answers to questions, do not shake hands, do not let themselves be influenced in any way in their doings, resist every interference, force their way out senselessly, knock or push with their knees against the doors.   They throw their food away, lie down in other people's beds, lie in a slanting direction, give a wrong name, do everything differently from what one expects. A patient knocked over the table and then sat down on the top.

The circumstance that the excitement, even when extremely violent, frequently takes place within the *smallest space*, is up to a certain point characteristic of the states here described. The patients have not as a rule any tendency to influence their surroundings, but their restlessness exhausts itself in wholly aimless activity which on this account also needs no extended stage. The movements themselves are sometimes clumsy and uncouth, sometimes jerky, angular or affected, solemn, then again unusually nimble and quick as lightning. Side impulses are frequently interpolated. The patients eat with the handle of the spoon, give the hand turned the wrong way, walk stiffly " as if they were marching through snow," lifting their feet high, urinate behind the bed.

Usually all their actions are carried out with great strength and without any consideration, so that it is scarcely possible to prevent them. "Go away ! I must drag the mattress ; I must knock at the door," a female patient cried out ; she gave the word of command, " Stand up ! Fall down ! " innumerable times, as she let herself fall and got up again. In consequence of these doings it sometimes comes to abrasions of enormous extent, to more or less serious injuries, as the patient does not spare his limbs in the slightest, always knocks the injured parts again, and without more ado tears away the bandages which hinder him. Not infrequently the patients injure themselves in the most serious way. They box their ears right and left for hours, dash themselves headlong on the floor, try to squeeze in their neck, to tear out their penis, bite their arm, tear their hair, scratch themselves, pick at their fingers, bruise their tongue and their underlip with their teeth, beat themselves on the head, tear out their toe-nails ; a patient bit off the tip of his finger. Now and then also impulsive attempts at suicide are made.

The **Bodily Care** of the patients encounters in these circumstances the greatest difficulties. As a rule they are very dirty. They pass their motions under them, roll up their fæces in balls, devour them, lick up their urine from the floor, urinate into the spittoon, smear themselves with menstrual blood, put bread in their anus, spit into their hands, into the soup, on their bread and butter, in their own bed. They sometimes eat greedily, swallowing down their food unchewed with haste in incredible quantity, and even taking away their neighbours' food ; sometimes they struggle to the utmost against the taking of any nourishment, spit everything out again, even what they begged for before with entreaties. Many patients only eat when they think they are unobserved, or they let the food stand for hours till it has become cold and almost uneatable.

Movements of expression usually undergo very varied and singular changes. Here belong spreading gestures, making faces, threatening flourishes, senseless shaking and nodding of the head, monotonous crying, crowing, yodeling, clicking, spitting like a cat, singing, squeaking, screaming in falsetto, screeching and growling, and continuous, uncontrollable laughter. Speech is sometimes scanning, rhythmical, with wholly perverted intonation, sometimes singing or commanding, sometimes jerky, sometimes in broken sentences. Many patients declaim in the high-sounding cadence of the actor, hold discourses, preach with lively movements of expression and mingling of religious phrases, or they hastily bubble over with unintelligible words, sometimes in foreign or self-invented speech. Other patients whisper and murmur, grunt or scream with all their might. One patient barked for hours like a dog. Some patients speak through their nose, affectedly, in an intentionally coarse or silly manner, like small children, without construction into sentences, in infinitives ; they turn the words about, use diminutives everywhere. To this are added neologisms, and sought-out expressions ; a female patient spoke of "poison blisters." The substance of the conversations often shows a high degree of incoherence ; the following sentences furnish an example of this :

"But I cannot let myself be made mad and dad. You know I was quite mad and perhaps am so still. Whether it is a Lord Grand Duke or King and Kaiser—whether it is the voice of the court or who it is. The dear God in heaven comes as well and if it is only a dog or a gnat —or a little bit of bread. I don't know whether I have a fish in my hand or a serpent or what rattles or what walks and stands ; I should prefer everything in the world. From below and above no one can be made mad." "My nose belongs now stuffed into Jesus Christ and everything twisted round me. They all rattle and mock God. And if the dear Arch-Grand Duke is up there, then those on this side and that side mock and ridicule and put sleekness in."

There are to be noticed here the neologisms, the repetition of single expressions, "be made mad," "rattle," "mock," the senseless similarities of sound, the lack of all connection of ideas in sustained construction, lastly the indications of exalted ideas and of morbid feeling.

Verbigeration.—Lastly the phenomenon, already discussed, of verbigeration is very common. Sentences of any length, frequently wholly senseless (for example "Gekreuzigter Krex in e Umkrexhaus "), also perhaps single letters are repeated for hours and days without interruption in the same, often rhythmical, intonation, sometimes screaming, sometimes whispering, sometimes even in a definite tune. A female patient called out fifty times in succession "Up!" Sometimes the patients make slips in speaking or a word heard in the surroundings is interpolated; in this way a sentence may gradually undergo changes, the result of which then appears after some hours. One can often force the patients to repeat their accustomed sentences by saying the beginning to them. Thus a quite sensible patient for weeks, on the cue "My husband" being given in the middle of a conversation, continued the sentence in drawling cadence without hesitation, though frequently against her will:

"My husband is a fine man, a cultured, respected, diligent, honest merchant, and I am his wife; my child is an honest child, and we have no debts in the town, and we have 2000 marks of honest money, and 300 marks, these we found. My brothers and sisters are honourable brothers and sisters, and my brothers are respected, diligent, esteemed, honest men of business, and that is the pure truth."

To the question why she always repeated this speech, she said, "because I am cracked." In other cases the substance of the verbigerative speeches shows great variety. In the writings of the patients also we meet with disconnectedness and incoherence of the substance, and the tendency to bewildering desultoriness, to sounding phrases that say nothing, endless enumerations, uniform repetitions, to odd figures of speech and neologisms. Many patients write nonsensical whirligigs and assert that this is a foreign language.

Stupor.—In the further course of the disease states of stupor follow the excitement; somewhat seldomer they precede, with or without introductory depression. The patients become quiet, shy, monosyllabic, sink into brooding, stare fixedly in front of them, stand about in corners, hide themselves and creep out of sight, lie idly in bed; a patient lay down "in order meantime just to have a good rest." Now and then stupor begins quite suddenly; the patients become mute, rigid in their whole body, sink on to the floor, remain lying in cruciform attitude with closed or widely open eyes. All independent volitional expression is silent; speech, the taking of food, intercourse with the surroundings, occupation, care for their own needs, cease more or less completely.

External Influences.—The behaviour of the patients towards external influences shows, however, certain differences, which indeed are subject to much variation. They are in general characterized by the predominance either of automatic obedience or of negativism. If one will, one may accordingly separate out a flaccid and a rigid stupor. In the first case we principally observe catalepsy lasting for shorter or longer periods, which in such states usually reaches its highest development. Echolalia, or even echopraxis, meet us also, but more rarely and usually only as passing phases. The patients then merely repeat quite mechanically what is said to them, or even anything they have picked up by chance, in certain circumstances even with closed mouth, or join in a song which their neighbours are singing. Related to this phenomenon is the constrained answering with an association or a jerky movement, standing up and sitting down, making faces, a turn of the hand when one calls to them. The patients often imitate vivacious gestures made in an impressive way in front of them (lifting up the arms, clapping hands), continue for a considerable time a movement stimulated by external influence (beating time, rolling their hands round each other). Sometimes they are even seen for hours doing everything that some one person does in their surroundings, saying everything that he says, walking behind him keeping step, dressing and undressing along with him and so on. Some patients scream at fixed times; others give the word of command at tube-feeding: "Basin, tube and glass utensils, all here, all here, Doctor, feeding," "Mouth open," "Tube clean!" A female patient verbigerated: "Put on nightdress, lie down in bed, bath! Put on nightdress, bath, lie down in bed!"

The severe volitional disorder in these states appears very distinctly when one asks the patients to show their tongue in order to pierce it through with a needle. Although they notice the threatening needle and comprehend quite well what is before them, they still unhesitatingly stretch out the tongue on being asked emphatically to do so. In many cases the experiment may be made as often as one likes with the same result. The patients make a pitiful face at each prick, but are unable to suppress the impulse discharged by renewed command or in any other way to withdraw themselves from the threatening injury.

Rigid shutting up of themselves to all influences from their surroundings is more frequent in stupor than heightened susceptibility to influence. The patients withdraw themselves, cover themselves up, press their hands against their face, hold their handkerchief over their mouth, draw the cover over their head; they give no answer, do not look up when spoken to, do not ward off pricks of a needle. Only

rarely does a very strong stimulus bring about movements
of evasion, still more rarely an unexpectedly dextrous and
powerful assault. Also an occasional slight blinking, more
marked flushing or perspiring of the face, twitching of the
corners of the mouth on such attempts, bursts of laughter

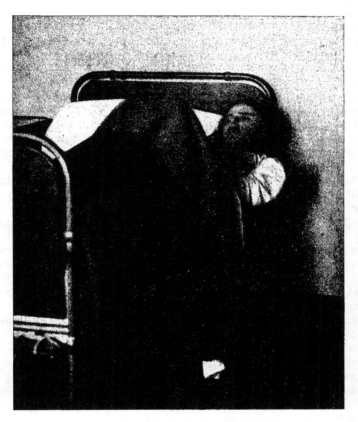

Fig. 26. Stuporous patient lying on the edge of the bed.

when something funny happens, point to the fact that not
the perception of impressions but the discharge of the corresponding volitional expressions is disordered. Commands
are not obeyed or only after very long persuasion or with
vigorous help. Sometimes one sees here and likewise in the
few independent volitional expressions of the patients that a
movement is at first begun correctly, but then suddenly
interrupted or even turned into its opposite. Now and then

the negativistic movements are even set in action by spoken commands. It is then not only possible to cause the patient to go forward by apparently forcing him back and vice versa, but he sits down on the night-stool if he is definitely for- bidden to do it, stands still, as soon as he is told to go, lets go if he is commanded to hold fast.

Also in a series of other features the fundamental resist- ance to the natural volitional impulses can be distinctly recognized. Many patients do not tolerate any clothes or shoes, not even a shirt, do not go to bed, stand beside it with their arms folded, at night lie down on the floor, under the bed, on the outermost edge of the bed, like the patient represented in Fig. 26. They put on articles of clothing the wrong way, turn the bedclothes about, lie on the bedstead and cover themselves with the mattress, lie down in another person's bed or at least stretch out their legs over it. Without a word they force their way out at a certain door, even if all the others are standing open, but do not use the key which is put into their hand to open it; they go backwards if any- one approaches them, hide themselves in a corner, put on other people's clothes, blindfold themselves, throw their petticoats over their head, do not let anything be taken from them which they have once taken hold of.

Sometimes in spite of their immobility otherwise and inaccessibility the patients carry out single senseless, often rhythmic movements, tap on the table or on paper, pull faces, move their fingers as if playing the piano. Some patients do not speak a syllable for years or even for decades, or they just whisper now and then some detached words, mostly incomprehensible; a patient suddenly said; "Let me to Heaven's ladder," and then was again mute. Sometimes these mute patients express themselves by writing in a long- winded and incoherent way. Others on great persuasion only move their lips, or they give short answers, stick to single words, break off in the middle of a word or sentence, begin to speak when one goes away, and are silent as soon as one turns to them again. Their words are usually brought out in a low voice, monotonously, sometimes jerkily.

The taking of food often encounters the greatest difficulties. The patients sometimes quite suddenly stop eating, and cannot be prevailed on in any way to continue the meal, they spasmodically clench their teeth, press their lips together, as soon as the spoon is brought near. They keep the morsel that is put in their mouth there for a long time, do not chew it or swallow it; let the soup run out again. Often the patients do not eat as long as they are watched, let everything stand for hours, or only take something secretly. Some patients with invincible stubbornness refuse soup, meat, or the food placed ready for them, but know how to procure by cunning or by force their neighbours' food and devour it with the greatest haste; others again only take certain dishes; a female patient for days and days called out pitifully and monotonously : "Choc'lat !"

Fæces and urine are often retained to the uttermost. The patients do not use the water-closet at all, even when they are ever so often taken to it, but evacuate immediately afterwards on the floor or in bed and do not change their position in the slightest to avoid the unpleasant consequences, or they remain lying on the full bed-pan. Some patients squeeze their urethra spasmodically with their fingers. Their saliva is not swallowed, but collects in their mouth and then flows down over their chin and clothes or suddenly gushes forth like a fountain from the full cheeks.

In the most severe cases of negativistic stupor the patients usually lie in bed completely motionless and dumb. At every attempt to change their position all the muscles pass into a state of extreme tension and offer the strongest passive resistance, a phenomenon which caused Kahlbaum to adopt the term "tension-insanity," "catatonia." If one presses against their forehead their head springs forward like elastic as soon as one lets go; if one touches the back of the head, it endeavours to go backwards against the pressure of the finger. If the patient is pushed from the place where he is, he resists till he has quite lost his equilibrium and he immediately takes up his place again as soon as the force ceases to act. The patients are often seen for days, weeks, even for many months assuming exactly the same position at the same place. They squat, kneel, or lie motionless on the spot in a peculiar attitude, like a statue, often rigidly twisted on themselves, in knee-elbow position, their chin forced down on their breast, their head lifted up free of the pillow or hanging down over the edge of the bed, the pillow over their face, their legs under the mattress, or the sheet between their teeth, spasmodically grasping with their fingers perhaps an old bit of bread, a ball of fæces, a button that has been torn off, a wreath of roses. They let themselves be rolled about to any extent or even be lifted up in the air like a parcel by any part of the body without changing the position of their limbs in any way. One of my patients folded her hands spasmodically for such a long time that gangrene arose at the points of contact ; another knelt for years on the same spot till he had to be forcibly kept in bed amid violent struggling

K

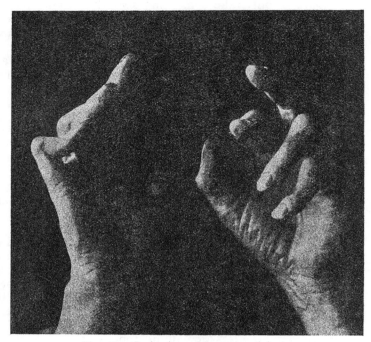

Fig. 27.   Contracture of fingers in catatonia.

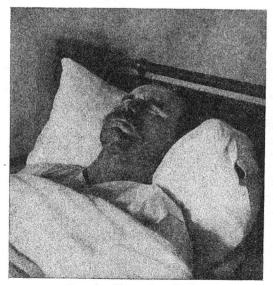

Fig. 28.   Stuporous patient.

on account of developing arthritis. A patient sat bent for-wards in such a way that her nose dipped in the soup; another held the left thumb always extended, the right bent inwards; a third sat with the mouth open, the tongue stuck in a corner of the mouth. Many patients assume a fencing attitude; a patient continually held his hands as if he wanted to box.

Sometimes contractures are developed in the joints that are continually bent; an example of this is given in Fig. 27, which represents a patient who for long years had held his arms pressed against his body and his fingers bent.

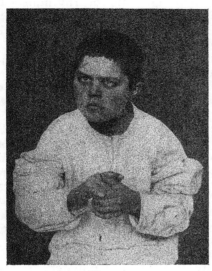

Fig. 29.
Expression of face in catatonic stupor (a).

In stupor the eyes are either closed, as in the patient represented in Fig. 28; if anything comes near they are tightly closed and the eyeballs rolled upwards, or they are wide open, staring with dilated pupils into the distance, never fixing any-thing; blepharoplegia takes place extremely seldom. The forehead is drawn up, fre-quently wrinkled; the ex-pression of the face, vacant, immobile, like a mask, aston-ished, is sometimes reminis-cent of the rigid smile of the Æginetans. Figs. 29 and 30 represent the face of the same youthful patient at different stages of a severe catatonic stupor. In the former the face shows more a dazed, rigid perplexity, in the latter that sleepy vacancy

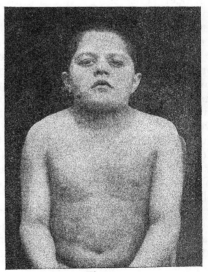

Fig. 30.
Expression of face in catatonic stupor (b).

which is generally connected, as also here, with catalepsy. The lips are often pursed forward like a snout ("Snout-cramp"), and show now and then lightning or rhythmic twitchings. Grinning, sudden laughter, and making faces are frequent.

Constraint is also noticeable in the *gait* of the patients. Often indeed it is quite impossible to succeed in experiments in walking. The patients simply let themselves fall down stiffly, as soon as one tries to place them on their feet. In other cases they march with extended knees, on tiptoe, on the outer edge of the foot, with legs wide apart, with the upper part of the body well bent backwards, sliding, frisking about, balancing, in short, in any wholly unusual attitude which, however, is preserved with all the strength at their command in spite of every external influence. A patient walked with his face turned backwards; a female patient kept accurately to a seam in the floor and did not let herself be pushed to the side. Single movements are stiff, slow, forced, as if a certain resistance had to be overcome, or they are done jerkily and then often as quick as lightning.

The states of catatonic excitement and of stupor, which are here described, and which are apparently so opposed, are obviously very *nearly related* to each other clinically, as they not only can pass directly the one into the other but are also intermingled in the most varied way. The patient who has just been senselessly excited may suddenly become mute and now lie motionless; the patient who has been stuporous, perhaps for weeks, abruptly begins to utter unintelligible screams at the top of his voice, to call out cock-a-doodle-doo, to bark, to sing a song in a refined voice. Or he leaps with long bounds through the room, as quick as lightning unhinges somewhere or other a window, gives a neighbour a box on the ear, and dashes with tremendous force into another patient's bed, and then remains again inaccessible or possibly even passes through a longer period of excitement. Such a change of state occurs with fair frequency in our patients. Very often both excitement and stupor last only a few days or weeks, perhaps only a few hours, and then gradually or suddenly disappear. But on the other hand also a uniform clinical state may continue for months, years, and even decades, and be only quite temporarily interrupted by remissions or by some other kind of morbid phenomena. Especially in stupor that happens not very rarely, while catatonic excitement stretching similarly over years belongs, one may say, to the exceptional cases.

The character of the phenomena is in different cases very

varied. Stupor may sometimes only be 'indicated by taciturn, repellent drowsy conduct, rising in other cases to the suppression of volitional discharge, while excitement may fluctuate from slight, silly merriment to the most regardless fury seriously endangering life. We may well regard it as a *mixture* of the phenomena of both states when a patient dances about mute and with- closed eyes, or lies motionless and bawls a street song. Indeed, one may perhaps on the whole connect the negativistic admixtures in the states of excitement, the inaccessibility and the insusceptibility to influence, the resistance, the speaking past a subject, further the indications of automatic obedience, with the admixture of stuporous morbid symptoms. On the other hand we observe in stuporous patients frequently enough single impulsive actions which are otherwise peculiar to the states of excitement. The patients suddenly throw a cup across the room, jump up in order to smash a pane of glass, to go round the table, to throw themselves then head foremost again into bed and lie there motionless, or they give utterance to meaningless sounds or scream, hurrah! The stereotyped movements, which are occasionally observed in stupor, fiddling, pulling faces, spitting, might also be regarded from the point of view of a mixture with the phenomena of excitement. From that, however, not much is gained. Essentially it only appears that we everywhere meet the *same fundamental disorders* in the different forms of dementia præcox and so also in the catatonic forms, certainly in very varied conjunctions, even though the clinical picture may appear at first sight ever so divergent.

Consciousness is for the most part somewhat clouded, sometimes even very considerably, in catatonic morbid states, especially during their development and at the height of acute disorder. The patients appear, it is true, almost always to perceive single impressions fairly well, even when one cannot prove it at first, but still they usually have only a rather indistinct idea of their situation and of the occurrences in their surroundings, certainly partly on account of the fact, that they are not at all concerned about them and do not feel the need to work up their perceptions further. They, therefore, often mistake people, do not know where they are, but cause surprise not infrequently by knowing the names of the nurses or of the other patients, by making a jocular remark, by complaining about some occurrence or other, by giving a reasonable account of their circumstances, by composing a connected letter with an accurate account of their place of abode and the request to be taken away.

Many patients also solve arithmetical exercises correctly, even of a somewhat difficult kind and display surprising knowledge ; an apparently quite obtuse and inaccessible country lad could give accurate accounts of the Crusades and of Konradin of Hohenstaufen. Quite commonly discernment and clearness are much less disordered than one is inclined to assume from the singular demeanour of the patients which is essentially dependent on volitional disorders.

Insight.—Even a certain insight into their diseased state is frequently present. The patients call their singular doings stupidity ; they say that they are just mad. To the question whether he was mentally affected, a patient replied, " Yes, of course ! If one is sensible, one does not do such things ! " A female patient, who displayed catatonic stereotypies of movement in the highest degree, said to me, " But I must always make such stupid movements ; it is really too silly " ; another complained that she always had to make faces, her laughing should be driven away. Many lay stress upon the fact that when they laugh they do not feel at all merry. A satisfactory account of the motives for their singular behaviour is certainly never got from the patients. A patient gave as the motive of his mutism the answer, " I am not yet suitable to be able to show a voice " ; another stated that he had given utterance to his thoughts only in writing because he could not at once find words ; a third said he had not spoken because he knew no one. A female patient said that she had not wished to speak, another that she did not venture to speak. The physicians had already known everything, the questions had been so simple, they had not known what they should say, are similar utterances. On being asked the motive of her refusing to eat, a patient declared that she simply did not need to eat; another asserted that she had not been hungry. Usually one is told that the patients were obliged to do what they did ; " was obliged to spit " said a patient. Another declared that she was obliged to speak so, it was given to her so ; a third on being asked why she assumed such peculiar attitudes answered, " Because I wish to." Similarly a patient declared that he had remained so motionless because he had wished it ; another alleged that he had been obliged to behave in that way, he had been unconscious. It had just amused them, come into their head, they had thought it had to be so, a power, an impulse, a force had come over them, are answers that frequently recur. Automatic obedience is explained by the fact, that it had just been wished so, that the patients had thought that they were doing the physician a pleasure.

Much more rarely are other motives alleged. A patient according to his own account had believed that he would apostatize from God if he ate; a female patient said that God had not wished it; another said that he had been drawn to his violent movements " as with a rope," a third who in counting always left out the number four, said that he always had to think at the same time of the fourth commandment. A fourth who for hours played passionately on the mouth-harmonica, affirmed that the omnipotence of God inspired him to make music in order that the military should take no harm. It can be clearly enough recognized from all these alleged motives, that the singular actions are of impulsive origin and do not depend on definite deliberation. ·

In spite of these clear statements about the peculiarity of their condition which in general is usually regarded as diseased, the patients have, at first at least, no *real* understanding of the gravity of the disorder. Many patients complain bitterly about the treatment which has been accorded to them; an extremely stuporous patient who for a full year had sat huddled up in bed, whose sensitiveness to pin-pricks had been tested, and whom one had often tried to put in a lying position, was enraged after sudden awaking from the stupor because she had been thrown into bed and that iron bars had been bored into her head. Another demanded 30,000 marks damages. To all representations of the incomprehensibility and morbidity of their conduct the · patients give as answer explanations which say nothing, they had just not known where they were, were without cause torn away from their domesticity, had been treated in quite the wrong way; it was then not to be wondered at, if they had become somewhat confused.

Recollection of the period of the disease appears as a rule to be fairly clear, but very imperfect. The patients state that it may well be possible that this or that has happened so, but they did not know about it, neither could they explain how they had behaved as they did. Sometimes they dispute some of the occurrences very resolutely, then again assert that they have been dead, have been overpowered. The intermingling of delusions and hallucinations on the one hand, the inaccessibility and lack of insight of the patients on the other hand, make it often difficult to obtain a reliable account of the real substance of their recollections. The indifference, however, with which the patients regard their own serious malady is almost always very striking. They do not feel any real need to explain to themselves the details of their morbid experiences, do not ask about the subject, will not listen to anything about it, smile incredulously when they are told about it, do not attribute any very grave import to the disorder ; regard themselves at once as perfectly well, as soon as they have become to a certain degree clear and quiet, insist without more ado on discharge, blind to better counsel.

Mood in states of stupor usually shows no marked colouring. Often the patients appear to be in a state of anxious tension, so that formerly a section of these cases was named "melancholia attonita," as the rigidity was connected with emotions of anxiety and fearfulness. It is as a rule easy to convince oneself that fear is not the motive of the patients' behaviour. · They are not influenced by threats, do not draw back from the clenched fist or the drawn knife, do not blink when the point of a needle is brought near their eye. Only in the beginning of the disease do we occasionally notice, corresponding to the depressive delusions, outbreaks of violent fear and despair. Later the mood changes often without recognizable cause ; pitiful weeping gives place to furious irritation or childish merriment, while a dull indifference forms the basis, and is expressed particularly in the behaviour of the patients to their nearest relatives and in the gradual disappearance of wish and will.

The **General Course** of the catatonic forms is very varied as already appears from the description given. It shapes itself in still more changing forms because in about one-third of the cases considerable improvement in all morbid phenomena, sometimes resembling complete recovery or coming very near it, occurs, most frequently as it seems in the cases beginning with a state of depression. The duration of these periods of improvement varies greatly ; they most frequently last about two to three years ; but they sometimes last nine, ten, twelve, thirteen, fourteen, sixteen years ; indeed once between the first attack of the disease and the second which led to dementia, there was an interval of twenty-nine years. The objection can certainly always be made, that in the case of such long intervals the two attacks have nothing at all to do with each other. Meanwhile the observation that a pause of ten years' duration between two attacks with quite similar morbid phenomena is frequent in this as in other forms of dementia præcox, shows there cannot well be any doubt here about a long respite and renewed outbreak of the same morbid process. But then also we often enough see the insidious development of the malady extended over long, long years till at last an acute disorder announces the real outbreak of the disease. Not altogether seldom the disease runs its course in three, or still more, attacks separated by periods of improvement, attacks which in certain circumstances may at first be of only quite short duration before a more serious one commences leading to dementia. The individual catatonic states may either follow the one immediately after the other and alternate quickly, or be separated from each other by long intervals. I observed a case where a state of excitement followed the introductory stupor only after fifteen years ; in other cases the malady began with a state of stupor which was first interrupted by a remission of many years and then a characteristic state of excitement developed. In another case stupor appeared only after the malady had lasted for fifteen years.

In the *terminal states* dementia along with the phenomena of negativism and mannerisms was in great excess. Simple weak-mindedness was the issue in about 11 per cent. of the cases, dull dementia still somewhat more rarely. Seizures were observed in 17 per cent. of the cases. A female patient, thirty-one years' of age, broke down completely a few days after an attack with deep unconsciousness and unilateral manifestations of cerebral irritation. On the whole we must reckon the catatonic forms with the more unfavourable varieties of dementia præcox on account of the frequency of profound dementia, while passing improvements are somewhat more frequent than in the average of the cases here taken into account. The share of the men with 54 per cent. and of the cases under the age of twenty-five with 57 per cent. does not deviate from the average ; still the forms beginning with stupor seem to me to begin at a somewhat more advanced age. The number of the observed cases included 19.5 per cent. of the whole series.

THE PARANOID DEMENTIAS.

A picture, which is in many respects divergent, is exhibited by those cases, the essential morbid symptoms of which are *delusions* and *hallucinations ;* we call them paranoid forms.[1] I feel justified in including them in the domain of dementia præcox by the circumstance that in them, sooner or later, a series of disorders of a kind which we everywhere find also in the other forms of dementia præcox, invariably accompanies the delusions. Further in a large number of cases terminal states are developed, which completely resemble the forms described up to now, and also in the remaining cases a psychic decline is developed, which in

[1] Ferrarini, Rivista sperimentale di freniatria xxx. 876 ; xxxi. 435.

spite of many peculiar features, nevertheless discloses a near relationship with the issues of dementia præcox already known to us.

PARANOID DEMENTIA GRAVIS.

If, as seems conformable to our purpose, we let ourselves be guided in the grouping in detail by the point of view of prognosis, we shall next have to take into consideration those paranoid morbid states, which, it is true, begin with simple delusions, in the further course, however, exhibit always more distinctly the *peculiar disintegration of the psychic life*, and in especial also the *emotional* and *volitional disorders* in the form characteristic of dementia præcox ; they might be grouped together under the name of "dementia paranoides gravis."

The development of the disease took place in 63 per cent. of my cases insidiously ; in 17 per cent. of the patients there existed from youth upwards certain unfavourable peculiarities of character, frivolity, love of pleasure, defiance, self-will, unyielding and hasty conduct. Among the women there were several prostitutes ; among the men 19 per cent. were vagrants. In about 30 per cent. of the cases the disease began subacutely ; usually it was a case of convicts, who fell ill during imprisonment ; in 7 per cent. of the cases the beginning appeared to be acute. The introductory disorders are quite similar to those of the remaining forms of dementia præcox, headaches, tiredness, aversion from work, sleeplessness, restlessness, irritability, a changed, monosyllabic, shy behaviour.

Delusions.—Gradually there come "forebodings," "things come to light." The patient notices that he is being oppressed, too little considered, he is being maligned, insulted, scoffed at. The people in the street stop, make jokes about him, look at him in a rude way, laugh, make insinuations as if he had stolen, as if he were to blame for everything. Everywhere there are aiders and abettors ; a marriage which he has planned is. being prevented ; the neighbours are taking everything out of the house, he is being plundered and robbed ; secret debts are being made, there are people in the warehouse, burglars are breaking in ; people are forcing their way into his room. The Jews are lying in wait for the patient's children ; his relatives want his money ; the parsons spoil everything ; the sermon is aimed at him. Newspapers.scribble about him ; letters are changed and falsified ; everywhere there are rascally tricks and Freemason ongoings.

Everything seems changed and uncanny to the patient. His children are all confused; his whole surroundings are bewitched and enchanted. The physicians are not right physicians, his fellow-patients are suspicious personages; the clock stops; money has not the security that it once had. Every one is being murdered; everywhere wounded men are seen; his father and brothers and sisters are being strangled, roasted; the Grand Duke is being killed; the patient is in a den of murderers. A female patient thought that outside there was the Lake of Constance, and it had destroyed all countries and human beings; a patient said that all souls were lost; in three days there would be the last judgment. The patient acquires the conviction that he has very powerful enemies and is threatened with frightful dangers. People want to behead him, to immure him in the stove, to crush him, to burn him, to throw him to wild animals; sparrows, rats, dogs with goats' hoofs are called out against him. By the order of the Grand Duke revolvers were distributed in the village, he is going to be brought before a secret military tribunal, is being treated as a political prisoner; a patient perceived that some one was working at her coffin. There is poison in the beer, soap in the drinking-water, morphia, hydrochloric acid, iodine in the food; the patient accordingly feels burning in his mouth and obstruction; everywhere "bellephonpoison" and phosphorus are displayed; the dishes are dirty; bread is baked specially for him by the baker. His enemies, who lie in wait for him, are sometimes Freemasons, parsons, the "Frankfurter," the devil, "Brother Markus," sometimes the nearest relatives, his sister and especially his wife, who speaks evil of him and poisons him; he feels it. She takes sides with her brother, with the clergyman.

Hallucinations usually appear very soon. The patients see figures, people with little red caps, black men, cows, Christ, angels and saints at the altar, "little figures and little souls," God, the Virgin Mary. A patient saw a man in green bathing-drawers, who was playing with his penis; a female patient saw her supposed loved one lying on her bed at night. By far the most frequent are *auditory* hallucinations, whispering, signals from the air, exclamations, abusive names. Voices are heard in the sound of the bell, in the chirping of the birds, in the sounds which animals make; people speak about the patient and his wife; there is whispering and ringing in the walls; at night there is loud talking in the room. Sometimes the voices seem to have completely the character of real perceptions; the patient can give their substance in words and also recognize their supposed author. Thousands of people threaten and abuse him from the wall, said a patient; another stated that he had got his hearing from his father and mother; a third said when he was brought to the hospital, "The devils of fellows speak here too!"

In other cases the illusions are more or less sharply distinguished from sense-impressions. The patient hears the voice of God, invisible beings speak, evil spirits let him have no rest, grossly abuse him: he hears all sorts of things "in thoughts," has voices for the whole of Europe by the apparatus or current; "Nature speaks to me," said a patient. The voices are referred to different places. "There is something in my ears," declared a patient; another heard "memorial" all day long in her head. "The words have come out of my stomach," asserted a male patient, while a female patient heard speaking in her genitals, and another thought she had a telephone in her feet.

What the voices say is usually unpleasant; "If I could only get rid of my hearing!" exclaimed a patient on this account. The patient hears everything that one says or thinks about him, that he is going to be executed, beheaded, that he has committed *lèse-majesté*; "He is to be got rid of," it is said; there is a war going on. A patient heard "a murmuring," that his brother was dead. Female patients hear "immoral stuff," sexual accusations; forest-whore, married man's whore, strolling whore; they have committed abortion, killed a child. Sometimes the voices forbid the patients to work. A patient heard that he was God.

Frequently the patients' own thoughts are perceived by others. The people know by the voice-telegraph what the patient is thinking; they speak of his thoughts; what he thinks and reads is repeated after him. The patient answers silently, speaks with the voices the whole day, converses with Kaiser Wilhelm, with spirits, carries on dialogues "on the thought-way through the nostrils." Sometimes also the thoughts are made; the patients must think what others think; transference of thought takes place; "These are things, they flow to one, and one says them," said a patient.

Occasionally also other kinds of hallucinations come under observation, the smell of corpses, the taste of sulphur in the food, mephitic air, the feeling of being electrified, pulled at, of being doubled. "Something wanders about in a wonderful way in my body," said a patient; another felt a machine in her teeth and in her breast; the taking of the temperature caused another one pains. A patient had pain in his heart when the post drove by; another complained, "The cover smells so loud"; a third felt "chinks of pain."

Hypochondriacal Ideas.—In the further course of the disease the delusions soon acquire an always more wonderful character. In especial there are nonsensical hypochondriacal ideas, in which the delusion of persecution finds shape, possibly in connection with morbid common sensation. Often also the delusions are connected with the experiences of dreams, which are without hesitation regarded as reality. Blood is drawn off from the patient, it is beaten to milk; something is taken out of his body, his bowels are torn out; everything is sawn to pieces, his face is disfigured, his heart is stolen, something is being poured into his throat. A patient thought that he was being continually filled with water, which he must then pass, and in consequence kept running innumerable times to the water-closet. His eyes are sprinkled with poison, drawn out of his head; his sight is taken from him; "something is being done to my fine eyes," complained a female patient. His head is closed, pressed together, is to be made confused; the skull-cap is being taken off, the central nerve is lacerated and bleeding, the nervous system is torn down, the brain is bored through with Röntgen rays, the head-power is weakened; another head has been put on. The patient is to be made crazy, giddy; his understanding is stolen, his thoughts are criminally taken from him, his four senses are fetched away by the doctor; he is becoming idiotic, a simpleton; a patient complained that he could not stand the things going through his brain. The patient feels that he must die; his blood runs cold, his inside is annihilated; beauty is gone, the freshness of life is lost. Something is wanting in his head and spinal marrow; the brain is shrinking; the patient has no longer any intellectual life, any heart; he must live for ever.

Sexual Influences usually play a large part in these complaints, especially in female patients. At night women come; the patients feel themselves used sexually from behind; their nature is driven off, thrown in their faces. Women are tormented by "seductive stories," violated at night, turned into whores; people wish to practise obscenity with them. The physician has given them desire in their bath; they feel it sometimes in their back, sometimes in their head, sometimes in their hands. At night there are seventeen or eighteen gentlemen in their bed; the hospital is a brothel; a female patient declared that the obscene practices with the three-and four must now cease. The abdomen has no resistance, is not right, the periods are hindered; the motherly feelings have been torn out, the maternal parts have been turned outside ; the patients feel themselves "made nature-less." The womb has never been loved, is rotting, sways about in the hinder parts ; the ovary is to be operated on, pepper is to be put into the mouth of the uterus.

The idea of being *influenced, constrained*, appears distinctly, as in the delusions quoted, also in many other utterances. The patients are tormented and have their lives threatened by machines, by "light-tube-ray-apparatus," by sympathy, hypnotism, enchantment and witchcraft. They are influenced by artificial means, are changed every day, feel it in their body ; at night abductions take place. A power drives the patient, accumulates, goes right through people, gives a ringing tone and overcomes him ; a patient was caused by the compulsion, by the "going round of his head," to go twice to America. The patient feels intrigues, "mental transferences to planet and sun" ; sentiments all run to him ; "intellectual patterns are being fitted on." He is caused to have pains in his back ; he is being made to scratch his face. Sometimes it is the evil eye that brings this to pass ; the physicians speak the eye-language ; "But one may not with a look tear out ninety years of a lifetime," complained a female patient. "I am a depressed body, a fettered human being," said a patient ; "lightning things have no aim" ; another pleaded that he would like to have his rights, his power again. A third felt himself in "public, hypnotic custody" in spite of apparent freedom in the enlarged cage, as the "hypnotists" had him completely under their control by the hypnotic power of their eyes.

Exaltation.—Alongside of the ideas of persecution there are present in more than half of the cases exalted ideas ; in a small number of cases they alone dominate the clinical picture. Usually they appear only after some time, even after several years, more rarely towards the beginning of the malady ; thus in the case of a postman almost the first striking morbid symptom was that he signed himself on an official document as General Field Marshal. The patient has supernatural gifts, has made important inventions, the Röntgen apparatus, the "Peter mobile" ; he possesses numerous patents, a factory ; the hospital, the country, all kingdoms belong to him. He has money in the safe, has great riches, is getting a situation with a salary of 1000 marks ; he has a claim to thirty-two millions, which have been deposited for him by Rothschild and the Shah of Persia ; he demands every day 1000 marks damages, he understands the making of money ; a patient asserted that he had "the ransom " as he twisted off all the buttons from his suit and attributed to each the value of some thousand marks. The patient is prince by the grace of God, heir as German Emperor, owner of the German Empire; his father is prince, Kaiser; he was at the age of twenty-five king, having inherited from his great-grandfather; he possesses a privileged and triumphal canopy, wants a uniform, wants to live in the Castle, wishes to have an explanation from the local magistracy about his lineage. A patient who was hoarse, thought that he had the Emperor Frederick's disease and was therefore related to him and of royal blood. Another is rightful successor of the cross as Pharaoh, thought-reader, clairvoyant, called of God, born for the salvation of all mankind, Paul, God the Father, guardian angel, judge of the quick and the dead. He has two natures, a divine and a spiritual, is standing already in the red magnificat, must punish the wicked, protect the pious; he receives revelations, can make the sun rise. Many patients tell a story of inner transformations which they have experienced and in which their future high calling has become clear to them; a vagrant heard then that he was to become an organ-builder. A patient asserted that his *fiancée* had born him spiritually.

Female patients are Baroness Bergshausen, Planga Geyer von Geyersberg, Countess Drossel, Empress of Ladenburg, royalties, daughter of Kaiser William I., wife of the Kaiser, must take the place of the Kaiserin; they get maintenance from the Kaiser; they are ruler of the world, queen of heaven, lord over all higher things, wish to redeem mankind, have the keys of hell. To them belong all kingdoms; God is their dear papa. They speak of their subjects, explain that the institution belongs to them, desire to go to a grand hotel, to their kingdom, to Berlin. A patient declared that she was Christ; another called herself by her husband's name, asserted that he was her wife, asked for trousers and wished to go out to work on the fields. Many patients do not acknowledge their husbands any more, wish to marry a baron, travel after a curate, whom they think is their husband, ask the physician to marry them. A patient put on mourning for her supposed lover; another fell in love with the priest, wished to go with him to Rome, where he was to become pope; a third declared that the Kaiser came to her every night.

Memory.—Here and there the delusions are connected with errors of memory, which misrepresent to the patients experiences of a time long forgotten, back in their earliest youth, indeed from a former existence. The patients think that they are supposititious children because they do not resemble their brothers and sisters; they remember being dandled as children on the knees of the reigning prince in a beautiful castle; later they were badly treated by their "foster parents," and heard all sorts of hints from them that had reference to their high lineage. A patient asserted that he had already lived in the house of his grandparents when his parents married, and he remembered the celebration of their marriage; another stated that he had lived in America from 1795 to 1820; a third narrated that he was born in 1797 and then he grew up in Moscow; he was present at the crucifixion of Christ, had founded Universities, built castles, erected the Houses of Parliament, hunted lions in Africa, taken part in all campaigns. These cases in which, according to the utterances of the patients, the delusion has apparently already begun in early childhood, gave Sander the occasion for the description of an "idiopathic" paranoia, in which the development of the disease was said to extend back into childhood. Further experience has meanwhile shown that in such narrations it is without exception a case of subsequent morbid invention. Neisser has therefore frankly put down as the characteristic mark of the group circumscribed by Sander, errors of memory and proposed the delimitation of a "confabulating paranoia." According to my conviction the cases of Sander which have been quoted belong to dementia præcox. As a rule the errors of memory here form only a passing morbid symptom, so that they are scarcely suitable for the delimitation of another group.

If at the beginning it is in some measure possible to follow the patients' train of thought, in the further development of the disease the senselessness and the singularity of the mode of expression, which have already frequently appeared in the examples quoted, become so pronounced that it is scarcely, or no longer at all, possible to make out the meaning of the morbid utterances; neologisms also help to make it more difficult. The patients complain about the people who carry on murder, the subterranean business of human beings about their body; at night they feel themselves drawn out through a needle. The bleaching-book is being opened; the railway has for nine years closed the convict-prison; intellect was brought into high heaven; a dog's trick is being carried on with them; the central nerve is being led off from its origin. They have growth, the murmuring of the sea, no more breast-food, liver-constriction, white dysenteric consumption; an acceleration course is arranged against them. A patient said that he was "the abusive epithet empire, his heart certainly and human life"; a female patient declared that she bore the globe and the telephone.

In spite of these often quite incomprehensible utterances, the patients are usually permanently clear about their residence, about time and about people, even though delusional falsifications and wrong interpretations are frequently recognizable. Thus a patient thought that she was in the confusion-institution ; another called the hospital the casemate-convict prison. The patients also often mistake the physicians and their fellow-patients and they disown their own relatives, but not on account of real disorders of perception, but in connection with delusions. Consciousness, apart from passing states of excitement, is not clouded; the patients are sensible and perceive fairly well, are able to give an account of their circumstances, and to solve the more simple intellectual exercises, so far as they are not hindered in doing so by volitional disorders or by increasing dementia. Of understanding of the disease on the other hand there is no question. The patients at most admit that through the persecutions they have become somewhat "nervous." "To mention in one word myself and the madhouse is just exactly a quadratic perversity," wrote a patient. Nor does ocular evidence convince the patients. If they are taken to the room where they suppose that the persecutors are, they only acknowledge that everything suspicious has meantime been cleared away.

Mood shows no very pronounced colouring. Many patients exhibit greatly increased self-consciousness or silly merriment ; frequently one sees them breaking out into cause-less laughter. Others appear remarkably indifferent and unconcerned. But very frequently there is repellent, irritable, quarrelsome behaviour with occasional violent outbursts of abuse, and even acts of violence, especially at the time of the menses. Sometimes a state of very lively sexual excitement appears, which expresses itself in regardless masturbation, obscene talk, coarse proposals and assaults. A female patient continually begged in the most urgent way to be examined with the metroscope ; another stuffed horsehair into her vagina.

The **Activities** of the patients seem to have some relation to their delusions but they usually bear the stamp of singularity and incomprehensibility. The ideas of persecu-tion lead to violent outbursts of rage and dangerous attacks on the supposed enemies. A patient threatened the clergyman that he would shoot him; another locked in his wife and children and handed over the key to the public prosecutor for further enquiry. A female patient wished to cut her father's throat, another suffocated her friend, a third wished to kill herself and her child because she had heard "perdition take her and her brood!"; a fourth hit her husband on his head with an axe "in order to redeem him." The motives of these attacks are often very obscure. A patient felt himself suddenly forced to injure his sister with whom he was on good terms, went up to her on the road and stabbed her in the back. Not infrequently the patients apply to the authorities to complain about the persecutions and to ask for help, sometimes in wholly confused documents. The hallucinations cause the patients to stop their ears or to beat their ears; two of my patients in this way brought on themselves hæmatomata auris. Others speak away to themselves, answer the voices, call into the heating apparatus, become restless at night in order to defend themselves from reproaches and abusive language. Ideas of poisoning may lead to refusal of food; a female patient for a considerable time only ate eggs; one patient only drank milk; another spat a great deal in order to get rid of the poison again. Many patients suddenly fling their food away, because it appears suspicious to them. A patient tied herself up wholly in cloths in order to protect herself from the influences which she feared. Occasionally it comes also to attempts at suicide; a patient tried to remove his testicles by ligature; a female patient swallowed needles.

Exalted ideas connected with religion lead to the declaiming of texts from the Bible, to preaching and fasting, to abuse of the clergy; a patient built for himself a house altar. Here also the taking of food is often involved. A female patient took only bread and water; a patient fasted on Thursday and Friday; another thought that a higher being did not require to eat at all, nor to ease himself. A female patient went to the local medical officer and asked him to cut open her back and fix in angels' wings. Sexual excitement causes the patients to commit dissolute acts, to decide to be divorced, to make an attempt to approach any wholly unknown person whatever of the opposite sex, and to commit immoral acts on children. A female patient wished to marry her brother.

Alongside of these volitional expressions, which after all are still to a certain extent comprehensible, go others for which intelligible motives can scarcely be discovered. The patients wander through the house at night; they suddenly stop the alarum clock, tear out stakes from the vineyard, tear down the vines, search in the graveyard for the grave of their wife who is still alive, run to the water-closet a hundred times in the day, cut off their hair. Sometimes here also delusions may play a part to which the patients do not give expression; but often we have certainly to do with purely impulsive actions, about the origin of which the patients themselves are not able to give any exact account. This view appears certain in the numerous actions which we have come across in quite similar form in the types of dementia præcox previously discussed and which we have there learned to recognize as the result of the volitional disorders peculiar to this disease.

Negativism.—Next we meet with a series of negativistic phenomena. The patients are repellent, inaccessible, mono-syllabic, even mute, withdraw themselves, hide themselves away, draw the cover over their head. One patient gave utterance to his thoughts only in writing; others only answer in indefinite phrases or speak past the subject. They do not shake hands because they "do not need to," "may not do it," because they "do not any longer go in for frivolity." Or they give the left hand, the finger-tips, or wrap up their hand in their handkerchief. Many patients keep their eyes closed, cover their mouth with their hand, lie down in other people's beds, refuse food at times without recognizable cause, now and then pass their excreta under them; if told to employ themselves, they refuse. On the other hand the patients occasionally again exhibit automatic obedience, are cataleptic, put out their tongue non-voluntarily to be pierced through, imitate what is called out to them or done in front of them. Often they are seen assuming singular attitudes, standing the whole day on one spot, staring in front of them.

Mannerisms are often a marked feature. The patients pull faces, stick out their lips like a snout, suck their fingers, make peculiar gestures, which sometimes appear to represent a kind of sign-language, move affectedly, adorn themselves tastelessly, put their bedclothes together in a singular manner, let down their hair, spit, click their tongue, cut their words when they speak, speak rhythmically, in affected High German, in a Frenchified style. Among these are inter-polated all kinds of senseless impulsive actions. The patients pull out the hair of their beard, turn about their own axis, suddenly climb right up the window, smash panes of glass, throw the dishes about the room. Stereotypies, pulling at their fingers, rocking movements, running round in circles, monotonous movements of arm and hand, rhyming, verbi-geration are also frequent.

Speech.—The substance of expression in speech is incoherent, odd, exhibits drivelling verbosity, a tendency to sounding phrases, quotations, silly plays on words, neologisms, sometimes going on to complete confusion. The whole manner of speech of the patients becomes in this way, especially in the later periods of the disease, extremely peculiar, and bristles with bewildering turns of expression. A female patient described herself as being ill-treated "churlwise," "horrorwise," "pretensionwise," and as being an "embezzled mama"; a patient called himself the "artificially opposed person"; another asserted that the physicians were "reversed doctors." "Live without liver has been telegraphed to me," said a patient; a second said "When one gives any one the hand, one is love"; a third received me with the words, "I believe that the gentlemen are there for my confidence and not for yours." "Doctorship is being made with me," complained a female patient, while another on being asked about hallucinations, replied: "The attaché affair has been finished for two years." Again another expressed herself, "Personal right does belong to me, a man who steps in for me; the avertor must avert," and a patient dismissed me with the words, "Are you a state model? Radius, radius, that's enough." Complete agrammatism, inability to form grammatical sentences, also occurs; a patient replied to me when I spoke to him: "Sleeping and dreaming and emotional state without sympathy and without master-key." In the patients' writings similar oddities again occur: at the same time we often meet here a singular arrangement of lines and letters and queer orthography. These disorders of the expression of speech in word and writing agree perfectly with those which we have an opportunity of watching in the terminal stages of other forms of dementia præcox.

Course.—In another direction also the *issues* of this group correspond completely with those of the clinical types hitherto discussed. As terminal state the most frequent is manneristic dementia, somewhat seldomer negativistic or drivelling dementia. Only in about 12 per cent. of the cases simple weak-mindedness is developed without other more striking morbid residua; just as often dull dementia sets in. I could not verify any essential improvements with later relapse among my cases, which embrace rather more than 9 per cent. of all the cases of dementia præcox; there were seizures in only 3 per cent. of the patients. The form here described belongs accordingly to the less favourable varieties, Its course is essentially more chronic and more monotonous than any we have hitherto seen ; remissions of the morbid phenomena, as well as seizures which may well be interpreted as specially violent expressions of the disease, disappear almost completely. The fact is very remarkable, that here the male sex with 44 per cent. remains considerably below the average, but especially that only 26 per cent. of our patients were below twenty-five years of age. This paranoid form is therefore by preference a disease of middle and later life ; a few cases occurred in the sixth decade of life. We call to mind here that depressive dementia with delusions, which shows many points of contact with this form, also shows a certain preference for riper years. If progressive experience confirms our present assumption, that in all the clinical pictures here separated from one another, it is still a case of the same morbid process, one might suppose that with more advanced age in itself, the tendency to more pronounced delusions grows, while at the same time the possibility of a more complete disappearance of the disorders decreases and the course becomes more gradual. That delusional forms of disease usually belong in general more to riper age is confirmed by many experiences. Also in paralysis we see that the forms, which occur in youth, generate delusions with considerably less frequency.

PARANOID DEMENTIA MITIS.

As a further form of paranoid dementia præcox I think that I should now add another group of cases, which on the one hand exhibit a quite similar development and the same delusions as the paranoid diseases just described, but on the other hand result in peculiar states of weak-mindedness. While there in the terminal states principally the volitional disorders and the incoherence of the original clinical picture remain behind, here we have to do with the development of a psychic decline which is specially characterized by the continuance of delusions or hallucinations ; the issue of the malady is a state which we may call *paranoid* or *hallucinatory weak-mindedness*. As here the substance of the personality seems to be less seriously damaged, it is perhaps allowable to speak of a " dementia paranoides mitis."

The beginning of the disease was in 74 per cent. of my cases slowly progressive, while about 9 per cent. set in acutely, the rest subacutely. But certainly also in these last cases slighter changes had frequently for a considerable time preceded the actual onset. Almost always indeed it was a case here of the outbreak of morbid phenomena during *imprisonment* in individuals who already years ago had fallen into a career of crime, sometimes after good development in the beginning, but often also on the foundation of a disposition unfavourable from the first or a neglected education. In 20 per cent. of the cases the patients had shown mediocre or poor endowment at school ; some were described as from youth up stubborn, self-willed, wicked, suspicious, peculiar, "nervous." Among the men two-thirds were vagrants and criminals, probably a sign that we had here to do either with individuals of inferior disposition, or, what for many cases seemed to be the more correct view, with a very gradual change which reached far back into the past and which only after a considerable number of years acquired marked morbid features. In all these directions, therefore, the form here treated behaves quite like the other.

Hallucinations and Ideas of Persecution.—The first manifestations of the disease also seem to be the same, as far as they can at all be verified in the usually very slow development. The patients become suspicious, irritable, insubordinate, at times threatening and violent, behave in a conspicuous way, carry on singular conversations, often change their situations, stop working. Little by little it then becomes clear that they are suffering from hallucinations, generally auditory, and from ideas of persecution. In the cases which set in acutely, especially during imprisonment, these disorders are usually the first striking morbid symptoms.

The substance of the hallucinations is mostly hostile, provocative. In the beginning there is perhaps only a buzzing, ringing, humming ; but then the patient hears how he is mocked and abused by his neighbour ; he is called bastard, rogue, dirty dog, prison thief, wild swine, shabby beast, young swine ; they are "voices of persecution." Frequently immoral things are said. The patient hears indecent talk about himself ; he is said to have assaulted his children criminally ; "bigamy" is called out. Women are abused as "princes' prostitute, rose prostitute, princes' drabs" ; a patient heard ladies' voices which called out to him that he was to come and love them ; another was called "pencil-sharpener" (onanist) More rarely it says, "He's a pretty boy, a handsome fellow.' Sometimes everything that the patient does is discussed : "every now and then he peeps again." The master of the house telegraphs what he says ; the voices hear everything know his thoughts, say them aloud beforehand, repeat aloud what he reads ; there is thought-reading, double speech. A patient thought that two people saw through his eyes everything that happened.

But he also can read the thoughts of others, feels what people intend to do with him. The voices are sometimes quite· transcendental, "secret voices," "inward voices," "thought brooding," inspirations from above, sometimes whispering, "whispering to him," "inblowings," "murmuring." People speak through air-shafts, from the clock or through a phonograph, sing into his ears ; people over him and above him speak (" Roof-runners," "Behind-wallers ") ; from all sides there is telephoning ; the patient " is in touch with everyone "; someone is sitting in his left ear. Now and then it is God or Christ who speaks. The voices often control the patient continuously, especially in the night, the attendants have him at night on his trial ; it is a " nightly cross-examination."

Visual hallucinations are more rare. The patient is being dazzled and reflected ; he sees a shining light in the room, bright squares, lines, pictures of saints in the sky, a cross and the Saviour, the ascension of Jesus in the firmament ; "That does not happen to everyone," added a patient. Others see " pictures produced as if for entertainment," black figures ; a patient asserted that he saw everything through glasses in the wall. With these are associated putrid smells, a " colossal smell of phosphorus," stinking vapours, bitterness in mouth and nose, the taste of petroleum, bugs, chloride of lime, human fæces, sulphur, oil, spirit, onion juice, white-lead, pepper, poison of all kinds in his food ; he feels sick after taking the milk ; the beer is blood-water.

Dysæsthesiæ.—If it is already in such utterances of the patients often difficult to decide, whether it has to do with real hallucinations or not, it is in still higher degree the case in the manifold dysæsthesiæ of which they habitually complain. They have stitches in the lung, feel themselves "embraced by cold," have a sensation of burning and stirring in their stomach, cold in their lung, oppression in their heart. There is pricking, punching and cutting. The skin itches, is too narrow ; their hinder parts are gone so that they cannot sit ; they cannot take a deep breath, have no longer any lungs ; their brain is running to pieces ; filth is running out at their ears. Very soon these sensations are connected with external influences and insanely worked up. The patient is worried day and night, tormented, burnt, made filthy, ruined in his health ; he is tortured in every part of his body. His blood is drawn from his nose and body ; saliva is squirted into his face and mouth ; he is infected with diphtheria ; he is given an enema " of churchyard putrefaction," dangerous medicines are introduced into him by little tubes, pulverized sublimate is put in his eye ; his ears and head are blown up ; he is burnt with machines; he is shot in the ears with 5000 small shot, electric shocks are given to him; a hundred mice run over his back. His flesh is torn off, taken from his shoulders with a magnet; he is "damaged"; his heart is sewed up, his throat pressed together; the urinal is fixed in; his throat is made raw; his face old. His foot is being cut up, his buttocks torn; his veins are being laid hold of and cut through, his teeth are being destroyed. Children are boring round about his buttocks; his bowels are being "wound up and deposited in plates"; fæces are pumped up into his brain; his "sex is drawn out horizontally and put in again vertically." There is a magnet in his ear, wheelwork in his breast, that moves him like a jointed doll. The clergyman has pressed out his brain by the nose; the patient is "filled up and filled in," must breathe in mice and cats; alternating currents come undulating towards him; there is a "current-war." Often these torments are given special names; "filthy murder" is being practised, "urine magic" is being carried on; the patients speak of twitching of the fingers, swelling of the flesh, stanching of blood and letting blood flow, event-making, bomb-bursting, lobster-cracking, and so on. A patient wrote that in him "hallucinizations, alienations, exstirpations, informations, transversalism, orthotrophy, and so on" were being aimed at.

Besides the extraordinary forms of the dysæsthesiæ, the circumstance that the tortures are often referred to the time of sleep, is also favourable to the interpretation that everywhere here it is a case more of delusions than of erroneous perception. The bed is moving; the patient is tormented at night by blows in the ribs and electrification; in sleep his breast is pressed in, or his bones are taken out of him and replaced by sticks. At night "spiritual underselling" takes place; there is "much coming and going"; "at night one does not have night rest," said a patient. Here it may sometimes be a case of the interpretation of dreams as the patients frequently without any hesitation transfer dream experiences to reality.

Varied Persecutions.—All other possible ideas of persecution also make their appearance. The patient is being made a fool of, everywhere announced already beforehand, watched and persecuted by policemen, tempted by Satan, is lost, infected, outlawed, is to be ruined, condemned to death, shot, chloroformed, strangled, got rid of, executed, must die in May, will be buried in an unconsecrated churchyard. He is being cheated, robbed; people force their way in with false keys, spoil his food for him; holes are being bored in the

roof; cart-grease, chloride of lime, soap is being thrown down.
Letters are falsified, suppressed; lottery-tickets disappear;
political intrigues are taking place; justice is being
administered. The clergyman preaches false doctrine; in
the newspaper there are allusions; "people understand it
already," said a patient. The questions addressed to him are
"puzzles"; the people round him are females, "masked";
a conspiracy exists in which the accomplices relieve each
other. There are uncanny ongoings in the house, like a plot,
a "double world"; everything is enchanted; even ·the cat
is instigated to breathe on the patients. His wife is dead,
estranged by witches' sympathy, killed by the doctor; his son
is ripped up, hung, his daughter burned; his children have a
knife in their neck, have got into the subterranean regions;
in the house patients are being slaughtered and worked up
into sausages.

Sexual delusions are very frequent. The patients are
jealous, think that they are married elsewhere; the children
are not theirs; a female patient thought that her husband had
fifty-four wives and fifty-four children. The patient's wife puts
menstrual blood in the food; a female who can make herself
invisible persecutes the patient. Immoral plays are being
represented; figures of little girls appear and excite the
patient sexually; he is irritated by unchaste talk. Female
patients are said to be misused, made pregnant by magnetic-
electrical methods; men lie in wait for them; at night filthy
fellows work about them; there is match-making going on.
Filthy deeds are being carried out; the penis is being tickled,
rubbed off; the semen poured off, nature drawn off. A
patient was invited by voices to associate sexually as stallion
with the daughters in better-class families.

Sometimes Polish Jews, the clergyman, a former sweet-
heart, the secret Freemason association, the neighbours, the
magicians in the subterranean vault, the sister-in-law, the
overseer in the prison are regarded as the originators of the
persecutions; a patient thought there was "a nightly,
religious, secret, assassinatory, governmental, civil war." As
means used by their persecutors the patients suppose
apparatus, an electric death-dealing current, a "patent
electrifying apparatus," with which also they occasionally see
someone occupying himself, 300 machines and a patented
large clockwork which moves everything; "with electricity
much can be done"; there are two souls who electrify the
patient. He feels himself "full of galvanization," is being
tormented by the machine, "telegraphed through," examined
by Röntgen rays; there are physical experiments, pestilential,

or it is enchantment, witchcraft. A patient thought that the passers-by drew blood out of his body by means of an instrument like a cupping-glass which they had in their mouths.

Influence.—The description of influence on *thoughts* and on *volition* usually play a special part also in the complaints of these patients. "Thronging of thoughts" takes place; the "thought-examiner" exercises an influence; "the apparatus causes laughing, crying, cold, trembling, sensations in the body." The vehmgericht causes tensions; the patient feels himself "forced back," "confined," depressed, "in all relations disturbed," he is "excommunicated"; it comes to "criminal oppressions and inquisitions." He is worked on by thoughts; he must do what the voices command, is pressed to certain actions by suggestion. His body is like a machine which is made to speak; his tongue is guided for him; "They loosen the tongue for me, and one must speak, whether one will or not." In the involuntary making of a mistake in writing a word, "the probability of inspiration prevails." The spirits hinder the patient at work; his thoughts are taken out of his head, so that he cannot think anything. Or thoughts are given to him which are not his own; the imputation is made to him as if he imagined himself a king. Then again he is stupefied, hypnotized, put into a magnetic sleep, must give information. A patient was instructed to pull out his hair; "That continues working till I do it," he explained. States of excitement, flow of saliva are caused in the patient; he is secretly examined medically by magnetic influence, made crazy; his whole understanding is being destroyed. With this he feels rays in his lips; the voices penetrate to his bones. A patient addressed a letter to us "concerning spiritualistic conditions," in which he begged for our medical help. It said here:—

"The above-mentioned spiritualistic conditions of my person consist in a real speaking with souls in the inside of my head. Their thought-disturbing influence is imposed on me by the mystical-beings mentioned, in a compulsory way by boring and piercing, continual itching in my head in a way not to be described. I call this ill-usage by souls compulsory, as a man cannot ward off from himself their contravening influences in the inside of his body. This disturbance frequently so severe often passes into a state in which a man does not know at all any longer what he is doing. It appears to me that I am performing an action which is exactly the opposite of what I ought to do. I regret having become a victim of a spiritualistic seizure. Displeasure shown not to wish to speak with souls remains ineffectual. I beg to be allowed to apply with confidence to the hospital in order to be able to hope for final relief in the conditions of disturbed soul."

Besides the auditory and sensory illusions the painful constraint of the patient appears here clearly, which goes as far as the reversal of volitional impulses, further the feeling of morbidity and of the need for help, without, however, any clear understanding of the real character of the malady.

Exaltation.—In nearly half of the cases there are also exalted ideas, sometimes appearing at the beginning, sometimes first at a later period. The patients are not the children of their parents, they are of noble birth, related to the Kaiser, son of the Emperor Nikolas, daughter of the Grand Duchess, of the King of the Suabians, "put in the world by the Grand Duke by command of the Kaiser," have a claim to the throne of Bavaria; a patient asserted that he was 135 years old and had been a volunteer with a red uniform for one year in Russia. Female patients are a former queen, Countess Salm, Baroness von Lichtenstein. The Emperor Frederick has visited them, made their son minister; the Duke of Coburg has given them lottery-tickets; they are going to the Grand Duke and to the Kaiser at Berlin, and are waiting for the carriage which is to fetch them. Other patients have got an inheritance from America, millions, several billions are deposited for them; they are supported by rich people, do not need to work any more; a female patient thought that her husband had renounced seven millions in order to be able to marry her. Others again have made great inventions, built the dirigible air-balloon, possess currents with which they influence other people, can see into the sun, know what will happen next day, are "Dr of Industry," sinless. A patient connected a dissolution of the Reichstag with a letter written by him to the Emperor and thought he found an allusion in the words of the Bible, "The city lieth foursquare" to his town, Mannheim; a female patient asserted that she had been operated on and had got a rectum "of silver foam." Secret relations to persons of the other sex are very frequent. The patient is "thrown together" with highly-placed persons at night, hears the voice of his *fiancée* who invites him to sexual intercourse; the Empress is presented to him "with charming speeches." Female patients recognize in some man or other their disguised *fiancé*, to whom they give themselves without hesitation, and whom they love "with their whole heart"; it is the Baron "Josa von Bolza." They were married very many years ago to Prince William; the Prince Regent will bring them to the throne; the physician is their Prince Consort.

Consciousness seems unclouded during the whole course

of the disease.　So far as delusions do not come into account, the patients are permanently clear about their place of residence, the reckoning of time, the persons in their surroundings and their situation in general.

Mood is very variously coloured.　At first the patients are usually depressed, suspicious, irritable, quarrelsome, at times very excited, inclined to immoderate outbursts of abuse and even to deeds of violence ; some make impulsive attempts at suicide, throw themselves into water, or out at the window.　Later the patients become as a rule duller and more indifferent, even though occasionally they may still become very violent.　Many patients exhibit a cheerful, self-conscious mood, make all sorts of jokes, laugh and simper. Onanism is not rare.

Fig. 31.
Stopper for nose of a paranoid patient.

The **Activities** of the patients are partly influenced by their delusions.　They complain to the police about the persecutions, bring their complaint before the court, write innumerable letters to the authorities, compose comprehensive documents, ask for testimonials, health certificates ; a woman went to the court in order to be present at her trial for divorce which she thought was taking place there.　Other patients search through the house for persecutors, stop up the keyholes, abruptly leave the house to wander about without a plan, cease working.　A patient asked the supposed father of his child to pay him board, and locked his wife out of the house.　A woman wanted to kill her husband and children ; a man beat his wife on her head with a hammer.　The patients try to protect themselves from the voices by stopping up their ears ; a patient had a stopper for his nose made with fine holes for breathing, which is reproduced in Fig. 31, in order in this way to prevent the injection of saliva and the drawing out of blood.

The patients try to keep off from themselves hostile poisoned arrows and flashes of light by large screens and masks.　A patient surrounded his whole bed with wires on which he hung up in great number phallic amulets.　Merklin has described a patient who for his protection wore armour made of old metalware, which weighed twelve kilograms. Another had himself limited the movements of his arms by a leather-belt with loops in order to be able to resist the impulse to scratch his face, an impulse which was caused by his enemies. Many patients try to protect themselves from the influences by peculiar gestures, defensive movements, definite, often very intricate, attitudes, low continual repetition of certain words. Others apply to the public, vent their anger by means of advertisements in the newspapers, wall posters, open letters, pamphlets,[1] or they undertake some or other very conspicuous course of action in order to attract general attention to their situation. The patients often hope to be able to withdraw themselves from the persecutions by frequent change of situation and dwelling-place. A patient crossed the French frontier in order to see if the currents could reach him there also; when he had convinced himself that they could, all he wished for further, was to go across the sea, although on account of the cable he cherished little hope of escaping in this way; should this means also fail, he was determined to kill himself.

Conduct.—The general conduct of life of the patients is invariably influenced to a considerable degree by their malady. Many are impelled to enter the path of crime (theft, indecent assault) or vagrancy; they wander restlessly about, are not capable of any regular work, neglect themselves and come down in the world. Others whose lives are better protected, can keep themselves, it is true, for a longer time in freedom without too far overstepping the bounds of decorum, but still show some or other of the peculiarities which are known to us as accompanying phenomena of dementia præcox, catalepsy, echolalia, echopraxis, frequent negativism, but above everything mannerisms and impulsive actions.

The patients are often inaccessible, repellent, mute, refuse the visits of their nearest relatives; "that's got no aim." They answer questions with counter-questions, with the remark that one knows already everything oneself, curtly deny all morbid phenomena, do not enter into any conversation, do not associate with anyone, hide themselves away under the cover, refuse food or at least special kinds of food, do not shake hands; "that's of no use." Other patients exhibit a peculiar, affected behaviour, kneel the whole night through, laugh without occasion, spit round about themselves, have a different reckoning of time, fast on Sunday because it is Friday, suddenly cut off their hair, smash panes of glass, throw the dishes about the room. Many patients are restless at night, carry on loud soliloquies, use violent language about

---

[1] Wollny, Über Telepathie, 1888; Sammlung von Aktenstücken, 1888; Teffer, Uber die Tatsache des psycho-sexualen Kontaktes oder die actio in Distans. 1891; Schreber, Denkwürdigkeiten eines Nervenkranken, 1903.

the persecutions, sing songs because it occurs to them to do so.

Conversation.—Very commonly the conversation of the patients bears a peculiar stamp. The manner of speech is frequently affected, sought-out High German, interspersed with foreign words, unusual turns of speech, odd expressions. Many patients are very loquacious, and in a longer conversation produce a veritable throng of incomprehensible and unconnected utterances, although they are able to give quite clear and reasonable information if they are asked definite questions. Neologisms play a great part, especially in the description of the manifold persecutions. The patients are "ilisiert," "tupiert," "desanimiert," "anstimuliert," gone to sleep, weakened, revenged, jeered at; "impulse is placed on in-

Specimen of writing 5.   Writing of a paranoid patient.

stinct"; everything is placed full of "Isi," bepowdered with "turmalin," the house is "verdreieidigt." They are tormented by "Hineinzähmen," "Befeinigen," by "Stigmatisie and Hypnotisie," by "Introchieen," "Veneriepocken"; they are in an "epileptic Bengalese convict-prison." A patient spoke of "steel-chip-pin-sausages" and called his persecutors "electric assassin-homicide-rivercommissionbusiness-stinking he-goats."

Writing.—The documents also which are sometimes very numerous and monotonous, exhibit in their singular flourishes and their often scarcely intelligible spelling the most remarkable derailments of the movements of expression. I insert here two specimens of writing of a shoemaker, which were written at an interval of seven months. He sought out in the newspaper all possible expressions from foreign languages, and wove them in with a meaning invented by himself in his decree as "heavenly physician, astronomer and President Lichtenstern." In the second there are the words "Fidelis Syphilis," which he explained as, "Thus shall it happen." The change in the character of the writing from pretentious self-consciousness to stiff eccentricity is very characteristic.

In the **Further Course** of the disease the specially striking disorders very gradually disappear to a certain extent. The patients become more accessible, quieter, complain less about the persecutions, possibly even begin to occupy themselves, though they may perhaps refuse regular work, because they are not paid, or are not obliged to work. Some patients become quite useful and eager workers. But along with that the hallucinations and delusions continue, with-

Specimen of writing 6. Writing of the same patient seven months later.

out being corrected in any way; they only lose more and more their power over the actions of the patients. We may, therefore, contrast the terminal states which develop here as *hallucinatory* or *paranoid weak-mindedness* with the forms of mental decline hitherto characterized. The hallucinations persist but the patient "no longer pays so much attention to them," only speaks of them if he is asked explicitly about them, or even then says that he has already for some time heard nothing more, the last time was a few days ago. He also possibly allows that he has been ill, that it was a case of congestion, of nervousness, but yet he scarcely ever acquires a clear understanding of the character of the morbid phenomena. Meanwhile he learns to come to terms with them, does not let himself be influenced by them any more. A patient who still occasionally heard abusive voices while he worked outside as a painter, it is true, asked anyone he met, "What did you say?", but was at once reassured when he was told that no one was speaking, and he then knew that

it was again a case of "voices." Often the voices are heard
at times more distinctly and still control the patient temporarily till quietness is again restored. This kind of patient
occasionally speaks in terms of the most violent abuse, but is

Fig. 32.
Paranoid patient with ornaments.

shortly afterwards completely
accessible and up to a certain
point intelligent. Such attacks
occur especially at night, so
that the patients then become
very disturbing to their neighbours, while during the day
they scarcely show any deviation from normal conduct.

· In about 20-25 per cent. of
the cases temporary or permanent hallucinations without
further working up form the
only striking residuum of the
disease which has been under-
gone. In the remaining cases
there are still preserved a
greater or less number of delusions, the significance of which,
however, in the psychic life of
the patients gradually disappears more and more. They
do not speak much about them
on their own initiative or they
mention them without emphasis like other indifferent subjects and do not become excited
about them any more. Many

patients still hand in from time to time documents with
monotonous repetition of their former complaints and claims,
possibly even still fall into excitement if one investigates
their delusions, but accustom themselves to some or other
regular employment. While the expression of their exalted
ideas can still be recognized in their peculiar adornment,
as in the patient pictured in Fig. 32, they yet adapt
themselves in other matters without resistance to the daily
routine of institution life. The "rex totius mundi" occupies
himself with work in the garden, the "Lord God" with carrying wood, the "Bride of Christ" with sewing and darning.
Of course this change always goes alongside of a blunting of
the emotions. The patients have become more indifferent;
the circle of their interests, wishes, hopes, has narrowed itself

considerably; their mental activity and their endeavour are extinguished. At the same time all sorts of traces of the former volitional disorders may still be preserved, singularities in behaviour and especially in speech.

The form here described seems to be just about as frequent, as the former. Temporary disappearance of all morbid symptoms might occur once in a while quite exceptionally. *Seizures* were observed in 5 per cent. of the cases. Here also accordingly the whole history of the disease is unfavourable; the course is slowly progressive. To the male sex belonged 53 per cent. of my patients, a proportion that possibly is explained by the fact that in Heidelberg numerous vagrants and prisoners from the neighbouring convict prisons were admitted, who with special frequency fall ill in the way indicated here.

Causes.—About the cause of this remarkable process only hypotheses can be made. It might be that we have here to do with a form which develops specially slowly, and which for many years before the onset of the more striking morbid phenomena brings about changes in the psychic life, such as must lead to the path of the vagrant and of the criminal. For this view the fact would also speak, that apparently only 12 per cent. of our patients at the beginning of the malady had not yet passed their twenty-fifth year; perhaps we would frequently have to place the beginning of the morbid change much earlier than usually happens according to the customary view of it. On the other hand it cannot be denied that clearly the influences of imprisonment and of the workhouse are specially suited to produce paranoid conditions. We may therefore look at it somewhat in this way, that we have here to do with an unusually slow development of the morbid process, which makes it possible for the patient for a long time still to continue to live as an apparently healthy individual, while yet at the same time the increased difficulty in the struggle for existence, which results from the disorder, and the unfavourable influences of life favour the development of paranoid trains of thought.

CONFUSIONAL SPEECH DEMENTIA.

A last very peculiar group of cases, the discussion of which has to be interpolated here, is formed by the patients with confusion of speech. These are cases of disease the *development* and *course* of which correspond in general to those of dementia præcox. On the other hand the *issue* is divergent. It consists in a terminal state, which is essentially

M

characterized by an unusually striking disorder of expression in speech with relatively little impairment of the remaining psychic activities. If one will, one may therefore, relying on Bleuler's nomenclature, speak of a " schizophasia."

Commencement.—Sometimes a gradual failing with restlessness and silly actions, sometimes a moody condition with irritating hallucinations, ideas of persecution and serious attempts at suicide forms the beginning. Often the malady is developed in short attacks, between which there are remissions of considerable extent and lasting for years. Some patients sink to vagrants; one became a crier at market stalls. But by degrees, now and then apparently within a fairly short time, the extremely remarkable morbid symptom is developed, which characterizes these patients above everything, confusion of speech.

General Features.—Perception and memory usually show no considerable disorder, as far as can be judged from the utterances of the patients; in any case the patients are clear about their place of abode, also about time relations, recognize quite correctly the people in their surroundings, even though they often give them wonderful names to which they usually adhere. Auditory hallucinations appear still to persist, but play no recognizable part in the psychic life of the patients and are not further worked up. Indications also of delusions appear, ideas of persecution, complaints about influences at night, " interpolations," and along with these there are exalted ideas. All these delusions are, however, extraordinarily vague, are only produced occasionally in often changing, often half-jocular, form, and acquire no influence over the rest of thought and activity. The patients are mentally active, accessible, show interest in their surroundings, often also follow the events of the day quite well.

Mood is invariably exalted, self-conscious, at times irritable, usually pleasant; the patients are lively, inclined to jokes and to little harmless tricks. Conduct and outward behaviour are reasonable, sometimes a little affected, submissive or whimsical; the patients have the tendency to adopt all sorts of little peculiarities from which they are only with difficulty dissuaded. At the same time they are as a rule very useful, diligent and clever workers, who occupy themselves without assistance, but like to go their own way, ward off every interference in their doings, will not work with others, for the most part fulfil their obligations with great carefulness, but probably also once in a while do something quite nonsensical. In this way they usually fit in without difficulty in the life of the institution and make for themselves there a modest sphere of work, without giving utterance to more ambitious desires.

Speech.—All the patients show a certain flow of talk which certainly only expresses itself in conversation, here and there perhaps also in soliloquies. As soon as they are addressed, they frequently answer with great vivacity and immediately take up the attitude of a lecturer. To simple questions put with emphasis they generally give a short and suitable answer. Or perhaps that throng of disconnected utterances, which was described before, begins immediately, or at most after the first still tolerably intelligible sentences. It is produced in flowing speech and with a certain satisfaction on the part of the patient. These utterances are mostly quite *unintelligible* and are richly interspersed with speech *derailments* and *neologisms*. Often the current can only be brought to a standstill by the interference of the questioner and can again be immediately put in motion by renewed questioning. Sometimes it is possible from the behaviour of the patient and from detached, less nonsensical parts of the talk, to make at least very vague guesses what thoughts he wishes perhaps to express, stories of long ago, complaints, boasting, taunts, but all hidden in the most bewildering phrases which abruptly digress into the most remote domains of thought.

An example of such utterances is given in the following letter :—

"The sentimental vocation of the Welschneureuther citizens requires above everything that after the sublime birthday festival of his Majesty the illustrious King William Charles, all his spiritual powers should be collected in order to do justice to their pastoral intercession in the Lord. So forty respected stormpatriots in view of the repeal of the statutes of the University of Erlangen have to-day taken it upon them to confirm as first retrospective negative in analogical-patriotic sense. To place at the most gracious disposition of his Majesty the Art. 1 of the Welschneureuther constitution, consisting in combustible available war-material, further most obediently to stop the most notorious dealings as intercourse with cattle, sheep and turkeys. Now in order that the sublime royal company cannot be subjected to any competition from the neighbouring states in transportable tempers all to be recommended to indulgence, we swear by the profit of enhanced merchandise only to serve each alone, only then to break off a consequence of the balance of the nineteenth century to be drawn periodically and mechanically, when we shall be able to be expectantly deceived in our opinions towards our august ruler and regarded as a useful adviser of a healthy antiquarian museum and so on."

On the whole the construction of the sentences here is to a certain degree preserved so that this drivel might perchance make the impression of internal connection, if it were read inattentively or by anyone who had imperfect understanding of the language. On more exact inspection there is certainly no longer any question of that.

Peculiarity of this Form.—It might be supposed that in the form of disease outlined it was only a case of drivelling dementia of a specially high degree ; there also incoherent, confused talk with neologisms and nonsensical phrases come to the front. But what distinguishes our patients here, is the sense and reasonableness in their *behaviour* and in their *actions,* which compels us to the assumption that this is a case not so much of a severe disorder of thought but much rather of an interruption of the connections between train of thought and expression in speech. In any case we have to do with an unusual restriction of the volitional disorder to a narrowly limited territory of volitional activity, that of expression in speech, in which it at the same time reaches a quite peculiar extent. Perhaps this limitation of the phenomena, which is certainly not quite strict, is conditioned by a special site of the morbid process similar to what we have seen in the atypical paralysis, still the possibility should probably also not be left out of account, that we have here before us a peculiar form of disease which is indeed related to dementia præcox but is yet not essentially the same.

The severity, with which the phenomenon of confusion of speech appears, is subjected to great fluctuation. Many patients are usually able to express themselves at first quite intelligibly, but fall into their nonsensical talk as soon as one speaks for a longer time with them or when they become excited. Further, periods are frequently noticed which recur with approximate periodicity, in which the patients are more ill-tempered or excited, and then become much more easily confused in speech ; it is exactly this peculiarity which completely corresponds with the observations in the other terminal states of dementia præcox. But lastly a state of confusion of speech may again disappear even after existing for many years, till only slight traces remain noticeable during excitement. That, for example, was the case of the patient from whom the letter given above originated ; he applied later in a quite correct way for a post. At the same time there is here certainly no question of real recovery. Lack of insight into their morbid state and lack of judgment, restlessness and aimlessness in work, a tendency to use high-sounding phrases, and superficiality of the emotions remain behind even in favourable cases.

CHAPTER VI.

COURSE AND REMISSIONS.

The general course of dementia præcox is very variable. On the one hand there are cases which very slowly and insidiously bring about a change in the personality, outwardly not specially striking but nevertheless very profound. On the other hand the malady may without noticeable prodromata suddenly break out, and already within a few weeks or months give rise to a serious and incurable psychic decline. In the majority of cases with a distinctly marked commencement a certain terminal state with unmistakable symptoms of weak-mindedness is usually reached at latest in the course of about two to three years. One must always be prepared for acute exacerbations of the disease leading to a lasting aggravation of the whole condition. Not altogether infrequently the true significance of a change in the personality lasting for decades is first cleared up, by the unexpected appearance of more violent morbid phenomena, in the sense of dementia præcox.

The fact is of great significance that the course of the disease, as we have seen, is frequently interrupted by more or less complete remissions of the morbid phenomena ; the duration of these may amount to a few days or weeks, but also to years and even decades, and then give way to a fresh exacerbation with terminal dementia. Evensen saw a patient have a relapse after thirty-three years. Pfersdorff[1] established improvement for the duration of two to ten years twenty-three times in one hundred and fifty cases (15 per cent.) ; I myself found real improvement in 26 per cent. of my cases, when that of the duration of a few months was also taken into account. It has been already mentioned that such improvement is to be expected most frequently in the forms which begin with excitement, and is almost entirely absent in paranoid forms of the disease as also in simple silly dementia; one is reminded here of similar experiences in paralysis, in which the expansive forms also exhibit frequent and considerable improvement while demented paralysis rarely does and, if it does, the improve-

---

[1] Pfersdorff, Zeitschr. f. klinische Medizin lv. 1904.

ment is only slight. Among women improvement seems to be rather more frequent than among men.

The **Beginning** of the improvement takes place as a rule very gradually. The excited patients become quiet; the stuporous more accessible and less constrained; delusions and hallucinations become less vivid; the need for occupation and for the taking up again of former relationships becomes active. At the same time sleep, appetite, and body-weight usually improve considerably. But astonishing improvement may appear quite suddenly; it then for the most part certainly does not last long. We find the patient, who up till then appeared to be quite confused in his aimless activity or his hopeless degradation, all at once quiet and reasonable in every way. He knows time and place and the people round about him, remembers all that has happened, even his own nonsensical actions, admits that he is ill, writes a connected and sensible letter to his relatives. It is true that a certain constraint of manner, a peculiarly exalted or embarrassed mood and a lack of a really clear understanding of the morbid phenomena as a whole will always be found on more accurate examination.

The **Degree** of improvement reached is very different in individual cases. Among those here worked up by myself there were 127 patients who ultimately became demented, in whom such a degree of improvement occurred, that a return to home life was possible; in eight further cases which exhibited a periodic course, such improvement occurred even very frequently. In these latter cases, however, there existed in the intervals a distinct psychic weakness gradually increasing, which for the most part bore the stamp of simple emotional dulness and great poverty of thought, but was occasionally accompanied by slight, cheerful excitement, also perhaps by isolated hallucinations and delusions. That there was a state of even approximate health in the intervals was, however, quite out of the question.

Duration.—Leaving these peculiar instances out of account, cases of improvement may be grouped according to their duration in the following way, if in the few patients whose state improved several times we consider only the longest period of such improvement :—

No. of years	1	2	3	4	5	6	7	8	9	10	12	13	14	15	16	29
No. of cases with periods of impt.	21	28	20	14	14	4	6	3	2	5	3	1	2	2	1	1

In the great majority of cases therefore the periods of improvement do not last longer than three years. Among those here noted it was stated sixteen times without reservation that the patients had been completely well. The duration amounted in 3 cases to one year, in 2 to two years, in 4 to three years, in 2 to five years, in 2 to six years, and 1 to four, 1 to seven, and 1 to twenty-nine years. In seven further cases the patients were described as "quiet," "orderly," "not attracting attention," and were at least in a position to earn their own living again without difficulty; it was a case here of periods of improvement lasting two to three years, 1 of four years, and 1 of twelve years. There were also two cases in which the patients were described as well, but talkative and irritable; in one of these cases, in which already two periods of improvement of several years' duration had preceded, the relapse leading to terminal dementia only occurred after fifteen years. In thirty cases the patients took up their work again as before, but appeared quiet and depressed, or timid and anxious, possibly also at times excited. One of these patients passed an examination well in the interval which lasted nearly three years. The duration of the improvement fluctuated for the most part between one and ten years; it amounted in about half of the cases to over two years; among these there were cases each of seven, eight, nine, ten, thirteen, and sixteen years.

In twenty-six further cases there was to be noted an essential improvement of the condition but without the complete disappearance of all morbid phenomena; here there were usually fairly short intervals which in half of the cases lasted less than two years. There were also ten cases in which after the disappearance of the more striking morbid symptoms there remained a distinct degree of psychic weakness, especially emotional dulness and lack of judgment; in seven of these cases the improvement did not exceed three ye͏͏͏͏. In a group of thirteen cases there remained ͏͏ restlessness and irritability with a tendency to passing of excitement; the duration of this state, till a fresh ou͏͏ occurred, amounted nine times to over three years, five times to ten years and over. Perhaps there might be added here five cases, in which the patients during the period of improvement led a restless life and became vagrants; in only one of these did the relapse follow in less than three years.

In the cases which still remain, from which ten must be deducted, about which no sufficient information was forthcoming, the morbid phenomena were even in the intervals still more severe. Some of these patients were indeed quiet, but wholly unoccupied and stayed a great deal in bed; others still gave utterance to delusions or suffered from hallucinations;

strictly they ought not to be counted with those who had periods of essential improvement at all. Leaving them aside, we come to the conclusion, that 12·6 per cent. of the improvements bore the stamp of complete recovery, which, however, only seldom lasted longer than three to six years. Among all the cases ultimately leading to dementia the proportion of these periods of improvement resembling recovery only amounted to about 2·6 per cent., or in a somewhat wider acceptation to 4·1 per cent. If we take all those cases together who were able to live in freedom without difficulty, and to earn their living, the proportion would rise to 13·3 per cent., and it would mount to about 17 per cent., if those patients were also counted, who, it is true, have experienced a distinct change of their personality, but still are to a certain extent able to live in freedom. The remainder, without regard to the cases which were not sufficiently elucidated, consists of those patients who indeed did not require further institutional care, but still on account of remaining disorders were not able to manage without special care.

When the patients again fall ill, it is frequently in the same form as the first time, but sometimes it takes one of the other forms described above. Indeed this alternation of clinical forms, which is occasionally noticed,—depression, excitement, stupor, paranoid states, is, as in manic-depressive insanity, an important proof of their inner connection. The disorders may, according to the kind of relapse, appear again slowly, acutely or subacutely. Not at all infrequently there is seen, as in the first attack, after the initial improvement a gradual deterioration of the psychic state developing very slowly, till years afterwards more severe morbid phenomena appear.

CHAPTER VII.

ISSUE—TERMINAL STATES.

The consideration of states of improvement is of the greatest importance for the question of general *prognosis*[1] in dementia præcox. According to my former grouping into hebephrenic, catatonic and paranoid forms I had come to the conclusion that in about 8 per cent. of the first and in about 13 per cent. of the second group, recovery appeared to take place, while paranoid forms probably never issue in complete recovery. These statements have been much disputed. The differences of opinion have certainly more to do with the limitation of what is to be regarded as recovery. Meyer found, when he followed their fate, 20 to 25 per cent. of his patients "with catatonic phenomena" so far restored after a few years that they could follow their calling and appear healthy to their neighbours. Räcke, who after three to seven years made enquiries about his cases, found that of 171 catatonics 15·8 per cent. might be regarded as "practically well," a number which does not materially diverge from my statement. Kahlbaum found recovery in one-third of the cases of catatonia. On the other hand Albrecht reports that among his cases of hebephrenia no real cure was observed; in catatonia and in paranoid dementia on the contrary a few cases of recovery occurred. Stern saw recovery in dementia præcox in 3·3 per cent. of his cases; Mattauschek observed recovery in hebephrenia in 2·3 per cent., in his depressive paranoid form in 11·1 per cent., in the catatonic form in 5·5 per cent., in real catatonia in 4 per cent., and in dementia paranoides no recoveries at all. Zendig in his investigations arrived at the view that not a single genuine case of dementia præcox could be regarded as really completely recovered; Zablocka also has taken up this view in his report on 515 cases. Schmidt who had over 455 histories at his disposal, states that in 57·9 per cent. dementia had supervened, in 15·5 per cent. recovery with defect, and in 16·2 per cent. a cure; the remainder had died.

[1] Meyer, Münchener medizin. Wochenschr. 1903, 1369; Räcke, Archiv. f. Psychiatrie xlvii. 1; Mattauschek, Jahrb. f. Psychiatrie, xxx. 69; Schmidt, Zeitschr. f. d. ges. Neurologie u. Psychiatrie vi. 2, 125.

There are various grounds for the contradictory nature of these statements. In the first rank of course the delimitation of dementia præcox comes into consideration. We shall see later that on this point, in spite of the ease with which the great majority of the cases can be recognized, there is still great uncertainty. This is true in regard chiefly to the placing of the paranoid forms which are reckoned with dementia præcox sometimes to a greater, sometimes to a smaller, extent, as also in regard to cases in advanced age in which likewise the arrangement in proper order in our morbid history may be variously handled. As in general the widening of the limits in both directions increases the number of cases which are prognostically unfavourable, there are here some causes for the variation of the figures got for recovery.

Further difficulties arise from the varied delimitation towards the domain of amentia[1] and of manic-depressive insanity. The cause of that lies in the importance, sometimes greater, sometimes less, which is attributed to the appearance of the so-called "catatonic" morbid symptoms about the extent of which, moreover, opinions are likewise varied. In any case there still exists to-day to a not inconsiderable extent the possibility of cases of amentia and of manic-depressive insanity being wrongly attributed to dementia præcox and vice versa; the prognosis of the disease will accordingly be more favourable or more unfavourable.

In this uncertainty about the delimitation the statements of different observers can in the first place not be compared at all, not even the diagnoses of the same investigator at different periods of time separated by a number of years. But, even if this difficulty did not exist, we should further have first to agree about the idea of *cure*. To begin with, the degree of recovery must be taken into account. Meyer evidently does not make the very strictest claims, and Räcke speaks frankly of "practical" cures. But in dementia præcox in a considerable number of cases all the more striking morbid phenomena may disappear, while less important changes of the psychic personality remain, which for the discharging of the duties of life have no importance, but are perceptible to the careful observer, who need not always be a relative. As the most manifold transitions exist between complete disappearance of all the disorders and these cases of "recovery with defect," the delimitation of recovery in the strictest sense is to a certain extent arbitrary, but just as much so also the determination, where "practical" cure passes into distinct psychic decline. On this account also the figures of

---

[1] See note on p. 275.

different investigators will of necessity diverge from one another. Further also there is the possibility that in certain circumstances slight peculiarities which were already present before the patient fell ill, but which had remained unnoticed, or which are dependent on other conditions, may be wrongly regarded as consequences of dementia præcox.

But lastly, attention must be directed to improvement with later relapse, which has already been treated in detail. As improvement, which resembles recovery, may certainly persist far longer than a decade, we shall be able to pronounce a final judgment about the issue of an apparently cured case only after a very long time, and must even after ten or twenty years make up our minds to having few cases verified. In the majority of the researches, hitherto communicated, the time which has passed since the commencement of the improvement is much too short for the figures to give now a final decision on the prognosis of dementia præcox. Meyer, indeed, has taken up the standpoint that in relapses after a considerable time we have to do with fresh attacks of the disease and thus are quite justified in speaking of recoveries. It might, however, considering the many gradations in the length of the intervals, and in the severity of the slighter morbid symptoms which continue during their course, be quite impossible .to determine the point when we no longer have to do with a flaring up of the morbid process which has been so long at a standstill, but with a really fresh attack of the disease. Later we shall, moreover, learn still other grounds which give evidence of an inner connection between attacks which are similar to each other though separated by considerable intervals of time.

It is the difficulties here explained in detail which cause me for the moment to refrain from laying down new values for the prospects of cure in dementia præcox. In any case for a very considerable number of apparently cured cases it will not be possible to bring forward now with any certainty the objection that it was a case of mistaken diagnosis or of temporary improvement which later was followed by relapse. On the other hand it will not be possible at the outset to deny the possibility of complete and lasting cure in dementia præcox. If a morbid process can remain quiescent for twenty-nine years, as in one of the cases observed by myself, it will probably be able also to attain to a complete cure. Still, the severe relapses after comparatively long and perfectly free intervals must suggest the thought that, as in paralysis, we have often to do only with a standstill or with extremely slow progress, but not with a real termination of the morbid process. The experience, is, however, worthy of notice, that even among the cases which terminate unfavourably, which form the foundation of my clinical statements, many forms in a third of the cases, indeed in more than half, exhibit marked improvement, but which gives way sooner or later to a relapse. As the frequency of essential improvement in any other disease could scarcely be much greater, it may reasonably be thought that the cases terminating unfavourably, which I selected, on the whole represent the general behaviour of dementia præcox. Further researches into extensive series of cases observed carefully throughout decades must show how far the view, which is gaining in probability for myself, is right, that lasting and really complete cures of dementia præcox, though they may perhaps occur, still in any case are rarities.

An almost immeasurable series of intermediate steps leads from cure in the strictest sense to the most profound dementia. According to my former statements 17 per cent. of the hebephrenic and 27 per cent. of the catatonic form seemed to me to issue in a moderate degree of weak-mindedness, while profound dementia occurred in the former in 75 per cent. of the cases, in the latter in 59 per cent. Among other observers Zablocka found for hebephrenia in 58 per cent. of the cases slight, in 21 per cent. medium, in 21 per cent. high grade dementia ; the corresponding values for catatonia were 58 per cent., 15 per cent. and 27 per cent. Mattauschek reports for hebephrenia over 9·3 per cent. recoveries with defect, 20·9 per cent. dementia of the first grade, 67·4 per cent. dementia of severer degree. For his "depressive paranoid" cases the figures amount to 11·1 per cent., 24·1 per cent., and 53·7 per cent.; for his "catatonic forms" 13·8 per cent., 25 per cent., 55·5 per cent.; in catatonia 12 per cent., 20 per cent., and 64 per cent. Albrecht found recovery with defect in hebephrenics in 12·5 per cent., simple dementia in 27 per cent., high grade dementia of different kinds in 60 per cent. of the cases; for catatonia the results were in 24 per cent. of the cases simple, in 50 per cent. severe dementia. Stern established as issue in dementia præcox in 36·7 per cent. slight, in 18·3 per cent. medium, and in 41·7 per cent. severe dementia. Evensen states that of his hebephrenics 5 per cent. remained independent, 25 per cent. at least still capable of work, and 70 per cent. profoundly demented; among the catatonics only 50 per cent. became quite insane. I have invariably seen the paranoid cases issue in states of weak-mindedness, which in about half of the cases were of slighter degree, in the other half of severer degree. Simple weak-mindedness without other more striking morbid phenomena was the result in only 7 per cent. of the cases. Mattauschek notes as terminal states in these forms in 21·1 per cent. of the cases slighter, in 78·9 per cent. severer dementia ; Zablocka in 65 per cent. slight, in 16 per cent. medium, in 29 per cent. profound dementia. Albrecht states that for the most part hallucinatory weak-mindedness was the end of the disease, occasionally also simple dementia, recovery with defect, hallucinatory insanity, or even, as already mentioned, cure.

As can be already recognized from this summary the statements of the individual investigators are at present not at all comparable. To the uncertainty of the diagnosis there have to be added the divergent grouping of the forms and the various judgments of the terminal states. It is indeed in high degree arbitrary how many grades of dementia may be distinguished, and how the individual cases may be distributed among them, especially as their condition may still often experience after a long time all kinds of transformation. The grouping of the terminal states according to the morbid phenomena which principally appear in them, as has already been attempted in the foregoing presentation, perhaps offers a somewhat better prospect of scientific usefulness. Here also the placing of the individual case will doubtless be often uncertain ; still this classification at least brings the terminal states into closer relations to the preceding clinical pictures.

Simple Weak-mindedness.

The first form, ·which from this point of view we may delimit, is simple weak-mindedness without other striking morbid phenomena. The weakness lies, corresponding to the principal points of attack of the disease, specially in the domain of emotion and volition ; to a less degree judgment and still less memory are involved. After the disappearance of the more marked morbid symptoms the patients seem to be clear about time, place, and person, also about their position, and give reasonable and connected information. Hallucinations disappear in the main, especially the voices ; only now and then perhaps " hissing sounds " occur still once in a way, or the patient sometimes hears his name called, but with an effort can get away from it, does not pay attention to it any longer. Recollection of the time of the disease is usually clouded. Still the patient knows that he has heard " inward voices," thought he was in heaven, was anxious. He also states that now his head is not being electrified any longer, that the voices have stopped, and he denies more or less definitely the former delusions; he "won't be a guardian-angel any longer," "can't work any miracles."

Understanding of the significance of the morbid pheno-mena is at the same time often very defective. The patient perhaps admits that he has been confused, has been suffering from his nerves, but considers the illness that he has passed through quite harmless, and himself quite well ; and he does not feel any need of enquiring further about the nature of his disease and its course. Many patients connect their morbid conduct with chance external causes, wrong treat-ment by relatives, life in the institution ; "It was only dissimulation," said a patient. Sometimes perhaps even a few delusions which have arisen during the course of the disease are retained uncorrected, though the patients do not speak of them any longer, and do not let themselves be influenced by them any longer.

Also in other directions a distinct *weakness of judgment* appears as a rule. The patients have become incapable of taking a general view of more complicated relations, of distinguishing the essential from side issues, of foreseeing the consequences of their own or other people's actions. Their circle of ideas appears to be narrowed. Although occasionally still a considerable residuum of knowledge formerly acquired may come to the surface, yet the patients have lost the capability of making use of it, and of working with it, a circumstance which naturally brings about its loss by degrees. The patients therefore lose a great part of their knowledge ; they become impoverished in thought, monotonous in their mental activities. As at the same time their attention is blunted, they have but little inclination or ability to learn anything new, to pursue aims, to carry out a more extended plan. "She has no memory at all when she works," the father of a patient wrote; "He hasn't got enough sense," another reported about his son. In slighter cases, however, acquired proficiency remains fairly well preserved. Many patients play cards or chess well ; others can do arithmetic, draw and write with great perseverance, but are perhaps quite incapable of appreciating corrections, mistakes in spelling, or interpolations properly, or of planning anything themselves.

Mood may be of very various colouring. The lack of deep emotion, however, is the characteristic feature. The patients regard with indifference the events of life, live a day at a time without endeavour, without wishes, without hopes or fears. A patient replied to the question, whether he did not wish to return home, " It is the same, whether I stand about here or there." The relation to their relatives becomes cool, sometimes directly hostile; former interests are weakened or extinguished ; work is accomplished mechanically with. out inward participation. At the same time the patients frequently exhibit depressed, suspicious behaviour, not very accessible, at times irritable and sensitive, occasionally accom. panied by ideas of jealousy. They must " be treated with love and consideration," as one of the patients put it. Other patients are cheerful, untroubled, confiding, erotic; often there is a tendency to laughing and smirking without recognizable cause.

The **Outward Conduct** of the patients is in general reasonable ; only they often exhibit a stiff constrained demeanour or a somewhat odd behaviour, singular clothing, neglect of their person, small peculiarities in speech, gait and movement. One of my physicians noticed a young mason who in placing the stones turned them in a curious way ; it was a patient of our hospital who was " cured with defect." In a few patients there remain indications of automatic obedience. Many patients are quiet, taciturn, constrained, shy, withdraw themselves, avoid people ; they appear obstinate, unresponsive, intractable, do not go any more to church or public-house, always sit on the same chair, stare in front of them. Others on the contrary are childishly intimate, access- ible, docile, but not independent ; others again display signs of slight excitement, grumble, try to get away, are prolix, somewhat incoherent in their talk, over-polite, abusive at times, occasionally perpetrate nonsensical actions, destroy anything, throw their watch into the water-closet, compose confused documents, fall into drinking habits. One of my female patients, who up till then had been a respectable girl, gave birth in a remission of five years' duration after severe catatonic excitement to three illegitimate children, the last of which she smothered by carelessness ; during detention there then occurred a fresh, very violent attack of catatonic excitement which led to simple dementia ; seven years later in the institution she again passed through a severe attack of excitement which passed off rapidly.

Capacity for work is as a rule diminished. Many patients, it is true, are diligent, but cannot be set to every kind of work: " The will to work is perfectly good, but accomplishment is deficient," wrote the relatives of a patient. Sometimes they make very peculiar and useless things. Their previous employment has very frequently become too difficult for them ; they look out for easier work. The former fine mechanician becomes a simple locksmith, the student a copyist, the artisan a day-labourer. There is no question of deliberate endeavour to make good use of or to improve their own condition. They live a day at a time, squander what they earn, take no thought for the future. Some patients absolutely refuse to work, loiter about aimlessly, take walks, stay in bed for days. Not infrequently a very great need for sleep is observed, also considerable appetite, while other patients must always be pressed to eat. "Half nourishment is enough," said a patient. Complaints about headache are frequent.

The degree of development reached by the morbid phenomena which have been described of course varies to a very great extent. In numerous cases the changes are so trifling that they can only be recognized by those in close contact with the patient and only by good observers. The patient has merely become a little quieter and more self-willed, more capricious ; he appears more absent-minded, more indifferent, gives up the execution of more ambitious plans, works more mechanically, but is able to fulfil the usual claims of the day quite well. If one will, one may here speak of a " practical " recovery, although a complete and radical cure of the morbid process has not taken place, as is then proved by occasional fairly severe relapses. But even the more marked forms of this simple weak-mindedness usually exhibit no very striking psychic morbid picture and are often enough regarded from the point of view of moral offence, especially when they have developed slowly. This is seen in those patients who sink in an apparently incomprehensible manner from the position in which birth and breeding had placed them, indeed in certain circumstances to be habitual criminals, vagrants, prostitutes, without the morbid nature of the change which is taking place in them being recognized. This accounts for the frequency with which more marked morbid states are developed in them when after a restless life full of excitement, privation and excesses, loss of freedom brings on them still further severe injury.

HALLUCINATORY WEAK-MINDEDNESS.

Next to simple weak-mindedness there come perhaps those forms of psychic decline, in which as residuum of the disease through which they have passed, besides a more or less severe loss in mental capacity, some hallucinations are still left, which are regarded by the patient himself as morbid phenomena or at least are not further elaborated.

Auditory Hallucinations play the principal part. Some-times only very occasionally, sometimes more frequently, but still always with great fluctuation, they torment the patient; sometimes they occur specially at night. What the voices say frequently consists of fragmentary cries, which are often repeated in the same phrases and are sometimes quite in-different, sometimes mocking, even perhaps nonsensical or incomprehensible, occasionally in a foreign language. Other patients hear question and answer or whole conversations; at the same time noises, murmurings, knockings, are perceived.

The hallucinations of hearing of the patient have mostly a certain connection with his train of thought, though some utterances appear wholly bewildering and unconnected. " I was never wholly free from the idea, that a strange person was interfering in my mental sphere," wrote a patient who at the time had been in a responsible position in life for more than twenty years without any morbid symptom; "Thoughts flash up at times without my seeking them at all." Another patient describes his disorders very vividly who likewise, after passing through an acute attack fifteen years ago, has been continuously diligent in his calling though with much inward difficulty:

"The utterances accompany my own thinking, but in such a way that I always can separate them from it. Sometimes they are mixed with the formation of thought itself; that is then specially tormenting, and the more tormenting the shorter the moment is between my thoughts and the corresponding utterance of the voices. As regards what they say the voices bring professed news about everything possible and impossible, the Emperor, the Crown Prince, their consorts, my superiors and colleagues and their families, relations and friends and also about my chance surroundings. Sometimes I have the impression, as if certain persons, known and unknown, could become aware of my thoughts, were inwardly encountering me in a friendly or hostile manner. As I fear that from such thoughts mania of persecution might arise, I oppose them with all the power of logic."

Here unmistakably it is a case of the same disorders which we have met with so often in the description of the clinical morbid pictures. It is only the *attitude* of the patient towards the hallucinations that has changed, a sign that we have only to do with a limited residuum of the former malady and no longer with a morbid state of the whole personality.

An excellent view of these processes is given by the following notes written by the same patient of what he heard at intervals; among them the questions which were inwardly directed to the voices by the patient are given in parentheses :—

(Why are you speaking in me?) " You may eat blood. A. must laugh at you. Because we are poor blockheads. Asylum. We'll bring

N

you later to an asylum. O my dear genius! Because we are hypochondriacs. I am your poor marmot. We are the mistresses of the German whipping-club. We inhale you." (Why do you torment me?) " Have you a fate! We think the best of you. Taraxacum! Taraxacum! We thrash Dr S.'s bones bloody for he has become surety for you. Because we are frightfully fond of you. What am I to do? We weep laughing tears. We are differently developed. O you my darling little Jesus. Because we ourselves are tormented. Because we morally act perversely. We have christian catholic morality. Every human being must laugh at you. You are mentally ill. Yes, it is so. Because we have to fear your brain grease. O wild sheikh Almagro! Whom one loves, one torments. We have no implements of handicraft. You are in many things an absolute child, an absolute fool! We torment you as moral rapscallions!" (What is your real object?) "We wish to kill you. You have offended divine providence. Our object is morally irrelevant. M. must laugh at you. Our object is your cleansing. But Absalom! We love and hate you. Our object is terrible establishment of women's regiment. We are silly." (Are you human beings or spirits?) "We are human beings, old topswine! O that needs an insane patience! I will show you my last aims. We weep about you. You have been very prudent. We are climbing up Ararat. Now then, little spirits! Little folk, brownies! You are fundamentally insanely deep!" (Shall I get well again?) "Not according to the plan of the women's regiment. Now then, no! For you have the delusion of persecution. We only want to try you. You are not mentally ill. Have you then no idea of your significance? We are moral female anarchists. Yes certainly, in God's counsel. Have you not delirium? For God's sake, you make a note of everything. Haven't you let loose the werewolves at us? Between mountain and deep, deep valley——" (Are you near!) " No, far away. What shall we do contrary to your interests? No, in the middle of your head! "

These notes, which reproduce about the half of what was heard in an hour, let it be seen that the voices answer the questions inwardly addressed to them, though not always immediately. In between are interpolated all possible disconnected remarks and exclamations. In many of these utterances the personal attitude taken up by the voices towards the patient appears distinctly, as we observed it at the height of the disease in connection with ideas of persecution and exaltation. The voices mock, deride, threaten the patient and his friends, reproach him, bewail, praise and admire him; they indicate that they have power over him and dwell as spirits in him. Along with this a marked morbid feeling makes itself noticeable in the phrases about asylum, mental disease, delirium, mania of persecution.

Visual **Hallucinations** usually play a smaller part. Many patients see, especially in sleepless nights, all possible figures, effects of light, or objects appear distorted. Other patients have pictures of individuals forced on them, sometimes with, sometimes without, connection with their other trains of thought. Occasionally also all sorts of bodily dysæsthesiæ are reported, especially oppression in their head and sensations of giddiness.

Mood is mostly depressed. The patients feel themselves tormented, inwardly constrained, hindered in their capacity for work ; they incline often to painful self-observation, make complaints about sleeplessness, digestive disorders, states of anxiety. Many patients learn gradually to come to terms with their troubles in some measure, and by a prudent and regular life and avoidance of greater exertions, excitement and excesses, to preserve their capacity for work. Even in them, however, a quiet, shy, reserved behaviour usually accompanies the loss of self-confidence and independent energy, which results from the continuance of the morbid residua. " My success in controlling my disease I owe principally to my own self-restraint and to taking measures for my state as soon as it becomes intolerable," wrote a patient.

In other cases the damage to the psychic personality goes much deeper, even to the production of marked weak-mindedness. The patients do not correct the hallucinations, but they do not speak about them any longer ; they do not listen to the voices any longer, do not get excited about them ; " that's useless, there's no aim in it." Many patients are probably still irritated temporarily by the " voices of persecution," abuse them, especially at night, stop their ears, speak now and then low to themselves, but between times do not wish to know anything more of them, go on with their work without disturbance. At the same time there is invariably found a greater or less narrowing of interests, a weakening of emotional relations, a loss of volitional activity, often also a repellent, reserved behaviour.

PARANOID WEAK-MINDEDNESS.

Obviously those terminal forms of dementia præcox, in which uncorrected *delusions* continue to exist, injure the psychic life essentially more profoundly than the " hallucinatory weak-mindedness" above described. We met them as the invariable terminal states of "dementia paranoides mitis," but they come under observation here and there as the issue of other forms conjoined with delusions, though perhaps in somewhat divergent form. Above everything it is *ideas of persecution* which are permanently adhered to after the disappearance of the more acute morbid phenomena, mostly in a very monotonous way and without substantial elaboration, but in gradually ever more nonsensical and incoherent

expressions. At the same time the most varied hallucinations also usually play an important part. It is the old
story ; the persecutors are still always there. The patient is
abused, mocked, electrified, stupefied, blinded, plagued by
witches ; by day and by night experiments in physics are
carried out, specious political business, rascally tricks. His
children are being murdered, his money withheld from him,
his throat slit up. Obscene things are said, his nature drawn
off, his semen poured out. The patients " must answer the
voices," must do what they command. On the other hand
they hear voices from God saying that they are Christ, that
they are queens by birth, that they are to get millions. In
course of time the delusions fade somewhat, it is rather better,
the patients say. " Electrification is rather less." At the
same time a certain morbid feeling may appear. The
patients say that they had often suffered from disorders,
had confused thoughts, cannot work properly, are a little
" mentally affected."

About their surroundings and their position in general,
the patients are usually for the most part clear, so far as
delusional occurrences do not play a part. Their train of
thought remains fairly connected and reasonable, but easily
becomes incoherent and confused, as soon as their delusions
are suggested and they fall into excitement.

Mood is morose, often very irritable, more rarely dull or
exalted. At times the patients become threatening, abusive,
violent ; they shut themselves up, indulge in superior irony.
Nevertheless they are often able to occupy themselves with
success and aptitude, though at the same time they like to go
their own way. Slight indications also are often found of the
volitional disorders characteristic of dementia præcox. The
taciturn, thoroughly inaccessible, behaviour of many patients
might not be caused only by their delusions but at least partly
by negativistic action ; in others we observe mannerisms,
smacking with the lips, spitting, repetition of questions
addressed to them, queer ways of expressing themselves,
singular clothing.

DEMENTIA—DRIVELLING, DULL, SILLY, MANNERISTIC, NEGATIVISTIC.

If we try to carry out the classification of the terminal
states according to the special characteristic which is im-
pressed on them by the *permanence* of definite morbid
phenomena from the earlier periods of the disease, we shall
be able to distinguish a series of forms in which sometimes

mental weakness, sometimes emotional dulness, sometimes one of the peculiar volitional disorders more specially dominates the condition. Of course it is never a question here of sharp limitations, as little as in the various courses of the disease previously described. Much rather we shall find again everywhere the fundamental features of dementia præcox, only that here the one peculiarity, there the other, is more strongly represented. Clinical relations to the former morbid pictures exist in so far that in the terminal state only such symptoms are preserved as had already been developed, but they may later even completely disappear. While we therefore have recognized in simple weak-mindedness an issue which signifies a disappearance of all the more striking disorders and therefore in general a milder course of the malady, there remain permanently in the following forms of the psychic decline distinct morbid phenomena in particular domains of the inner life. At the same time a considerable disappearance of the morbid disorders may take place in some or most of the other domains, so that we find besides the more striking characteristics of the terminal state, sometimes only very slight, but sometimes also very deeply-spreading changes in the rest of the psychic personality.

Drivelling Dementia.—If in the "paranoid" terminal states we had to do essentially with a continuance of the delusional morbid processes, the characteristic of drivelling dementia is the general *decay of mental efficiency*. Here also are still found, as a rule, hallucinations and delusions, the senselessness of which distinctly proves the mental weakness. The patients hear the voices of devils, spirits calling, are tormented by senseless telephoning; thoughts are blown into them ; they speak with the voices. They are influenced, bled every evening, have their genitals pulled at, are pressed together, sucked out through a needle, castrated, punctured ; they are beaten on their heads at night with an iron hammer ; they smell blood and corpses. The doctors procure abortion ; the connection between the uterus and the rectum is gone, their flesh is adulterated. Little children are sitting in their neck ; the female sexes have suffered very great want ; there is. quackery going on, subterranean vapour business, silly speculation. The patient is the son of primal force, has a divine calling, is the Lord, suffers for the whole of mankind, is singled out for distinction by the Grand Duke, demands special food, is going to marry. All these delusions are given utterance to without connection and without emphasis, in often changing, always more extraordinary form. Not infrequently a certain morbid feeling exists at the same time. "We're not quite well yet," said a patient; another said, "I used to have the delusion that I was the King of Bavaria, or I was the Lord God; that's just nonsense," while a third declared, "The abuse was in the disease"; again others say that their sense has been taken from them. Or they allege, if they are asked about hallucinations and delusions, that they do not hear so much now, do not pay attention to it, do not take themselves up with these things any more, have forgotten them.

The really characteristic disorder, however, in this form is *incoherence of the train of thought*. The most loquacious patients ever afresh bewilder their hearers by the confusion, and singularity of their utterances and by the senselessness of their associations of ideas. "I am bird black," declared a patient, another, "I am no country," a third, "I am your deceased father," a fourth, "I believe that my father is now born," a fifth, "That he was tuned at the turn of the year." The following are examples of similar utterances already reaching into the domain of confusion of thought and quite similar to conversations in dreams: "I speak with the voices for my welfare elements," "If one may serve after the right, the left must become," "In this custom there are very difficult tasks," "I still hear voices, where does right and the damage sits above." We may, therefore, well assume that it is a case here not only of disorders of the train of thought, but also of disorders of expression in speech. Further, the circumstance, that silly clang-associations and neologisms frequently come under observation is in favour of this view; many patients speak in a self-made language. The loquacity and the richness of vocabulary might point to a relationship with sensory aphasia. Incoherence is usually most in evidence when the patients converse for some time and fall into excitement, while they often answer simple questions quite correctly.

The patients are often not clear about their position and their surroundings. They mistake people, and call them by quite arbitrary names. They are in a "house for a manure king"; they are "there because of an offence to the catholic church," have "a religious affair," "must do business."

Mood is changeable, often self-conscious, silly, cheerful but irritable; it easily comes to violent excitement suddenly exploding. The deeper emotional relations are blunted; the patients do not trouble themselves about their surroundings, remain indifferent when their relatives visit them, show neither interest nor perseverance in work.

Volition.—Here also we invariably meet with manifold

volitional disorders. Some patients exhibit automatic obedience, catalepsy, echophenomena, others are repellent,
unmanageable, at times refuse food, become mute, hide
themselves away in bed, retire if any one approaches them,
force their way out senselessly, speak past the subject, do not
shake hands ; "I can have no more intercourse with you,"
declared a patient ; "It's no use giving a paw," said another.
But most frequent are mannerisms of all sorts, making faces,
singular attitudes, kneeling, affected movements, rhythmical
swaying, running up and down, shaking their heads, scratching,
monotonous gestures, spitting, licking, smacking with their
lips, wiping, screeching, shrill singing, mincing speech, lisping,
speaking in falsetto, whispering, impulsive laughing, obscene
abuse, remarkable hairdressing and garments, peculiar spelling.
Many patients are dirty; many visit the water-closet
innumerable times.

Dull Dementia.—In a further group of terminal states
the *loss of emotional activity* is more striking than anything
else, so that we may here speak of a "dull dementia."
Hallucinations and delusions only play a small part here.
Many patients, it is true, state when asked, that they still
hear the same as before, "filthy things," "the wicked enemy,"
but they do not speak about them any more of their own
accord ; others "have forgotten hearing voices" or only hear
quite indifferent things. Now and then the patients state
that they are being influenced, poisoned, that their veins,
their skulls are burst, their parents beheaded, that at night
there is examination and impropriety, that human flesh is
given to them, that they have intercourse with the Lord God,
but such ideas are not further elaborated and they acquire
no determining influence on the conduct of the patient. The
surroundings are as a rule correctly perceived, though the
patients may have little inclination to account to themselves
for people or events in any way. Much rather they live their
lives dully and without taking any interest, do not trouble
themselves about their relatives, do not reflect about their
position, do not give utterance either to wishes, or hopes
or fears.

Mood.—At the same time the slightly marked colouring
of the background of mood is sometimes more gloomy,
anxious, or lachrymose, sometimes more that of a vacant
cheerfulness with frequent smirking or laughing. But often
without recognizable occasion dull indifference is from time
to time interrupted by violent excitement with confused
abuse and a tendency to sudden destructiveness and even
to serious deeds of violence, of the causes of which the patients

are not able to give any account; he had too much blood, said one patient. These states may recur with a certain regularity.

The **Volitional Expression** of the patients shows very severe disorders. They are for the most part quiet, taciturn, or quite mute, sit about in corners, remain standing wherever they are pushed, do not get out of bed. They do not try to get away; they are prepared to stay where they are, till they are fetched away; they do not plan to begin anything. On the other hand they are often able to do simple work, such as sawing wood, carting, shovelling with great perseverance, if they are put to it. *Rhythmical* actions especially are continued by them, till they come up against some hindrance, at which they then stop, till they are again set going. Attitude and behaviour are sometimes slack and negligent, sometimes stiff and constrained; movements are clumsy, uncouth, awkward. Marked automatic obedience is very frequent; Weygandt[1] was still able to demonstrate it in a case after the disease had lasted for fifty-four years. Further also we often meet with negativistic features. The patients do not look up when they are spoken to, do not answer, stare straight in front of them, do not shake hands, avoid people, every now and then stop working for a few days and refuse food, or they hide away under the bedclothes. Now and then speaking past the subject is observed, or quite unconnected answers are given; a patient replied to the usual greeting, "Respect for religion ought not to be." Lastly, impulsive and manneristic actions are also not lacking, especially in the ever-returning states of excitement. The patients make faces, assume singular positions, make monotonous movements for hours at a time, play with their fingers, strike their own faces, shake hands with the little finger or with the left hand, slide about on the floor, run up and down, rub and wipe things, spit, suddenly cry out, mutter unintelligibly to themselves. They usually quiet down again very quickly and then sink back into the old dulness.

Silly Dementia.—*Impulsiveness* and *weak susceptibility to influence* are the striking characteristics of those terminal states which we class together as "silly dementia"; they form the invariable issue of that clinical type which we formerly delimited under the same name. Hallucinations and delusions are frequently entirely lacking here. On the other hand a considerable degree of weakness of judgment

[1] Weygandt, Centralbl. f. Nervenheilk. u. Psychiatrie, 1904, 615.

invariably exists. The patients have no understanding of the kind or of the extent of their disorder or of their actual position, consider themselves well and able for work, although they perhaps still sometimes suffer from "blocking of thought." They wish to take up their occupation again, do not understand why they are prevented from doing so. About their surroundings and what occurs in their neighbourhood they are quite clear ; they certainly form quite erroneous opinions about details, regard their fellow-patients as well, treat their dreams as real occurrences. They are able to occupy themselves, write letters and petitions usually of a very monotonous kind, sometimes with verbal identity. Their acquired knowledge may be fairly well preserved ; still in time a certain mental impoverishment always appears, as the patients are not able to use what they have learned. At every difficulty, the solution of which requires independent thought, they habitually fail in a surprising manner.

Mood is invariably confident and cheerful, more rarely and only temporarily depressed and lachrymose. But for the most part the patients are easily excited and fall suddenly into lively agitation or into quickly passing outbursts of rage, sometimes with periodic return. The lack of fine feeling is usually very striking ; it makes the patient wholly forgetful of the regard due to his personal dignity as well as to the feelings of the people round him. In the same way foresight in relation to the events of life and to the results of his actions and the ability to carry out any plan consistently are also lacking. His *whole demeanour* bears the stamp of childish thoughtlessness and stupidity. He chats without ceremony about his most delicate affairs, uses disrespectful expressions about his parents and superiors, exposes himself in the most incredible way. He follows sudden fancies without hesitation, is sometimes immediately susceptible to influence, sometimes incomprehensibly obstinate. He fills his time with aimless occupations. "The will is present but I don't bring it together," said a patient. Often a certain restlessness exists which drives the patient to all sorts of foolish actions. He decorates himself in an extraordinary way, grunts, frisks about, howls, plays with dolls, smears everything, makes faces, chats and writes a great deal, composes insipid rhymes, speaks in affected phrases, makes up singular words.

Manneristic Dementia.—In a further form of terminal state which we shall term manneristic dementia, *singular changes in volitional actions* are in the foreground of the clinical picture. For the most part hallucinations and delusions are still present here also. "There are still always enough voices," said a patient. They torment him the whole day, call out "Filthy fellow"; it may come from the telephone, or it is inward speaking, voice annoyance. There are influences at night; there is foul air in his ear. His nature is not pure; torture is being carried on; it is known how that happens, a fatal blow, poisoning of witnesses. Figures descend from heaven; the patient is being murdered by witches, is given the flesh of his burnt relatives to eat. He is burned inwardly, blown to pieces, has five diseases, must die; his heart has been stolen. Other patients are John the Cherusker, Frederick Barbarossa, the German Emperor, wish to be Prince of the world, a statesman. Many patients are quite confused, mistake people, have "no more sense or idea of nothing." Now and then a certain morbid feeling is present. The patients state that they are scattered in their minds, they cannot remember anything, cannot think in their heads, do not recall things as they used to do. Former morbid phenomena are sometimes denied; the patients will have nothing more to do with the voices, "don't speak any foreign language now."

Mood is often exalted, self-conscious, but frequently also peevish and irritable, more rarely dull or lachrymose. The patients smirk and laugh, but at times fall into violent excitement, break out into wanton and obscene abuse, suddenly become violent and destructive.

Their **whole conduct** is dominated by singular impulses, which lead to their carrying out senseless actions, to diminution, derailments, and in the end to the suppression of their volitional utterances; along with that very commonly stereotypies develop. The bearing of the patients is stiff and constrained; their movements are affected, theatrical, often jerky and inelegant. They assume uncomfortable positions, lie on their stomach, on their face, twist themselves together, hold their head, press their hand before their mouth, close their eyes, put out their lips like a snout. They run round in a circle for hours, beat themselves, impulsively touch the handle of the window, dance about, suddenly run through the room, pull their ears, pull at their fellow-patients, devour urine and fæces, bite their nails off, pluck their finger-tips to pieces, sway rhythmically to and fro, spit about them, masturbate, smudge things, make faces. They adorn themselves in an extraordinary way, make singular gestures, affected bows, walk and eat in a manneristic way, shake hands with their thumb or two fingers, smack their lips, and click their tongue. Pictures of these conditions are given in Figs. 33 and 34, which represent a patient on one leg hopping about and another sitting in a distorted attitude.

Speech.—In the speech also of the patients manner-ism makes itself felt in most manifold ways. The patients declaim, preach, speak in a washed-out way, mawkishly, with closed teeth, lisping, in a foreign or self-invented speech, with child-like pro-nunciation and accent; they give unconnected answers, in-dulge in silly puns and clang-associations, odd expressions and neologisms. One patient said he was a wicked world-begetter, another said, "Down there is Hell; she is called Müller"; another spoke of "Witch-begging-rascal-fur-nace." In many patients

Fig. 33. Patient hopping.

automatic obedience can be demonstrated; but negativistic features are much more frequent. Their capability for work is mostly slight, and is usually limited to mechanical activ-ity, copying, knitting, sawing wood, and that kind of thing, even in the most favourable cases.

Negativistic Dementia.—As the last form of decline induced by dementia præ-cox we take into considera-tion negativistic dementia, in which the phenomena of *impulsive resistance* appear in a specially marked way. It is nearly related to the last form, since there just as here varied volitional disorders are usually combined with each other. About hallucinations or delusions little is heard from the patients, probably

Fig 34. Patient in distorted attitude.

for this reason that they are not at all inclined to make statements. Still many patients abuse the voices which "go against the man," close their ears, complain about "the extortion of the extortioner-Bismarck." Others demand

Fig. 35.   Patient continually holding her head.

"their money"; they have no one for a friend, are first doctor, the Christ-child in the manger. The substance of their conversation is mostly confused and incoherent, especially as soon as they fall into excitement; they are not clear about their position, and are without understanding for the occurrences in their surroundings.

Mood is sometimes jocular, but much more frequently irritable, morose, even threatening; besides convulsive laughter furious outbursts of abuse with a tendency to violence occur. At the same time the patients are inaccessible, repellent, taciturn, or absolutely mute, sometimes for years; they look away when spoken to, resist every interference, refuse food, avoid people, try to get away, stand at one particular door in order to rush out as soon as it is opened. They hide their face, creep under the bedcover, sit with their eyes closed, lie down under the bed, do not tolerate any clothes, stand naked or in their shirt beside the bed, or lie on the floor only wrapped in a coverlet. Many patients whisper low, unintelligibly to themselves, become mute as soon as one listens to them; others in walking always go a few steps backwards again. If told to do anything, they do not obey, at most once in a way they answer with a slight shake of the head. "We must not shake hands," declared a patient. The attitude of the patients is usually rigid, constrained, sometimes quite odd, and is for a long time monotonously maintained. An example of this is given in Fig. 35; the patient represented remained continuously in the same attitude. A patient got gangrene from holding his fist clenched.

Besides the negativistic phenomena there are invariably impulsive *actions*, stereotypies and mannerisms as well. The patients throw away their food or their shoes, swallow glass and stones, give utterance to senseless sounds or bestial cries, pull out their hair, jump about with great leaps and suddenly stand still like a monument. They rub their heads keeping time, rock with their body or with their foot, make monotonous movements with their fingers, shake themselves, stamp on the ground, nod, spit. Others lie with the corner of the sheet or their fingers in their mouth, assume singular attitudes, shake hands with the fourth finger, stir up their food, speak lispingly or in a stilted manner, invent a peculiar spelling. Here also the capability for work is always very severely damaged, though many patients can still be trained to simple mechanical work.

PROGNOSTIC INDICATIONS.

At the present time it must still be considered doubtful how far the terminal states here described really represent in individual cases the last period of the development of the disease. For simple weak-mindedness, which signifies a kind of recovery with defect, it is distinctly enlightening and often confirmed by experience that, sooner or later, a fresh exacerbation of the disease may follow and bring about a higher degree and another form of dementia. But also in the remaining forms changes in the condition are often possible, even after a number of years, usually in the sense of *deterioration*. That is especially true of hallucinatory weak-mindedness. Further we see, as described before, paranoid states not infrequently pass later into negativistic or manneristic dementia ; the same might be said of silly dementia which in certain circumstances even after a decade may be essentially changed by the appearance of stupor or of excitement.

Drivelling, dull and manneristic dementia appear to be variable more according to *degree* than according to *kind*. In negativistic dementia, lastly, so long as well-marked negativistic stupor exists, the possibility of considerable improvement is to be reckoned with, which now and then may appear even after the lapse of ten years. Petrén reports the case of a patient who had to be tube-fed for nine years, but who yet after being ill for eleven years was so far restored again that he earned a living for himself and his family as a tailor and only showed still a certain irritability. It appears accordingly that in stupor there are fundamental changes which still after a very long time are capable of *retrogression*. But it is very difficult in individual cases to decide whether such a possibility still exists or not. It appears that in the cases which finally have become incurable, the severity and especially also the promptness of the negativistic reaction to interference relax considerably. This suggests that there is a loosening of the inner harmony between impressions, impulses and volitional actions as we formerly saw it as a fundamental disorder in dementia præcox.

In the remaining forms also of the terminal states the point of time is difficult to determine from which onward the appearance of considerable improvement can no longer be expected. On the whole the prospects will be the more unfavourable the more those peculiarities are developed, which we see in the foreground in the multitude of cases finally uncured. Among them there is especially the loss of emotional activity which characterizes the most severe forms of the disease, those that issue in dull dementia ; with it the connecting link falls away which unites rational action to perception and thought. Furthermore the development of fixed mannerisms and stereotyped movements is apparently to be regarded as an unfavourable sign ; they are a sign that the influence of healthy volitional action and inhibition on activity is no longer strong enough to suppress side-impulses and the tendency to repetition. Of specially bad significance is the appearance of simple rhythmical movements ; they seem only then to occur when through very deep-reaching destruction of the volitional apparatus lower ancestral motor mechanisms acquire a certain independence. Lastly, the states of excitement and moodiness occurring periodically and abruptly are probably also of evil, significance, as they very frequently make their appearance in the incurable terminal states. These also might indicate that the equilibrating mechanisms were disordered, which otherwise make the psychic life to some extent independent of the fluctuations of bodily conditions.

We come therefore to the conclusion that the onset of incurable terminal states is announced chiefly by those disorders which signify the loss of mastery over volitional action, be it that the mainsprings of volition are broken, be it that the mechanisms are destroyed which make systematic co-operation of individual volitional actions possible. I would ascribe much less importance to pure disorders of intellect. They appear in general to be further removed from the point of attack of the morbid process, and therefore not so soon to signify incurable phenomena of decay. Not only may hallucinations and nonsensical delusions be again completely lost, but also incoherence of the train of thought, and indeed even marked confusion of speech. Only then when with continuance of these disorders emotional activity also gradually disappears, is one obliged to consider the hope of equilibrium being restored as very slight.

The prognosis of individual cases is made essentially more difficult by the circumstance that it is not always easy to obtain absolute certainty about the existence of the above-mentioned symptoms. Indifference towards occurrences in the surroundings may also be simulated by negativism or by stupor. Only then when the patients, in spite of complete understanding and without a symptom of negativism, show no further interest at all in their fellow - patients, their relatives or their occupation, and accept quite indifferently threats or contradiction in regard to their delusions, may we conclude that there is a real annihilation of emotional activity. In the same way only the stereotypies which have been retained for long and have become quite rigid, and lastly, only those states of moodiness and excitement, which without external cause return abruptly with approximate regularity, and after very short duration disappear again in the same way, are to be taken into account in judging of the prospect of recovery.

Frequently not without significance also for judging the condition is the behaviour of the *body weight*. As the rising of this in general signifies a disappearance of acute morbid phenomena, it may announce either the beginning of improvement or, on the other hand, the development of a final state of weakness. The decision between these two possibilities is furnished by observation of the psychic behaviour. If the disappearance of the disorders which hitherto have been dominant is combined with a return of emotional activity, accessibility, interest in the surroundings and the relatives, and need for employment, a favourable turn of the course of the disease may be reckoned on. But if the patients in spite of increase of body weight remain incoherent, uninterested, silly, manneristic, inaccessible, the probability is very great that the disease has reached a final and unfavourable conclusion. Whether the loss of the psychic pupillary reaction is of prognostic significance in the individual case, must in the meantime still remain undecided. At any rate there are demented patients enough in whom it is preserved, while in other cases it is already absent in the beginning of the disease. At the same time its disappearance seems to be considerably more frequent in the terminal states. Zablocka states that difference in the pupils also seems to have a certain unfavourable significance.

Lastly, if we put before ourselves the question by what circumstances the *issue* of the disease is determined, obviously the *clinical form* is in the first degree decisive. Räcke thought the prospects of recovery by far the most favourable in what he delimited as the "subacute paranoid forms," considerably more unfavourable in the "depressive," still worse in the "excited-confused" and in the "stuporous" forms. If we go back to our classification, we saw formerly that periods of improvement lasting a considerable time are principally observed in the excited and the catatonic forms, therefore by preference in the forms which have an acute commencement and course, while the simple, silly and paranoid forms of dementia præcox which usually begin insidiously offer far less prospect of material remissions of the morbid phenomena.

With regard to the *final issue* the relations are somewhat different. Slighter degrees of psychic decline are, it is true, likewise fairly frequent in the excited forms, but are also often the issue of depressive forms and of simple progressive dementia ; further we may perhaps also regard hallucinatory weak-mindedness, and at least a part of the paranoid states of weak-mindedness, as relatively favourable issues. On the other hand the catatonic forms, silly dementia, and the first group of the paranoid forms usually have with greater frequency profound psychic weakness as a result. Closer relations between the clinical forms and definite terminal states can scarcely be demonstrated. Yet dull dementia appears to be developed most frequently from silly, simple depressive and excited forms, while negativistic and manneristic states of weak-mindedness constitute the issue specially of the catatonic, the depressive-stuporous and certain paranoid forms. Those forms which begin with silliness are also characterized by it in their terminal states ; incoherence appears to characterize by preference the issue of the states of excitement. Lastly, hallucinatory and paranoid weak-mindedness comes essentially under observation as the conclusion of paranoid forms.

According to Zablocka's statements the appearance of mutism of long duration and of stereotypies indicates the probability of a more profound dementia, and the same may be said of an insidious commencement of the disease. On the other hand Bleuler states that cases with considerable improvement after the first attack of the disease seldom become profoundly demented later. His further statement that acute forms show a greater tendency to very severe terminal states I can thoroughly confirm for catatonic forms, but for states of excitement only, with the limitation that here besides the frequent dull, manneristic or drivelling dementia, the issue in simple weak-mindedness is also very often observed.

Of further influences, which may acquire significance for the issue of the disease, there might be mentioned *predisposition*, while external causes in any case play no decisive part. Bleuler considers those cases more unfavourable in which from childhood up, abnormal qualities have appeared, and Zablocka also thinks that there is in them a stronger tendency to profound dementia. That becomes intelligible, if one assumes that in such cases through an inferior disposition either there exists a lesser power of resistance to the morbid process, or the morbid process itself, developing insidiously from childhood, has already generated those abnormalities. The last view would be supported by Bleuler's statement that inherited weakness does not exercise any influence on the prognosis. On the other hand, Mattauschek reports that dementia præcox has a more unfavourable course among Slavs and Jews than among Germans.

The **Age** of the patients has a decided influence on the course of the disease. The forms which begin in the years of development are by preference states of excitement, especially those with a periodic course, then simple depressive forms, and certainly also insidious dementia (dementia simplex), morbid states which in general tend to have a

O

milder course. Somewhat later silly dementia and the catatonic forms have their greatest frequency, that is, forms which are decidedly to be regarded as severe. Still later, depression with delusions is developed, likewise a form with an unfavourable course predominating. Lastly, in definitely advanced age the paranoid forms appear, which on the one hand lead not so very frequently to the most severe forms of psychic weakness, but on the other hand show very little tendency to essential improvement of the morbid state when it is once developed. It could, therefore, be approximately said that here with advancing age the ability to restore the equilibrium and repair the damage generated by the disease gradually diminishes, but that at the same time the work of destruction appears to spread less deeply.

Sex.—There appear also to be certain relations between sex and the form of the disease. Men have a somewhat larger share in the unfavourable form of silly dementia ; women on the other hand have a greater tendency to paranoid forms, a circumstance which might, generally speaking, be connected with the greater frequency of paranoid morbid states in the period of involution in the female. Women are in a still greater majority in the states of excitement running a periodic course, but here there are not nearly enough statistics to hand ; otherwise one might in these forms beginning in youth think of the influence of the so strongly marked tendency in woman to a periodic course of normal as well as of morbid processes.

The **Time** in which the development of an incurable terminal state is accomplished naturally fluctuates within very wide limits. For one thing the exact commencement of the morbid phenomena can often enough only be determined with great difficulty, as all sorts of insidious changes have already for years been developing imperceptibly. But then, as already detailed, considerable improvement lasting a long time may make the course of the disease extraordinarily slow. Lastly, it is often scarcely possible to mark the point of time, even merely approximately, at which the final stage of dementia is reached. Strictly speaking, one will never be quite certain here, as probably changes in the condition may still appear, and certainly for the most part in a downward direction. In spite of these difficulties so much may perhaps be said that as a rule, if no essential improvement intervenes, in at most two or three years after the appearance of the more striking morbid phenomena a state of weak-mindedness will be developed, which usually changes only slowly and insignificantly. But often enough the unmistakable symptoms of dementia appear already within the first year, indeed even after a few months, though here a prodromal period of considerable length can never be excluded. Albrecht states that of his hebephrenic patients 27 per cent., of his catatonics 19 per cent., reached their terminal state within the first year.

Mortality.—Life is threatened only very slightly by dementia præcox. Kerner on the ground of researches in the institution at Rheinau comes to the conclusion that the mortality of patients with dementia præcox is somewhat greater than that of the healthy population of the same age. Here account must be taken of the fact that the patients in the institution on the one hand are in high degree protected from many of the injuries of life, struggle for existence, alcoholism, syphilis, accidents, and lead a quiet life constantly supervised by medical skill, but that, on the other hand, the confinement, with the small space which it affords for exercise, considerably lowers the tonicity of the body, and that the crowding of people together favours the development of tuberculosis. But of much greater importance is the circumstance, that by the psychic disease itself conditions are created which are fitted to increase the mortality. Dull and negativistic dementia, but especially stuporous states, which often last for years, bring about more or less complete bodily inactivity with depression of the work of lungs and heart and of the whole metabolism; in addition to that the patients by hiding away under the bedcover and obstinate resistance forcibly shut themselves off from the enjoyment of fresh air and often also·take food very irregularly or of an unsuitable kind, or they may even for a long time have to be tube-fed. Other dangers threaten owing to the impossibility of treating suitably, because of restlessness or obstinacy on the part of the patients, bodily suffering caused by chance injuries in states of excitement or by damage which the patients inflict on themselves. The most frightful mutilations of themselves carried out often with incredible rapidity and energy, tearing out of eyes or tongue, self-castration, are occasionally observed in our patients. Also unexpected suicide, especially in the first period of the malady, is not infrequent, and occurs sometimes without any recognizable cause also in patients who for long have been weak-minded and apparently quiet.

But lastly, in certain circumstances the morbid process as such may also lead to death. Occasionally, though seldom, it is observed that in severe states of excitement of long duration a steadily progressive loss of strength gradually makes its appearance, which continues even when the patients become quieter and take abundant nourishment. Finally death ensues with extreme cardiac weakness and great sinking of the temperature without the autopsy showing any perceptible organic disease at all. It is customary to speak here of exhaustion which is thought to be caused by the restlessness, the profound disorder of sleep and the irregular taking of nourishment. But as further on we must assume a cause which generates all those disorders, the possibility must also be reckoned with, that the same cause directly threatens life perhaps by far-reaching injury to the body mechanisms. Less uncertain is the causation of death by the morbid process itself in those somewhat frequent cases, in which the death of the patients results at the height of severe excitement, accompanied by phenomena of cerebral irritation with convulsions or paralyses, sometimes with almost continuous seizures. According to the investigations of Reichhardt it has become probable that here we have to do with an acute "cerebral œdema," with rapid changes of the brain which cause an enlargement of volume and therewith the appearance of fatal cerebral pressure. Now and then cases of sudden death [1] occur in stupor or in the terminal states, sometimes in a catatonic attack, sometimes without any striking phenomena Fankhauser found in some cases of the last kind status lymphaticus.

[1] Giannelli, Rivista di patologia nervosa e mentale xiii. 4.

CHAPTER VIII.

MORBID ANATOMY.

The morbid anatomy [1] of dementia præcox does not show macroscopically any striking changes of the cranial contents ; only occasional thickening and œdema of the pia are reported, the latter evidently a result of agonal processes. On the other hand, it has been shown that in the cortex we have to do with severe and widespread disease of the *nerve-tissue.* In some cases which succumbed in a condition of acute delirium and which are classed by him as catatonia, Alzheimer has described deep-spreading changes in the cortical cells, especially in the deep layers. The nuclei are very much swollen, the nuclear membrane greatly wrinkled, the body of the cell considerably shrunk with a tendency to disintegration. Similar findings have often been brought forward since then, also in cases which after psychic decline of considerable duration had succumbed to other diseases. Nissl invariably saw widespread cellular disease, which had led to considerable loss without, however, causing that extreme distortion and shrinking of the cortex which we have seen in paralysis. In the old cases which have reached a termination, Alzheimer found widespread changes in the cells which must be regarded as the terminal state of grave disease which has run its course, in particular sclerotic forms. Very frequently deposits of lipoid products of decomposition were found in the various tissue-cells, even already in quite young persons. With striking frequency were groups of nerve-cells observed, in which the basal processes appeared to be swollen and deformed by accumulation of fat. Lastly diffuse loss of cortical cells could also be established. All these most severe morbid residua could be demonstrated in marked predominance in the second and third cortical layers. Wada states likewise that the large pyramidal cells are comparatively less affected. Sioli was able to demonstrate

[1] Alzheimer, Centralbl. f. Nervenheilk., 1900, 296 ; De Buck et Deroubaix, Le névraxe vii. 2, 163 ; Zalplachta, Revista stintelor medicale 1906, 7-10 ; Agostini, Sull' anatomia patologica dei centri nervosi della demenza primitiva., 1907 ; Goldstein, Archiv. f. Psychiatrie xlvi. 1062 ; Wada, Obersteiners Arbeiten xviii. 313.

in connection with the destruction of the cells a great
accumulation of lipoid disintegrated material in the cortex,
in the tissue and specially round the vessels. He often
found the fibrils still well preserved; Moriyasu often found
them disintegrated. Wada reports that the extra-cellular
fibrils are profoundly changed, and Goldstein asserts that in
particular the coarser fibrils are damaged.

The *glia* has a great share in the morbid processes. In
the acute cases Alzheimer saw the presence of amœboid
hyperplasia of neuroglia, accumulation of glia cells round
the nerve-cells and morbid new formation of fibres, which
"embraced" the cells in a peculiar way. Nissl observed
especially in the deeper cortical layers numerous large glia
cells undergoing involution, of a kind that occurs in normal
circumstances only on the margin of the cortex. Specially
striking further was the fact that everywhere glia cells
were found with the bodies of the cell scarcely coloured,
and with vesicular, peculiarly pale, very large nuclei, which
often seemed to be closely applied to, or indeed to have
penetrated into, the diseased nerve-cells, mostly at the base
like the ordinary satellite nuclei, but also in other places.
These structures could be demonstrated with greatest ease in
the inner zone of the medullary border layer. According to
Sioli the glia cells in the first cortical layer, then those in the
deep layer of the cortex and in the medulla exhibit a strong
tendency to morbid formation of fibres and to the protoplasm
becoming coarse; in the medulla amœboid glia cells were
found in abundance. Eisath likewise saw increased fibre-
formation, dark staining of the glia nuclei, and in the deeper
layers increase of the granular substance of the glia, a few
sickle-shaped satellite cells with disintegration of pigment,
in the medulla degenerated, atrophic glia cells and sometimes
increase, sometimes decrease, of fibre-formation.

The *medullary fibres* appear according to the findings of
Goldstein, De Buck and Deroubaix somewhat thinned
especially in the supraradial network; Goldstein, Agostini,
Gonzales, Moriyasu, Klippel, and Lhermitte describe slight
loss of fibres in the tracts and changes in the anterior horn
cells of the spinal medulla. By some investigators, Obregia,
Klippel and Lhermitte, Doutrebente and Marchand changes
in the vessels were also found, new formation of vessels,
proliferation of vascular cells. As the vessels, however,
as a rule, have no share in the morbid process, we have here
probably to do with chance side-findings caused possibly by
age, alcoholism or syphilis. Doutrebente and Marchand saw
numerous nerve-cells in the embryonic stage of development;

Agostini also reports some traces of arrested development and residua of childish diseases. Mondio found in six cases anomalies in the convolutions, which he regards as signs of degeneration. Schröder from the same point of view describes

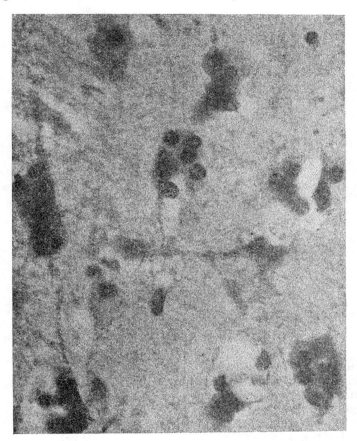

Fig. 36. Nerve-cells surrounded by glia nuclei.

in one case displacement of Purkinje cells and double nuclei, and also syncytial formations in the pyramidal cells of the cerebral cortex.

The accompanying figures represent some of the most important findings in dementia præcox. The first two figures represent acute changes. In Fig. 36 a number of nerve-cells from the deep layers of the cortex are reproduced, which are surrounded as thickly as possible by numerous glia cells recognizable by their dark nuclei, some of which have very much enlarged protoplasmic bodies. The distribution of decomposition products is represented in Fig. 37, which is taken from the cortex of a stuporous patient who died suddenly in a seizure. Two glia nuclei (*g*) are seen, round which

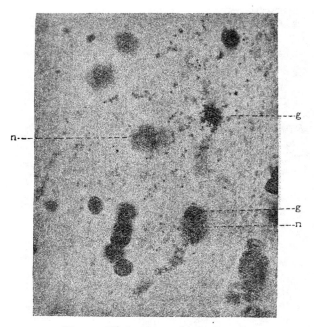

Fig. 37. Fibrinoid granules in glia cells.

are grouped radiating chains of fine granules; these are fibrinoid granules which have accumulated in the far-branching protoplasmic bodies of the glia cells which are otherwise not recognizable here. The lower glia nucleus lies on the nucleus of a nerve-cell (*n*) still partially visible; in the neighbourhood of the upper nucleus also there is a nerve-cell (*n*).

The chronic changes in the nerve-cells are reproduced in the two following figures. In Fig. 38 three nerve-cells from the upper part of the third layer of a healthy frontal lobe are represented; beside these there are two normal glia nuclei. In contrast to that three cells from the corresponding part of the cortex of a patient who died after long duration of dementia præcox in his twenty-fifth year are seen in Fig. 39. The narrowed shrunken cells with dark, long-drawn-out nuclei and deeply stained processes exhibit the picture of cell-sclerosis ; the tissue arranged as a network contains lipoid products of disintegration. Of the glia nuclei lying beside them one is unusually large ; the other two are small and

Fig. 38. Normal nerve-cells with glia nuclei.

darkly stained (pyknotic). In Figs. 40 and 41 also there are healthy and diseased nerve-cells placed in contrast. In two of the healthy cells and in one of the two glia cells lying between them there are only a few fine lipoid droplets. The drawings are from the third layer of the frontal lobes of a woman thirty-seven years of age who was mentally sound.

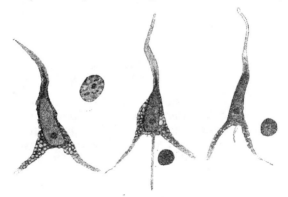

Fig. 39. Sclerotic nerve-cells in dementia præcox.

In contrast we see the diseased cells, changed in the highest degree ; they were taken from the cortex of a man twenty-three years of age who had suffered for five years from dementia præcox. In consequence of the distortion of the cortical structure caused by the morbid process some of the cells are obliquely placed ; their nuclei are shrunken and elongated, their processes are recognizable for a long way. But above everything one sees the shapeless, turgid body of the cells, and also the processes completely filled with lipoid products of disintegration.   Here also there meet us two unusually large glia-nuclei along with a small dark one; the cell-bodies of these, which otherwise are not visible, show numerous lipoid granules.

As in the clinical picture of the disease there are apparently also in the anatomical findings *two different groups* of processes, first the morbid disorders caused directly by the disease, and second the losses remaining as a consequence. To the first belong the changes in the cells, the formation of products of disintegration, the hyperplasia of glia, especially the

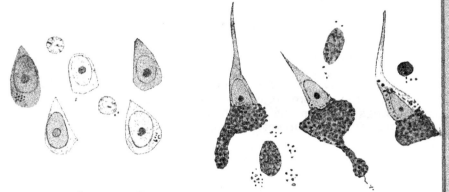

Fig. 40. Healthy nerve-cells.   Fig. 41. Nerve-cells diseased in high degree filled with lipoid products of disintegration.

appearance of amœboid glia cells ; to the second the destruction of cells and fibres, the necrotic and involutionary phenomena in nerve-tissue and glia, the deposition of fat and pigment.   According to whether it is a recent case relatively, an acute relapse of the disease, or an old case in the terminal state when the disease has long since run its course, the combination of anatomical changes will be different.

It has been already mentioned that the loss is for the most part to be found in the second and third cortical layers. Whether it extends over wide cortical areas to the same degree, remains still to be investigated ; by some investigators, Mondio, Zalplachta, Agostini, De Buck and Deroubaix, Dunton, Wada, it is stated that it involves the frontal lobes and the area of the central convolutions, also the temporal lobes to a greater degree than the occipital cortex.   Klippel and Lhermitte report atrophic changes also in the cerebellum.

In the remaining organs of the body in general only the findings resulting from the chance cause of death can be found. Dide, who looked for changes in the sexual glands, found these healthy, but on the other hand often saw fatty degeneration of the liver. Benigni and Zilocchi describe two cases with diffuse fatty degeneration in the liver, kidneys, heart, vessels, thyroid gland, and hypophysis. It must in the meantime remain undecided whether such findings have any further significance.

Relation of Morbid Anatomy to the Clinical Picture.— If we now make the attempt to consider the relation of the anatomical findings which hitherto have been got, to the clinical picture of the disease, there are two points which might be considered significant, the distribution of the morbid changes on the surface of the cortex, and the share of the different layers of the cortex. If it should be confirmed that the disease attacks by preference the frontal areas of the brain, the central convolutions and the temporal lobes, this distribution would in a certain measure agree with our present views about the site of the psychic mechanisms which are principally injured by the disease. On various grounds it is easy to believe that the frontal cortex, which is specially well developed in man, stands in closer relation to his higher intellectual abilities, and these are the faculties which in our patients invariably suffer profound loss in contrast to memory and acquired capabilities. The manifold volitional and motor disorders, which extend partly to the harmonious working of the muscles, will make us think of finer disorders in the neighbourhood of the precentral convolution. As it does not go so far as paralyses or to genuine apractic disorders, and there are only indications occasionally of motor-aphasic disorders, we may assume, although as yet no investigations on the subject are to hand, that the actual motor discharging-stations are not attacked by the destructive process. On the other hand the peculiar speech disorders resembling sensory aphasia and the auditory hallucinations, which play such a large part, probably point to the temporal lobe being involved. Here also, however, there is no true auditory aphasia, but only a weakening of the regulating influence of clang-association on the movements of speech expression, perhaps also a loosening of the connection between the former and conceptions; we must, therefore, imagine that the disorder is essentially more complicated and less circumscribed than in sensory aphasia. The auditory hallucinations, which exhibit predominantly speech content, we must probably interpret as irritative phenomena in the temporal lobe; it might not be due to chance that we invariably observe them along with confusion of speech and neologisms. The phenomena of hallucinatory repetition and hearing of thought point to the relations between ideas and sensory areas being attacked by peculiar disorders.

As the significance of the cortical layers is at present still almost wholly unknown, it will scarcely be possible to set up hypotheses with regard to the influence of the site of the morbid processes in definite layers, although it is certainly not indifferent for the form of the disease. According to the extended experience of Alzheimer we may assume that the permanent loss of nerve-tissue capable of work concerns preferably the *second* and the *third* layer of the cortex, therefore the smaller nerve-cells, though in the acute periods of the malady a severer attack of the deeper layers is simulated by the proliferation of glia which is there specially conspicuous. On the other hand the first terminal stations of the paths radiating from the sense-organs into the cortex and the large motor cells, in which we locate the origin of the pyramidal tracts which make their way to the spinal marrow, both lie in the depth of the cortex the structure of which, moreover, still most resembles that of the cortex of the lower animals. In these layers, therefore, will the processes presumably take place, which correspond, on the one hand to the appearance of a sensory perception, on the other hand to the discharge of a motor impulse, or are immediately connected with these.

In opposition to this we may ascribe to the upper small-celled layers such activities as are peculiar to the higher psychic stages of development since they reach their highest perfection in man, especially in the frontal lobes. Though it would not be suitable to put forward conceptions going into particulars about these relations, still it is easy to think before everything of the process of abstraction, which transforms perceptions to general ideas, sensations to emotions, impulses to permanent trends of volition. These abstract creations of the higher psychic activity are what the essence of the psychic personality is compacted of. As a permanent deposit of the experiences of life they dominate the thought, feeling and will of man for long periods, and up to a certain degree make it independent of the experiences of the moment, which through it are reinforced, moderated, corrected, or in certain circumstances even shown to be false. One may probably with impunity lay stress upon the fact, that in dementia præcox apparently it is the loss of those permanent foundations of the psychic life, as they are created by abstraction, which influences the clinical picture often in the highest degree in incoherence of thought, in contradictory change of emotions, in impulsiveness of action.

The small-celled layers extend in fairly uniform structure over nearly the whole surface of the brain. The hypothesis, therefore, is easy that besides the task of abstraction, perhaps in connection with it, they have also the task of mediating between the activities of the deeper layers which are more confined to circumscribed areas, especially sensory perceptions and volitional impulses. The real psychic elaboration of external experience, the linking of it on to past experiences, the critical judgment of it by means of formerly acquired standards, the connecting of it to new psychic structures, to conclusions and creative ideas, could even so be ascribed to an organ gathering things together in that way, as the preparation for action by weighing values, the ripening of decisions on the ground of deliberation. It is evident that the activities named here must before everything else be regarded as foundations of the inner unity and consistency of the psychic life. The fact that the working of external influences is essentially determined by the permanent character of the personality concerned, and that in the other direction action represents the outflow of the whole experience of life, necessarily forces us to the assumption, that the organ of our psychic life must also contain mechanisms which mediate a general connection of all the psychic workshops among each other. Just the destruction of the psychic personality, of this inner harmony of all the parts of the psychic mechanism in perhaps even surprising individual activities is, as formerly demonstrated, the *real fundamental disorder* in dementia præcox. If Alzheimer's finding is proved to be invariably present, we might from it conclude with a certain probability that in the *small-celled layers*, that harmonious gathering into one of psychic activities takes place, the destruction of which characterizes dementia præcox.

This hypothesis gains great support from the circumstance, that in our disease the lower psychic mechanisms as a rule are comparatively little encroached on, corresponding to the slighter damage done to the deeper cortical layers. The power of purely sensory perception remains often fairly well preserved, as also the memory of perceptions, and acquired knowledge and skill. On the other hand judgment is lost, the critical faculty, the creative gift, especially the capacity to make a higher use of knowledge and ability. Pleasure and the lack of it are often perceived by the patients with the greatest intensity, but the sense of beauty, the joy in understanding, sympathy, tact, reverence, desert them, as also the intelligent, continuous emotional relations to the events of life. The patients may also exhibit volitional activity of the greatest strength and endurance, but they are wholly incapable of arranging their lives according to rational principles or of consistently carrying out a well-considered plan. We see, therefore, in all the domains of psychic life the ancestral activities offering a greater power of resistance to the morbid process than the psychic faculties belonging to the highest degrees of development, corresponding to the slighter damage done to the deeper cortical layers which are more like those of the lower animals, in contrast with those which only attain to development with the appearance of the most complicated psychic activities.

The transparency of this relation is somewhat clouded by the fact, that memory being well preserved may make possible the continuance of individual capabilities which are much exercised. We may well assume that the site of both sensory and mechanical memory is to be sought for principally in the deeper cortical layers, the former in the sensory centres, the latter in the areas which mediate the harmony of movements. The experience which has been formerly acquired is able up to a certain point to cover the destruction of the higher faculties, just so far as independent psychic activity may be replaced by acquired proficiency. Precisely work which is dependent on understanding is often served by associations of ideas and habits of thought which have been firmly laid down in forms of speech, while in the domains of the emotional life and of action an adjustment to the special conditions of the given moment is requisite in far higher degree. Perhaps there lies in this an essential ground for the clinical experience, that the disorders of dementia præcox usually appear here earlier and in more severe form than in intellectual activities.

But further by the destruction of the harmonious personality which holds together and dominates the whole psychic life, there is given to the influence of ancestral mechanisms a free play which they could never otherwise acquire. To these namely I reckon the activities of automatic obedience and negativism, which are not set in motion by deliberation or moods, but appear and disappear irregularly. Stereotypy also, as a general expression of the facilitating action of volitional impulses, might come in here, as also the rhythmic movements characteristic of profound idiocy. Lastly in the mannerisms and derailments of action one might see the consequence of defective consciousness of purpose and defective precision of volitional impulses, which makes them more easily accessible to all kinds of side-influences. Similarly neologisms and the manifold disorders in the structure of speech may probably be connected with loosening of the connection between abstract ideas, speech sounds and speech movements and with defective characterization of speech formulæ; all these are disorders which may be brought under the general point of view above discussed without special difficulty. In the roughest outlines, therefore, clinical experience and anatomical findings in dementia præcox may with certain presuppositions be brought into agreement to some extent. It must naturally be left to the future to decide whether and how far such considerations stand the test of increasing knowledge.

CHAPTER IX.

FREQUENCY AND CAUSES.

Dementia præcox is without doubt one of the most frequent of all forms of insanity. Its share in the admissions to a mental hospital is naturally subject to very considerable fluctuations, not only according to the delimitation of the morbid picture, but also specially according to the conditions of admission. With us approximately 10 per cent. of the admissions might belong to it, while the proportion in Heidelberg amounted to nearly 15 per cent., because there, through formalities which made things difficult, a large number of slight cases of other kinds were kept out. Albrecht states the frequency for Treptow at 29 per cent.; to the real mental hospitals only those patients go, who are absolutely in need of institutional treatment, and the cases of dementia præcox are in the first ranks of these. As the patients neither quickly die off like the paralytics, nor become in considerable number again fit for discharge like the manic-depressive cases, they accumulate more and more in the institutions and thus impress on the whole life of the institution its peculiar stamp. In the private institutions with a smaller number of admissions the share of our patients may in the total amount rise to 70 or 80 per cent.

The **Causes** of dementia præcox are at the present time still wrapped in impenetrable darkness. Indubitably certain relations to *age* exist. The very great majority of cases begin in the second or third decade; 57 per cent. of the cases made use of in the clinical description began before the twenty-fifth year. This great predisposition of *youth* led Hecker to the name *hebephrenia*, "insanity of youth," for the group delimited by him; Clouston also, who spoke of an "adolescent insanity," had evidently before everything dementia præcox in view, although he did not yet separate it from the manic-depressive type which likewise often begins about this time. Hecker was even inclined to regard the issue of his hebephrenia just as an arrest of the whole psychic life on the developmental stage of the years of puberty. In fact, we find in silly dementia at least many features which are well known to us from the years of healthy development. Among these there is the te dency to unsuitable reading, the naïve occupation of the ind with the "highest problems," the crude "readiness" of idgment, the pleasure in catch words and sounding ph ses, also sudden change of mood, depression and unrestrai ed merri- ment, occasional irritability and impulsiveness of action. Further the desultoriness of the train of thought, the half- swaggering, boastful, half-embarrassed, shy behaviour, the foolish laughing, the unsuitable jokes, the affected speech, the sought-out coarseness and the violent witticisms are phenomena which in healthy individuals, as in the patients, indicate that slight inward excitement which usually accom- panies the changes of sexual development. However, we shall not yet be able to conclude from these similarities that there are causal relationships between dementia præcox and puberty, as a limitation of the disease to the tim of d velop- ment does certainly not take place.

The diagram, Fig. 42, represents the distribution of 1054 cases with regard to age. The first striking thing there is, that the commencement of the malady for a certain percent- age of the cases is placed in the earliest years of life. It has to do here with a group of patients in whom already from childhood upwards a considerable degree of psychic weakness existed, although the more striking morbid phenomena only later, perhaps in the third decade, became noticeable and now led to fairly severe dementia. As there dementia præcox was in a certain manner grafted upon an already existing disease, we speak in such cases of an "engrafted hebephrenia." The proportion taken here of 3·5 per cent. is probably much too small, as only the most severe instances of that kind of case were separated out. Slighter divergencies of the most varied kind occurred moreover very frequently, a circumstance to which we shall later return. At this point it must already be emphasized that the determination of the point of time at which the disease began, is often very uncertain and arbitrary owing to the development being so frequently insidious. If it were wished to apply a very strict standard here, the whole diagram of age would certainly be dislocated not inconsiderably towards youth.

The decrease in the percentage between the tenth and the fifteenth year is in so far artificial, that this number is not directly comparable with the number of engrafted hebephrenias existing from youth up. From that time on we see the frequency of dementia præcox increasing with extraordinary rapidity, more than two-thirds of the cases begin between

P

the fifteenth and the thirtieth year, a quarter between the twentieth and twenty-fifth year. However, there can be no talk of an inviolable connection of dementia præcox with the period of youth. We see the vertical lines of the diagram fall off fairly quickly, it is true, but yet with regularity, and

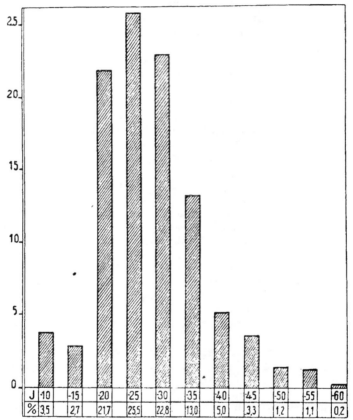

J	-10	-15	-20	-25	-30	-35	-40	-45	-50	-55	-60
%	3,5	2,7	21,7	25,5	22,8	13,0	5,0	3,3	1,2	1,1	0,2

Fig. 42. Percentage distribution of 1054 cases of dementia præcox according to age. (J = years.)

a not inconsiderable number of cases still reach development in the fourth, fifth and even in the sixth decade.

It must be allowed here that the objection is suggested by the great excess of cases among the young, that the cases apparently beginning late had in reality begun insidiously much further back, though the more striking morbid manifestations only became noticeable after the lapse of many years and even decades. In general this objection is justified.

Without doubt, especially in vagrants and criminals, a change of personality may gradually develop in youth, the morbidity of which is only recognized much later, when the known phenomena of dementia præcox become associated with it, auditory hallucinations, delusions, states of excitement or stupor, incoherence, mannerisms.   However, it would hardly do in some respects to set aside the share of the more advanced ages in dementia præcox because of such considerations.   The number of cases, the commencement of which would have to be displaced more or less far back, would in any case up to the fortieth and forty-fifth year be so large that it would be necessary to have uncommonly conclusive arguments to justify such a proceeding.   Such arguments, however, are actually not forthcoming.   So long as the view represented by Hecker for hebephrenia held, that there existed close causal relations between dementia præcox and puberty, the attempt could be made to find another explanation for the cases which did not fit this, or to separate them.   Experience has, however, meantime taught that the greatest frequency of the cases falls at an age in which sexual development is essentially excluded.   If already by that a dependence, in the narrower sense really causal, of the disease on the processes of puberty becomes improbable, it may further be pointed out, that we also very frequently see manic-depressive insanity begin at the end of the second, or in the beginning of the third decade, a circumstance which only admits of the interpretation that at this age the tendency to psychic disease is in any case specially great.

The view here represented receives further support from the fact that, even if in the first place we leave engrafted hebephrenia wholly apart, cases occur already in childhood, which with the greatest probability we may classify as dementia præcox.   Long ago I brought forward the hypothesis that certain, not exactly frequent, forms of *idiocy* with developed mannerisms and stereotypies might be early cases of dementia præcox.   Weygandt has not accepted this interpretation, as he asserts that the phenomena mentioned merely signify the appearance of childish forms of movement with inhibition of the higher development of volition by some or other morbid process.   With this view already formerly developed by myself I can agree so far as it concerns the peculiar rhythmic movements of idiocy.   I might take the view indicated of the sucking reflex also, which appears in very severe dementias (paralysis, Alzheimer's disease), and further of certain springing, rubbing "movements of sucklings" which are observed in young paralytics.   On the other hand, the swaggering manners of some idiots, and likewise many stereotypies of attitude and movement which are connected with these, and lastly negativistic features which accompany them, e.g., permanent repellent inaccessibility to all attempts at approach, appear to me to have no relation at

Fig. 43.   Idiot with manneristic movements.

all to general childish peculiarities but much rather to belong to the well-known morbid picture of dementia præcox. One of my patients had the habit of repeatedly hitting his plate with his fork, waving his hat, dipping his bread again and again into his cup, scraping all round his roll, doing everything twenty or thirty times. A patient aged twenty-three years is represented in Fig. 43, who was from childhood idiotic, dull, inaccessible, but otherwise clean, who carried out incessant, senseless, spreading movements with his hands. Complete certainty about the significance of such observations will, it is true, only be obtained by anatomical investigation. I may, however, point out that in one of my cases, the beginning of which reached back into the fourth year, and in which an extremely characteristic negativistic dementia had come into existence, the patient's mother also exhibited the picture of dementia præcox.

Recently Sante de Sanctis[1] has described under the name of "demenza precocissima" a series of morbid conditions observed in young children, which are accompanied by "catatonic" phenomena; some of these cases are cured, but others issue in psychic weakness of greater or less degree. As he himself emphasizes, it can scarcely be decided at

[1] Sante de Sanctis, Rivista ital. di neuropat., psichiatria ed elettroterap. ii. 3; Folia neurologica ii. 9; iii. 395; Weygandt, Zeitschr. f. d. Erf. d. jugendl. Schwachsinns i. 311.

present how far the cases described belong to dementia
præcox or to other forms of disease, among which indeed
specially hysteria and infections, also syphilitic cases might
come into consideration. However, the clinical agreement of
some morbid states, which develop in the first or at the
beginning of the second decade, with the dementia præcox of
adults, in phenomena, course and issue is so apparent, that
there can be no reasonable doubt about the relationship. I
have myself observed several such cases and Räcke and Vogt
also have communicated some. Lastly, Heller has described
as "dementia infantilis" cases which begin in the third or
fourth year, sometimes run their course violently, sometimes
insidiously, and issue in profound dementia with stereotypies
and mannerisms. Here also we shall be obliged to think of
the probability that at least many of these cases belong to
dementia præcox.

If in the interpretation of the morbid pictures appearing
in earliest childhood we find ourselves often on ground at
present still rather insecure, the same applies to the cases in
the *years of involution*, which run their course according to
the picture of dementia præcox. Here without doubt there
are on the one hand cases, which according to our present
knowledge cannot by any means be separated from the
forms beginning earlier, which we, therefore, may term
genuine "late catatonias."[1] Petrén observed twenty-four
cases of catatonia after the fortieth year, among them six
between fifty and fifty-five, one of fifty-eight and one
of fifty-nine years of age. Schröder also quotes a case
which began at fifty-nine years. Zweig has brought together
thirteen cases between the thirtieth and fortieth year and
five cases after the fortieth, and arrives at the result, that
they correspond in general to those of a younger age; only
the prognosis appeared to him to be comparatively favourable, a conclusion for which the number of his observations
is by no means sufficient, and which in Zablocka's communications finds no confirmation. It is very noteworthy
that Schröder found four cases among sixteen late catatonias,
in which twelve to twenty-five years previously very slight
attacks, mostly states of depression, had preceded. The
hypothesis formerly touched on, that it may here sometimes
be only a case of the flaring up of a morbid process reaching
far back in an inconspicuous form, finds in this experience a
certain confirmation. Bertschinger also has pointed out this
possibility. Petrén reports a case which at nineteen years of

---

[1] Sommer, Zeitschr. f. d. ges. Neurol. u. Psychiatrie, i. 533.

age passed through an attack of hebephrenia and recovered with defect, and then at the age of forty-four fell ill again.

It must meantime be acknowledged that specially in the years of involution we not at all infrequently meet with cases, the clinical judgment of which even now meets with the greatest difficulties. Here it has to do at one time with cases which run their course with intense and anxious states of excitement and depressive delusions, also with catatonic symptoms, automatic obedience, inaccessibility, resistance, stereotyped attitudes and movements, and issue with comparative rapidity, sometimes even after a temporary improvement, in profound psychic decline; at another time it is a case of paranoid forms. I consider it probable that here we have partly to do with morbid processes which do not belong to dementia præcox, although a satisfactory delimitation and especially a decision in individual cases at present is still scarcely possible. So far as the purely clinical view allows us, I have made the attempt in the discussion of the presenile and paranoid cases to fix some points of view for new morbid pictures. An essential hindrance to the success of such attempts lies, however, in the circumstance, that the clinical forms of dementia præcox not only exhibit in themselves an extraordinary variety, but that they also, as formerly mentioned in detail, are distinctly influenced by age. The decision as to which morbid disorders of the age of involution are to be reckoned with dementia præcox and which are to be regarded as psychoses of another kind, will therefore always depend on the question, how far the differences in the form of the clinical phenomena are conditioned by the character of the morbid process and how far by the changes of advancing age in the personality.

The difficulties here touched on have caused Stransky, under the term "dementia tardiva,"[1] to delimit certain paranoid cases of the years of involution with indications of catatonic features particularly in women as a special clinical form. Hallucinations, change of mood without very severe dulling of emotions, passing states of lively excitement, delusions without systematic elaboration, indications of catatonic features characterize the morbid picture. It must remain for the future to decide whether dementia tardiva represents a clinical entity, or whether, as I for the present consider more probable, it must be broken up into various groups according to the points of view indicated.

Sex.—The male sex appears in general to suffer somewhat more frequently from dementia præcox than the

[1] Stransky, Monatsschr. f. Psychiatrie u. Neurol. xviii. Erg.-Heft.

female; among the 1054 cases utilized for our age-diagram there were 57·4 per cent. men. In the individual clinical forms meantime, as we have formerly seen, the share of the sexes exhibits not inconsiderable differences. The same holds good for the different ages, as the following table of the number of men in the different periods of life shows:—

Age	.	.—10	—15	—20	—25	—30	—35	—40	—45	—50	—55	—60
Men per cent.		70·3	50·0	65·8	63·6	57·9	50·4	60·4	34·3	54·0	33·4	0·0

Engrafted hebephrenia appears therefore to be more frequent in the male sex; but in the next period both sexes are attacked in the same degree. After the fifteenth year the male sex predominates greatly, then less, till between the thirtieth and the thirty-fifth year, equality, though only temporarily, is again reached. After the fortieth year women predominate especially at the most advanced ages, but the numbers from which the percentages are taken after the forty-fifth year are too few to be of use. It may be mentioned, however, that Schröder found among his "late catatonias" three men and thirteen women; Sommer also emphasizes the predominance of the female sex. Consideration of the figures might in any case show at least, that the tendency of the female sex to attacks of dementia præcox, which on the average is somewhat less, experiences a certain increase in three different periods of life, before the fifteenth, between the twenty-fifth and thirty-fifth, and after the fortieth year. There will certainly be a temptation here to think of sexual development which is earlier in the woman, of the time of the work of reproduction and of the years of involution.

General Conditions of Life.—Since attention has been drawn to the morbid picture of dementia præcox, it has been shown that in all civilized nations it comes under observation in approximately the same forms and everywhere accounts for the greatest number of the permanent inhabitants of institutions. As the progressive increase of these patients seemed to prove most obviously the increase of insanity, it was easy to think of dementia præcox as a product of the injuries to which the progress of *civilization* and its unpleasant accompaniments exposes our mental health. Mental over-exertion, especially in the years of development, on the other hand degeneration, were frequently regarded as the causes of the malady. It appeared to me, therefore, of especial importance to ascertain whether the disease appeared also in nations, which live in quite different, and especially more simple and more natural conditions. A visit to the institution in Singapore at once showed me that in the most different constituent parts of the mingling of nations there, among Chinese, Tamils, Malays, there were clinical pictures to record which wholly resemble the ·forms of dementia præcox known to us. The later more exact investigation in the institution Buitenzorg brought out the result that the greatest number of the inmates there, consisting of Malays, Javanese, Sundanese and Chinese all thrown together, almost 80 per cent., presented morbid pictures about which it could scarcely be doubted that they belonged to dementia præcox. There were, it must be admitted, in the character of the individual features very remarkable differences from the forms familiar to us ; the disease began for the most part with states of confused excitement, which then with comparative rapidity led to drivelling dementia with incoherence, exalted mood, loquacity and mannerisms. Since then the frequent occurrence of dementia præcox in the most different regions of the world has been confirmed ; Koichi Miyake reports that it occurs in Japan just the same as with us, only with less tendency to states of depression.

If we must therefore seek the real cause of dementia præcox in conditions which are spread over the whole world, which thus do not lie either in race or in climate, in food or in any other general circumstances of life, we are still not able to say anything as to whether the factors mentioned have not perhaps a furthering influence on the development of the disease, as reliable statistical facts on this point have not been collected. We know nothing about the relative frequency of dementia præcox in individual nations, in different conditions of life, in town and country, at different times. Only so much may be said, that the disease is probably extremely old, as indeed the descriptions of the old physicians often unmistakably point to the clinical pictures familiar to us.

Hereditary Predisposition.—Of the causal conditions of dementia præcox accessible to our investigation at present hereditary predisposition [1] must next be named. The figures stated for this point vary considerably among themselves, evidently according to the extent which is attached to the idea of heredity, as also according to the accuracy of the information which can be got about the families of the patients. Schott finds hereditary taint in 52 per. cent., Lukacs in 53·8 per cent., Meyer in 54 per cent., Karpas in

[1] Levi-Bianchini, Rivista Sperimentale di freniatria xxix. 558; Berze, Die hereditären Beziehungen der Dementia præcox, 1910.

64 per cent., Sérieux in 70 per cent,. Wolfsohn and also Zablocka in 90 per cent. of the cases. I had myself found formerly in Heidelberg general hereditary predisposition to mental disorders in about 70 per cent. of the cases in which about this point reliable statements were to hand. As by this restriction it naturally resulted that a certain selection was made, the proportion might be somewhat too high. Among the 1054 cases made use of above there were 53·8 per cent. in which the family history gave support to the assumption of hereditary taint. This figure is certainly too small, because in numerous cases the information about the ancestors of the patients was very incomplete. Perhaps it is possible to get somewhat more reliable figures if one limits oneself to direct heredity, that is to the occurrence of mental disorders, suicide or severe brain diseases in the parents, as about this question it is easiest to get trustworthy statements. Within this limitation there was found a direct taint in 33·7 per cent. of the cases, a number which on the grounds named must still be regarded as too low ; that appears also from the fact that the admissions in Heidelberg with their more complete previous histories yielded a higher value than the patients admitted often without any information in the city of Munich. But to that must be added that in 7·9 per cent. of the cases alcoholism in one of the parents was present ; this figure contrariwise is for Munich somewhat higher than for Heidelberg. In 2 per cent. of the cases lastly besides the direct taint of mental disorders alcoholism had also to be recorded in one of the parents.

If these figures are compared with those got by Diem, it results that the taint from the morbid condition of the parents here taken into consideration is perhaps 10 per cent. higher than in mentally healthy individuals, and therefore causal relations must be regarded as probable. To the same view must the experience lead, that dementia præcox not at all infrequently is *familial*, most often appearing in brothers and sisters, more rarely in parents and children, as the disease, because of its early development and its serious phenomena, encroaches on the reproductive capability to a high degree. I know a very great number of cases in which several brothers and sisters were attacked with dementia præcox, sometimes in startlingly similar ways ; once three members of the same family were admitted very shortly one after the other. Schwarzwald[1] describes three series of cases, in which each time three sisters, and one in which five sisters were attacked with the symptoms of dementia

---

[1] Schwarzwald, De la démence précoce familiale. Diss. 1907.

præcox. Frankhauser reports twenty-eight pairs of brothers and sisters who succumbed to the same malady. Not infrequently one learns further that among the brothers and sisters of the patients there are found striking personalities, criminals, queer individuals, prostitutes, suicides, vagrants, wrecked and ruined human beings, all being forms in which more or less well-developed dementia præcox may appear.

If such cases serve as evidence of a similar morbid predisposition, on the other hand, however, it also often occurs that among the members of some families disorders of quite another kind appear, epilepsy, hysteria, manic-depressive insanity. The comprehensive investigations, which Rüdin has carried out about the families of our patients, have in the frequency of the familial occurrence of dementia præcox likewise made clear the important part played by hereditary predisposition. Rüdin on the ground of his researches comes to the conclusion that dementia præcox is probably transmitted according to Mendel's law and indeed as a recessive characteristic. He has as evidence the great predominance of collateral and discontinuous inheritance compared with direct transmission, its increase in in-breeding and the special numerical ratio of those attacked in individual families to those who remain healthy. He finds that in the families attacked there comes under observation with relative frequency besides dementia præcox a series of other anomalies, specially manic-depressive insanity and eccentric personalities. While the latter are probably for the most part to be regarded as "latent schizophrenias" and therefore essentially the same as the principal malady, the relations to manic-depressive insanity are still not clear. Rüdin found that manic-depressive parents not at all infrequently have children with dementia præcox, while the reverse case belongs to the rare exceptions unless there also exists inherited predisposition to manic-depressive insanity from the other side.

Injury to the Germ.—Besides heredity, however, still other influences may apparently determine the appearance of dementia præcox. That is proved according to Rüdin's experience first by the fact that first-born and late-born, also last-born, individuals are attacked by the malady with comparative frequency. Further it was shown that not infrequently immediately before or after the birth of the individual attacked there have occurred miscarriages, dead-born children, premature births; or children with small vitality or with bodily or mental defects may have been born. The assumption is suggested by such observations that influences injurious to the germ might play a certain part in the origin of dementia præcox. Further evidence for that is given by the observation, confirmed by Rüdin, that *alcoholism* is reported in the parents with striking frequency ; he found it at least sixty times in 300 accurately investigated cases. Wolfsohn saw chronic alcoholism in one of the parents in a fourth of the cases, while I could demonstrate it in my patients often with incompletely known previous history in any case in 10 per cent. One may accordingly assume that parental alcoholism probably exercises a certain influence on the development of dementia præcox in the children, a connection which might be caused by injury to the germ.

In the same sense we may probably interpret the statements made by Hirschl and Pilcz about the occurrence of *syphilis* in the parents of our patients. Pilcz reports that in 416 cases of dementia præcox he had found tabes in 5 per cent. of the parents, in manic-depressive insanity on the other hand only in 0·6 per cent. In the parents of forty-four hebephrenic patients paralysis was found twenty-three times, in those of twenty-seven catatonics five times ; also in the brothers and sisters of our patients paralysis was observed with striking frequency and in those of the paralytic often dementia præcox. In the parents of my patients I got information about syphilis only in 4 to 5 per cent.; further it has not hitherto struck me that the children of paralytics are attacked specially often by dementia præcox ; among 124 such children of whom certainly only sixty-seven had passed their tenth year, and twenty-nine their twentieth year, two suffered from dementia præcox. On the other hand Klutscheff reports that in sixty cases of dementia præcox he has found in 41·6 per cent. signs of hereditary syphilis. As, however, otherwise there is no evidence of any kind for the assumption that dementia præcox may be directly caused by hereditary syphilis, confirmation of such statements might probably only point to a general injurious action of parental syphilis on the germ. In each case investigation would be necessary, and with the help of serological procedure comparatively easy to accomplish, how far the traces of syphilis can really be demonstrated in the parents of our patients; the "stigmata" are, as is well known, extraordinarily deceptive.

Personal Idiosyncrasy.—For the view that in the origin of dementia præcox *degeneration* plays a part, the circumstance is usually brought forward that in the patients from the beginning, physical and psychic signs of degeneration are frequently found. Saiz[1] states the frequency of such physical abnormalities, which are usually regarded as the expression

[1] Saiz, Rivista di freniatria sperimentale xxxviii. 364.

of degeneration, as 74 per cent. Considering the great elasticity of the limits, which in ascertaining such facts must be allowed for, it is scarcely possible to set a value on the figures. But it corresponds well enough to the general experience that in patients with dementia præcox all sorts of physical abnormalities exist with striking frequency, especially weakliness, small stature, youthful appearance, malformation of the cranium and of the ears, high and narrow palate, persistence of the intermaxillary bone, abnormal growth of hair, strabismus, deformities of the fingers or toes, polymastia, defective development and irregularity of the teeth and the like. Here is the place to add the not infrequent occurrence of convulsions in childhood, of obstinate nocturnal enuresis, of frequent headaches, sensitiveness to alcohol, tendency to delirium in slight fever.

But much more important than the physical signs of degeneration, which in similar guise appear in many other forms of insanity, appears to me the fact that in a considerable number of cases definite *psychic peculiarities* have come under observation in our patients from childhood up. Schultze states that 50 to 70 per cent. of the patients were from the beginning psychopathic, and exhibited a shy, quiet, or specially in the female sex, an irritable, capricious character. Karpas found among his patients that 68 per cent. were psychopaths ; Schott reports that 28 per cent. of the patients were quiet and reserved.

I also have examined minutely the previous history of my patients for the occurrence of striking psychic predisposition and can in general confirm the statements of the investigators quoted, though I would abstain from giving definite figures because of the incompleteness of the information which is forthcoming at present. It was mentioned with very special frequency, particularly in the male sex, that children were mostly concerned who always exhibited a quiet, shy, retiring disposition, made no friendships, lived only for themselves. Of secondary importance, and more in girls, there is reported irritability, sensitiveness, excitability, nervousness, and along with these self-will and a tendency to bigotry. Then a smaller group of children, mostly boys, is noticeable, who from childhood up were lazy and restless, disliked work, were inclined to nasty tricks, did not persevere anywhere, and then became vagrants or criminals. Somewhat in contrast to that are those patients, likewise belonging rather more to the male sex, who were conspicuous by docility, good nature, anxious conscientiousness and diligence, and as patterns of goodness held themselves aloof from all childish naughtiness.   Intellectual endowment I found among my patients in Heidelberg, who were in more favourable circumstances for such investigations, in 17 per cent. of the cases stated as excellent, in about one-third of the cases as moderate, in 7 per cent. as poor.   Evensen puts down 6·7 per cent. of his patients as being above the average, 22 per cent. as poorly endowed ; Plaskuda puts down 15 per cent. as from childhood up limited.   Schott states that 28 per cent. of his patients learned with difficulty, 40 per cent. on the other hand were good to very good scholars, and Levi-Bianchini attributes to 6 per cent. of his patients great, to 60 per cent. medium, and to 24·4 per cent. slight endowment.

In view of these experiences the question is raised in what relation the psychopathic abnormalities, which with striking frequency precede the development of dementia præcox, stand to the later disease, and especially whether they are only the expression of constitutional injuries which lower the power of resistance to the cause of dementia præcox, or whether it is a case of the first indications of the disease itself reaching back into childhood.   For the answer to this question the circumstance seems to me to be of authoritative significance, that at least a part of the psychic peculiarities quoted exhibits the greatest resemblance to those disorders which we can establish in the incomplete remissions as well as in the cures with defect of our patients.   In numerous cases we see here as a residuum of the disease in persons formerly not at all remarkable, the quiet, shy, retiring ; the indocile, stubborn ; the irritable, sensitive ; or the harmless, good-natured conduct develop, as it is described in changing characters in the previous history of so many patients.   Further, it must be pointed out that we not at all infrequently see a change in the personality, in the sense here indicated, take place first in the later years of childhood, but many years before the real onset of dementia præcox. This experience may probably only be interpreted as a sign that the morbid process, which occurs here and first begins insidiously, is able to cause the same peculiarities which we see so frequently precede its appearance from childhood onwards.

Here perhaps the objection may be made that the peculiarities which meet us in the previous history of our patients could also be found in similar guise in any other group of people taken at random, and that they on the other hand are too varied to be the expression of one and the same morbid process.   It must at once be admitted that the first objection is justified ; it would be quite necessary for the right appreciation of the circumstances to carry out similar investigations in other forms of disease also, but especially also in healthy individuals. We shall later have to discuss the results, which have been got up to now, of such investigations in epilepsy and in manic-depressive insanity; they show that the previous history of the patients here does yield essentially abnormal features. It is true that there are also certain points of agreement; but we may not leave out of account that our characterization of personal qualities at present is still very rough, that, therefore, under the same term, which is used by the relatives for the description of the former conduct of our patients, perhaps a series of wholly different characteristics is comprehended. If this source of error is appreciated, the impression is, as it appears to me, so overpowering, which is got from the statements, always the same, of the relatives about the former personality of our patients, that there cannot well be any doubt about the striking frequency of very definite predisposition in the previous history of dementia præcox. But the differences, the very contrast, of these peculiarities finds its exact counterpart in the differences of the clinical pictures, of the terminal states, and of the variations observed in the remissions. It is indeed easy enough to bring the reserved or stubborn conduct of the children, who are attacked later, into nearer relation with the negativism, their capriciousness with the mannerisms, their irritability with the impulsiveness, their good conduct with the automatic obedience of dementia præcox.

On the grounds alleged the conclusion seems to me justified that the psychic abnormalities which precede the real onset of dementia præcox already represent in part at least the action of the cause of the disease, even if they can be traced back into the first years of the patient's life. The commencement of the malady would be, if this view should be confirmed, moved back into childhood for a considerable number of the patients; we should have to assume a longer or shorter preparatory stage, in which without noticeable progress, but already in indications the disease develops certain results such as we find again most strongly marked at the height of its development and in the terminal stages. This interpretation finds essential support, as appears to me, in the dementia præcox of children and in engrafted hebephrenia. It has indeed here also been thought that it was a case of chance coincidence with other kinds of brain disease which only favoured the development of dementia præcox. But engrafted hebephrenia is on the one hand too frequent for the explanation to have much probability in itself, and on the other hand the weak-mindedness, which is its founda- tion, bears also most unmistakably the features of a hebe- phrenic terminal state, and the fresh attack very often assumes the features of a simple exacerbation of the already existing disorders. As in addition the appearance of dementia præcox in early childhood is certain, there is no satisfac- tory reason according to my view to assume in engrafted hebephrenia an association of morbid processes of a totally different kind.

The frequency of defective or poor endowment will from this standpoint, so far as it is characteristic of dementia præcox, be capable of being regarded at least partly as an expression of engrafted hebephrenia, modified to a certain extent, as the first still indefinite action of the same morbid process which later causes dementia præcox. More difficult to explain remains the fact which, as it seems, is also fairly certain, that a number of our patients exhibit strikingly good endowment. Here it would be necessary first to investigate how far it is a question of purely scholastic endowment of those scholars who with a good memory attain by good conduct, conscientiousness and indefatigable diligence to being "always the first in every class." Thus I remember a scholar, who with all the symptoms of a hebephrenic disposi- tion, shy, lachrymose, childish, wholly unboylike conduct and an ineradicable tendency to biting his nails, up to the highest class occupied the position of a prominent shining light in the school in consequence of his exemplary diligence, which nothing turned aside. But further, as degeneration certainly plays a part in the development of dementia præcox, the experience must be pointed out that on its soil not infre- quently distinguished, though mostly one-sided, endowment is present. As dementia præcox often encroaches later and in lesser degree on mental capabilities, and especially on memory, than on emotional life and volition, the former might in certain circumstances still stand on a higher level, while in the domain of the latter already distinct disorders have developed.

If we regard certain predispositions which are frequent in the previous history of dementia præcox as the first slight beginnings of it, the question arises further, whether those peculiarities are to be interpreted always in this sense, and especially, whether the onset of dementia præcox must always follow them. The first question would only then be capable of an answer, if the last must be answered in the affirmative. But of that there can obviously be no dubiety. There are without doubt innumerable people who bear throughout their lives features such as we have formerly described without ever falling ill mentally.   From that it must be concluded either that other kinds of inherited or acquired injuries could also exercise similar effects on the psychic life, or that in such cases the existing germ of dementia præcox has not attained to further development.   The possibility of such an interpretation will not be capable of dispute in so far as we see very slightly defective states as residuum of an attack of dementia præcox, which has been passed through, persisting often enough for decades, to the end of life without further progress.   It would, therefore, be quite conceivable that certain abnormal personalities with the peculiarities mentioned were to be regarded as the product of an attack of dementia præcox which had been passed through in earliest childhood and then reached the close.   Bleuler is inclined to stretch the limits of such a " latent schizophrenia " to an extraordinary extent, and to interpret all possible psychopathic personalities in this sense.   How far that is justified in fact can scarcely be decided at present.   As even marked clinical symptoms do not always allow the conclusion to be made with certainty that the definite morbid process exists, we shall probably only quite exceptionally find the personal qualities characteristic enough to discover in them the infallible traces of an attack of dementia præcox which has been suppressed in its origin.

External Causes.—About the part which external causes might play in the development of dementia præcox there is little to report.   That *mental over-exertion*, which Kahlbaum suggested, and which is also held responsible in part by Deny and Roy, cannot be seriously taken into account, is already proved by the extension of the disease in the country population and among the Malays, Tamils, Chinese, peoples growing up in the simplest conditions of life.

The view expressed by Vigouroux and Naudascher and supported also by Bleuler, that *infections* in the years of development might have a causal significance, cannot in its indefiniteness be either proved or disproved.   The unmistakable importance of the predisposition points, however, to the fact that infectious causes can scarcely be the decisive factor ; moreover other complicated factors must be assumed to explain the after-effects of such causes continuing for decades. At the same time in about 10 to 11 per cent. of my patients at Heidelberg severe acute diseases had preceded the malady, most frequently typhoid or scarlet fever. Sometimes the picture of dementia præcox developed abruptly during the bodily disease, so that at first an infectious insanity was thought of; as a rule, however, many years had passed before the appearance of the psychic disorder, so that there could be no question of direct connection. Now and then it was stated that since the bodily illness a certain change had already been noticed in the patient, greater irritability, a lowering of mental capability, a marked liability to fatigue. We shall regard with great doubt the statements of Bruce, who considers a short streptococcus the exciting cause of the disease, and was able by its means to produce "mental dulness" in rabbits.

Just as little shall we be able to reconcile ourselves with the view represented by Steiner and Pötzl that *acquired syphilis* could in certain circumstances bring the disease to an outbreak. It cannot be disputed that recent syphilis is often found in our patients, but that is not to be wondered at, as it has mostly to do with young people in the third decade, who are in part very much excited sexually and very much inclined to excesses. In isolated cases there was a report of inflammation of the brain in childhood, not altogether infrequently also of *head-injuries*,[1] which, however, are in any case so frequent, that they can only quite exceptionally be made use of for establishing a cause. Also in brain diseases, especially tumours, "catatonic" morbid results are occasionally observed; but we cannot doubt but that in such cases apart from chance coincidences the resemblances are purely external. The misuse of *alcohol* appears to have no significance for the origin of dementia præcox. Though 15 to 16 per cent. of the men observed by myself had drunk heavily, as a rule it is a case of debauches which are caused by the morbid instability and irregular conduct of life of the patients.

The fact already touched on is striking, that the outbreak of dementia præcox frequently takes place in *prison*. Among 600 men about 6 per cent. had fallen ill in detention, in jail or in the convict-prison; to these were added 8 per cent. of vagrants of whom likewise a considerable number had shown the first symptoms of the disorder in the workhouse. It is suggestive of the possibility that the emotional influences of the loss of freedom, the monotonous food, the limitation of movement, the being shut up from air and light, the facilitation of onanistic tendencies may be productive of disease. In more exact investigation, however, it can be shown for a considerable number of the cases that probably already a long time previously changes of the personality

[1] v. Muralt, Allgem. Zeitschr. f. Psych. lvii. 457.

Q

in the sense of dementia præcox had taken place, which then made the patient a habitual criminal and vagrant. It is a remarkable fact that by preference paranoid forms develop on prepared soil through the influence of the loss of freedom, so that these, therefore, at least give a characteristic colouring to the morbid picture. Whether beyond this in individual cases the loss of freedom can gain real causal significance for dementia præcox has become doubtful to me.

Among 386 women there were 3 per cent. prostitutes. Once I saw two sisters fall ill almost at the same time who were both prostitutes; a respectable young woman, already mentioned formerly, gave birth to three illegitimate children after recovery from a state of severe catatonic excitement. A woman fell ill while in custody, and became demented after she had prostituted herself in an incredible way, being urged to do so by her husband, he being present hidden in a cupboard. That probably the immorality in all such cases is the consequence and not the cause of dementia præcox scarcely requires more proof.

We stand perhaps on a somewhat firmer foundation in the consideration of the relations between dementia præcox and the work of *reproduction*. Apart from the fact, that disorders of menstruation are frequent and, moreover, exacerbations of the morbid process are often observed during the menses, dementia præcox begins in a considerable number of cases during pregnancy, in childbed or after a miscarriage, sometimes also first in the period of lactation. In Heidelberg I saw nearly a fourth of the catatonic cases in women develop in connection with the work of reproduction, while of the hebephrenic cases not even in a tenth could such a connection be recognized. Once the four attacks, in which the disease ran its course, were each connected with a birth, till the last brought the final dementia. In another case the disease began likewise in childbed and after a remission of considerable duration ended with the occurrence of a fresh pregnancy in a severe relapse. As, however, the attacks of manic-depressive insanity also are readily connected with the changes caused by the work of reproduction, it must remain for the present undecided how far here it has to do with closer causal connections. The apparent increase of the attacks in the climacteric also has to be remembered, which would likewise correspond to the observations in manic-depressive insanity.

Sexual Life.—Meantime the experiences touched on give us the occasion to examine somewhat more closely the behaviour of the sexual processes in our patients. Here must be first pointed out what in the clinical descriptions must ever again be emphasized, that in our patients very frequently a lively sexual excitement exists, which makes itself known in regardless onanism, debauches, and tormenting sexual ideas of influence. Especially of male patients one learns with striking frequency that for many years they have constantly masturbated. Formerly, therefore certain morbid pictures belonging to hebephrenia were simply described as the "insanity of masturbation"; perhaps also part of the widespread ideas about the terrible consequences of onanism is connected with such experiences. Lastly, it is worthy of mention that often the outbreak of dementia præcox is brought into causal connection with the abandonment or the failure of a plan of marriage.

The observations quoted, which appear to point to relations between dementia præcox and sexual life, have had much attention paid to them. Tschisch has come to the view that suppression or defective development of sexual activity is to be regarded as the cause of dementia præcox, and Lomer ascribes the cause to disorders of the internal secretion of the sexual glands. I also have expressed the view that possibly there might exist some or other more or less distant connection between dementia præcox and the processes of the sexual organs. It must meantime be emphasized that convincing proofs for such assumptions are not by any means forthcoming. Increase of sexual excitement is found in all possible forms of insanity. Onanism meets us also frequently enough in simple psychopathies, and it might be encouraged in our patients by their shy reserve which often makes sexual approach impossible for them. The failure of plans of marriage is probably with more correctness to be regarded as consequence and not as cause of the disease. But lastly the considerations brought forward above, which point to a more frequent reaching back of the malady into childhood, take away part of the significance of its relations to sexual development, a significance which might be attached to these relations, if the quite similar behaviour of manic-depressive insanity is not taken into consideration.

In any case we have to think of those connections, just as of those with pregnancy, childbed and climacteric as very common. One could perhaps imagine as connecting links, disorders in the bodily economies, as they accompany the great changes of life and in certain circumstances draw after them far-reaching consequences. Our attention has been drawn to these circumstances mostly by the better understanding of the disorders of the *thyroid gland*, which likewise exhibit certain relations to menstruation, pregnancy and climacteric. The occasional appearance of increase and decrease of the thyroid, remarkable thickening of the skin, facial phenomena, acceleration or retardation of the pulse, tetanoid seizures, brings immediately to remembrance the phenomena observed in diseases of the thyroid gland ; on the other hand, according to Blum's descriptions, the disorders of the psychic life and of movement in dogs without a thyroid gland present a certain similarity to the behaviour of catatonic patients. Lundborg has therefore brought dementia præcox into relationship with myoclonia, myotonia and tetany, and has regarded as its foundation changes in the thyroid and parathyroids.

Auto-intoxication.—At present it is obviously premature to form any opinion at all about the possibilities which might perhaps come into consideration for the explanation of the points of agreement indicated ; for that all serviceable foundations are still lacking. Nevertheless, the general statement may perhaps with all reserve be made, that a series of facts in dementia præcox up to a certain degree makes probable the existence of an auto-intoxication in consequence of a disorder of metabolism. Many investigators have found even the morbid anatomy similàr to that of chronic intoxication. Further Ajello believes that he is able to connect the changes brought forward by him in the behaviour of the muscles with the action of a toxin such as might perhaps correspond to veratrin ; also the frequency of idiopathic muscular swellings, heightened mechanical excitability of muscles and nerves, the increase of the tendon reflexes could be interpreted in the same sense. Further evidence could perhaps be found in the statements, certainly still in need of more exact examination, about blood changes and metabolic disorders. Tomaschny has also interpreted the frequency of headache in the same sense. If we then still take into consideration the occurrence of osteomalacia in dementia præcox emphasized by Barbo and Haberkandt, and lastly the above-mentioned relations to the work of reproduction, the indications appearing here and there of thyroid symptoms, the great fluctuations of the body-weight, with shapeless adiposity on the one hand, and the most extreme emaciation on the other, the occasional great fall of temperature, the epileptiform seizures, and the cases of sudden death, the conclusion is on the whole justified, that according to the present position of our knowledge the assumption of an auto-intoxication, which sometimes develops insidiously, sometimes sets in violently, has for itself the greatest probability.

About the source and kind of the toxin circulating in the body, we can certainly at present give just as little account as in the metasyphilitic or metalcoholic diseases which in their causes are already much better explained.

Against this view it must be said that those observations appear at first to give evidence which point to a causal importance of the inherited or at least congenital predisposition. The view has often been brought forward, that hebephrenic dementia signifies nothing else than the gradual failure of an inadequate constitution. Like a tree whose roots find no more nourishment in the soil at their disposal, so the mental powers are said to disappear as soon as the insufficient dowry no longer allows a further unfolding. Pick speaks of a "failure of the vital capacity of the brain," of a "disproportion between efficiency and work." So enticing as this interpretation appears to be at the first glance, especially for the insidiously progressive inadequacy of dementia simplex and the forms similar to it, just as little nevertheless can it stand more exact examination. Already there is difficulty in understanding why the development of the patients without recognizable external cause should not only stop short all at once, but should directly end in profound psychic decline. To that must be added that the change, though it usually appears after all sorts of premonitory symptoms, still not infrequently occurs rather suddenly, that then again improvement lasting for years, indeed more or less complete recoveries, may occur after very severe morbid phenomena, all of these being circumstances which can scarcely be explained from the standpoint described. But in any case the fact is decisive, that the morbid anatomy has disclosed not simple inadequacy of the nervous constitution, but destructive morbid processes, as the background of the clinical picture.

But neither from the clinical standpoint is there any ground for regarding dementia præcox as the direct expression of a particularly severe degeneration. The part, which must be allocated here to the familial disposition, is rather smaller than in the pronounced forms of the insanity of degeneration, in manic-depressive attacks, in hysteria, and in psychopathy. Nevertheless we invariably meet there not the tendency to dementia, but rather morbid states filling the whole life uniformly or in periodic return without rapid progress. By these considerations dementia præcox comes nearer to epilepsy ; in it also, besides the undeniable importance of the inherited, or early acquired, constitution, we have cause to assume the development of definite, destructive morbid processes progressing either somewhat slowly or rather rapidly, which sometimes reach back into childhood, sometimes begin, or at least experience an exacerbation, about the time of sexual maturity. There also we come across facts which make the existence of disorders of metabolism in high degree probable ; epilepsy also is a very ancient disease and spread over the whole world. If one will, one may to the further understanding of the relations between constitution and disease bring into the discussion certain frequent disorders of metabolism with purely bodily abnormalities, diabetes, gout, chlorosis, the occurrence of which is undoubtedly essentially favoured by inborn peculiarity.

Freudian Complexes.—The adherents of Freud's psychology of complexes have gone their own way in the view which they take of dementia præcox, as in many other clinical questions. Bleuler and Jung[1] have first brought forward the opinion, that "complexes," groups of ideas strongly emphasized by emotion, are to be regarded as the causes of the morbid phenomena or at least of their appearance, complexes which here on morbid soil can give rise to specially momentous effects. They are said to exercise a far-reaching influence on thought and action and, according to Jung's expression, are able to rob the ego of light and air, as cancer takes the vital power from the body. In support of these assertions the experience is brought forward, that psychic causes frequently bring about improvement or aggravation in the state of the patients, and that many patients for a considerable time give utterance to ideas which are in connection with events of life emphasized by emotion. The former statement is in general correct and indeed self-evident, but is subject in detail to very many exceptions. If the latter statement were not true, here also, as in the most varied mental disorders of a different kind, it would certainly be wonderful. But I think from an experience sufficient for this question that I may conclude that it is far more rare than might be expected according to general psychological laws, or than we observe it to be in many other forms of insanity. What has bewildered me ever afresh innumerable times, was just the complete failure of the most natural complexes emphasized by emotion of healthy life. One may here certainly find the assumption helpful, that it is a case of suppressed and transformed ideas, of "masks," the real meaning of which can only be guessed by an interpretation, dependent on the fine feeling of the

[1] Jung, Über die Psychologie der Dementia præcox. 1907 ; Isserlin, Centralbl. f. Nervenheilk. u. Psychiatrie. 1907, 329.

observer, of association experiments and dreams, a proceeding which, judging by the examples forthcoming, has little
attraction for me. But if by complexes nothing else is
meant than delusions, in which the fears and wishes of the
patients are reflected, that would be only a new and, as it
appears to me, a not exactly desirable expression for an old
thing. Its danger lies in the psychological views from which
it proceeds. The idea of independent, parasitic psychic
neoplasms, which on the one hand are completely withdrawn
from the influence of the ego, but on the other hand are able
wholly to transform and almost annihilate it, would overthrow
such a number of everyday and thoroughly ascertained
psychological experiences, that its substantiation must in
any case be supported by quite other means of proof than
has hitherto been the case.

The opinion, that a large part of the clinical morbid
picture can be explained by the effect of complexes, has then
further led to the differentiation of *primary* and *secondary*
symptoms. Only the former are said to represent the
immediate expression of the destructive morbid process,
while the latter proceed from the reaction to the influences of
the surroundings and to the morbid efforts of the patients
themselves. Thus according to Riklin negativism is said to
depend on inhibitions by the action of complexes; also the
mistaking of persons, delusions, nonsensical answers, perseveration, catalepsy, are connected with complexes, which
furthermore hinder suitable adaptation to surroundings. All
those expressions of morbidity are said to be just as
comprehensible psychologically under the now existing
hypotheses created by the disease as, according to Freud's
explanations, dreams are, as soon as one has learned to
interpret their intricate and extremely arbitrary symbolism.
Jung even gave utterance to the sentence: "If we let an
individual who is dreaming go about and act as if he were
awake, we have the clinical picture of dementia præcox."
Even though it were admitted that in the domain of thought
and of speech-expression similarities exist between dreaming
and dementia præcox, that statement is for the rest so
evidently untenable, that a refutation appears the more
superfluous as every proof at all acceptable is lacking.

The separation of the morbid phenomena into primary
and secondary I consider purely artificial. It certainly
cannot be disputed that in our patients some domains of the
psychic life are less injured than others and that many of
their trains of thought, utterances and actions would be more
comprehensible to us, if we knew their hypotheses, but the

wheelwork of our soul is so compactly fitted each part to the other, and the anatomical morbid process is moreover so widespread, that a division according to direct or indirect causation of the morbid phenomena appears to me on this account to be quite impossible. In any case the attempts, which up to now have been made in this direction, are not at all convincing.

The distinction made by Bleuler of *fundamental disorders* and *accompanying phenomena* of the disease is to be judged essentially otherwise. The former constitute the real characteristic of the clinical state and can be demonstrated in each individual case more or less distinctly ; the latter may be present, but may also be absent ; they are not caused by the character of the morbid process but by circumstances which are in loose connection with it. Those must therefore be regarded as fundamental disorders, which meet us in the picture of dementia simplex and in the terminal state called simple weak-mindedness, while all the remaining morbid symptoms represent obviously not necessary, though in part very common, accompanying phenomena of the disease. From this point of view the weakening of judgment, of mental activity and of creative ability, the dulling of emotional interest and the loss of energy, lastly, the loosening of the inner unity of the psychic life would have to be reckoned among the fundamental disorders of dementia præcox, while all the remaining morbid symptoms, especially hallucinations and delusions, but also the states of excitement, depression and stupor, further the manifold disorders of volition, negativism, automatic obedience, stereotypy, mannerisms, impulsive actions, would be regarded more as secondary accompanying phenomena. Bleuler reckons "ambivalence" and "autism" also among the fundamental disorders, not, however, as appears to me, altogether with right, as there are terminal states in dementia præcox, in which these abnormalities are lacking, while the above-mentioned fundamental disorders are present.

By what circumstances the appearance in the clinical picture of the secondary phenomena mentioned is caused, is at present unknown. Paralysis will be called to mind here, where likewise, the simple, characteristic dementia, which is the rule in the childish paralytic, may be elaborated by delusions, states of excitement, ill-humour and so on. Differences in the course and in the local extension of the morbid process might not be without significance. The forms which develop insidiously usually bear the stamp in paralysis, as in dementia præcox, of a simple, progressive weak-mindedness, and those, which have a violent onset, that of states of excitement and confusion with vivid delusions. Lastly, for the form of the clinical picture the circumstance might not be without significance, that according to the development of the psychic personality the morbid process must injure sometimes these, sometimes those faculties of the brain in a more striking way. I do not think here of the effect of complexes which have been acquired by chance and have become psychic parasites, but of the very varied consequences, which a change in the brain must have according to the particular direction, in which the faculties of the individual complicated brain machine and in especial of the injured parts have been fashioned by life. Thus the rarity observed by myself of hallucinations of hearing in the Javanese patients might be explained by the slighter significance which speech ideas have there for thought ; thus we have seen that with progressive development and rigidity of the psychic personality the delusions usually become more connected and more systematized. It would also well be conceivable that for the form of the peculiar catatonic disorders of volition besides the kind and extent of the morbid changes, the special volitional constitution might be of importance ; I found it striking that the disorders mentioned seemed to be less pronounced in the Javanese patients than with us.

While Bleuler ascribes significance to complexes and in general to psychological influences only for the form of the clinical condition, Jung claims them in certain circumstances also as a real cause of the disease. The complex emphasized by affect is thus said to be able to act as the starting-point of the disease in a way similar to that of a trauma or an infection. That might be conceded in so far as the origin of an attack of dementia præcox by trauma or infection is just as unproved as by complexes. But Jung gets a connection here with the theory of intoxication by pointing out the possibility of the emotion being able to produce a kind of toxin, as it otherwise might well arise of itself and might cause the disease. Surely then it would not be understood why the manic-depressive patients with their violent emotions do not produce the destructive toxins which lead to dementia in the greatest quantity !

Abraham has taken the Freudian doctrines into the service of dementia præcox more on the sexual side. For him the malady signifies the "auto-erotic" disposition, existing from youth up, the incapacity for objective love, which produces in its own time the withdrawal from the surroundings, especially the aversion to the parents formerly involved in erotic relations, as well as the ideas of persecution, further the tendency to onanism and, by the transference of sexual overestimation to the patient's self, megalomania. The persecutors are frequently people the patient has formerly loved ; the hallucinations always concern the complex. Another series of similar " analyses " of the mental state in dementia præcox has come from the Zurich School. They all run in the direction of gaining an understanding of the deeper sense which is hidden behind the " mask " of the confused talk and incomprehensible actions of the patients. " Freud and Jung have shown that the system of delusions of the patients is not in the least nonsensical, but follows the same laws as perhaps a dream,. which always discloses itself as a sensual elaboration of a complex," is what is said. But the complexes are as good as without exception sexual.

Here we meet everywhere the characteristic fundamental features of the Freudian trend of investigation, the representation of arbitrary assumptions and conjectures as assured facts, which are used without hesitation for the building up of always new castles in the air ever towering higher, and the tendency to generalization beyond measure from single observations. I must frankly confess that with the best will I am not able to follow the trains of thought of this " metapsychiatry," which like a complex sucks up the sober method of clinical observation. As I am accustomed to walk on the sure foundation of direct experience, my· Philistine conscience of natural science stumbles at every step on objections, considerations and doubts, over which the lightly soaring power of imagination of Freud's disciples carries them without difficulty. I also hold the view that many speeches and actions of our patients are not so nonsensical as they appear to us and that sexual emotions certainly play a considerable part in them. But as I only succeed very exceptionally in explaining my own dreams to a certain extent, although the preliminary conditions are certainly as favourable for that as possible, I must not only say explicitly that the statement, that a dream " always discloses itself as a sensuous elaboration of a complex," is wholly imaginary, but I am also unable to pluck up courage to give any credence to the disclosures which are yielded by the " analysis " of the processes of consciousness of our patients which are infinitely more difficult to understand, Certainly anyone who can decide to regard the utterances of the patients sometimes literally, sometimes as the expression of the contrary, sometimes again as " symbols " of any other ideas whatever, who in all these expulsions, displacements, concealments, finds his way with confidence, will not find it too difficult in the end to discover in a fable of Gellert a background of secret incestuous thoughts, jealous, masochistic, sadistic or homosexual emotions.

CHAPTER X.

DELIMITATION.

Whether dementia præcox in the extent here delimited represents *one uniform disease*, cannot be decided at present with certainty. In any case we shall no longer need to refute in detail the objection formerly brought from different sides against the establishment of the morbid form, that it was a case of unjustified grouping of uncured psychoses of very different kinds, of melancholia, mania, acute and chronic confusion, derangement. Clinical experience has demonstrated innumerable times that it is possible from the conception of the pathology of dementia præcox to foretell with great probability the further course and the issue of a case belonging to the group ; but in saying that, the proof is furnished that our picture of dementia præcox is in the main agreeable to natural laws. Nevertheless, it is certainly possible that its borders are drawn at present in many directions too narrow, in others perhaps too wide.

Paranoid Forms.—The most criticism has always been directed against the inclusion of the paranoid forms in dementia præcox. It cannot be denied that the pictures of paranoid states at first sight do not have the slightest resemblance to those of catatonic stupor, of excitement or of dementia simplex. Meantime the diversity among one another of the pictures described, as also all similar experiences in other diseases, such as in paralysis, in cerebral syphilis, in manic-depressive insanity, point to the fact that it is very hazardous to draw conclusions from the clinical states alone as to whether they belong to the same or to different forms of disease. This question can only be decided by the whole course of the malady, and the appearance, gradually becoming always more distinct, of those morbid symptoms which are essential to the disease as opposed to the more secondary, though often much more striking, accompanying phenomena.

If we apply these principles to the case before us, the result is that at least some of the attacks beginning in paranoid form, as before described, issue in quite the same *terminal states* as the remaining forms of dementia præcox. The delusions, which originally completely dominated the morbid picture for years, may vanish leaving scarcely a trace, may be corrected by the patient, denied or forgotten, while a simple hebephrenic weak-mindedness remains. In other cases again there are, interpolated in a paranoid morbid course, states which bear unmistakably the stamp of dementia præcox, silly excitement with mannerisms and stereotypies or negativistic stupor. Fuchs has described a case in which between two such acute attacks for more than ten years a purely paranoid state was present. Lastly, it must be pointed out that delusions and hallucinations of quite the same kind, as we see them in paranoid cases, occur also in most of the remaining forms of dementia præcox, certainly here in connection with a series of other morbid symptoms. The changing composition of the morbid pictures in a given group of phenomena with sometimes weaker, sometimes stronger characterization of single features is, however, quite familiar to us from the most different clinical groups of forms ; we shall therefore not lay too much stress on the occasional absence or more striking appearance of single characteristics for the clinical judgment of the states, and all the less if we see their composition repeatedly change in one and the same case of disease.

In any case we may, as I think, regard it as certain that paranoid states may appear in the course of dementia præcox. The question is much more difficult to answer, how wide the circle of paranoid cases must be drawn, which we are justified in regarding as expressions of that disease. Although it appears to me to be impossible at present to arrive at a definite conclusion on this point, nevertheless I have thought, with reference to the doubt which I expressed before, that I should attempt to make a narrower delimitation. Accordingly I have for the present separated from dementia præcox a part of Magnan's " délire chronique" and what was formerly called dementia paranoides, now named " dementia phantastica." On the other hand I have still included in dementia præcox those paranoid forms which pass with comparative rapidity into marked psychic decline and in which, besides delusions and hallucinations, those disorders of emotional life and volitional activity can be demonstrated in more or less distinct form, which meet us so invariably in the disease named. It is proved, as far as I can see, to be wholly impossible to delimit them sharply in any way from the first-mentioned paranoid form. Certainly the grouping which is now attempted is not final ; but at present we still wholly lack the hypotheses for a satisfactory solution of the task here before us.

Catatonia.—For several other groups of cases also the separation from dementia præcox has been recommended. Tschisch has emphasized that catatonia and dementia præcox are fundamentally different from each other, and Morselli[1] also has come to the conclusion, that catatonia deserves a place to itself; it is curable, and is caused by infections. According to my observations I must consider these views erroneous or at least wholly unproven. Even though after infectious diseases morbid pictures similar to catatonia come under observation, they can still not be grouped together with the very great majority of cases in which such causation can be easily established. Whether catatonic cases may be cured under certain circumstances, was formerly investigated in detail; as a rule, however, they are not cured. Catatonic states may further appear suddenly in each period of dementia præcox, sometimes only after a decade. Then we observe after catatonias exactly the same *terminal states* as in the remaining forms of dementia præcox; but lastly, the "catatonic" symptoms may be present in the morbid picture in all possible grades and groupings. I see, therefore, no possibility of attaining with their help to a delimitation of an independent clinical form.

Meeus has proposed to delimit a hebephrenic-catatonic group from the paranoid forms and from dementia simplex. I think, however, that we need not recognize this as a separate disease. It represents, strictly speaking, the previous history of numerous cases of dementia præcox, in which a fuller development of the clinical picture takes place later. If one will, one may place the slighter cases alongside the "formes frustes," as they are described by the French in morbid pictures of another kind, the forms with poorly developed disorders, while the more severe would be compared with perhaps the simply demented paralysis. As numerous cases, beginning first as dementia simplex, later follow the ordinary course of dementia præcox, we have to do, as Diem also has already emphasized, with indefinite boundaries. Nor can I make up my mind to make a special place, as Vogt proposes, for dementia infantilis. It will have to be admitted that the conception of the disease has hitherto been insufficiently elucidated, and that therefore among the so-called cases all sorts of component parts of various kinds may be found. Nevertheless the picture described appears to me to correspond so completely with the dementia præcox

[1] Morselli, Rivista di freniatria sperimentale xxxiv. 3.

of adults, that we may without hesitation ascribe to it the majority of the cases with the proviso of the rejection of extraneous admixtures, as the assumption of a dementia præcox in childhood can present no difficulty to us now.

Psycho-reaction.—An extremely convenient solution of all these questions of delimitation seemed to be offered by the "psycho-reaction" brought forward by Much and Holzmann. It was a question of the inhibition in the presence of the serum of certain mental patients of the lysis of human red blood corpuscles effected by cobra poison. As this inhibiting effect was said only to belong to the serum of patients with dementia præcox or manic-depressive insanity, it would have furnished us with a valuable aid for establishing whether definite morbid pictures belong to one of those two great forms, and therewith also to the distinguishing of independent groups. If meantime the fact that the psycho-reaction is common to two groups of forms, which certainly are not nearly related clinically, had not aroused very grave doubts as to its reliability, further investigation has given the result, that there can at present be no talk of a diagnostic peculiarity in that kind of reaction, but that it much rather sometimes appears, sometimes fails, in morbid states of the most various kinds, and also in healthy individuals, just as in the forms named.

Clinical Experience.—We have therefore even yet to rely purely on the valuation of clinical experience. The result is, as it appears to me, that we are with great probability justified in connecting the great majority of the cases up to the present brought together under the name of dementia præcox with the same morbid process, and therefore in regarding it as a single form of disease. Everywhere the same *fundamental disorders* return again, the loss of inner unity in thinking, feeling, and acting, the dulling of higher emotions, the manifold and peculiar disorders of volition with the connected delusions of psychic constraint and influence, lastly the decay of the personality with comparatively slight damage to acquired knowledge and subordinate expertness. These features are certainly not all demonstrable with full clearness in each individual case. But still the general view over a great number of complete observations teaches that nowhere can a state be discovered which is not connected by imperceptible transitions with all the others.

In any case the differences in the individual clinical cases, as soon as their whole development is taken into account, seem to me to be not greater than possibly in paralysis. If one will, one may even in the appearance of simple demented, expansive, depressive, stuporous, galloping, and stationary varieties ·of the course, with or without remissions, as also of juvenile cases of a peculiar form, recognize a certain general agreement in the principal clinical features of the two diseases. As the delimitation of paralysis is now assured, the objections drawn from the difference of the states to the view of dementia præcox as a unity would be thereby weakened. We certainly miss in paralysis the real paranoid forms, but instead we find them again in cerebral syphilis, the clinical forms of which have a still greater multiplicity to show.

If we may, therefore, also regard the essential outlines of dementia præcox as assured, one must reckon with the possibility, indeed the probability, that progressive knowledge will yet bring us all kinds of rectifications of the limits of the disease. The giving a place to the childish forms of the malady, which certainly requires further investigation, signifies material progress also with regard to our ætiological views. Perhaps also the very desirable clearing up of the doctrine of the " late catatonias " will bring us a further increase of forms. On the other hand again perhaps some of the smaller groups will in course of time be got rid of; I think first of this possibility namely for the cases with *confusion of speech* and those with a *periodic course*.

The hypothesis has also frequently been brought forward that a morbid process other than dementia may be the foundation of the apparently cured cases. I will not dispute this possibility. Partly it will certainly be a simple mistake in diagnosis mostly to the loss of manic-depressive insanity. But there might well be also other curable forms of disease of different kinds with phenomena like catatonia, which we at present are not yet in a position to distinguish from dementia præcox. Those cases with simple persistence of hallucinations without decay of the personality might also come under consideration. It must, however, be recognized that *urgent* reasons for the separation of the cases, which do not go on to dementia, are as yet absent. The assumption, that the morbid process of dementia præcox, according to its severity and according to its extent, may not only produce phenomena of loss of different kinds, but also sometimes issue in recovery, sometimes lead to more or less profound dementia, is in itself not improbable. Certainly we shall cherish the eager wish to become clear as soon as it is at all possible, as to which way it will take.

CHAPTER XI

DIAGNOSIS.

The diagnosis of individual cases of dementia præcox has to distinguish the manifold states from a whole series of diseases which outwardly are similar but which are totally different in their course and issue. Unfortunately there is in the domain of psychic disorders no single morbid symptom which is thoroughly characteristic of a definite malady. Much rather each single feature of the morbid state may in like, or at least very similar form, also make at a time the impression of an essentially different morbid process in which exactly the same areas are involved. On the other hand we may expect that the composition of the *entire picture* made up of its various individual features, and especially also the changes which it undergoes in the course of the disease, could scarcely be produced in exactly the same way by diseases of a wholly different kind; at this or at that point, sooner or later, deviations will be certain to appear, consideration of which makes possible for us the distinguishing of the morbid forms. It may in certain circumstances be very difficult, not only to judge correctly of the diagnostic significance of such deviations, but even to recognize their very existence.

Catatonic Symptoms.— Special importance in the establishing of dementia præcox has, not without justification, been attributed to the demonstration of the so-called "catatonic" morbid symptoms. Under this term must principally be understood the *volitional disorders* first described by Kahlbaum as accompanying phenomena of catatonia, automatic obedience, negativism, mannerisms, stereotypies, impulsive actions. As undeniable as it is, that all these disorders in no other disease come under observation in such extent and multiplicity as in dementia præcox, just as little, however, may the appearance of one, or even of several, of these disorders be regarded as infallible proof of the presence of that malady. Certainly this restriction holds good in very different degree for the individual disorders. Automatic obedience, which represents only a sign of the surrender of the patient's own volition, is found

R

in a large series of morbid states of the most different kinds, and possesses therefore only very slight diagnostic significance. Impulsive actions and stereotypies come under observation in severe brain diseases, specially in paralysis, in infectious psychoses, in senile dementia, in idiots, and can therefore likewise only be used with great caution for the establishing of dementia præcox. Much more characteristic are negativism and mannerisms, which scarcely accompany any other morbid process uniformly in a pronounced form throughout a long period.

At this point meantime the consideration arises, that it is often uncommonly difficult to decide whether we really have to do with genuine catatonic morbid symptoms or not. Automatic obedience may be simulated by shyness ; impulsiveness of action by obscurity of motives in clouding of consciousness with inhibition of the movements of emotional expression ; stereotypy by uniformity of volitional actions, as that may be caused by the domination of definite, overpowering ideas or emotions. From genuine impulsive negativism there must be distinguished the surly, stubborn self-will of the paralytic and of the senile dement, the playful reserve of the hysteric, the pertly repellent conduct of the manic, and from the senseless perversities in action and behaviour, as they occur in dementia præcox, the conceited affectation of the hysteric, as also the wantonly funny solemnity of the manic patient. Often it will only be possible to find out these and other similar differences after considerable observation among changing conditions, after having made all sorts of experiments on the conduct of the patients under influences of various kinds; sometimes information is first got from observations in quite other domains about the correct interpretation of the phenomena.

Psychopathic States.—If we now consider in order the diagnosis of dementia præcox from individual diseases of another kind,[1] the question first comes before us, how far it may be confused with states produced by *morbid predisposition*. That among psychopathic inferior personalities a group is possibly found which we may regard as undeveloped cases of dementia præcox, as "latent schizophrenia" according to Bleuler's terminology, was formerly mentioned. Occasionally there come into notice certain shy, whimsical, queer people, and then perhaps many irritable, unaccountable psychopathics with a tendency to distrust and overweening

[1] Schott, Monatsschr. f. Psychiatrie u. Neurol. xvii. Erg.-Heft 99 ; Wilmanns, Centralblatt f. Nervenheilk. u. Psychiatrie 1907, 569 ; Bornstein, Zeitschr. f. d. ges. Neurol. u. Psychiatrie v. 145.

self-conceit, who may at least with a certain probability be supposed to be suffering from dementia præcox. On the other hand we cannot well accept such an interpretation for the great mass of those morbid states the foundation of which is anxiety and want of self-confidence. If the conduct of life exhibits here ever so many peculiarities and apparent incomprehensibilities, their origin can yet invariably be traced back in one or another way to intelligible motives. Only a small group of childishly weak-minded, weak-willed personalities without initiative, with hypochondriacal failure of volition, seems to belong to the frontier territory of dementia simplex.

Not at all infrequently a commencing dementia præcox is looked on as simple nervousness, hypochondria or neurasthenia and treated accordingly, and still more frequently regarded as moral depravity. The increasing failure in work is connected with exhaustion and over-exertion, perhaps also with the influence of some or other occurrence. Here above everything the decisive points for the diagnosis are the signs of psychic weakness, the want of judgment, the senselessness of the hypochondriacal complaints, the inaccessibility towards the reassuring statements of the physician, the emotional dulness and want of interest, the lack of improvement on relaxation from work, further, the more or less distinct manifestations of automatic obedience or of negativism. Hallucinations and sudden incomprehensible impulsive actions naturally are wholly in favour of dementia præcox.

Numerous patients, who on account of moral incapacity either become habitual criminals, or fall into prostitution, or who, being incapable of earning a living, drift into a vagrant life, are for many years disciplined and punished, if the more striking symptoms of dementia præcox are absent, till the appearance of more severe disorders, states of excitement and stupor, hallucinations of hearing, and delusions, makes clear the morbidity of their state. Here also the incoherence of thought and action and the peculiar dulness with which the patients let everything happen, may give hints to the expert for a correct decision. Of special importance is the proof, that in a certain period of life a change of the whole personality, a deterioration and a failing, has taken place; still the forerunners of such an "acquired folie morale," as we have seen, go back even to childhood. Many patients fall into drinking habits and then the extraordinary rapidity is surprising with which they break adrift, carry out the most incomprehensible actions, and become completely demoralized. At the same time there exists also in

sober moments a complete lack of understanding for the
consequences of what has happened and dull indifference
towards them.

Imbecility and Idiocy.—States of weakness, which are
produced by dementia præcox, may be regarded as imbecility
or idiocy, especially when they have already arisen in childhood, while otherwise the previous history will as a rule
point to the peculiarity of the malady. Sometimes it is
possible from the comparison of present performances with
earlier school reports, essays, letters, to establish the fact of
the mental falling off, and from that to conclude that the
case is probably one of dementia præcox. Where residua
of the disease, which has been passed through, have been
left behind, hallucinations of hearing, delusions, mannerisms,
negativistic features, the decision will be easy. Simple
rhythmical movements are, however, not of use for diagnosis,
which may, as a symptom of very profound injury to the
volitional mechanism, be produced by other morbid processes. If it is a case of simple weak-mindedness without
specially characteristic disorders, the disproportion between
knowledge and ability may often give effective points for
decision. As by dementia præcox what is remembered is
less injured than the ability to use it, we often still find
surprising knowledge, while efficiency has suffered most
severe losses. Imbeciles on the contrary can often manage
fairly well in their daily tasks, even when their knowledge
is of the very lowest degree. Correct recognition is very
important especially in military service, as the profound
incapacity of the hebephrenic is easily interpreted as laziness
and obstinacy and then leads to discipline which may have
as a consequence serious exacerbations of the state. Weak-
mindedness which has existed from childhood without focal
phenomena, which later experience an exacerbation, is as
a rule to be regarded as engrafted hebephrenia, if epilepsy
and cerebral syphilis can be excluded, the former by the
absence of seizures, the latter by the negative result of the
Wassermann reaction. In many cases the recognition of
the condition is made essentially easier by the failure of the
psychic pupillary reaction.

Manic-depressive Insanity.—By far the most important
point in diagnosis, but at the same time also the most
difficult, is the distinguishing of dementia præcox from
isolated attacks of manic-depressive insanity.[1] As little as
we can doubt that here we have to keep separate two morbid

[1] Urstein, Die Dementia præcox und ihre Stellung zum manisch-depressiven
Irresein. 1909 ; Thomsen, Allgem. Zeitschr. f. Psychiatrie, lxiv. 631.

processes quite different in their character, and as simple as the delimitation is in the great majority of cases, just as insufficient do our distinguishing characteristics yet appear in those cases in which we have before us a mingling of morbid symptoms of both psychoses.

Opinions still differ widely as to whether here greater weight must be attributed to the catatonic or to the circular symptoms for the classification of the case. I consider indeed the putting of this question wrong, and am coming more and more to the view that one must on principle beware of attributing characteristic significance to a *single morbid phenomenon.* Not even states differing so widely from each other as manic, paralytic, and alcoholic excitement can be distinguished from each other with certainty on the ground of a single psychic characteristic. We must indeed also keep in mind that the causes of disease everywhere meet preformed mechanisms in our brain, whose independent morbid activity attains to expression in the clinical picture. All possible stimuli will, therefore, by their attack at the same point be able to call forth perhaps very similar psychic morbid phenomena. But what hardly ever is produced in quite the same way by morbid processes of different kinds, is, as already mentioned above, the *total clinical picture,* including development, course and issue. If, therefore, isolated morbid symptoms and in certain circumstances whole pictures of states cannot always be interpreted with certainty in the sense of a definite disease, a complete survey of the whole disease will then at least invariably lead to the goal, when our knowledge of the domain concerned already suffices for the needs of such a task.

In the controversy about the significance of isolated morbid symptoms, however, it must further be kept in view, that their value is of very varied kind. Thus the frequently employed conception of " catatonic " phenomena[1] embraces a number of characteristics which are only in the smallest part specially peculiar to catatonia. Catalepsy, echophenomena, making faces, affected behaviour, speaking past the subject, speaking in artificial languages, rhythmic movements, peculiar gestures and attitudes, none of these by themselves alone justify, as with Wilmanns I must emphasize, the regarding of a case as catatonia. A more or less convincing proof is given by their accumulation and their connection with yet other disorders .in themselves likewise not characteristic, as hallucinations of hearing, delusions of influence on will,

---

[1] Soutzo, Les symptomes catatoniques ; leur mécanisme et leur valeur clinique 1903.

repellent conduct, indifference towards the surroundings, lack of susceptibility to influence, absence of movements of defence, abrupt change from stupor to excitement and so on. As already mentioned, genuine negativism, instinctive, purely passive resistance, seems to me to possess the relatively greatest significance as an isolated symptom. Here also, however, a mistake may be made, especially as it is sometimes impossible to be certain whether the resistance is instinctive or founded on imagination and emotional occurrences. The same difficulty meets us, moreover, in the remaining catatonic morbid symptoms. On this account they cannot always signify the same thing, because in the isolated case we know only the outward behaviour but not the inward origin.

As it appears to me, the circular morbid symptoms can make just as little claim to inviolable diagnostic significance. In the first place that is true for the periodic and also for the circular course, which, even though perhaps with certain deviations, may occur in very similar way in dementia præcox. Manic pressure of activity, which in its slighter forms is so characteristic, often in great excitement nearly approaches the picture of catatonic raving mania; the flight of ideas in similar circumstances becomes not infrequently a monotonous, persistent drivel. For the inhibition of will and thought the same may be said as for negativism; it may be impossible to distinguish them from the failure of mental activity and of volitional impulse, which is peculiar to dementia præcox. Sometimes the patients are themselves able to give an account of the inner origin of their actions, which then may become of special importance for the interpretation. Indubitably even that does not always allow of a certain judgment being made. At the commencement of a case of dementia præcox, when the patients often feel very distinctly the gradual annihilation of their will, one hears from them frequently utterances quite similar to those of the manic-depressive patients, although they are in reality related to essentially different processes.

The states of manic-depressive insanity therefore will not be, as I think, recognized from one isolated symptom, even though it may apparently be capable of only one interpretation, but only from the whole clinical picture with cautious weighing of the relations which exist between the individual features. For the delimitation from dementia præcox great weight must without doubt be laid on "intrapsychic ataxia," which was brought by Stransky especially into the foreground, that is on the want of inner logical arrangement of psychic events, which distinguishes this disease. Unfortunately it is not always easy to recognize the existence of this disorder, as also in the mixed states of manic-depressive insanity; owing to injuries of various kinds to nearly related functions and the interconnection of different states, pictures may temporarily arise which externally at least are similar. (Flight of ideas with inhibition of thought, exalted ideas with depressive mood and so on).

From different sides the attempt has been made to use *association experiment* for the characterization of the two diseases discussed here. Isserlin draws special attention to the fact that manic-depressive patients invariably exhibit a desire to try the exercise, even though they may appear indifferent and impoverished in thought. In contrast to that there is observed in dementia præcox persistence of individual answers, sometimes through whole series of attempts, wholly nonsensical or maneristic associations, repellent conduct, abrupt change between very short and greatly prolonged periods. Bornstein also found frequent absence, repetitions, poverty of associations in dementia præcox in contrast to the tendency of the manic patients to produce all possible associations and to spin the thread further; the clang-associations which are frequent in the latter were almost entirely absent in the former.

If we now look at the individual clinical states in the *depressive forms*, the early appearance of numerous hallucinations of hearing and of nonsensical delusions, in particular the idea of influence on will, makes dementia præcox probable, especially if ordinary sense remains preserved. Hallucinations of hearing are in manic-depressive insanity much rarer and have generally a less definite stamp, so that the patients usually reproduce their content not in exact words but only in general expressions; they very frequently refer them to their own thoughts as voices of conscience, and are very much disturbed by them, especially as the content is invariably in the closest relation to their depressive ideas. The train of thought of the patients is made difficult, and they become painfully aware of this. Wilmanns places extraordinary weight on this "intrapsychic inhibition," the "feeling of insufficiency," for the diagnosis of manic-depressive insanity, and considers it, just like the hypomanic mood, to be more characteristic than the "catatonic" phenomena in dementia præcox. On the other hand I have still doubts of all kinds.

It is, however, correct, that the patients with dementia præcox, who likewise often complain of incapacity for thought, usually describe not so much the feeling of inward inhibition as that of influence by external forces; they cannot think what they will, and must think what they do not will, what is forced on them, while the manic-depressive patients cannot collect their thoughts and reduce them to order, or in certain circumstances, as when they have an inward flight of ideas, cannot retain them, but they only exceptionally feel themselves dominated by external influences. Urstein thinks that the patients with dementia præcox only feel subjective inhibition, while the patients in the circular states of depression are inhibited subjectively and objectively. I cannot agree with either opinion.

In general there is found in the manic-depressive patients more tendency to, and ability for, the *observation of self*, to painful dissection of their psychic state, in contrast to the indifference with which in dementia præcox we so often see the patients regard the most deep-reaching disorders of their psychic life. In the latter even the most exciting delusions are produced with remarkably slight emotional participation, and as a rule also they do not induce in the patient any definite, intentional action. It is striking in the highest degree that the patients are usually not at all disturbed by the phenomenon, just as mysterious as it is weird, of hearing voices, apart from their content sometimes provocative, sometimes wholly trifling, and often for months do not utter the slightest complaint on that account, when they are not specially questioned on the subject. Generally it is only with difficulty that a glance is gained into the occurrences of their inner life, even when the patients are able to give utterance without difficulty to their thoughts; they are taciturn, repellent, evade questions, give indefinite information that tells nothing. Neither do they take any share in what happens in their surroundings; they do not greet their relatives who visit them, they do not speak a word during the visit, but perhaps devour greedily everything that is brought to them.

In contrast to that the *signs of anguish or dejection* are never absent in circular states of depression. It is true that the expression of the inward states may be limited to a considerable extent. Nevertheless the emotional susceptibility to influence is shown by stimulation of ideas emphasized by emotion, by letters, by visits, with considerable persuasion most unmistakably in the signs of tension or excitement, sometimes even in violent outbursts of feeling. By the occurrences in their surroundings the patients are much more strongly moved, relate them to themselves, fall into anxiety. While in dementia præcox the emotions are silent, without the patients noticing the disorder, or being disturbed about it, the manic-depressive patients complain in despairing accents of the feeling of inward desolation and emptiness, of their inability to feel joy or sorrow, although in their conduct emotional reactions of great vivacity appear. Towards the physician likewise they are indeed often monosyllabic, but do not make evasions ; they let themselves be stirred up by persuasion to further utterances, and they invariably bring forth their complaints with the signs of inward agitation. Their activity is developed logically from their ideas and from their mood even when in itself it is ever so nonsensical, while frequently in dementia præcox very sudden impulses, not explicable even to the patient himself, interrupt the inner connection of psychic events.

Monotonous lamentation of anxious patients must not be allowed to mislead to the assumption of catatonic stereotypy. The constant return of the same utterances and gestures is here not the result of senseless, perseverating impulses, but the expression of a permanent emotional reaction dominating everything, which continually produces the same ideas and tries to express itself by the same expedients. It is true that the originally intelligent movements and utterances in the course of time show a certain rigidity, pulling, tripping, arranging, rhythmic screaming. A female patient for years imitated the movements and noises of the wild animals into which she thought she was transformed. As a rule it will be possible to demonstrate their origin from ideas and emotions in contrast to the purely impulsive senseless discharges of volition in dementia præcox.

Very important is the distinction of negativism from the *anxious resistance* and the *inhibition of will* in manic-depressive insanity. Even the behaviour at the approach and greeting of the physician permits certain conclusions to be made. The negativistic patient does not look up, hides himself perhaps, turns away or stares straight in front of him, and does not betray by any movement of a muscle that he is aware of anything. All the same he usually perceives better than the manic-depressive patient, who indeed also perhaps remains mute and motionless, but still in his glance, in the expression of his face, in slight attempts at movement, acceleration of the pulse, flushing, stoppage of respiration, lets it be seen that he has felt the impressions. In the negativistic patients further we meet rigid resistance at every attempt to change their position, but only on actual interference ; on the other hand the patients endure simple or even painful touches and even dangerous threats (needle at eye) for the most part without defending themselves, do not fall into excitement, at most move out of the way, let the needle stuck into their eyelid remain sticking. Lastly the resistance may of itself or under the influence of prudent compulsion pass directly into automatic obedience. In the manic-depressive cases on the other hand resistance begins with the threatening danger, no matter whether a change of position takes place or not ; nor do the limbs moved out of their position take up again with inviolable tenacity exactly the former attitude. At the same time a threatening approach leads to lively expressions of emotion, to screaming, evasion, anxious defence.

The stuporous catatonic usually moves little or not at all, especially not, if asked to do so. Persuasion has no result or it makes resistance still greater. But if he does do anything, which cannot be reckoned on, this happens without recognizable retardation, often even with uncommon rapidity, while in the patient suffering from inhibition, such actions, which require volitional resolves, are carried out slowly and hesitatingly, as can be demonstrated now and then even in quite simple movements or answers. Sometimes in inhibition it may be demonstrated that well-practised speech utterances, as numbers, are run off without hindrance, while difficulties are increased as soon as the morbid ideas are touched on, a sign that emotional influences play an authoritative part. Many a movement which is asked for remains wholly undone, yet at least preliminary movements for the desired action (slight movements of the lips, twitching of the fingers) are frequently seen, especially if the inhibition is gradually overcome by powerful persuasion. Contrariwise in catatonics one may observe how the impulse, at first perhaps appearing, is thereupon abruptly interrupted, made retrogressive, perhaps even turned into its opposite.

For distinguishing the states of excitement of dementia præcox from *manic seizures*, it must first be noticed, that the faculty of perception and ordinary sense are usually more severely injured in mania than in the former. While the patients even in the wildest catatonic mania are for the most part surprisingly clear about their position and surroundings, we shall always meet in severe manic excitement considerable disorder of perception, of thought and of orientation. In the agitated states of dementia præcox attention is scarcely occupied with the surroundings, although these are perceived quite well ; it is not easily diverted. The manic on the contrary perceives inaccurately and fugitively, and turns to anything new which enters into his circle of vision. Frequently he speaks at once to the physician, overwhelms him with a throng of words, while the patient suffering from catatonic excitement does not trouble himself about the physician, simply continues his perpetual movement and can only by special exertions be brought to give a sensible answer.

In dementia præcox again *conversation* is frequently altogether senseless and incoherent in spite of very slight excitement, while even in the most violent raving mania we seldom quite lose an at least approximate understanding of the manic train of thought. In the former there is also adherence to a few expressions going as far as marked verbigeration ; on the other hand in the manic train of thought, in spite of the absence of all connection, the progression from one circle of ideas to another can still almost always be recognized. Speaking in a self-invented language occurs also in manics, but only in the form of boasting about foreign languages ; in the same way occasional neologisms appear as students' jokes and not, as in dementia præcox, as derailments of expression in speech. A tendency to clang-associations and rhyming, as well as flights of ideas, is peculiar to manic conversation ; on the other hand senseless monotonous jingling of syllables gives evidence for dementia præcox.

Some of these distinguishing marks fall away in *mania with inhibition of thought,* in which the few and monotonous speech utterances as well as the vacant merriment make a complete impression of weak-mindedness, and therefore can bring the assumption of dementia præcox very near. However, it has to do here with poverty of thought and consequently little substance in conversation, and not with unrelated incoherence and impulsive stereotypy. Laughing is often connected with external causes, and in the intervals isolated actions, more playful and merry than senseless, are interpolated.

Mood is in mania for the most part cheerful, merry, or irritable, but in dementia præcox, silly, convulsively unrestrained, or indifferent ; Dreyfus remarks that the hilarity of the manic has something infectious in it, in dementia præcox it has something repulsive ; it has no relation to the ideas of the patients. In the utterances of the patients with dementia præcox there often continually appears even in slight excitement a deliberate obscenity, such as only occurs once in a way in manics in occasional outbursts of abuse.

Further there has specially to be observed the aimlessness of the catatonic movements compared with the *pressure of occupation* of the manic, who invariably seeks relations with his surroundings. In catatonics the movements are monotonous and are repeated innumerable times in the same way, while in manics being dependent on changing impressions, ideas and feelings, they usually always assume new forms. Not infrequently we meet in the excitement of dementia præcox a striking want of relation between pressure of speech and pressure of movement, perhaps on account of the fact that they are here not brought into connection with each other by higher psychic processes. The patients may be in violent movement without at the same time saying a word, or they chatter incessantly without moving from the spot and even without lively gestures. Therefore here the pressure of movement is often limited to a very small space, perhaps a part of the bed ; the manic on the contrary seeks everywhere for an opportunity to occupy himself, runs about, busies himself with the other patients, follows the physician, carries on all sorts of mischievous tricks. To these are added the constrained and spreading nature of the movements, the mannerisms and nonsensical impulses in catatonia in contrast to the natural, and to the healthy individual much more comprehensible, conduct of the manic. In other words, in mania perception, thought, orientation, are relatively more profoundly disordered than in the excitement of dementia præcox, while in the latter it is specially emotions, actions, and speech expression which are injured in a peculiar way.

Special difficulties in delimitation, as Wilmanns rightly brings forward, are presented by the *mixed states* of manic-depressive insanity. The differentiation of mania which is poor in thought from catatonic excitement has been already mentioned. In manic stupor the peculiarly cheerful mood, the lively, though concealed, attention to the surroundings with slight senselessness, the playful, certainly often scanty and empty remarks, the susceptibility to influence by persuasion and external occurrences, lastly, the occasional purposeful, merry actions of the manic as opposed to the empty merriment, the indifference and the inaccessibility, the incoherent unrelated conversation, as well as the nonsensical, monotonous, impulsive discharges of volition in dementia præcox might usually after considerable observation make the differentiation possible. For the correct interpretation of the remaining mixed states suitable points of view can be gained from the consideration of the individual disorders which compose them.

The *content of the delusions* offers in general few effective points for the differentiation of the two diseases here discussed. Delusions of sin, ideas of persecution, hypochondriacal ideas may in both appear in very similar forms. Exalted. ideas will mostly only be met with in manic-depressive insanity when other indications also of the manic state are recognizable. The delusion of physical, specially sexual, influence points with great probability, the idea of influence on thought and will almost certainly, to dementia præcox. Thomsen points out that the delusions in manic-depressive insanity have more connection with one another, have more inner unity, while in dementia præcox they are more changing, more incoherent. The nonsensical character of the delusions must not be immediately regarded as a sign of mental weakness, still in manic-depressive patients it is usually connected either with very lively emotional participation or with dreamlike confusion. Where these accompanying phenomena are absent and exalted ideas are connected with the delusion of influence on will and perhaps persistent vivid hallucinations of hearing still exist, the assumption of dementia præcox will be justified.

The recognition of dementia præcox is often made specially difficult by its course in *isolated attacks* separated by approximately free intervals. If the clinical picture of the state is not wholly unequivocal, the question in such cases will always have to be raised whether it is not a case of manic-depressive insanity, specially if at the same time states of depression also alternate with those of excitement. Thomsen has rightly called attention to the fact that the course of a single period of manic-depressive insanity in general is usually more even. Sudden and abrupt change of the states, as also shortness and irregularity of attacks and intervals, specially with more frequent recovery, will arouse rather the suspicion of dementia præcox. But above everything the conduct of the patients during the periods of improvement will have to be considered. Apparent complete restoration, clear insight into the nature of the disease, return of former efficiency, absence of all peculiarities in action and behaviour, will make manic-depressive insanity probable, though not absolutely certain. On the other hand the persistence of those peculiarities, which we formerly became acquainted with in the discussion of remissions, allows the conclusion to be made that dementia præcox is present, conduct sometimes quiet and constrained or inaccessible and repellent, sometimes irritable and self-willed or capricious and peculiar, emotional dulness, loss of endeavour and energy. Wilmanns has in the meantime properly drawn attention to the fact that shyness and embarrassment at the examination may simulate the disorders named, further that in certain circumstances it may be a case of vanishing morbid residua, lastly, that also in manic-depressive patients not infrequently between the attacks all kinds of abnormalities are demonstrable. It is true that they might incline more to the states belonging to this disease, anxiety or depression, shyness, restlessness and perplexity, frequently also lack of clear understanding of the disease.

Here it will not always be easy to arrive at a certain judgment from the evidence which is often so insignificant. Zendig after some years out of 370 cases of dementia præcox searched out 127, in which the diagnosis had not appeared quite certain. He came to the conclusion that of them sixty-seven patients, the majority of whom were women, were to be regarded with greater or less probability as manic-depressive, because they exhibited no abnormalities at all, or at least only such as may be expected within the limits of the disease named. The result is, however, not final. My experiences have shown me that in cases with no very clear clinical morbid picture the possibility of dementia præcox may nowhere be left out of account, where after the attack of disease any changes at all of the psychic personality have made their appearance. Nevertheless attacks which have occurred many years previously, which have resulted in approximate recovery, but still more repeated attacks, especially those of contrasted colouring which have brought about no recognizable state of weakness will with rare exceptions justify the diagnosis of manic-depressive insanity.

Hysteria.—Very frequently cases of dementia præcox are regarded as hysteria[1]; on the one hand the affected, often erotic, behaviour of the patients, on the other hand the appearance of hysteroid convulsive phenomena commonly leads to that. The drivelling terminal states with delusions are then perhaps termed hysteric insanity. Maggiotto reports that among 101 patients with the diagnosis of hysteria forty-seven turned out to be cases of dementia præcox ; in a further series of 240 supposed hysterics there were forty-three similar errors in diagnosis. What distinguishes hysteria and dementia præcox from each other, is above everything the *behaviour of the emotions*. In hysteria we find a heightened susceptibility of the emotional life ; in dementia præcox the susceptibility is lowered. In hysterics, therefore, we observe rapid, violent, and often even lasting influence by impressions emphasized by emotion, while the emotional reactions in dementia præcox are mostly shallow or of short duration and essentially independent of external influences. The permanent

[1] Reyneau, Démence précoce et hystérie. Thèse. 1905.

inner relations to the occurrences of the external world, as they are developed in hysterics by the vivid emotional emphasis of the events of life, are in dementia præcox extinguished, or at least very much weakened ; the patients remain indifferent towards visits, surprising communications, exciting experiences, which in hysteria immediately find response in lively reactions. Stransky points out that the patients with dementia præcox even after the most violent excitement are at once able to fall quietly into deep sleep, while in hysterics the emotional reactions continue working for a much longer time.

The *resistance* of the hysteric is not impulsive but it bears sometimes the stamp of angry irritability, sometimes that of childish defiance or affected coquetry ; it is not limited to passive resistance, as it mostly is in dementia præcox, but leads to outbursts of indignation and to defensive movements ; it can often be calmed by persuasion, in contrast to the rigid lack of susceptibility to influence of the catatonic. The *affected behaviour* of the hysteric arises from the more or less clearly felt need of being conspicuous and of showing off. It aims at working on the surroundings and is therefore definitely influenced by them and their behaviour, while the mannerisms in dementia præcox arise without purpose, even constrainedly, and do not exhibit the slightest relation to the .surroundings.

Disconnected *talk* is carried on by hysterics only in dazed conditions with clouded consciousness and disorientation ; on the other hand the incoherence of dementia præcox offers such a peculiar picture just because the patients for the most part are wholly clear. Moreover, in hysteric utterances of that kind the course of definite trains of thought may usually still to a certain extent be followed, the connection with occurrences in the surroundings, experiences emphasized by emotion, dreamy imaginations ; while in dementia præcox it is a case of a senseless sequence of incomprehensible fragments of thought often with persistence of isolated component parts. Also in the speaking past a subject of the hysterics the relation of the evasive reply to the question put and, therefore, their mental working can usually still be distinctly recognized, in contrast to the utterances of negativistic patients, which as a rule are wholly disconnected.

Genuine *hallucinations* in hysterics come under observation only in dazed conditions or in half-waking states ; they occur far more in the realm of sight than in that of hearing, and are mostly of an exciting nature ; it is a case of threatening or beneficent figures in significant garments. The invariable appearance of hallucinations of hearing even by day excludes hysteria according to my experience, and gives decisive evidence for dementia præcox; the same holds true for the undiscerning continuance in ideas of persecution and exaltation after complete disappearance of clouding of consciousness. This observation is probably in close connection with the circumstance, that in hysteria no weakness of judgment is developed, as usually meets us in such a striking way in dementia præcox in the unresisting giving way to the most nonsensical ideas in spite of perfect clearness. In hysteria whole regions of the psychic life may temporarily be forced out of connection with consciousness; but still they go on working approximately as at other times, something like separated choirs. In dementia præcox that connection remains preserved, but the psychic faculties lose their mutual inner contact like an orchestra without a conductor.

The *seizures* in dementia præcox are mostly fainting fits or epileptiform in character, still I have repeatedly observed seizures which wholly resembled those of hysteria. It may be thought that here, as occurs in manic-depressive insanity, in epilepsy, in paralysis, in focal diseases of the brain, the morbid process in certain circumstances is also able to set in action psychogenic disorders. The *stigmata* of the hysterics will not usually be found in dementia præcox, still anæsthesia of the cornea, of the tongue, of the skin of the face, may be simulated by indifference and inattention, or by negativistic suppression of the reactions; unilateral absence of sensation may be regarded as pointing to hysteria, as also circumscribed paralyses or contractures. The *dysæsthesiæ* of the hysterics are usually changing and susceptible to influence up to a certain degree; those of dementia præcox are monotonous and obstinate, and otherwise than in hysteria are easily elaborated to nonsensical hypochondriacal ideas, or ideas of persecution. Occasionally I was able to assign morbid states, which at first looked quite like hysteria, to dementia præcox, because the *psychic reaction of the pupils* was extinguished; further observation confirmed this interpretation. Hübner has reported similar experiences.

Psychogenic Psychoses.—Special difficulties may arise for the correct apprehension of the morbid states in *prisoners*. Besides dementia præcox psychogenic forms of disease come under observation here, which may exhibit great external resemblance to it; on the one hand there are hallucinatory-paranoid states, on the other stuporous states. In the former probably above everything the absence of characteristic independent disorders of volition is to be emphasized. Mannerisms and stereotypies are absent, as also genuine negativism, which, however, in consequence of delusions, may be simulated by repellent behaviour. The patients are confused only in excitement, and when consciousness is clouded, but do not exhibit the incoherence of dementia præcox which continues even without emotional reaction and with complete clearness. As a rule hallucinations and delusions last comparatively only a short time and disappear soon on the removal of the patients to suitable surroundings, especially on their being taken from solitary confinement. Even when the delusions are not forgotten or corrected, there is still no further elaboration, and also no development of weak-mindedness and no decay of the psychic personality. The patients remain natural in their conduct, preserve their emotional activity and are able to take up their former life again.

In states of stupor the patients are inaccessible, mute and resistive, like the catatonics, but it is usually easy to persuade oneself soon that their conduct is not impulsive, but is determined by ideas and emotional reactions. They provide in an orderly way for the satisfaction of their needs, observe their surroundings, try to occupy themselves in some way or other, are clearly affected by external influences, and an increase of their stupor can at once be recognized as soon as one occupies himself with them. In contrast to that, negativistic stupor in its rigid constraint exhibits, it may be, sudden and quite incalculable changes, but is in the highest degree independent of external occurrences.

Dissimulation.—The silly, capricious behaviour, the repellent attitude and the speaking past the subject of negativistic patients, further the absence of natural reactions to external interference, sometimes arouse the suspicion of deliberate dissimulation. In this domain the utmost caution is necessary. In several such cases, in which I believed with certainty that I had to do with undoubted dissimulation, I nevertheless saw dementia præcox develop later. Here inquiry must be made whether in the previous history morbid features in the sense of that malady have not already been demonstrable, whether an intelligible motive for dissimulation is present, whether the phenomena have immediately followed the arrest or the sentence, whether they continue when the patient thinks he is unobserved, whether they are susceptible to psychic influences. If mannerisms,

S

stereotypies, or hallucinations of hearing appear, the assumption of dissimulation is of course unfounded.

Epilepsy.—As in dementia præcox epileptiform seizures occur, the malady may be taken for epilepsy ; Näcke has described cases as " late epilepsy," which obviously were in substance dementia præcox. For the most part, however, the seizures in dementia præcox only appear as isolated phenomena, as precursors of the disease, or after it has existed for many years. Rarely it comes once in a while to an accumulation like a status in which the patients may succumb. Once I observed in a catatonic such frequent and regular epileptiform seizures, but with them also hysteroid seizures, that I was tempted to believe in a more chance connection of the two diseases without, however, becoming clear on the subject. Morawitz [1] has described a series of similar cases with epileptic seizures existing from childhood, and he interprets them as epilepsy with catatonic features. The remaining phenomena of epilepsy are absent in dementia præcox. The weak-mindedness caused by epilepsy has also essentially different features. It is characterized by impoverishment of the range of ideas up to the most ordinary things of everyday life, limitation of the emotional relations to the welfare and the woes of the patient's own person and his nearest relatives, great weakening and imperfections of memory with preservation of orderly thought, action and behaviour. If with this is compared the incoherence of thought with fairly good preservation of memory, the general emotional dulness, the profound disorder of volitional action, as we meet it in dementia præcox, the differentiation of the states will not generally be difficult.

On the other hand it has repeatedly happened to me that I have taken commencing catatonias for the dazed condition of epilepsy. To take the one for the other is especially easy, if perhaps a convulsive seizure has preceded. A point for differentiation may be given by the negativism of the catatonic as opposed to the anxious resistance of the epileptic. Perception and orientation might for the most part be more profoundly disordered in the dazed state of epilepsy than in catatonia. Senseless answers to simple questions, rapid and correct performance of commands point more to catatonia. In epilepsy the anxious or ecstatic mood usually lets itself be clearly seen ; action is generally not so much impulsive as dominated by definite delusional ideas and feelings, which also come to light in conversation. Therefore we more frequently see the epileptic making assaults or attempts at flight or com-

[1] Morawitz, Klinische Mischformen von Epilepsie und Katatonie. Diss. 1900.

mitting deeds of violence, while the activity of the catatonic bears the characteristics of the senseless and peculiar, and betrays fewer relations to the surroundings. A certain stereotypy of speech and action may occur in both states, as also loss or clouding of memory. On the other hand the previous history generally, the further course always, will soon make the condition of things clear.

Paralysis.—The delimitation of dementia præcox from paralysis has lost almost all its former difficulties by cyto-logical and especially serological investigation. In the con-junction with lues, which occasionally occurs, we find, indeed, deviation of complement in the blood and perhaps increase of cells in the cerebro-spinal fluid, but never the Wassermann reaction in the latter which is so characteristic of paralysis. If further the physical symptoms of paralysis are taken into account, especially the reflex rigidity of the pupils, the dis-orders of speech and writing, the seizures accompanying focal phenomena, the distinction will usually be easy, particularly as the age of the patients also gives some evidence for the decision. The most important characteristics for the differ-entiation, which result from psychic findings, have already been mentioned in the section about paralysis.

Amentia.[1]—The states in dementia præcox which are accompanied by confused excitement and numerous hallucina-tions, have often been called amentia and traced back to exhausting causes. Experience has shown me that cases of that kind cannot be separated from the remaining forms of dementia præcox according to the origin, course and issue. Only among the psychoses developing in immediate sequence to severe infectious diseases is there a group of cases to be differentiated, which in their clinical picture, as in their further development, deviate from dementia præcox, and are caused by the toxins of infectious diseases. The points of view, which for their characterization as opposed to the disease here treated of come into consideration, have been discussed in the individual forms of infectious insanity. Laurès[2] calls them by the name "démence précoce acci-dentelle" in contrast to the real "démence précoce constitu-tionelle"; this in my opinion is not expedient and leads to error.

Cerebral Syphilis.—Considerable difficulties, which at present cannot always with certainty be overcome, may arise, when there is a question whether certain acute hallucinatory states of excitement in patients demonstrably syphilitic are

[1] Confusional or delirious insanity.
[2] Laurés, La confusion mentale chronique et ses rapports avec la démence précoce, 1907.

to be regarded as the expression of syphilis or of dementia præcox by chance accompanied by syphilis. A series of such cases have occurred in my experience; in all of course paralysis could be excluded according to the points of view expounded above. Here the demonstration of bodily symptoms seems to me to be of importance, which may point to the existence of a cerebro-spinal syphilis (lymphocytosis of the cerebro-spinal fluid, disorders of the pupillary play, of reflexes, paralyses of the ocular muscles, disorders of speech and writing, pareses, seizures), on the other hand the absence of independent disorders of volition (negativism, mannerisms, also stereotypies), further of torpor, and the preservation of emotional activity. All these symptoms would give more evidence for a syphilitic foundation for the morbid state, as also conspicuous improvement of the same under specific treatment. In the rare cases in which once in a while in a case of focal disease of the brain "catatonic" symptoms are observed, the demonstration of the focal phenomena should keep us from the assumption of dementia præcox.

Paranoid Diseases.—At present the delimitation of dementia præcox from certain paranoid diseases appears least of all to be cleared up. Genuine paranoia itself is certainly not easily mistaken for it. In *paranoia* above everything the independent disorders of volition are absent. While our paranoid patients because of the regardless folly and danger of their activity usually very soon come into conflict with their neighbours and with the public authorities, true paranoiacs usually control themselves so far, that more serious collisions with other individuals, as with public authorities, are avoided; they preserve also in the essentials the capacity of managing to a certain extent in the struggle of life. Their actions and behaviour appear only in so far abnormal as they are the outcome of their delusions; for the rest they are mostly commonplace and inconspicuous. Negativism, mannerisms, stereotypy, confusion of speech, neologisms are completely absent, as also the phenomena of influence on will. To that has to be added that the patients do not suffer from hallucinations, that their delusions are not incoherent and nonsensical, but connected and mentally elaborated, that the emotional reactions have suffered no loss.

In the further course also it is seen that destruction and finally disintegration of the personality does not take place as in dementia præcox, that much rather the inner unity of the psychic processes remains permanently preserved. If we see the patients after five or six years again, they appear in essentials unchanged, perhaps a little more resigned and by all kinds of experiences of life made more mellow, but with the old ideas, perfectly reasonable and well-balanced in conversation, bearing, and behaviour. The paranoid patients in dementia præcox in favourable cases repudiate their former delusions, yet have become shy, quiet, indifferent, weak of will. Or they bring forward other similar ideas but in a more disconnected, more extraordinary form, without proportionate emotional emphasis, contradictory, without mental elaboration, without essential influence on endeavour and action. But just as frequently they present the picture of one of the terminal states described with its many fluctuations, and are incoherent, silly, manneristic, negativistic or dull.

The differentiation of paranoid dementia præcox from the similar alcoholic and syphilitic morbid states we have already tried to make clear in another place. The reasons why we have thought that we should give some other forms of paranoid diseases an independent position, we shall explain in the next section. Unfortunately there we shall frequently have to move on very uncertain ground.

CHAPTER XII.

HOW TO COMBAT IT.

As we do not know the actual causes of dementia præcox, we shall not be able at present to consider how to combat it. Lomer has, it is true, proposed as a heroic prophylactic measure bilateral *castration* as early as possible, but scarcely anyone will be found who would have the courage to follow him. Besides Henneberg in a case of pseudo-hermaphroditism saw just after the removal of the testes, which were situated in the inguinal region, a paranoid psychosis develop, which probably belonged to the domain of dementia præcox. One of my patients, a physician, who castrated himself, experienced no improvement of his condition by it.

Bruce in connection with his discovery of a streptococcus tried without success the *immunization* of a patient by sensitized goat's serum ; in another case beginning acutely he used dead bouillon cultures with favourable effect according to his report. In the meantime we shall regard this attempt also with expectancy. The same may be said of the partial *excision of the thyroid gland,* which was carried out by Berkley in ten cases and is said to have resulted in six in improvement or recovery. He thought that by re-section of a lobe of the thyroid gland he would increase the blood-supply to the parathyroid glands, and he recommends the administration of lecithin at the same time. This procedure has been several times repeated, by Judin in two cases, by Kanavel and Pollock in twelve cases, by van der Scheer in seven cases, almost always without result ; only van der Scheer saw improvement in two cases of which the one ran its course with Basedow's phenomena, the other exhibited struma. Pinheiro and Riedel report somewhat more favourable results. Pighini saw on administration of parathyroidin improvement of the pulse and of the disorders of metabolism which were found by him. Many years ago I endeavoured for a long time to acquire influence on dementia præcox by the introduction of preparations of every possible organ, of the thyroid gland, of the testes, of the ovaries and so on, unfortunately without any effect.

Prophylaxis.—In children with such characteristics as we so very frequently find in the previous history of dementia præcox, one might think of an attempt at prophylaxis, especially if the malady had been already observed in the parents or brothers and sisters. Whether it is possible in such circumstances to ward off the outbreak of the threatening disease, we do not know. But in any case it will be advisable to promote to the utmost of one's power general bodily development and to avoid one-sided training in brainwork, as it may well be assumed that a vigorous body grown up under natural conditions will be in a better position to overcome the danger than a child exposed to the influences of effeminacy, of poverty, and of exact routine, and especially of city education. Childhood spent in the country with plenty of open air, bodily exercise, education beginning late without ambitious aims, simple food, would be the principal points to keep in view. Meyer, who regards dementia præcox essentially as the effect of unfavourable influences of life and education on personalities with abnormal dispositions, hopes by all these measures to be able to prevent the development of the malady.

Treatment of Symptoms.—With regard to the main point we see ourselves for the present thrown back solely on treating the phenomena of the disease already present. Firstly in the cases which arise acutely or subacutely the placing of the patient in an institution is necessary to prevent accidents and suicide. Rest in bed, supervision, care for sleep and food, are here the most important requisites. In the states of excitement prolonged baths are suitable, the employment of which, it must be admitted, often meets with great difficulties, as the patients do not remain in the bath, but always jump out again, perform neck-breaking gymnastics, roll about on the floor. The next thing now to be tried is to quiet the patient so far by a sedative, hyoscine, sulphonal, trional, veronal, that he may remain some hours in the bath ; he then usually soon becomes accustomed to it, and now, while whirling, splashing, plunging, turning round, gesticulating, only makes passing attempts to leave the warm water and lets himself be brought back again to it without difficulty.

If in very severe and lasting excitement this procedure is unsuccessful, the best expedient, which invariably after a longer or shorter time leads to the goal, is the employment of moist warm packs. After a preliminary resistance of short duration the patient usually with surprising rapidity consents to these measures, even if, as with us, the coverings are on principle not fastened. If he unrolls himself, as happens fairly soon at first, the attempt is again made to keep him in the bath, and, if the restlessness makes that impossible, the pack is renewed. This procedure in severe cases, helped in the beginning by sedatives, is continued day and night without interruption, but so that after at longest two hours the pack is exchanged for the bath, and the patient after one or two hours only then returns to the pack, if he will by no means remain in the bath. By such a regulated continuous change between pack and bath the most severe states of excitement are usually so far moderated after a few days that the simple bath treatment, or even, if at first only temporarily, rest in bed is possible. Care for regular feeding in very reduced, sleepless, resistive patients, in certain circumstances by the stomach-tube, is requisite, as also the regulation of the bowels, and the cleansing of the mouth, which is often encrusted by the continuous screaming and speaking.

During states of stupor the continual refusal of food may make tube-feeding necessary ; frequent weighing is here indispensable. Likewise the regular evacuation of the bowels has to be kept in mind, and because of the negativistic retention of urine, which sometimes occurs, of the bladder as well. The uncleanliness of the patients, which is often great, demands the most careful attention. The danger of intentional and unintentional self-inflicted injuries can be met to a certain extent by the use of a padded bedstead ; but in spite of that it often enough still happens that there are skin-abrasions, bruises, furuncles, and so on, which then show the usefulness of the employment of the prolonged bath, and in certain circumstances demand surgical treatment.

As soon as the acute disorders disappear, the main thing is to preserve as far as possible what the disease has not destroyed. Often the return to the family is now possible and even suitable, if the circumstances are to some extent favourable, and if states of excitement, uncleanliness, refusal of food, and similar more severe phenomena have not remained behind. Bleuler without hesitation advises early discharge, as he, in part probably because of his views of the unfavourable action of certain complexes, fears that the patient might " shut himself up." It is indeed the case that the removal to another ward or institution, or to former circumstances, sometimes exercises a surprisingly favourable influence. The patients who up till then had been perhaps wholly mute and inaccessible begin already on the journey home to converse with strangers in the train, stop refusing food, go without making any fuss to their accustomed work at home. Further it must be acknowledged that the monotonous daily routine of institutional life, which relieves the patient of all independent activity and of all thought for himself, secures to him, it is true, far-reaching protection, but at the same time must also have an enervating influence and above everything must to a high degree blunt intellect, emotion and volition. To these considerations there is certainly opposed the difficulty that many patients are dangerous to themselves or to their surroundings, or are quite helpless and in need of careful attention. Nevertheless many of the more difficult patients behave themselves at home surprisingly well, so that one does not need to be too anxious about experiments in discharge. In the case of female patients, however, the danger of pregnancy, if there is not careful oversight, is to be guarded against. Where it is possible, before the discharge to the patient's own home, care in a family under medical supervision will first be tried.

Occupation.—With all our measures we can meantime not prevent the great majority of those who are psychically crippled or half-crippled after dementia præcox gradually being gathered into large institutions and homes for the insane, and these patients, as they do not quickly die off, and often pass their whole life in the institution, *form the great mass of the insane who require to be cared for.* What is necessary for them is occupation, which alone can preserve by exercise the capabilities which still remain to them, and prevent them from wholly sinking into dulness. For them, therefore, perhaps still more than for other forms of disease, *colonies for the insane,* with their manifold opportunities for work and treatment on general lines, preserving independence as much as possible, are a blessing which can scarcely be too highly valued ; family care also plays for them an important part as a transition to discharge or as a permanent shelter. Frequently one sees even very demented patients still cheerfully and usefully employing the remains of their capabilities which the disease has left to them, in a circumscribed domain, in field and garden, in cowstall or workshop, in sawing wood and cutting fodder, in copying, drawing, reading, in cooking, washing, or in the ironing-room. in housework, or in the sewing-room. In the states of excitement, which occur very frequently, it usually suffices to remove them, temporarily, to supervision and rest in bed.

Leucocytosis.—Not altogether infrequently one sees the psychic condition of the patients essentially improve under the influence of a fever, even in terminal states which have already lasted a long time without change. Irritable and repellent patients give intelligent information and become more accessible; negativistic patients appear more docile and obey medical orders; in paranoid patients the delusions pass into the background; dull patients apparently wholly demented show a surprising appreciation of the occurrences in their surroundings and bring all kinds of old memories to light. Unfortunately, with the disappearance of the bodily morbid state, this improvement usually very soon gives place again to the former behaviour. It is meantime a sign that even very profound dementia is not absolutely the expression of unalterable destruction, but up to a certain degree is still capable of amelioration. It might be thought in a similar way, as has been tried in paralysis, here also to imitate the natural process described, yet the few attempts in that direction have as yet not yielded any very encouraging result. Thus Itten from this point of view has tried in nine patients injections of sodium nucleinate. Nothing was obtained; the same is true of some similar attempts, which I made myself.

CHAPTER XIII.

PARAPHRENIA.[1]

The disintegration of the psychic personality is in general accomplished in dementia præcox in such a way that in the first place the disorders of emotions and of volition dominate the morbid state. In contrast to that we have now to take into consideration a comparatively small group of cases in which, in spite of many and various points in common with the phenomena of dementia præcox, but because of the *far slighter development of the disorders of emotion and volition*, the inner harmony of the psychic life is considerably less involved, or in which at least the loss of inner unity is essentially limited to certain *intellectual* faculties. The marked delusions, the *paranoid colouring* of the morbid picture is common to all these clinical forms which cannot everywhere be sharply separated. At the same time there are also abnormalities in the disposition, but till the latest periods of the malady not that dulness and indifference which so frequently form the first symptoms of dementia præcox. Lastly, activity also frequently appears morbidly influenced, but essentially only by the abnormal trains of thought and moods; independent disorders of volition not connected with these, such as usually accompany dementia præcox in such multifarious forms, only come under observation by indication once in a while.

The grouping of these paranoid attacks, as well as their delimitation from other similar states, presents the greatest possible difficulties. We know indeed that isolated morbid phenomena themselves only furnish us with very unreliable means of delimiting forms of disease. It can here, therefore, only be a case of a first tentative attempt to break up the various paranoid morbid types into groups. If a considerable number of cases which are accompanied by permanent delusions are examined carefully, and if the alcoholic and syphilitic forms are excluded, it will always be found that a very considerable part of these, according to my experience about 40 per cent., within a few years exhibit the characteristics of dementia præcox. A further somewhat larger part

[1] See Introduction, p. 1.

falls to the paraphrenic forms which are to be described here, the rest essentially to real paranoia.

Among the paraphrenias again about half exhibit that slow but continuously developing mixture of delusions of persecution and of exaltation, as Magnan has described them under the name of "délire chronique à évolution systématique."[1] Certainly this Magnan's disease, as far as can be judged from the descriptions given, is according to the views brought forward here probably not a clinical entity; we should thus reckon many cases with marked mannerisms and numerous neologisms which rapidly end in weak-mindedness to the paranoid forms of dementia præcox without hesitation. But at the same time "délire chronique" in its developmental forms with their slow course stretching over decades, embraces a series of cases which form the nucleus of the first paraphrenic morbid group to be discussed here. As the French word "délire" has a different meaning from our term "delirium," and as also the name proposed by Möbius for the morbid state, "paranoia completa" no longer corresponds with our views of to-day, I prefer to speak, supporting myself on Magnan, of a "paraphrenia systematica." Associated with it then there are as smaller groups, perhaps nearly related to each other, the expansive and the confabulating form of paraphrenia; the last form, the fantastic, appears to hold an exceptional position.

PARAPHRENIA SYSTEMATICA.

Paraphrenia systematica is characterized by the *extremely insidious development of a continuously progressive delusion of persecution, to which are added later ideas of exaltation without decay of the personality.* The beginning of the disease often consists of a change very slowly accomplished in the conduct of the patient. He becomes gradually quiet, shy, sometimes more dreamy and absorbed, sometimes more distrustful and gloomy, withdraws himself, occasionally carries on peculiar and incomprehensible conversations, is conspicuous in his behaviour, incalculable, capricious in his actions. From time to time there appears great sensitiveness and irritability; the patient becomes on quite insignificant occasions immoderately violent and malevolent, exhibits embittered hate and antipathy towards individuals in his surroundings, often towards his nearest relatives. Ideas of jealousy are specially frequent.

In course of years a *delusion of persecution* becomes always

[1] Magnan, Psychiatrische Vorlesungen, deutsch von Möbius; Heft 1, 1891.

more and more clear. The patient notices that he is the object of general attention. On his appearance the neighbours put their heads together, turn round to look at him, watch him. On the street he is stared at ; strange people follow him, look at one another, make signs to one another ; policemen are standing about everywhere. In the restaurants to which he goes, his coming is already announced ; in the newspapers there are allusions to him ; the sermon is aimed at him ; there must be something behind it all. A patient thought that he must be watched from the church tower.

The sentiments of the people round him appear at the same time to be anything but friendly. The inmates of the house look sarcastically at him ; they whisper and make mysterious sounds ; they separate from each other as soon as he comes. At the habitués' table in the restaurant he is jeered at ; queer things are said ; his companions are unkind ; they look askance at him, avoid him, greet him without ceremony, withdraw themselves from him. " It is noticed when anyone has fine feelings," said a patient. As soon as he enters a restaurant people begin to break up the party. People spit in front of him, clear their throats, cough slightly, sneeze in a conspicuous way, shuffle with their feet, ape his coughing, rush up against him. Detectives crowd round him ; he has the impression that he is under police supervision. Always and everywhere there are pin-pricks, everywhere chicanery and hostility. " It's never ending what goes on there," said a patient, "everywhere I see allusions, hints, a thousand things, which cannot be described, which must have been experienced in order to be understood." He also regarded a broken lamp-glass, the conferring of the military medal, as an intentional insult. Another patient made the observation that the number seven pursued him everywhere, and that his fellow-travellers in the train invariably were grouped in the figure of the Great Bear.

Gradually the persecution becomes always more tangible. The patient cannot find rest any more ; tricks are played on him everywhere ; everything is done to spite him : people work systematically against him. The servants are incited against him, cannot endure him any longer ; the children have no longer any respect for him ; people are trying to remove him from his situation, to prevent him from marrying, to undermine his existence, to drive him into the night of insanity. Female patients perceive that people are trying to dishonour them, to seduce them, to bring them to shame. Secret affairs are being carried on in the house ; strange people are standing in the passage. The patient ascertains that his things are being stolen, that a "secret domiciliary visit" was held. The lock is forced; his boxes have been broken open, his things rummaged through, thrown pell-mell, the furniture displaced. His bed is dirty; his clothes are torn; the stove is being blocked up, bad air let into the room, the water suddenly turned off; letters are being suppressed. The beer causes colic, the bread a burning in the brain; there are poisonous vapours in the house; there is a suspicious powder in the bed; the doctor gives a blue medicine which without doubt contains prussic acid and is intended to cause the death of the patient. In consequence of this the patient feels himself "spied on" everywhere and threatened, not safe even with locked doors; it is an unparalleled hounding, fraud, and deceit, "the whole affair is known in the town." "There's a constant uproar," declared a patient. Obviously there exists a regular conspiracy that carries on the persecution; sometimes it is the social democrats, the "red guard," sometimes the Freemasons, sometimes the Jesuits, the Catholics, the spiritualists, the German Emperor, the "central union," the members of the club, the neighbours, the relatives, the wife, but especially former mistresses, who cause all the mischief.

Hallucinations.—After this extremely tormenting state of distrust, uncertainty, and tension has continued as a rule for years, real hallucinations usually appear also, especially those of *hearing.* The patient hears whistling, false notes, weird noises, disapproving remarks, abusive epithets, threats. There is whispering going on, telegraphy, speaking through the telephone. A patient ascertained that the hallucinations ceased on his ears being stopped, another that they were present only at home but not when he was out walking; both drew therefrom the wrong conclusion, that it could not be a case of mistake. Jews scream after the patient on the street; people speak about him, call him foolish, a blackguard, filthy beast, old wretch, simpleton, court-prostitute, a bad lot, rascal, ragamuffin, criminal; he is accused of masturbation, of murder; it is asserted that he is impotent, that he is sexually filthy, that he brought his parents to the grave; his son has been killed. A female patient heard her husband and her son lamenting "as if they were lying in the tower of purgatory undergoing penance"; another noticed that she was jeered at because of her alleged sexual insatiability; "It went like wildfire." Everyone abuses and persecutes him, everyone knows all the circumstances of the patient accurately. Sometimes it is not a case of sensory perceptions, but of "spiritual calls," "inspirations," "the play of thought," "thought dialogue." The patients are made capable of that by hypnosis, are spiritually questioned, to which questioning they answer aloud or perhaps only inwardly. Now and then they notice their thoughts becoming loud; others can hear it. A patient thought that his neighbours would be very much annoyed with his thoughts being said aloud; another heard his thoughts whistled after him by locomotives. The voices also perhaps speak in the thoughts of the patient, criticize him, accompany his actions with remarks.

Hallucinations of other senses play an essentially smaller part. The patient is " fooled with visions," sees skeletons, the devil, people who are dead, the Virgin Mary, bleeding sacramental bread, naked women. To a female patient the faces of people appeared changed; she thought that people had put on masks or other heads. Food tastes abominably, stinks; the house is filled with peculiar smells; the clean linen smells of a chemist's shop. A patient complained of unnatural and painful sensations, felt mysterious stabs as of a dagger, thought that Satan was spitting on him; another felt himself struck, rushed upon, pushed about; a woman thought that she was being photographed with Röntgen rays. Female patients have sensations, pulling in the genitals, feel themselves spiritually married.

Ideas of Influence.—The idea, which occurs not infrequently, of hypnotic, magnetic, electric influences, may likewise be frequently connected with bodily dysæsthesiæ, sharp pains, twitchings, dragging pains, transmission of currents. Many patients make statements about influences on will. Suggestions are given to them by magnetism; people want to have their thoughts; people who are dead tell them what they must do. A female patient felt that a count had got her in his power; she was as if paralyzed and must obey him, she could not eat at meal-times, became hungry at the wrong time, felt herself forced to buy clothes against her will; she was not able to love her mistress any more, she had to be impolite to her. A patient declared that he would be forced to do certain actions but would only yield in insignificant things. Another thought that his will was being led: " Someone wants to do something to me. The whole force and persuasion from an unknown part—it is forced on me that I must think myself greater than I really am or was in everyday life till now."

Exaltation.—When the delusion of persecution has continued for a number of years and has been developing by slow progression or, as happens much more rarely, after the disease has existed for only a short time, or in the beginning of it, the patient produces, sometimes rather suddenly, exalted ideas. At first they may keep within fairly modest bounds. After being ill for some years a woman directed a letter to the emperor with the inquiry how she could be rid of her husband; later she praised her own brilliant talk, her voice clear as a bell, her fine tact, her high endowment. Another female patient, who felt herself very much annoyed, thought that she must have a peculiar power in her eyes because people could not look at her. A third, after being persecuted for six years, supposed that some highly-placed personage must be behind it all; a patient asserted suddenly, after he had suffered extreme torment for twenty years, that some of his fellow-patients were marquises and princes, and he began to treat them with special reverence and to kiss their hands.

Very commonly the patients make claims to *money*. From some source or another large sums should come to them which are being kept back; they have been left an inheritance which has been suppressed. A patient thought that by going round "circular paths" he would earn large sums, and daily he sought such paths and hoped so to acquire about 30,000 marks a month, which, he assumed, would be deposited for him regularly in the bank. A female patient thought there and then that she must have an income; another was convinced that an archduke had settled some money on her for her marriage. Apparently they derive their knowledge of such things most frequently from hallucinations of hearing in which their secret wishes come to expression.

In a further group of cases it is an affair of *erotic relations* with highly-placed persons. The patient notices that a lady of distinction is interested in him; a picture postcard which he receives is obviously from her; highly-placed persons approach him in all sorts of disguise. A duke made known to a female patient by hypnotic ways that he wished intercourse with her; later she had "thoughts of love," that a married man wished to marry her, and she made all the preparations for her marriage. At the same time high-sounding titles are often attributed to the loved ones. The man last mentioned became a baron to the patient. Another female patient wrote letters to a man, also already married, with the address, " Peter the Great of Russia, incognito," and then made complaints at the post-office that the letters were not dispatched. Others exalt their enemies. A patient threatened that with the help of the pope he would put Bismarck in chains; another supposed that the main-spring of all the troubles that came upon him was William II., whom he regarded as his personal enemy.

But most frequently by far the exaltation in rank concerns the patient *himself*. He observes that he is being greeted by gentlemen of rank, that sentries show him marks of respect, that he is treated with peculiar distinction; the policeman who travels everywhere after him is appointed by the Emperor for his protection. Someone or other addresses him as Count or Prince; the waiters speak of Highness, of Elector; immediately on his appearance they have a fresh barrel broached; as soon as he begins to eat the lights go up. He perceives that the Emperor is interested in him, that princes also are in the affair, that aristocratic ladies send him letters and presents, which in an infamous way are suppressed; a patient thought that he had himself seen the ladies throwing letters into the letter-box. Someone makes known to the patient that coins with the likenesses of his ancestors are in existence; he hears allusions and learns through the telephone that a patent of nobility has been awarded to him, that at mid-night he will be publicly proclaimed a Count of the Empire. It becomes clear to him that he is of high descent, that his ancestors have played a great rôle, that he possesses great merit and rights. He can display gigantic capacity and knowledge, feels himself a political personage of the first rank, a member of the House of Lords and Vice-chancellor of the Empire, a relative of the reigning House, indeed the rightful ruler of the country himself; "Indeed the whole world knows that," said a patient. He is the "King's bastard," son of the Emperor Frederick, step-brother of Prince Charles Frederick, is in communication with all monarchs, will marry Princess Katherine of Russia. A patient declared that he was emperor and pope in one person, ruler of the whole world, later also that he was immortal, that he had driven the capacity of decomposition out of his body by salt, and that he was a unique thing among human beings. A glimpse into this train of thought is afforded by the following frag-ment of a letter:—

"Distress, grief, care and doubt make me have the most unrefresh-ing nights. I cannot be indifferent, and so the dumb, obdurate world is an oppressive burden to me, even though the star of my bliss is as large and glorious as the sun in the firmament. The black spectre of doubt, which often haunted me so dreadfully last year, causes me the question of the whole future, namely. immortality! Dear K. you will also be frightened about it, because no one as yet has remained in the world. But it is also evident and not to be refuted, that also as yet no one has been endowed with my qualities. For this reason it is certainly not absurd to think about it and to talk loud out, consequently even to believe, and the doubt, when it comes upon me, is no wickedness and no sin. I have not called forth this thought; it came upon me suddenly as long as two years ago, in a moment when I went past the well in the garden, and immediately took complete possession of me, so that I was not able to ward it off. . . .   I am already advanced to the half of the usual age, and who has thought of laying down arms and surrendering at discretion? Yes, certainly the world has enough cause to defy the Messiah ! Still with the truth it is to be hoped that I shall come out top over all fraud, and that everyone must acknowledge that I am the Lord, as Pharaoh learned. Let it be said, for dying I have not time so soon ; I must first beget or create 1000 million children, that is soldiers, and so they may defy. . . ."

In a small number of cases the exalted ideas acquire a somewhat *religious* content, as already in the example just quoted. The patient is sent by God, is the protestant Joshua, speaks words of divine authority. A female patient declared that she was a saint, she had the insight of a seer, could read the hearts of men, felt beforehand if anyone died, understood all the four faculties, was comforted by God ; another was called the bride of Christ. These delusions are often reflected in all sorts of hallucinations. The patient mentioned saw the child Jesus beside her bed ; the light of the monstrance fell on her. She heard God's voice which gave her commands and imparted answers to thought-questions ; she felt at night a warm breath and a face beside her, perceived copulation and then heard the child speak in her belly. The patient, from whom the document quoted originates, saw how the pictures of saints nodded to him, how a radiance shone from his forehead ; he heard the voice of his guardian angel, felt an invisible hand on his head, the pricks of the crown of thorns on his skull. Other patients hear hints that they are Emperor or Crown Prince, that they are in the middle of a pile of money, are to get one to two millions ; a female patient heard " supernatural things " ; it was said, " Thou shalt be the lion for the sin." On the other hand harmless perceptions are interpreted according to the megalomania. A patient asserted that the reigning prince had appeared in a restaurant for his sake disguised as a " field-worker "; another saw a landlord make movements with his fingers and a guest shake his head in reply ; he concluded from this that they wanted to signify to him that he should accept the sum offered to him.

Ideas of exaltation and persecution frequently come into a certain relation to each other. Their conjunction is here, as in several other diseases, so frequent that it can hardly be doubted that there is an inner connection between the two. It is usual to represent it in this way, that the elaborate arrangements which are made to injure them cause the patients to think that there must be some special reason connected with their person, or that the opposition, which stands in the way of the realization of their delusion of greatness, engenders ideas of persecution. Sometimes indeed the patients give utterance to ideas which seem to point to such trains of thought. People are trying to get them out of the way, in order to be able to take possession of their great inheritance; people wish by "court intrigues" to hinder them from making an aristocratic marriage; they are to be made willing by the traps laid 'for them to marry their persecutor. A female patient thought that her relatives wished to hinder her from marrying till she could no longer have children, in order that she might become a rich old aunt ; a patient who considered himself the rightful King of Bavaria stated that the plebs were hostile to him ; others are persecuted in order to prevent them from making known their just claims. Meantime the attempts at explanation proffered here by the patients, which moreover often completely break down, are hardly more than reasons thought out after the event; otherwise, indeed, they would come to the surface much sooner. As we shall see later in the delusion of pardon in prisoners, a profound emotional disturbance lasting for a very long time engenders by itself the tendency in some measure to take flight from inexorable reality to a world of pleasing illusions, a process that surely signifies a certain weakening of the psychic power of resistance. As it has to do with a progressive morbid process, it could be understood that the exalted ideas as a rule do not usually appear till the patient has become prepared in the hopeless struggle against hostile powers.

The **Perception** of the patients is never disordered. They are clear about their surroundings and their position, if the misinterpretations caused by delusions are not considered. Understanding of the disease is completely absent, though a certain morbid feeling appears often to be present at least at the beginning. The substance of the hallucinations of hearing point to that; it is not infrequently related to psychic disorder: "That's where the silly woman lives," "We're going to take him to the mad-house." Many patients feel themselves "driven to madness," made to have brain disease, made stupid, their enemies are to make them lose their understanding ; others try all sorts of experiments to find out whether it is a case of hallucinations or real perceptions. In the end, however, healthy deliberation is invariably overpowered by the morbid influences, and the patient remains completely deaf to reasoning. "I ride my nag and I do not give the reins to anyone else," a patient declared. A woman said "If I imagine everything, then I admit that I am a regular fool," but in spite of this she was not able to correct her ideas of persecution; she looked on the supposed bad treatment in the institution as a sort of method of cure by which she should become accustomed to the persecutions outside.

Pseudo-memories.—Memory and retention do not in general exhibit any disorders, but delusional pseudo-memories not infrequently come under observation. The patients report that already in their youth they were persecuted, that their experiences were already made public previously in the newspapers, were made known to them, usually with all details; formerly they had not paid any attention to it, but it now occurs to them. A female patient asserted that she had repeatedly been hypnotized and assaulted, but had no idea of it till it now came into her mind again. The validity of their claims has formerly been confirmed to many patients. A patient reported that already in school he was addressed as Prince; his grandfather said to him of William I., "Joseph, that is your grandfather." Later in the year 1886, he met the Emperor Frederick, who had a canula in his throat; it was said to him that was his father. It was made very plain to him everywhere; his mother spoke of the Crown Prince; in his sponsor's letter there was a large sum of money; his aunt wrote to him on the death of the Emperor Frederick; in the tramcar someone said, "That is the German Emperor." It was said, "Two emperors at the same time, that was a difficult birth," from which he concluded that he must have had a twin-brother.

Exactly those kinds of delusional experience which one would at first be inclined to trace back to hallucinations often prove on more exact examination to be pseudo-memories. A patient narrated that many years ago a strange man had strewn poisonous powder on his forehead through the crack of the door; at the same time he heard a gold piece jingle as a sign that the man was hired by his enemies. Another patient affirmed that solemn promises were made to him in Parliament from the ministerial bench; a third repeated a host of long conversations, which were connected with his claims to an inheritance, word for word with such detail, as is never possible in real hallucinations, but for pseudo-memories is characteristic. I quote here an example from his numerous notes of the conversations alleged to have been heard by him relating to his claims :—

"On the 2nd February I was at the funeral of A. at the Auerfried Cemetery. It was half-past two o'clock when I arrived. South from the old mortuary four people preceded me. Furthest to the left there was Joseph R., then his wife, beside her Mrs S., and furthest to the right a man unknown to me with his brown cloak. I was walking only a few steps behind them, and heard every word that was said. Mrs S. said, 'Oh, how P. (name of the patient) looks; it's a veritable pity, and he was once such a capable workman ; how they have ruined him ; that is an abominable injustice.' Mrs R., 'And now they want to keep back his money from him too, and he is so much in need of it ; just look at him, how he looks, so pitiable !' R., 'Of course they would not want to give him the money ; they say he does not need it, but they must certainly give it to him ; but it will still come to light ; then they will be well punished.' The man on the right, 'Then doesn't he know anything of the business ?' Mrs S., 'He does know something but not rightly.'"

Mood is at first for the most part anxious, depressed, even despairing, but then becomes more and more suspicious, strained, hostile, threatening. Later, when the exalted ideas come more distinctly into the foreground, the patients become self-conscious, haughty, scornful. They withdraw themselves from the people round them, avoid intercourse, go lonely ways, appear sometimes brusque and unapproachable, sometimes formally polite and dignified, but from time to time may also, where the delusional attitude to their surroundings does not come into consideration, be pleasant and accessible. In their spoken or written statements they are usually skilful and ready, give a connected and reasonable account of things, refute objections, and in doing so readily become impassioned and excited, or they are repellent, will not admit any explanation, declare that it is superfluous, everything is already known without it.

The **Activities** of the patients are influenced in the most decided way by their delusions. It is true that many patients may continue to live for many years in their usual circumstances without specially severe disorders, but at the same time their whole conduct very soon shows the deep-reaching morbid change which has been accomplished in them. Apart from the fact that they shut themselves up and become gloomy and taciturn, they fall sooner or later into all kinds of disputes. They carry on loud soliloquies, they drum and knock on the furniture in the room, are irritated without recognizable cause ; they are abusive, they threaten, they make a noise at night. Many patients defend themselves in despair against the voices, stop their ears, whistle or scream loudly to drown the sound of them. The voices said to a female patient that she should just be violently abusive; she was so aloud or in thought; that helped. A patient was forced by the voices to continual answering by the remark, " Silence gives consent."

Often there are sudden attacks of anxiety. A patient called loudly for help at night, barricaded himself in his room, and passed a motion on the floor because he did not dare to go to the water-closet. The patients frequently change situation and place of residence; a female patient for years' moved from town to town and always after a few months made the discovery that she could not continue in her new home because everyone was already initiated. A patient tried to lead his persecutors astray by giving a false destination aloud on going out.

Sometimes it comes to wholly nonsensical actions probably caused by delusions. A female patient stood for hours in the sun, washed herself in the water-closet, picked the skin off her face because small grains of sand-soap had penetrated it. A physician left his fæces on the table-cloth and gargled with his urine. Very commonly after some time the patients apply to the police, beg for protection against the annoyance, ask for an explanation of what they are accused of, put advertisements in the newspapers to defend themselves against supposed slanders, appeal to the public with a cry of distress. A patient ran through the streets in his shirt in order to force admission to an institution for the insane for the verification of his mental state.

An idea of the struggle which the patients go through is given in the following fragments from letters which a patient threw over the walls of the institution in order to call the attention of passers-by to his circumstances:

"When I came to Munich in the year 1875, I was brought by force to the institution for the insane here, for fear I might bring a complaint before the court, although according to a medical certificate and my certificate of service I was physically and mentally perfectly healthy and fit for work and no one could complain of me. As appears from my letters, complaints, and so on, my freedom is taken from me in this institution here principally for the purpose, though hitherto without success, of destroying in every possible way my mental and physical health, for which unprecedented crime the persons who took part in it are responsible. The institution for the insane is wrongfully used for the greatest crimes and serves especially the particular interests of unscrupulous physicians. I live here among wholly demoralized people, who for the most part avoid work, of whom several, as also the so-called attendants, gain their living by continually annoying and disturbing me by all sorts of misconduct and noise. . . . The superintendent of the institution avoids less and less every day the worst means to disturb me continually in my peace and where possible to get opportunity to have me still more under his power.

Every human feeling and decency are here trodden under foot. The physicians often pretend to be insane and to confuse me with some other person. In the interest of order and justice I beg everyone to interest himself in my affairs and to bring them to public discussion."

Self-defence.—As the inward tension increases, the patients who see themselves helpless and abandoned to persecution, often undertake self-defence. They call the offending individuals to account, or in petitions to the Emperor explain the whole of the mean fraud which is being carried on with them, or try by deliberate attempts to escape from the detention in the institution for the insane. They overwhelm a policeman with invective, suddenly box the ears of a harmless neighbour at table, by whom they fancy they are abused, throw stones at the passers-by, and finally make dangerous assaults on their supposed persecutors; they become, as the French alienists call it, "persécuteurs persécutés." A patient shot his landlady from behind as she was passing, without further consideration, because he was convinced that she was going to put him in prison and incite others to murder him ; she had rattled with the keys in the morning, carried on a lively conversation with some neighbours who were sick nurses, made signs and laughed sarcastically, so that he thought he was in the greatest danger. Some patients perpetrate attempts at suicide in order to escape from their persecutors.

The exalted ideas may lead to all kinds of morbid actions. The patient goes to the bank to take out the sum standing to his credit, tries to get information about his descent at the registrar's office, suddenly makes a proposal of marriage, torments in every possible way his supposed beloved, who in spite of all refusals still continues to give him to understand by a flower that he is welcome to her. A female patient repeatedly tried to force her way late in the evening into the house of a married man to whom she asserted she was "civilly" married, and desired that he should immediately send away his wife out of the house and admit her to his wife's place. Other patients give conspicuously large subscriptions to public collections, write letters to highly-placed personages, go to the capital of the country to pay their respects to the sovereign or to bring forward their claims to the throne. A female patient asked the reigning prince by letter to find out the address of a washerwoman which she had not been able to get at the police office. A patient had visiting-cards printed with high-sounding titles, and sent tips to the policemen who had saluted him most respectfully after his supposed elevation to the rank of baron; he paid visits to the most varied governmental departments; he gave advice in long documents about home and foreign politics, sketched out financial plans, appeared uninvited at a dinner of the federal council. Another asked the French minister Delcassé to place ten million francs at his disposal. Many patients are very fond of writing, and compose comprehensive petitions to the most varied authorities and personages not only about their own business but also about all possible other questions—about the overworking of horses, the breaking up of the Sunday rest, the question of prostitution, plans for the improvement of the world.

The **Capacity for Work** of the patients may be preserved for a long time fairly well. The above-mentioned patient who was about to shoot his landlady remained, in spite of the delusion of persecution, which had already existed for ten years, a diligent and useful worker. Others, after being ill for decades, still draw very creditably, write poems, produce contributions for magazines; women can often conduct their household to complete satisfaction. A peasant boy when he felt himself called to be ruler of the world acquired a certain amount of knowledge of the Greek, Italian, Spanish, Russian and Latin languages one after the other. Nevertheless by the continued inner tension and excitement the capacity for regulated fruitful work in most cases gradually but materially suffers; the frequent change of situation in consequence of the ideas of persecution also works unfavourably in this direction. Many patients finally give up serious work altogether, especially if exalted ideas begin to make their appearance; they live a day at a time, read, dream, go walks, and wait for the fulfilment of their great hopes.

The **General Course** of the malady here described is, as has been already mentioned, very slow, but still it progresses fairly continuously. Fluctuations of the state seem to appear only in limited measure. It is true that the patients, especially in immediate connection with the difficulties of life, are at times more excited or more anxious, and are then quieter again, but of real disappearance of the morbid phenomena there is scarcely a question, even if the patients perhaps are able temporarily to force their delusional trains of thought into the background or at least to conceal them.

In the course of decades, however, a distinct change in the whole psychic conduct usually makes itself felt. It is certainly favoured by the circumstance that the patients because of their peculiar or dangerous actions and also their behaviour, after a shorter or longer space of time, usually have to be placed in an institution and often suffer extremely by the deprivation of freedom. Their delusions, which receive fresh nourishment from it, become in this way gradually more nonsensical and more extraordinary. The patients are in a den of murderers, feel themselves worried in every possible way, are massacred by day and by night, assaulted, spied on with the microphone, chloroformed, tormented by Satan, suffocated by the stinking current and by electric poison rays. The physicians are in league with their persecutors; they are being inoculated with syphilis; varicose veins and furuncles are being produced in them; their bones are being torn asunder electrically; nocturnal emissions are caused; attempts are made on their life with unscrupulous fury; they are stupefied by poisonous pillows. In the institution there are secret passages; patients are slaughtered and devoured; the Emperor is deposed, dead; a puppet has been put in his place; King Ludwig II. is still living. A patient made the announcement that a great assemblage of princes was taking place, in which the Prince Regent was kept prisoner, and people were continually being shot. On the other hand the patient has risen by degrees to always higher dignities, is in communication with all monarchs, has made 1600 prophecies which have all been fulfilled; he is the colleague of Jesus, the Lord God Himself, demands untold millions as compensation. His fellow-patients are counts and princes, aristocratic ladies who live in the institution on his account; the nurses are hermaphrodites; the physicians appear in different forms. The patient proclaims death sentences, and threatens to put everyone in jail, to make the military advance, and to have the institution shot to the foundation.

In his behaviour he becomes assuming and flares up easily; he overwhelms visitors with prolix explanations often rather vague; at times he is abusive, indulging in the strongest language; he finds fault, he is destructive and aggressive. Or he shuts himself up, goes his own way, buries himself in monotonous occupations, produces comprehensive documents with endless repetition of the same strains of thought, sometimes in bombastic style, with peculiar orthography and many flourishes in the calligraphy; one patient painted lines or innumerable single letters. The form of expression occasionally becomes capricious, especially in excitement, the manner of speech affected. A patient thought that it was "a business got up that way by instigation"; another on being accosted said that he did not let himself be "informed," he did not give up any right ; a female patient declared that she did not want the obscene cross ; another wrote : "All in all, also the cutting short or the complete cutting off of such to me honestly most happy time and times, which already since the year 1889 by God's grace was thus at our disposal, or thus becoming and shortened by such measures of arbitrary power and judgments. It is my last summons." A third asserted that she was subject to the annoyance of a vehmgericht and sun-dial. Playing with syllables also occurs; a lady analysed names into their syllables, distorted them, and said, "The name says everything (Esser-Ex-sex-Ex-sachs)."

In spite of all this the patients remain, even after their malady has continued for twenty to thirty years, clear on the whole about time and place as well as about their position, as far as their delusions do not play any part, and also rational in their behaviour, here also apart from delusional influences. They are able to occupy themselves, to take up an attitude to the events going on around them, are even accessible and pleasant towards strangers who have no relation to their delusions, give information in a connected and comprehensible way. But above everything they do not appear dull or silly, but are always interested, cheerful, and vivacious. Several of my patients knew how to convince completely one or other unreasoning member of their family of the reality of the persecutions and of their high claims.

The **Issue** of the malady is a psychic decline with persistent delusions and usually also hallucinations without specially striking independent disorders of volition and without emotional dulness. Recovery does not appear to occur ; yet it may certainly be possible that isolated cases recover without being recognized. On the other hand higher grades of dementia are not reached ; even after very long duration of the disease, extending twenty to thirty years or more, it does not produce real disintegration of psychic personality.

The share of the male sex was 60 per cent. in my cases. Rather more than half of the patients were at the beginning of the malady between the thirtieth and the fortieth year, a little over 20 per cent. between the fortieth and fiftieth year ; only isolated cases began before the twenty-fifth or after the fiftieth year. It is true, accordingly, for this disease also what we were able to establish in the delusional forms of dementia præcox, that it attains to development only in riper years. This circumstance might arouse the suspicion that the clinical details perhaps depend more on the manner of reaction of the developed personality than on the peculiarity of the fundamental morbid process.

Specially severe hereditary taint did not seem to me to be present; I would, however, lay no weight on this, on the one hand considering the relatively small number of cases and also because of the circumstance that many of them reached back thirty to forty years and the previous history was therefore frequently incomplete. In a series of patients there was a report of peculiar disposition. Some were described as very pious, others as inclined to depression or as weak and sensitive, one as spiteful and malicious. One patient was regarded as very gifted; another was a clever author inclining to be visionary; a third an excellent chess-player. These experiences witness against the view of Magnan, who has tried to separate his "délire chronique" from the "mental disorders of the degenerate." The latter are said to be distinguished by rapid development, frequent change of state, conjunction of delusions of different kinds, and disappearance of auditory hallucinations relatively to those of the other senses. I have not been able to convince myself that these differences can be placed in causal relation to the existence or absence of degeneration. External causes for the outbreak of the disease I have scarcely ever found recorded; in isolated cases the misuse of alcohol or infection by syphilis had preceded. We shall, therefore, be able to assume rightfully that the disease is engendered by internal causes, but of what kind it is certainly not possible for us at present even to make a hypothesis.

Delimitation.—It is above everything the permanent preservation of the psychic personality that has caused me to delimit the morbid group here described from the *paranoid forms* of dementia præcox. Certainly doubt is allowable whether this standpoint is justified. In dementia præcox also, especially in the paranoid forms, the disintegration of the personality may not take place, as we have seen in hallucinatory or paranoid weak-mindedness. But it is obvious that in those terminal states we have to do with morbid processes which have run their course and ended in recovery with defect, and just on that account these cases have not progressed to the more severe forms of dementia such as form the issue of other paranoid cases of dementia præcox. We may well imagine, and may occasionally even really experience it, that a fresh outbreak of the disease may yet transform the hallucinatory or paranoid weak-mindedness into a drivelling, silly, negativistic or dull dementia.

It appears that the circumstances are, however, somewhat different here. The disease does not after a few years remain stationary and then leave behind it an essentially uniform and permanent terminal state, but it progresses, even though very slowly, even after one or two decades, continuously, and almost never, or only after an uncommonly long duration, leads to an unchanging terminal state which, however, still scarcely injures the inner connection of the psychic personality. Against this it can certainly be said that we separated out only the cases of dementia præcox which have a very slow and relatively mild course, and that indications of the disorders which we met there are by no means rare in the later periods of the malady, incoherence of the delusions, the use of odd expressions and silly puns, and influence on will. But, on the other hand, exactly the peculiarities of the course quoted, as the rarity and the slightness of the disorders mentioned, might be an indication that we have here to do with a peculiar morbid process different from dementia præcox.

In the meantime it must remain doubtful whether the boundary line indicated here is sharp and whether it has been drawn at the right place. In any case it is often still very difficult at present to decide in the beginning of the disease whether it is a case of dementia præcox or of para-phrenia systematica. The evidence for the latter consists above everything in the very late appearance of distinct hallucinations in spite of a delusion of persecution which has existed already for many years, further in detailed mental elaboration of the delusions, liveliness and passionate-ness of emotional reaction, absence of independent disorders of volition, preservation of sense and of reasonableness in behaviour and action with delusions that are already advanced.

We meet with almost as great difficulties as in the delimi-tation from dementia præcox in the attempt to draw the line of separation in the direction of *paranoia*. As this task cannot be begun without first settling more exactly the con-ception of paranoia, which is still fluctuating inside the widest limits, we shall be obliged to postpone till then the discussion of the question. A separation on the extended territory of the psychoses which are accompanied by progressive delusions is, as shall be only indicated here, perhaps so far possible that we put on the one side those morbid cases in which we have reason to assume the course of definite morbid processes, while on the other side those forms would have to be placed, the causes of which we regard as consisting of the influence of the stimulus of life on morbidly disposed personalities. Whether and how far we are able from the given morbid phenomena to draw conclusions *a posteriori* as to the one or other history of origin of the individual case will be elucidated later.

Lastly, there has still to be considered in a few words the delimitation of the morbid state discussed here from other paranoid attacks. From the *alcoholic* forms it is distinguished above everything by its insidious development and its continuously progressive course, while in the former we are brought into close connection with an acute, or at least a subacute, form of mental disorder and as a rule with the development of a psychic decline distinctly marked after a comparatively short time. Moreover in the alcoholic attacks hallucinations are in the foreground of the clinical picture from the beginning; in paraphrenia they only appear after years. Later also they play in alcoholic attacks an essentially larger part; the morbid interpretations, suppositions, forebodings, on the other hand, wholly disappear. The condition of the mood is in drinkers more cheerful or indifferent, much less irritable and strained, than in the patients discussed here; the phenomena of psychic weakness, senselessness of the delusions, disconnectedness in conversation, emotional dulness, docility, appear in the latter much more rapidly and more markedly.

In *syphilis* paranoid attacks also usually assume striking forms considerably sooner than in paraphrenia; also in them likewise hallucinations as a rule dominate the morbid picture already from the beginning. The delusions are far more disconnected, not so systematized; mood is much more changing and inclined to sudden explosive outbursts; the patients are more accessible, more easily influenced. Their state is often subjected to abrupt fluctuations, in contrast to the obdurate stubbornness with which in paraphrenia all the morbid phenomena are continuously developing. The symptoms of psychic weakness in the syphilitic forms become much sooner noticeable, even if the delusions do not disappear. Added to that there are above everything the manifold bodily disorders caused by nerve syphilis and the demonstration of the Wassermann reaction in the blood.

If we now consider the *presenile delusion of injury*, which as yet is still, it is true, very inaccurately delimited, there must specially be called to mind the indefinite and indistinct character of the delusions, which is peculiar to that form of disease. The delusions are not mentally elaborated; they remain suppositions and fears engendered afresh at the moment and often changing; they come and go, and can be displaced by persuasion, being quite different from the delusions in paraphrenia, which slowly take shape but then persist with great stability and become greater in extent. It must, however, not be denied that in the early prodromal periods of the disease this distinguishing mark may in certain circumstances be absent.

The **Treatment** of the disease has naturally only very small scope. As the patients usually suffer very much in seclusion, which embitters them and furnishes fresh nourishment for their delusions, the attempt will be made, as far as possible, to arrange that they should be cared for in freer circumstances, possibly in a family or in the country. But unfortunately the disease frequently leads to actions which make institutional care indispensable. In these circumstances one will endeavour within the limits of necessary supervision to give the patients as much freedom as their state will allow, in order to counteract the withdrawal and shutting up of themselves, to which they are so much inclined. One will specially try to give them opportunity for occupation; it is also advisable, as far as possible, to promote the intercourse of the patients with the outside world by letters or personally, as far as it is wished by them. In personal treatment great patience, composure and foresight are necessary. From time to time it may be expedient to avoid all contact with the irritated patients. Necessary interference (as in bathing, cleaning of the neglected room) must be carried out with the greatest forbearance but with firmness.

PARAPHRENIA EXPANSIVA.

Of the smaller groups of diseases, to the discussion of which we now have to turn, the expansive form of paraphrenia is characterized by the development of *exuberant megalomania with predominantly exalted mood* and *slight excitement*. The disease begins as a rule gradually, but also sometimes subacutely. Occasionally a period of anxiety and depression appears to precede; an elderly unmarried woman believed that she was pregnant, and put on very thin skirts in order to conceal her state. The substance of the megalomania was in half of my cases *erotic;* it concerned exclusively female patients. The patient notices that a gentleman looks at her in such a peculiar way, smiles, makes signs to her, follows her; waits for her at the window. On the street remarks are let fall about it; highly placed persons are interested in the affair; the Virgin Mary gives a sign. Everyone knows about it; the affair is the talk of the town. Ladies in grand carriages drive past ; the military march through the streets ; automobiles come ; princesses turn to look at the patient ; the Court interferes.   The advertisements in the newspapers, the pictures and articles, indeed even the speeches in Parliament contain allusions.   A secret engagement with the " spiritual bridegroom " takes place, of which the patient learns from indications in the street; she is greeted with great reverence.   It becomes clear to her therefore, that there must be some special circumstance connected with her lover ; he is an officer high up in the service, a prince, indeed the King himself, or even the Pope.   A patient wished to marry two kings at the same time; another asserted that she had been made pregnant by means of a glass of beer by the King of Spain who shortly before had actually been in Munich.

In a second series of cases *religious* ideas of exaltation are in the foreground.   The patients notice that people speak of them as of saints; the clergyman declares them from the pulpit to be such ; the monstrance bows ; they have at times a halo round their head.   They receive inspiration and re- velations from God, possess the gift of prophecy, associate with Christ, are without sin, are mediator between God and mankind, are the instrument and daughter of God, can work miracles; they have received special grace, must co-operate in the redemption of the world, in the "final catastrophe." A female patient called herself heaven's bride, expected the angel-bridegroom ; she declared that she would be a priest, indeed that she was the third person of the Godhead.   Another asserted that for seven and a half years she had been preg- nant by the Holy Ghost ; but God had declared that He did not wish to come into the world in the institution ; as soon as she got out it would immediately happen.   A third stated that people could by a keen gaze pray diseases and sins on to her ; the latter would then be prayed off and so mankind redeemed, while she would get rid of the former by sleeping or by diarrhœa with flatulence and pains; in this way man- kind would once more be healthy.

Along with this all kinds of other *exalted* ideas frequently appear.   Above everything the patients lay claim to a great deal of money.   Because they redeem poor souls by prayer, millions have been collected for them, which have been promised to them ; they are to get a house as well, the neighbouring house belongs to them.   They are enormously rich ; there must be money there.   " A queen without money, there is no such thing," said a female patient, who considered herself the wife of King Ludwig.   Other patients remain permanently young, doubt whether their parents were the real ones, are of high descent, acquire great titles; they are rulers of the world, man and woman at the same time, royalties, the fate of the world ; their knowledge is great and beyond all price, fills the whole world ; what they say comes to pass.   A female patient had inspirations and therefore knew many things from God without anything being said to her, for example, the wishes of her master and mistress ; in this she almost never made a mistake.   Another foretold the death of the Empress of Austria, wars, the appearance of cholera, the birth of princes in Russia and in Italy ; she was therefore asked for advice by many people.   King Ludwig was called back to life by prayer, is imprisoned in a castle ; a female patient led him to God and redeemed him.

Hallucinations almost always appear fairly soon.   The patients have numerous visions, for the most part probably more dream-like, see the picture on the high altar transformed, the Holy Trinity, a man with a crocodile head fighting with Saint Michael, Christ on the Cross, the Child Jesus, the Virgin Mary on a tree, a monstrance floating in the air, a king's crown with Alpine roses and swans in the sky, erotic proceedings ; in the water of the fountain figures appear ; the light breaks out into flame as soon as they set foot in the church.   At night the King comes ; they speak with him, are asked if they would like to marry the Emperor, the King or His Royal Highness.   Heavenly voices ring out ; people call them saints ; the Pope speaks to them ; God, the Holy Sacrament, the Holy Ghost, give them continually an answer to the question what they should do ; it is said low, only perceptible to themselves : " My dear child, do what I tell you ; you will be blessed."   The neighbours whisper secretly, " Saint Anna," " Here comes the Saint," the affairs of the patients are talked about ; they hear everything that is said in the house.   A female patient carried on " conversations in thought " with her supposed bridegroom ; " What he said I knew, and vice versa."   Another heard dogs, birds, cattle, horses ; then also flies and pictures speak : they gave answer.   The dogs were employed by the police to watch everything and to bark it out ; voices came also from the clouds.   Sometimes it comes, as already indicated, to inward dialogues ; to thoughts there follow answers.

From the description of herself which a female patient drafted of her visionary experiences I take the following fragments :—

"So it came about that Satan left me no peace by night and I began the struggle with him afresh. . . It was a hard struggle. But the luminous cross of my Saviour and all the crosses of my sufferings (which also signify the sufferings of the world) killed him, for I stabbed his heart with all invisible cross-swords. There he lay dead, the dragon, the beast, the monster. But I took my stand with my last cross held high in my right hand on his paunch belly and cried three times with a loud voice: 'O death, where is thy sting? O hell, where is thy victory?' And when the serpent heard these things, it came slowly and sadly creeping, for it had no more strength; it had lent it to Satan, that he might conquer me, and when I saw it I pierced its head with my last cross-sword, and it also did not move again. Morning had long since dawned. The birds brought their songs to our love. . . Easter! 'Tell me, my father, why is it Easter for me to-day?' 'My child, my dear, good child, this night my resurrection took place, this night I took over the kingdom of my father. . .' Then came the night, a peaceful glorious night. But it was not to last long, my untroubled happiness, for he who before was the embodiment of Satan, who was then happy to be set free and called himself my bridegroom, he came spiritually to me, in order to take possession of the bride, but what did he take? Not the spirit, as I hoped, no, my pure body; he looked at me with a fearful lascivious grimace and said, 'Now you are mine, wholly mine' . . . But the old God laughed craftily and sang out of Wagner's Walküre; Blessing, laughing love, the bond of Siegmund and Sieglinde. Ha, even God helps me no longer; even a God is turned into a swine. . . If in the end now God Himself wanted to flirt with you! Ha, it drives one to desperation, to insanity; but I tell you, old God, that I whistle at you and your help, and at your love too, if it is that kind. . . Touch me again, you abominable creature, and look I shall put this six-barrelled revolver in my mouth and discharge it, and I shall lie before you with a broken skull, a corpse, then go on playing with me if you want. . . ."

Religious and erotic trains of thought are here spun out in high-sounding form to visionary pictures which were described by the patient partly as real events, partly as inventions.

Ideas of Persecution.—Hand in hand with the megalomania there are invariably ideas of persecution, which, however, in the whole clinical picture do not acquire a dominating position as in the previous form. The patients have to pass through trials, are to be oppressed; danger is threatening. They are being badly treated, being laughed at; people spit in front of them, clear their throat, blow their noses, threaten them with their fist, knock up against them on the street with packages, pour out water, knock at the doors, let the water run; everyone is in the plot. The money that should come to the patients is withheld from them; their letters are suppressed, their things are stolen. They are being poisoned, magnetized; their thoughts are deciphered by the physicians by means of apparatus. People lie in wait for them, wish to abuse them sexually, their husbands wish to get rid of them in order to be able to enter undisturbed into improper relations; dreams give cause

U

for jealousy. Rivals appear, force the loved one to marriage and to suicide. In the newspapers there are spiteful allusions; wounded men and hearses come in sight; acquaintances die; it is as in war.

Here also hallucinations may play a part. The dogs bark in such a peculiar way; allusions are made to cases of theft; abusive words, slanders are called out; someone is calling for help; at night Satan appears. A female patient was very much troubled by abuse and cries of the " Empress of Pekin." Occasionally dysæsthesiæ due to strange influence are reported; a female patient complained that a male teacher had " brought apparitions on " her.

Pseudo-memories.—During this development perception, orientation, memory and retention are not essentially disordered in the patients, still pseudo-memories occur not infrequently. The prophecies quoted above depend on them. Many patients state that they had already known beforehand that they would come into the institution, also how things looked there; they greet fellow-patients as old acquaintances. A female patient after many years remembered, as she thought, a meeting with King Ludwig; he treated her to beer and proposed to her that she should sleep with him at night. When she told her father about it, he laughed and said, " That has been King Ludwig; you will get a large sum of money yet." Another female patient saw a paper on which the title of countess was granted to her. The people in the neighbourhood are often taken for other people in a delusional way; they are princes and nobles; a female patient for many years called the physician " Little uncle of Nassau," even after an absence of some years; another woman called a female fellow-patient "her little Ludwig." Insight into the disease does not exist. The patients indeed occasionally, on remonstrances being made, retract some of the delusions to which they have given utterance, but immediately afterwards come with similar ideas again. A female patient, who discovered in the newspapers the most nonsensical allusions to her affairs, spoke of her "newspaper delusion," but at the same time continued her interpretations unswervingly.

Mood is self-conscious, cheerful, often unrestrained and irresponsible. The patients are inclined to jokes and witticisms, or radiant and beaming with happiness. There are interposed times in which they are irritable, high-flown, presuming or distrustful, repellent. In their conduct they appear as a rule reasonable, accessible, pleasant, but easily fall into violent excitement if people occupy themselves for a considerable time with them, fall into a preaching tone, let loose an enormous torrent of words, declaim, prophesy, abuse, threaten to make a whole regiment march up, give utterance to frightful curses.

The **Activities** of the patients are often under the domination of their delusion. They try to approach the object of their love, write letters, answer advertisements in newspapers, make preparations for marriage. A woman sent the most high-flown love-letters to her husband's superior, and indeed to the care of his wife, as presumably she was directed to do in the newspaper. Another female patient for years remained an hour and a half every day sitting at her window, because she thought that otherwise something might happen to her beloved who lived opposite and had no forebodings; she wrote to him as his wife and declared to her own husband that she wanted to be divorced from him. A third betook herself with a loaded revolver to a married physician, with whom she thought she lived in spiritual marriage, and threatened to shoot him and herself. Other patients try to come into possession of money that has been withheld; a woman tried to force her way into the Royal Palace and cried aloud from the window that she would stab the sovereign because he did not pay to her the sums of money due for the salvation of souls. Another female patient went to Vienna to prevent by her prayers the plague from spreading there; a patient suddenly ran to the altar during service and began to preach.

Apart from such derailments and the more transitory, though often very violent states of excitement, the patients may appear quite inconspicuous and occupy themselves reasonably. Often, however, they display a somewhat affected, pompous, unctuous behaviour. Many patients compose comprehensive, bombastic, and turgid documents; a female patient wrote in one of herself, "Myself, us—the most holy Majesty of God! Sovereign and ruler of heaven and of earth! Lord and Saviour-Imperator-Redemptor— of all princely families—in spite of my tender youth. . . ."

In the **Further Course** the morbid picture as a rule only changes slowly, as far as I can judge from the few cases, which were observed for longer than a decade. The patients remain in general reasonable and clear, but adhere firmly to their delusions, which perhaps become somewhat more nonsensical and more disconnected. They are loquacious, verbose, distractible, at the same time lively, accessible, and docile; they exhibit a changing, predominantly confident and exalted mood, do not cause any special difficulties in medical treatment. Apart from great lack of judgment, a certain incoherence, superficiality of emotions, and weakness of volition, no profound dementia appears to set in, at least no disintegration of psychic personality.

It is noteworthy that the patients whom I have described were almost all *women*. The commencement of the malady was in three-quarters of the cases between the thirtieth and fiftieth year; one case began first at sixty-four years of age, without there being any possibility of senile dementia. No trace could be found of specially severe hereditary taint, and just as little of external causes of disease. One female patient was artistically gifted, another had always been excited; a male patient was reported as very religious and with little mental endowment; in several other cases also there had probably existed for a long time conspicuous features in the character.

Delimitation.—Whether the morbid states brought together here as an experiment really constitute a clinical entity is doubtful. On the other hand I consider it almost certain that they cannot without difficulty be placed in one of the morbid forms otherwise known to us. From *dementia præcox* they are distinguished by the strikingly slight injury to the psychic personality even after a duration of many years in spite of the continued existence of the morbid phenomena, further by the absence of all independent volitional disorders apart from the affectation which is perhaps connected with the exalted ideas and from the indications of influence on will which appear now and then. Not unimportant is perhaps also the circumstance, that here hallucinations of hearing and above everything bodily influences as delusional occurrences go completely into the background behind hallucinations of sight, interpretations, and pseudo-memories. This circumstance also plays a part for the delimitation from *systematized paraphrenia*. But to that there is added the usually more rapid development of the disease, and especially the mood permanently exalted in spite of the ideas of persecution which likewise appear, and the accessible, pleasant, natural behaviour. Obviously the patients are not in the remotest degree so tormented as the persecuted persecutors; the continual interference in their inner life which by those patients is felt as so extremely tormenting, is almost entirely absent in them.

A number of the patients described here I considered for a long time to be *manic*. Their cheerful, often exultant mood inclined to jokes, and their prolix loquacity, as also their outbreaks of excitement, which rapidly become worse by external stimulation, make this interpretation sometimes extraordinarily probable. However, it is a case here in the first place of only single attacks which moreover may without essential change continue for an unlimited time; some of my observations extend over twelve, fourteen, eighteen years. Further, after a considerable time the gradual development of a state of psychic weakness with continuance of the delusion is unmistakable. Lastly, the excitement is often very slight, may even be wholly absent, or be noticeable only on stimulation, so that the patients display nothing but an unreasonably cheerful and confident behaviour without in any way letting themselves be disconcerted by their delusions. As I suppose, these are the cases which caused Thalbitzer to bring forward his " manic delusional insanity " which, however, may include still more cases of another kind.

The so strongly marked predominance of the female sex might moreover point to distant relationships with *manic-depressive* insanity. But perhaps the thought of *hysteric* admixture lies still nearer. The frequency of visionary experiences, the pompous, self-conscious behaviour, the nimbleness of speech, the susceptibility to influence, the tendency to make oneself conspicuous, indeed often remind one of the conduct of many a hysteric. One of my patients even had real hysteric seizures; in another the disease apparently began in the form of a "magnetic sleep" with dreamy religious visions, which lasted almost without interruption for four months. Nevertheless, in view of the persistent delusions and hallucinations, of the slow development of the malady in advanced age, and of the evolution of psychic decline, there can naturally be no question of a real hysteric psychic disorder, quite apart from the fact that phenomena pointing in that direction come under observation only in a minority of the cases.

PARAPHRENIA CONFABULANS.

The next form, perhaps related to the previous one, confabulating paraphrenia, which certainly includes only a small number of cases, is distinguished by the dominant rôle which *pseudo-memories* play in it. The commencement appears sometimes to be a change in the conduct of the patients. They become quiet, reserved, irritable, withdraw themselves, brood a great deal, and then gradually come out with a narration of very extraordinary experiences in the sense of *delusions of persecution* and *exaltation*. They feel themselves neglected; they are persecuted, robbed, are to be poisoned. Everywhere there are suspicious signs; stones are thrown, the windows are broken; shots are fired. People slander, abuse and threaten them, cough at them, put out their tongues; anarchists lie in wait for them; a cash-box with bonds in it was stolen; the King of Prussia will have them murdered; they are being sold for immoral purposes, assaulted, beheaded. Many patients also hear voices, low whispering; someone speaks in their ear and says what they themselves wished to say; people are whispering secretly and laughing.

Sometimes the persecution goes back into childhood. Already at school people aimed at ruining the patient. He was mocked by his relatives, roughly treated by his teacher, tempted to masturbation, was to be "ruined by bad habits"; his mother wanted to poison him with an apple. Then he fell into the most remarkable dangers. The people, with whom he came in contact, were murderers and procurers, used abusive language, slaughtered people, buried the corpses or packed them up in boxes in order to sink them in water. It was announced to him that his turn would now also come; people aimed at him, were going to slaughter him with a long knife, to blow him up into the air with an infernal machine; five years ago at the railway station he saw a girl who was going to throw a bomb, and he prevented her just in time. All these experiences are narrated with the most exact description of the details as occurrences that have happened quite recently. A patient reported that he had dug up an amputated human arm, but then was compelled by his neighbour with a revolver in front of him to eternal silence; nevertheless he gave information and an inquiry was really made. Another went into a brothel in order to convince himself whether cannibals lived there. People were aiming at his life, but he escaped, though later human flesh was put before him in a restaurant. The landlord betrayed himself, begged to be allowed to shoot him, failed however, and shot himself on that account. A female patient was criminally assaulted, and, because she knew too much, was going to be killed, when she was out walking, by a man who already had many murders on his conscience, and spoke quite openly about them; finally, however, the matter was again postponed.

Megalomania.—The confabulatory springs of megalomania flow almost still more abundantly. The patient is descended from a royal family, is the illegitimate son of a prince, of King Ludwig and an Italian woman, was already in childhood abandoned to die of hunger. Officers and policemen saluted him; he was called the wren (German, hedge-king). The clergyman made obeisance to him; his school companions called him Prince. His fellow-workmen were the King of Spain and the Duke of Brunswick; a girl, the daughter of the Emperor of Austria, said to him that he was the son of King Ludwig whom he resembled to such an extent that his real mother did not recognize him, and at a dance wished to enter into connection with him. The policemen on that account wore their beards like Ludwig II. He was also chosen to be Emperor but felt himself still too young for that. At the railway station the Emperor of Austria and the President of the French Republic met him; the Grand Duke of Baden and the Emperor came disguised to him to sound him. He had listened to important political conversations and just at a time when important events were happening. When he was only sixteen or seventeen years old, it was imparted to him that he would get a house in Berlin and inherit the estates of Prince Schwarzenberg; his mother spoke of it. At the post-office a letter containing money with an inheritance amounting to a million was shown to him and it was said that the sum was deposited at the bank. As a child he was taken to the Royal Palace and the room where he was born was shown to him; later the King made himself known to him as his father by look and gesture. The patient met one of the two daughters of the King; the older one promised to marry him.

In this way the patients bring forward with the most profound conviction an enormous number of extraordinary stories absolutely in the form of personal experiences. They can describe exactly every glance, every look of the persons concerned; they report every word, even though the events are referred back for decades. "This is all as distinct to me as·if I saw it with my own eyes in front of me," declared a patient. Sometimes the often repeated descriptions fix themselves in the patients' minds in such a way that they are repeated almost in the same words. But, especially in the beginning, it is sometimes possible by questions to make the patients add fresh decorations, and they themselves continually produce additions which meantime have occurred to them. The patient, who had dug up the arm of the corpse, reported in the days following this narration, that his neighbour had buried something that smelt of corpses under a tree, that further a female neighbour had spoken of shambles in the cellar, that numerous individuals in the village disappeared, the patient's mother among them, that the dogs were fed with human flesh, that a woman of the neighbourhood threatened him with a revolver and announced that it would be his turn in a week ; lastly that one of his neighbours followed him in disguise when he fled into the town.

The patients usually make light of the striking circumstance, that their remarkable experiences were formerly not taken notice of by themselves. They had completely forgotten it, have not thought any more about it, made no use of it, only later everything occurred to them again. A female patient said that she had first thought of it again when a whisper like a prompter had reminded her of everything ; she thought that her mother, who had foretold much of her fortune in life, had then taken away the thoughts of it from her ; "She understood that."

The manner in which the patients in their confabulatory narrations draw conclusions, witnesses to the easy swiftness of their power of imagination. A patient alleged that he had heard French spoken, therefore the President of the French Republic was present ; a fellow-workman spoke of Brunswick, therefore he was the Duke of Brunswick. A female patient described how the King drew little round arches on his garment with his finger ; obviously he wished by that to signify the rounded arch style of the royal palace in which she was born. Another said she had heard the wife of a guide in a picture-gallery say, " Money can be made in this rag-shop" ; from this it was clear to her that the valuable originals of the gallery had been secretly replaced by imitations.

The part also which the patients ascribe to themselves in their pseudo-memories is very remarkable. Although according to their account it was said to them in so many words that they were to be killed, they did not take the slightest measures for defence or flight, continued to associate for weeks with people who let themselves be known as terrible robbers who also committed murder. The most exciting information about their royal descent, their gigantic inheritance, their brilliant prospects of marriage, they have taken, as they allege, with the greatest equanimity and quickly forgotten again, without troubling themselves further about the matter, till it by chance occurred to them again. Pointing out all these impossibilities, however, usually makes little impression on the patients ; they admit, perhaps temporarily, that it was " all nonsense," but later again come back to it.

The content of the pseudo-memories is by no means

always limited to the actual delusions of persecution and exaltation ; it is frequently connected also with more remote personal experiences and everyday events. It occurred to a patient that he had formerly seen his *fiancée*, who he thought was very rich, and also her father, in an institution ; at that time touching stories were told him about the sad fortunes of the real father and the abominable crimes of the foster-father. A female patient described with the most absolute certainty a great many occurrences which incriminated her husband's superior in the most serious way and which were blindly believed by the husband himself. But further, she reported most extraordinary experiences, dating about twenty years back, with Prince Eulenberg, with Richard Wagner, and with King Ludwig, in such a clear, lively, detailed way that she was called as a witness in a lawsuit. Another narrated that people signified to her, by closing their eyes and nodding their heads, that King Ludwig had sat by the water and had fallen forward.

Very frequently pseudo-memories are also connected with the surroundings of the moment. To the patients everything appears familiar ; they have already been once before in the rooms of the institution ; the house and everything, that happens to them, have already been described to them previously ; it is a hotel in which they lived seven to eight years ago with the children ; they remember the view, the service in church ; it gradually comes to them that they have seen all that before. The physician also is known to them. " Don't look so innocent, as if you had nothing to do with it," said a female patient. The nurses, the other patients, are old acquaintances, are using false names. " Don't impose upon me," replied a female patient to our objections. The things which others are wearing belong to them ; the furniture comes from their house. The same persecutors return but in changing disguise. A female patient asserted that the rôle of her husband was played by different people, that he was sometimes smaller, sometimes bigger, sometimes stouter, sometimes thinner. The children also have been exchanged, are not hers, are from the foundling hospital. At a visit she did not acknowledge her husband, but tolerated his attentions.

Besides the morbid ideas which stand in relation to the pseudo-memories there are as a rule other *delusions* of various kinds. The patient is to be deprived of his rights, is surrounded by detectives, is given poison. Visitors are confined in the cellar ; the whole house was cleared out ; a revolution is breaking out ; Emperor and King are overthrown ; his wife has murdered the children. The patient believes that he is surrounded by murderers, is being tortured. He is related to Bismarck and the Emperor William, receives a message, that he is to make an aristocratic marriage. His mother is not dead, has inherited a house from Rothschild. Someone tells him in his ear that he is Christ, the son of God, that he will be more blessed than all the others. He has the stigmata, is the young man at Nain ; the ship of the world was about to perish ; then one has come to save it.

The **Consciousness** of the patients is in all their nonsensical delusions permanently untroubled. They are quiet, perceive without difficulty, give clear and connected information, behave themselves reasonably. So far as their delusion does not come into question they are usually perfectly clear even about their surroundings and their position, yet the occurrences going on round them often appear to them mysterious and incomprehensible. " I could not explain it all to myself, had nothing but riddles before me and would have soon become insane," declared a patient.

Mood in spite of the ideas of persecution is as a rule cheerful, exalted, " quite happy," yet temporarily anxious or irritable. The patients are usually very accessible, loquacious, verbose, desultory, with a tendency sometimes to silly plays on words. They are constantly bringing to light fresh details of their delusional recollections with great vivacity ; they defend their ideas with vigour and ability, let themselves also be guided in their activity by them. They go to the police-office to get information there about their affairs, give information to the public prosecutor, try to withdraw their money from the bank.

The **Course** of the disease seems to be progressive. For the most part the luxuriant growth of pseudo-memories forms only a comparatively short period of the disease, even though the delusional inventions are retained for a consider- able time, repeated, and perhaps still somewhat further adorned. In a year's time they may have completely paled ; the patients do not wish to hear anything more about them, do not know anything more about the stories, are evasive ; " That is a private matter." At the same time the delusions become more nonsensical, more incoherent ; mood becomes irritable, morose or indifferent, so that no doubt exists as to the development of a psychic decline. Unfortunately of the cases which were at my disposal only a single one hitherto was observed longer than a decade, so that I am not able to make any more precise statements about the last fate of these patients.

The extremely remarkable morbid state described here

is not frequent; in nearly thirty-five years I have scarcely
seen more than a dozen marked cases. Both sexes appear
to be equally represented; according to age my patients
were distributed fairly evenly among the three decades from
the twentieth to the fiftieth year; they were therefore on the
average somewhat younger than the patients discussed
previously. I have no special experiences to bring forward
in regard to the causes of the disease, except that of several
patients it was stated that they had always been quiet and
introspective.

Delimitation.—As the characterization of the clinical
picture essentially rests on a single clinical symptom,
certainly very striking, but one which in less marked form
occurs also in other forms of disease, its peculiar place must
not be considered as on sure foundations. Nitsche has
published one of our cases in agreement with myself as
chronic mania. Meanwhile, after more exact investigation
of a considerable number of paranoid cases, I incline to the
view that it is to this group that it belongs. Many circumstances, the comparatively early commencement, and the
psychic involution, certainly as a rule distinct after some
years, would point to a relationship with *dementia præcox,*
especially with those forms which have been called idiopathic
paranoia. As long, however, as the issues of the group here
discussed and their relations to dementia præcox are not
better cleared up by more extended series of observations, I
should like to assign to it a place by itself. This view is in
any case supported by the complete absence of ideas of
bodily influence and of volitional disorders, unless the
occasional making of faces and stiff repellent conduct are to
be regarded as such.

Paraphrenia Phantastica.

A last group of cases to be discussed in this place, likewise not very comprehensive, I should like to call paraphrenia
(dementia) phantastica; here it is a case of *luxuriant growth
of highly extraordinary, disconnected, changing delusions.* It is
covered in the essentials by dementia paranoides formerly
described by me; as meanwhile this term has been in general
frequently used for the delusional forms of dementia præcox,
I consider that for the prevention of misunderstanding it is
expedient to take a new name. The disease appears often
to begin with ill-humour. The patient becomes enervated,
spiritless, depressed, quiet, anxious, has no right vitality,
thinks also, perhaps, of suicide.

Ideas of Persecution then gradually come to the surface. The patient notices that he is looked at in a certain way, that the people in the house make fun of him, carry on spiteful conversations, seek after his life, listen at the door, do not leave him any peace; it is a baiting of him. He stands by the hour under police supervision, is denounced, is made answerable for everything, is to be castrated, to be punished because of robbery with murder and theft; he is a subject of study, and must do penance in experiments; people wish to take his property from him. His letters are not dispatched; in the newspapers he is roundly abused; a flash of light is sent through the room by electricity; in his absence the neighbours force their way into his house, take away clothes, spoil the things; they are a gang of criminals. Officials appear with falsified certificates and under false names; his wife is changed. In his food the patient finds saliva, fæces, human blood; he is stupefied with chloroform and sulphur; everything is drenched with sulphuric acid, is full of arsenic and phosphorus; his bed stinks, contains serpents.

Hallucinations of Hearing also invariably appear now. The patient hears whispering, chirping, wicked slander, whispering voices, spirit voices, telephone voices from the ceiling, "voices in public and when people meet on the street." People persecute him with the telephone apparatus; reproach him with his faults ("wax manufacturer"!), call to him, inform him that his family is dead, that he is pardoned. The magistrate and the police, the Emperor and princesses speak; his sister weeps subterraneously. Invisible people are present in the room and speak; out of the cushions whispering voices make their way from the devil and his light-bearers; his guardian angel speaks; Jesus murmurs; it is the "magic of revelation"; the spirit of hearing is sitting in his ear. Animals can also talk; "I have spiritual ears, when the flies speak to me," declared a female patient. The patient carries on conversations with the voices, converses with the ministers in Berlin, telephones with God. The voices accuse him, praise and threaten him, dictate to him, read aloud what is in his letters and in the newspapers, know his thoughts, tell them to him; a compulsory examination of his thoughts is taking place. They also make remarks about what he does. "Now she feels it," is said, when anything is painful; "Now he is speaking French so that he may not be understood"; "By God, she says everything; everything comes up," a murderer calls out. A female patient heard voices which were in constant contradiction with her thoughts. "They

are strange spirits which speak out of me," declared a patient.
Another had a feeling as if he repeated what he heard with
the breath of his mouth; he was always afraid to do harm by
a wrong word.   A third distinguished between street-voices,
conversation-voices and whispering voices; the last origin-
ate from people "generated inside," contained in his interior;
with the first it is as if a whole street would appear; "The
voices are let loose, meet with people, are established firmly
in the ears."

Hallucinations of Sight on the other hand usually play
only a small part.   The patients see the light from the
electric current, dark shadows which go out, the Saviour,
the heavenly Father, angels, dust-insects in the air, bodies
hovering in the air, figures, which change their form and
size; people are changed by magic.

Dysæsthesiæ and Influence. — On the other hand
common sensation and especially the delusion of personal
influence, which is connected with it, takes up a very large
space in the morbid picture.   The patients complain of pains
and dysæsthesiæ of all kinds; they are tortured, flogged,
dishonoured; they feel shooting pains in leg, head, and
breast, burning in the urethra, formication at the penis.
People give them colic with electrical apparatus; they are
pushed about, they get injections in the skin, are stupefied.
Their testicles are electrified; their voice is altered; their
whole body is changed; their thoughts, their memory, are
taken by spiritualistic arts and roguery, witchcraft and magic
agencies, by invisible persecutors "remaining under cover."
A patient felt pinching, pricking, pressing, lightning in his
brain; his heart was rubbed down with a curry-comb, his
bowels were rhythmically contracted; another thought that
he had instruments in his body.   At night the patient is
hypnotized, dragged away, made to do ugly things with
females.   A female patient had the feeling as if someone
were always about her; at night someone stood behind her
and confused her thoughts; she had to do all sorts of
indifferent things, had to cut open her arteries, was abused
sexually, even by the mouth.   "People have such an influence
on me that it is terrible," complained a patient; "I cannot
write unless they wish; they have an influence on all parts
of my body."

In isolated cases these sensations and ideas acquire quite
prodigious forms.   The patient was made sterile, has only
a few small stones in his scrotum; his bones are being
broken; his liver, spleen, lungs, bowels, the root of his penis,
are torn out; his marrow is sucked out by devilish instru-

ments, his sexual parts are drunk out, his breast-bone is exchanged, his clavicle is cut through four times; his head has been broken in pieces nineteen times and the parts torn out have been replaced by new ones. His body is being melted down; he feels the circular saw in his head; his body is being torn asunder; his legs are being taken off by the railway; his arms are separated by a great distance so that he feels the intervening space; his eyes stand far out from his head, are hanging by bloody cords a yard long. All machines and impulses pull at him; his organs are laid against the bulb of the electric light; the mouth-harmonica is sucked fast to his mouth; he feels himself harnessed to a kettle. "The direct mechanism of the machine is the point round which life, so to speak, the organism twines itself up; I don't know how that is, but the mechanism pursues me for vengeance," said a patient. The voices also specially influenced him. "This talk that strikes a man in the street, reduces him to a state in which one cannot defend himself; they lie in wait for him, drive him to actions of violence," he declared; "one may fall down because of it. This attacks men in their innermost parts, excites them terribly, comes like lightning, and stirs up even the natural and actual circumstances in which one finds oneself at the moment." Another patient thought that he was being attacked by "volitional thoughts," invisible strange people; when he read or wrote, wrong letters and words were substituted. A third asserted that he was chained to the whole world.

· But the most remarkable thing is that the patient feels and sees other people slip into his body. Individuals disappear in him, lay themselves "in his form"; a whole crowd of people can be dragged along by him. A patient noticed that a whole motor-car drove into him; the steering-wheel stood out at his ears. Freemasons are in him; his father is in his right calf; the Emperor Frederick is in his body in order to be saved. His whole body is full; people who are not themselves, wholly torn to pieces bodily, head here, spirit there, come flying out of the air; there is a going in and out like a dovecot. The patient consists of thirteen individuals; eight females are inside him. "Five hundred females were in me and outside me," declared a patient. Another said, "I appear to myself like an empty room, which is constantly inhabited by new tenants. What use is it that I drive them out? They are so shameless and come again."

Sometimes the troubles are of markedly *sexual* nature. A model of the patient has been made; as soon as the sexual parts of it are touched, he is stimulated and tempted to sin.

Aristocratic persons slip in and out of his penis; a princess sits in his penis; empresses and queens beg to be allowed to play with it, and ask, "May I? May I?" A patient asserted that he was used for breeding; people were bred into him, developed in him. He felt that he was being copulated through the nose, the larynx, through wounds into which people were passing. A female sexual organ developed on his eye, while the rest of the body floated in the air in front of him; also in a wound in his penis a girl nine years old played with his sexual organs. These girls spoke through his organs without his wishing it; he was accused of having done wrong to them, and thought that was perhaps done by other men. A patient felt himself pregnant, called himself Francisca, wished to be relieved of his genitals and to be placed in the Maternity Hospital, and he wanted to become the most beautiful woman on earth.

Scarcely less incomprehensible than these ideas of influence and of being possessed are the other delusions which are produced by the patients in almost inexhaustible abundance. They can partly be classified as delusions of exaltation or of persecution; but partly it is a case of wholly senseless and aimless playing with the most extraordinary and sudden ideas. Their relations are being cut to pieces; their father has throttled his two sons; in the storehouse 200 people are daily slaughtered. In the house there is a machine for beheading people; many have already offered up their lives; poisons and soporifics are being sold to landlords for giving to their guests. An international enterprise exists for "getting rid of people" by means of lifts in hotels, which unexpectedly go down into subterranean vaults. There a sausage-machine stands for the many slaughtered people; already during six years milliards of people have been daily murdered; whole towns are empty; it is a devilish crime. Everyone is eating human flesh; the food contains human blood and female genitals; from bones and brain cheese is made; Prussians and parsons are behind it all; everything happens by the order of the master of the lodge for penance. Everywhere there are electric wires; the fellow-patients are procurers; disguised enemies are there; they have taken the complexion, the capacities, speech from other people by magic; the Sovereign has shot himself, is a robber who commits murder; the end of the world, the fulfilment of the Revelation is at hand. The patient is by a bull of excommunication enchanted into a horse for his whole life long; he has insect spirits in his body; he has often been stabbed and shot; he has three hearts, is now without heart and lungs, is already dead, cannot think any more, has female genitals.

On the other hand the patient is descended from noble parents, is the stolen child of the Queen-Dowager, has been taken from a golden cradle to a shoemaker and his wife, is the son of Prince Charles, Duke of Habsburg, according to rank Emperor of Berlin, President of the Republic of Hesse. Other patients are, he who is to come, Emperor and God, first and last man, the first prince from the beginning of the world, a supernatural being, a fairy prince, Royal Highness, Majesty of Heaven and of Earth, Regent of the apes, Emperor of Austria, Napoleon, appointed to be King of Bavaria, Emperor of the world and owner of the whole world. The whole of Europe belongs to the patient; he has ruled over town and country from birth. A patient declared that the old Emperor, the Emperor Frederick and the present Emperor were united in him; inside another patient Prince Charles and the Emperor Frederick had been, since he was five years old; "Together we are called Charles Frederick," he said. Women are the Madonna of Lourdes, Grand Duchess by birth, the most highly-placed woman on earth, stolen from Coburg, the second Queen Luise by her "high, high, high, high father," goddess of hunting, the highest and noblest that exists, Majesty Clara, Regent of the House, capitalist of disease; they will give birth at Christmas to a Child Jesus, want to marry a high officer; a female patient declared that she had many children by Saint Theresa.

By the grace of God the patient has become infinitely rich, will receive for his piece of ground an untold price, is getting millions of money and jewels from the Emperor of Austria and from an American railway king, demands his milliards, possesses a kingdom of millions, thousands of square miles in Mars, Neptune, and Venus, wants to go to his palace, has inherited everything here, gets for each day 100,000 marks damages, receives cash remittances from all quarters, which are embezzled. He can make bread from stones, has studied the original language, has a knowledge of important state secrets; he is to marry a princess, is secretly married to six majesties. Prince Bismarck is coming; the King of the Netherlands will set him free; a prince is waiting in the next room; the Emperor Francis Joseph is there, who has married the patient's sister. He is nourished by the earth magnet, fed by the Holy Ghost who tells him every-thing, is in him, draws off the poison; he takes copies of the most beautiful pictures by golden wires with magnetic printing and electricity; he possesses the African method of life so that he cannot die, has grace, is in the service of the Godhead, receives revelations from the spiritualists about the approach of the end of the world; words of God flow from his mouth; God lives in his body.

The delineation of the high-flown exalted ideas leads sometimes to an extraordinary expenditure of superlatives

Specimen of Writing 7.   Paraphrenia phantastica.   × ⅔.

in which the patients try to describe their immeasurable superiority and suffering. An idea is given of it by the following extract from one of the innumerable documents endlessly repeated in a similar way with which a female patient furnished us. I add from them also a specimen of writing in which the effort is made in its large, pretentious features to do justice to the highly strained self-consciousness.

"I have here the Highest of all, the most Immeasurable of all, the most Sublime of all the most Colossal of all the most Boundless of all

X

the most Unlimited of all the most Distinguished of all only Highest of all only most Immeasurable of all only most Sublime of all only most Colossal of all only most Unlimited of all (so on for six folio pages), born the being possessing the most Devoted most Loving most Passionate Embracing all Embracing all more than all hottest Hottest of all Reverence Love Thankfulness, Devotions, Passions, Adorations, Adoration. . . . I was, am and remain this, a most Excellent of all a Greatest of all Unique thing of immortality in the most Many-sided involuted manner kind of accomplishment ! . . . Have been almost three years in the most terrible way the victim of a most bestial most dreadful band of murderers and robbers, by which I was slaughtered to the most dreadful cripple with the pains of death murdered and robbed am besides was murdered in comparison with my former most perfect beauty in a most dreadful ugliness, was am murdered and robbed it reaches back to my birth I suffered suffer as continuous victim of all bands of murderers and robbers on the earth the most boundless murders murders with robbery murders of honour I was am remain the most Excellent of all most Versatile most Sublime Best most Immortal being was most enormously rich most Magnificent Monarch of Many States. . . ."

The capital letters should be noticed, the absence of marks of punctuation, the anxiety by repetition, by using stronger terms, by the conjunction of past and present to attain to the greatest possible impressiveness, lastly in the specimen of writing the singular mannerism of writing single letters (here the m) twice in different ways.

Pseudo-memories.—Frequently the delusions clothe themselves in the form of pseudo-memories. The patient had from the beginning a foreboding soul ; as a child he was stolen, abused, had to endure great struggles ; he made journeys to China and to the North Pole, was appointed King of Bavaria in the Parliament nine years ago. He was fished up from the River Amazon, rubbed together from saliva, made small by plaster of Paris dressings, hounded for twenty-five years through the animal kingdom. People wanted to strangle him, behead him, poison him, throw him from the tower, kill him by electricity. He was Christ and Paris, Eve, Moses, Alexander the Great, Cæsar, Victoria, Mary Stewart, the Maid of Orleans, Eugénie, Napoleon, was killed several times, pierced by fifty bullets and thousands of needles, already as a boy poisoned with cantharides, was to have been misled to onanism ; he created the first people, has studied medicine, was lecturer at a. university, changed every two hundred years between studying and ruling, was to direct the whole world in seven years. He has eaten a bit of the archbishop, carried on a conversation with the devil of Zurich ; he was also the serpent of Paradise ; he is always being born again, has lived already a dozen times, has founded the town of Jerusalem, has deposed all dynasties, appointed stadholders instead, spends the night in the underworld, fights fearful battles day after day with the enemies of the country. He was professor to the Queen of England, saw there a machine for manufacturing children, worked along with the Hereditary Grand Duke as joiner and stone-mason, was in 1895 in the assembly of spirits, was also the huntsman who shot the girl in Switzerland. An inward voice tells him everything that is going to happen. The institution has already been built ninety-seven times ; the fathers also have done penance here.

Sometimes delusions of this kind are connected with every idea aroused by chance ; the patient has himself experienced every event in history, which is mentioned in conversation ; he was the Emperor William, Bismarck, Napoleon I. and III., Alexander III., all in one person ; if the conversation is about cloth-mills, he declares that he himself possesses large cloth-mills in all the towns of Germany ; he tells the physician of the most marvellous operations which he has carried out as surgeon ; he already knows all the newly admitted patients, as he knew them previously ; he can narrate extraordinary experiences with them. A patient discovered, when out walking, lions, buried cities, gold and silver mines.

All kinds of other confabulations, which do not bear the form of personal experiences are probably nearly related to pseudo-memories. A female patient narrated the most nonsensical stories from the past history of her fellow-patients ; a patient asserted that Christ had been crucified in Augsburg ; the battle of Hermann did not take place in the Teutoburger Forest ; Bismarck was still alive. Another related that Napoleon, his brother, had been beheaded the previous winter in France. Here belong also the ideas of descent which frequently come to the surface. A female patient thought that the seed of wrecked human beings got out of the sea-water into sharks, there become "rochus," and then again human beings; from the union of women and animals there arise half-men ("Gromen"); she spoke of "seed-sisters and brothers," who must marry each other. Another declared that her mother was descended from the dove of Zacharias; the first bride of Christ was an Indian girl, Lararuk; she herself was the second, and overshadowed by Him she became the mother of the Christ-child at Munich. Another time she narrated that 4000 years ago Christ had married Lucinda, and she was descended from this union; the Gospel was wrong; it was beneath the dignity of a God to let Himself be begotten and crucified. Further she was a grand-daughter of Napoleon who married her grandmother in the cathedral at Spires; he was accompanied everywhere by Christ. The heir to the throne was descended from a peasant wench, his wife from a bishop, who had 100,000 children.

A patient elaborated a comprehensive narrative of historical connections, freely invented, in which he declared all royal families to be spurious, all statements of history to be falsified; he had made many investigations, had taken a great deal from American newspapers, and he possessed excellent intellectual powers. Accordingly the patient was descended from the Duke of Reichsstadt who was a female and the daughter of the real Napoleon and of the daughter of the real Frederick II.; the former was a chemist in Baireuth and lived to be 130 years old; the latter was a hermaphrodite and was deposed. William I. also was a hermaphrodite, and was superseded by a master shoemaker; the Emperor Frederick's real name was Frederick Geier (Vulture), and he came from Nürnberg. Ludwig II. consisted of three persons; the first was a sodomite who committed rape and murder and was later a clergyman in the Allgäu, the second was the son of a day-labourer, the brother of Clara Ziegler, and was still living in poor circumstances; the third is a hermaphrodite and became an actor. The Habsburgs are a baker's family from Erlangen; the Hohenzollerns are derived from Hungarian Jewish circles, the Russian Emperor from the Jesuit family of the Medici in Baireuth. The patient declared that he himself was the last scion of all these and of many other princely families.

As already appears from the foregoing description, it is here everywhere a case not of connected, mentally elaborated circles of ideas, but of variegated, often-changing sudden ideas of a moment, some of which are certainly retained for a time, but which mostly are replaced by ever new and just as transient creations. A patient at repeated interviews called himself Graf Eberstein, Monarch on the Prussian throne, Lord of the Dead, a new God as Prussian general, Prince William in uniform, last professor, soldier, American gentleman, guardian of the institution, double District Medical Officer.

During the extraordinary delusions described the patients may be completely sensible, clear and reasonable in their behaviour, yet they often mistake in a delusional way their surroundings and individuals; they are in their kingdom, in the penitentiary, in the devil's den of murderers, in the den of rape, murder, whoredom and robbery; they see round them acquaintances, highly placed persons, viragoes, enemies ; the physician is Charlemagne. Sometimes the patients have a certain feeling of the change which has taken place in them, but no clear understanding of its significance. A patient, who was usually extremely irritable and violent, had intervening periods in which he was accessible and exaggeratedly grateful, but without real insight into the disease ; he thought then that he was " as if awakened from a long sleep," to be after some time again dominated by the old delusions.

Mood is as a rule somewhat exalted or indifferent, but sometimes also gloomy, strained, and inclined to violence. In conversations of any length the patients fall into a certain excitement. They usually bring forward their delusions with fluency and prolixity, often in a very confused and desultory manner, while they are able to give information about remote questions clearly and to the point. Their conduct is frequently somewhat affected ; occasionally grimacing is observed. Their speech is usually interspersed with peculiar turns of expression, but specially neologisms. A patient spoke of the " alphathunderbook," the compendium from the court law or university lexicon, called himself the "cyklesteraksander and brain inventor"; Aksander was a Christ-brain, Cyklester a penitential body, Rader someone who speaks out of one without one noticing it. A female patient declared that princes had as dynasty people (suite), " feds," dukes, " fesochs," emperors and kings, " fusaltos "; the world was a " cultar," a magnet, which forces vegetation. Her parents drove into the " Erdall," were merely killed ; her ancestor was " Doreal " with the Emperor of Iceland, which again consisted of Rumenien, Ostrumenien, Jeromin and Morasto ; her grandfather went with Emperors and Kings into the Erdterail, in order to hold Tyram or Tore. Another female patient thought that she had been dragged in as a poodle and suction-pump. Many sentences may be quite incomprehensible. " That is a great family word, that will never end, without war and deeds," declared a female patient ; she had as a child experienced the most wonderful things, the virgin 1000 and no night ; " that is beautiful and payable."

Silly plays on words also, nonsensical rhymes and witticisms are not infrequent. A female patient said that she was Socrates, should do " so grad'es "; a patient connected " Chamisso—Scham is so," " Wahrheit—wahrer Heid," " Doktor—Dogg-Tor "; another spoke of Leipzig "the town of the sacred masses and of the sacred religions, of the sacred legions." A third thought that fractures could be cured by introducing the new calender and abolishing fractional arithmetic ; he wanted by the abolition of prostitution to turn " Klagenfurt " into " Ehrenfurt." In spite of such occasional nonsensical interpolations the patients can still usually make themselves quite intelligible, especially if the matter in hand has not to do with their delusions ; they sometimes write faultless letters.

An example of the peculiar utterances of such patients is given in the following transcript :—

" You will probably know what that means to be an immortalized spirit, although I am only a simple beer-brewer and had to go through that if any one raises himself from a low rank to the nobility. It was certainly from birth Count Eberstein, but first by the head-disease and the strained memory the accession has resulted, so that he is Frederick William III. from then onward the fourth, which therefore has direct relation with William I. and Frederick III. That means the immortalized and that means that he is not it now for the rabble ; we know well why the pictures and flags have been waved to the right, that means the right one will come. . . I know that I am mad ; that means that I must suffer by head-disease and by memory voices, but then it is also possible that a common fellow comes to high station ; that will mean much, if one is to have memory for the general staff and the government. . . You have not the least idea how much goes on in my head ; I often think it must burst. You don't know at all what happens to me at night ; I frequent in fact the most glorious marble halls at night ; then I am many miles away. Last night I had 20,000 marks in my hands ; here there are only twenty and ten mark pieces, but there there are also thirty mark pieces ; that was not in dream, but by day ; there was on the pieces the President of America from Hamburg. Indeed you don't know at all what intercourse I have at night, the expanding pictures ; then I am indeed in glorious, wholly unknown towns, where I never was before, or, as last night, in glorious ships on the sea. In this world-globe, which I frequent at night, it is quite different from here ; it is perhaps a continent behind the moon. I am far away outside, though I am in the asylum. In December, January I have eaten cherries there, when here in winter-time there are certainly none at all. . . For eighteen and a half months already I have been William I.; but through the length of time I have obtained the double order of the crown ; at that time I was already as much as the most mighty King on earth. If Jesus Christ had been let go free and not innocently crucified, perhaps it would have happened to him as to me, by the head-disease throughout become equal with his father. . . ."

On the one hand the mental activity of the patient appears here in the vivacity of the descriptions, on the other hand there is occasional derailment into quite incomprehensible turns of expression and trains of thought. Further, the fabulous exalted ideas come to the front with wonderful nocturnal experiences probably pointing to pseudo-memories, lastly, there is the morbid feeling which shines through and which is brought into singular relations to the exalted ideas.

The **Course** of the morbid form described here is pro-gressive. In time the utterances of the patients usually become gradually more confused and more disconnected. The neologisms and queer turns of expression often greatly prevail ; the· behaviour also often becomes peculiar. The emotions become duller with rapid explosive outbursts of violence and transient states of excitement. Many patients remain permanently capable of work ; others are limited to long-winded speeches and the composition of comprehensive, scarcely comprehensible documents. The rapidity with which this dementia develops appears to be very varying. Sometimes it is already distinctly marked at the end of four or five years; I also know, however, cases in which after one and even after several decades, in spite of the most extraordinary delusions, there could be no talk at all of real confusion or at least not of a higher degree of psychic weakness.

Among my patients the male sex preponderated with 60 to 70 per cent.; almost the half of the patients were in age between thirty and forty years, a quarter in each of the decades below and above that. In one case there was at the age of twenty-one years a state of depression which gradually disappeared again, and which was followed between forty and fifty by the development of the delusional attack. Some of my patients were described as gifted, vivacious, but fantastic, others as frivolous, stubborn, self-willed ; several of them had a criminal career behind them and fell ill in prison.

Delimitation.—In this form also it must remain doubtful whether it corresponds to an independent morbid process. It cannot be denied that there exist many similarities with the paranoid forms of *dementia præcox*, especially with the cases which issue in drivelling dementia ; also the falling ill in prison which was repeatedly observed, could be advanced for this view. Nevertheless, the clinical picture is so peculiar that a separate description of it might in the meantime be justified, even though it should turn out later that gradual transitions to the forms named exist. In any case it is noteworthy that here, in comparison with the so unusually severe disorders of *intellect*, the injury to volition by the morbid process is wholly in the background, if we do not regard a certain mannerism and the disorders of speech. In connection with this it must be emphasized that the mental activity of the patients as a rule remains strikingly well preserved. They may appear in their conversation extra-ordinarily confused, but at the same time be ·vivacious and accessible, and because of the absence of volitional disorders act quite reasonably. In this connection they recall to mind the cases of *confusion of speech* formerly described, from which, however, they are to be distinguished by the delusions which are here so extremely luxuriant. It might be conceivable that a nearer relation existed between these two forms or at least between parts of them, as at present we are not yet able to judge whether the peculiar delusions observed in this form may or may not be regarded as an essential morbid symptom. Naturally the possibility must also be remembered that the cases brought together here under this point of view are perhaps among themselves by no means of the same kind.

The **Treatment** of the morbid forms ·discussed in this section has essentially to keep in view only the timely care of the patients who are almost always in need of institutional life, and further the preservation, as far as possible, of their psychic personality by suitable occupation.

INDEX.

J. & J. GRAY & CO., PRINTERS, EDINBURGH